MW00627592

"Grounded. Real. Embodied. This book gives you actual tools to not only survive the 'waking up' journey but to thrive. Sydney delivers a powerful and charismatic life-enhancing manual to support you to own your true power and be the change you wish to see on this planet."

—**Aaron Kleinerman**, bestselling author of *The Embodied Man*, speaker and facilitator

"*I'm Ascending, Now What?* is another entertaining and illuminated guide by Sydney Campos into the different realms of consciousness and human awakening. Read this book as your own bedside manual to accessing personal empowerment using spiritual principles in the modern world."

—**Alison Sher**, author of *The Millennial's Guide to Changing the World*

"Sydney Campos's new book makes ideas about the illusive spiritual term 'ascension' very accessible and very human. Her highly entertaining, well-informed writing helps the reader embrace their unloved parts and realize that their essential nature is an evolutionary force for this nexus point in history. This is the highest order of a self-help book, because she deeply reinforces what Joseph Campbell said: 'The privilege of a lifetime is to become who you truly are.' At the conclusion to this marvelous treatise we understand 'consciousness' as the perception of ourselves as all that is, and the process of ascension comes from a life well lived."

—**Alan Steinfeld**, author of *Making Contact: Preparing for the New Realities of Extraterrestrial Existence*

"*I'm Ascending, Now What?* is a most compelling book by powerful author-teacher Sydney Campos. Meeting the human experience in our true spiritual identity, it effectively covers a lot of life-changing territory. She breaks down complex topics like consciousness, contrast, nervous system dysregulation, along with inner-child and shadow work, taking them out of heady terrain, and making it all understandable and approachable. Pure spiritual nourishment for anyone living on a planet at this time. And if you're a highly sensitive empath, it's an absolute, all-supporting must! Embrace it for all the answers that point you back to your ultimate spiritual teacher: yourself."

—**Kris Ferraro**, bestselling author
of *Your Difference Is Your Strength, Manifesting,*
and *Energy Healing,* international energy coach and speaker

"In *I'm Ascending, Now What?* Sydney guides us in how we can be ourselves, stand in our power, and live the kinds of lives we truly desire. For anyone earnestly seeking to awaken to what's possible in creating their reality, I highly recommend this book as a starting point. Enjoy your journey!"

—**Laurie Handlers**, author of *Sex & Happiness: The Tantric Laws of Intimacy,* speaker, facilitator

"*I'm Ascending, Now What?* is a thought-provoking guide for anyone experiencing a spiritual awakening. This book delves into the challenges and opportunities that come with this transformative journey, offering practical advice and wisdom to help readers navigate the process with grace and understanding. Whether you're just beginning to sense a shift or are well into your ascent, this book is a roadmap for understanding and integrating the changes in your life. With its insightful and compassionate approach, *I'm Ascending, Now What?* is a must-read for anyone seeking a deeper understanding of the human experience and the path of embodied ascension."

—**Sheila Darcey**, author of *Sketch by Sketch*
and founder of SketchPoetic

"Sydney ties together lessons learned over many lifetimes within this lifetime, giving you a step-by-step framework to help overcome awakening and step into your divine ascension. A must for anyone looking to advance into personal mastery."

—**April Pfender**, founder of Golden Light Alchemy
and author of *The Complete Guide to Chakras*

"Another magnificent read by author Sydney Campos. This book is packed with insights and essential practices for individuals exploring the pathway of ascension."

—**Sherianna Boyle**, author of *Emotional Detox Now*

"What does it take to dissolve the chains of lack and limitation that hold us in captivity? Here Sydney is revealing a revaluation process that invites in the perfect answers to every life situation that presents itself. The expansive exercises and practices at the end of each chapter are priceless. The artful weaving together of personal experiences combined with life-changing awakening practices make this book a highly prized addition to the serious seeker's library. As you connect with a higher polarity, you find yourself needing guidance and practices that are difficult to find in this world. Sydney has compiled an array of teachings that help you to connect with answers to every life situation. The expansion practices at the end of each chapter help you stand tall as you move from fear-based patterns into your Divine self, so love wins every time."

—**Leisa Peterson**, author of *The Mindful Millionaire*, CFP, money coach, business consultant, and spiritual teacher

I'M ASCENDING,
NOW WHAT?

ALSO BY SYDNEY CAMPOS

The Empath Experience: What to Do When You Feel Everything

I'M ASCENDING, NOW WHAT?

Awaken Your
Authentic Self, Own Your Power,
Embody Your Truth

SYDNEY CAMPOS

ST. MARTIN'S
ESSENTIALS
NEW YORK

First published in the United States by St. Martin's Essentials, an imprint of St. Martin's Publishing Group

I'M ASCENDING, NOW WHAT? Copyright © 2023 by Sydney Campos. All rights reserved. Printed in the United States of America. For information, address St. Martin's Publishing Group, 120 Broadway, New York, NY 10271.

www.stmartins.com

The Library of Congress Cataloging-in-Publication Data is available upon request.

ISBN 978-1-250-85982-2 (hardcover)
ISBN 978-1-250-85983-9 (ebook)

Our books may be purchased in bulk for promotional, educational, or business use. Please contact your local bookseller or the Macmillan Corporate and Premium Sales Department at 1-800-221-7945, extension 5442, or by email at MacmillanSpecialMarkets@macmillan.com.

First Edition: 2023

10 9 8 7 6 5 4 3 2 1

To all who are here to remember and remind. I love you, keep going.

CONTENTS

A NOTE FROM THE AUTHOR

Everything is turning on nowadays, and simultaneously turning up, all the way up, to eleven on a scale of one to ten. Make that one hundred and eleven. Our bodies are becoming more alive, our spirits are coming online. They were there all along, of course, but we are becoming more aware than ever. We are feeling it all. We are remembering at the speed of light what we are really made of and what we are truly capable of creating and experiencing in these fantastic lives we've been gifted. Welcome to the infinite game of awakening more deeply into ourselves.

Awakening can feel like a real mess at times though, can't it? If you've ever—in the span of one day or maybe even in an hour or two—experienced a new dimension of happiness or even bliss, a deeper peace than you've ever felt before, only to crash a few moments later into a pile of emotional muck, crying on the floor, remembering something from when you were five that's finally now rearing its head to be processed out of your body: *Welcome, you're in the right place.*

It's no small feat learning how to use these bodies and their infinite spirits driving behind the scenes. I wish I had a book when I was born about what life was going to entail; something, anything, to help guide me along the path of awakening so maybe . . . just maybe . . . there wouldn't have had to be so many risks and experiments leading up into this moment. It's been hard, but it's also been real. I suppose really living entails risks and experiments along the way—this whole thing feels like a grand experiment, and maybe it's a sweet relief for us all to have permission to call it like it is and stop trying to be perfect and have everything figured out all the time. As if that were even possible, as if that were even our job.

Ascension is another term for awakening—perhaps you've heard it before amidst the spiritual jargon that's been taking up more space in the mainstream lately? Ascension might seem to imply an upward and outward journey, into Heavenly realms or into perhaps another dimension. Definitely not anywhere on Earth. Plus, frequent references to ascension commonly show images of spirits ascending out of bodies into celestial planes—signifying a completion of the human journey, the game of life completely mastered.

But this journey we may identify as ascension is actually more inward than anything else, at least in my experience. And the point isn't to ascend outward and upward into the celestial plane but more so to be fully here, on Earth, in these bodies, as our true selves. Quite a tall order indeed—but then again, we wouldn't be here unless we were capable of accepting the divine invitation. We got this.

A friend once said, "Welcome to Earth, the greatest party in all the multiverse." Amen. How might this be a perfect way we can relate to this whole journey, to ourselves, and to all the other players in the game? The farther I go on this path of awakening, it really does feel like a game—perhaps even one of our own creation. **The pages to follow are a series of invitations, inquiries, and practices for us to relate to life, to ourselves, and to one another in new ways**—as though we are all playing a game together. Let's ask:

How can it all be more filled with ease and even fun?
How can we feel more the ways we want to feel?
And, most of all, how can we enjoy the show?

Ready to rock?
Let's do this!

When you come to the end of all the light you know, and it's time to step into the darkness of the unknown, hope is knowing that one of two things shall happen: Either you will be given something solid to stand on or you will be taught to fly.

—Edward Teller

INTRODUCTION

Awakening is not at all a linear path. Is there such a thing as a linear spiritual path anyway? Somehow it seems we're taught to go step by step in a straight line as we grow into new jobs, relationships, or other roles, but looking back, doesn't it mostly seem that we zig and zag and spiral around more than we ever go in a straight line? I much more resonate with the image of an upward spiral for envisioning our evolution—we are always growing and evolving, that's for sure, but the route isn't direct and it's unique for each and every one of us. We have our own course charted in our custom-designed direction. Maybe some would call this destiny, but who knows what that really means. Perhaps we're here to explore this *now* together? What do you think?

When was your first awakening moment? Can you remember? Sometimes those moments can feel like an overwhelming sense of gratitude for being alive, even amidst a seemingly mundane experience that normally might have even felt kind of ordinary and underwhelming. Have you ever had an experience of a deeper presence than you've ever felt coming over you, almost stopping your heart or amplifying your sense of your own heartbeat so that it feels like it's beating like a drum through every cell? Or maybe you've felt the presence of an energy, or a spirit, in your space or out in nature—and it surprised you a bit but on another level you felt that this experience was so familiar. You remembered this kind of feeling as though you had lived it in another time.

In these moments it seems we remember ourselves. We see there's more to us than what we've always thought and certainly more than we've been taught to notice or value. The cool thing about these kinds of experiences is that we can have them infinitely, and each time they can deepen and shift and create new openings in our understanding of reality and all elements therein.

Lately it is getting more and more common for people to seemingly *come to* in their awakening. They awaken sometimes slowly or sometimes suddenly. They feel immense energy, their senses turn on with height-ened intensity and awareness, they become conscious and aware of their bodies in new ways and they start to see the bigger pictures of the world and the greater games we are all playing together. They start asking about their purpose, about the deeper meaning to life, and about how they can feel even more connected to themselves, their inner voice, and all the as-pects of life they love.

Our hearts are opening and our spirits are coming online more power-fully than ever before—our intuitions are turning on, we are remembering that we are energetic beings capable of pure magic and that there's nothing woo woo or weird about being conscious, attracted to healing and well-being, or starting to resonate with new things that elicit a more positive, expansive feeling. This is who we are:

- We are here to grow, expand, and evolve into new ways that feel better and better.
- We are here to experience peace within and with all.
- We are here to create incredible realities that expand beyond what we've ever been taught is possible.
- We are here to pioneer new templates and examples of what it means to be human, of what it means to be a spiritual being having a human experience.
- We are here to truly know ourselves and each other as we really are.
- We are here to be real.

It's time, now more than ever, to drop the masks we've been taught to wear to be safe or protected and reveal what's been shining radiantly beyond the superficial trappings of our various identities all along.

What if all of our issues, even the greatest of our global challenges and all the humanitarian and environmental crises therein, are actually the result of humans not living in alignment with their higher consciousness guidance?

What if all of our crises are the results of us not loving and caring for ourselves?

What if the way we treat and think about ourselves is the way we ulti-mately treat the Earth and all its living inhabitants?

Simplifying such vast issues in such a brief manner might sound like a huge generalization—I get it. Our minds that are used to intellectualizing, over-rationalizing, and over-complicating everything may find it challenging to understand a more simple truth, especially when the truth is often an immediately felt sensory experience as opposed to a rational one.

> **"Earth is a school for mastering how to manipulate energy. It's the most difficult school in the universe. Only the bravest souls sign up for this assignment."**
> **—Dolores Cannon**

Ascension in the simplest sense means being real and truly living. It's the invitation we all have loudly staring us in the face now to become radically intimate with ourselves, with our true purpose in this life, with our understanding of reality, and how we can create precisely what we desire into being and so much more. Do we believe ourselves worthy of such an experience? Maybe not all the way, not yet—but do we believe we can reside in this space of knowing our truly infinite value and worthiness, beyond everything else we've been taught, beyond all conditions?

There's only one way to find out. Let's practice and venture forth into the great unknown, together. Remember, we're never alone—no matter how much this belief might have guided our operating systems until now. As we get to know ourselves more completely and intimately, as we learn to accept and love ourselves just as we are, we allow ourselves to be truly seen. And when we are allowing our truth to shine through, we attract greater resonance into our lives in every way: through more aligned relationships, more aligned opportunities, and more ease and grace overall. Some might call this abundance—a feeling, a knowing, that all of life is supporting you to win and experience joy and success. We'll get more into this later.

I'm Ascending, Now What? is a collection of invitations and inquiries into practicing greater intimacy, connection, presence, and authenticity within ourselves and with all of life. It is a series of steps toward awakening one's true self, one's higher self, one's intuitive knowing, and everything in between. It is a portal of sorts—into new realities and dimensions of happiness, purpose, and fulfillment. It can be whatever you want it to be, of course, as this is your own journey that you get to design along the way. You are the creator of it all, which we will practice remembering together in the pages to follow until it becomes more natural to think of ourselves in this way.

> **"Healing is finding our way home—and then
> eventually remembering we are already here."**
> **—Kristy, Akashic facilitator training student**

HOW TO USE THIS BOOK

I hope this guide becomes a close, personal friend that you'll feel welcome to write in, record notes in, highlight, and bookmark in all the ways that feel good for you to make it your own. What I mean to say is—this book can be thought of as an interactive living being that's designed for you to play with and engage with as you would with a real-life human guide, by your side. I'll be here every step of the way along the path, walking with you through the journey upon us and I promise, we'll have a lot of fun even while exploring the sometimes deep, dark depths of consciousness and being.

There are a few things to keep in mind while engaging, which you can of course feel free to take or leave as you prefer. This is *your* journey after all, and together we're going to practice discernment in really listening and trusting what you want, what works for you, and what doesn't. So when I say take what you need and leave the rest—please do exactly that.

**"Life will give you whatever experience is most helpful
for the evolution of your consciousness."
—Eckhart Tolle**

Here you are completely allowed to walk (and practice walking) your unique, authentic walk and question everything along the way. If you ever read something in here that doesn't resonate, explore what comes up and see what might be there underneath an initially presented trigger. Maybe you have a better idea about how to conceptualize or say something? That's awesome and I hope that's often the case, especially when you find your own language that articulates most clearly for you the answers you seek.

What if we were all the smartest people in the room, and even then we still have no grounds for comparison because we are each seeing reality in completely unique ways that work for us? Imagine how much we could learn and explore together if we were holding ourselves and each other in this level of reverence.

Here are some guidelines to entertain for our journey ahead:

1. **Own your own experience and celebrate it:** In the pages to follow you're invited to continuously tune in with your own journey and relate to what's offered here from your own vantage points and understanding.
2. **Check comparison and judgment at the door:** Everything shared here is shared with the intention of supporting you in connecting more deeply with yourself, your own journey, and your own capacity to navigate your own most perfect path. What does it feel like to let go of judgment and comparison as a means of discerning one's position along the path?
3. **Take yourself, me, and everyone else off the pedestal:** Let's practice deprogramming ourselves from the various projections and roles we've held and put on others. Let's take the pressure off to be

perfect or to be anything other than exactly who we are, now. *Who we are being is all that's required.*

4. **When a practice resonates, stick with it and see what happens (consistency is key):** The pages that follow are full of stories and lessons, bookended at each chapter's close with attunements (practices) to embody the concepts we just learned. The numerous healing practices and modalities shared here aren't just called *practices* for no reason—they are meant to be practiced. If you find a practice that really resonates and supports you in feeling and being more how you want to be, stick with it and see what unfolds. Oftentimes practices that feel great for us, when done consistently, can have hugely positive impacts in our lives, usually in more ways than we can ever even imagine.

5. **Practice the pause:** Every once in a while you'll see a bolded statement and invitations for deeper practice highlighted in the text. These are reminders to pause to consider the lesson at hand and integrate and reflect on how you're feeling about all you're receiving. Take a deep breath, take five—how are you relating? What's it like to move at your own pace? Take as much time and space as you need before proceeding along your unique path.

6. **Practice keeping an open mind and an open heart:** Stay open and receptive to new potentials and directions that can come through and surprise you when you least expect it. What's it like to be a beginner, a fresh new student, completely open and receptive to learning new ways of being and thriving?

7. **Wear your beliefs and personality like a loose garment:** Ascension is a path of stripping away all that is not true and all that no longer serves to reveal what's underneath—the real you. Are you ready to loosen the grip on your personality, identities, and beliefs so you can expand beyond what you've been taught and experience something new, perhaps something more true, more you?

8. **Explore your authentic expressions and conceptualizations:** If you come across any guidance or insight shared here that really hits a strong cord of resonance, see if you can explore sharing the concept in your own words to really embody your authentic

understanding and knowing. You can even practice sharing the insight with a friend who might love to explore this with you.

9. **Be open and receptive to support in all the ways it shows up:** As you are engaging with the content to follow, especially if you commit to doing the practices that are designed to help shift your reality and consciousness in new ways, life is going to shift to surprise you with support, new forms of abundance, and greater overall resonance. Be open to receiving the gifts that are going to present themselves on your path—even the gifts disguised as triggers are opportunities to grow and heal.

You're signing up to activate a new level of awareness and overall consciousness in our journey together, so get ready for life to adjust accordingly. You may find that certain triggers arise to help you navigate through healing that you're ready to face and complete. You may relate within some of your relationships differently and see where dissonances have always been—but with your new awareness, you'll be too sensitive to stick around and play the same old unconscious games. It will be time to let go.

> **"With a *strong* commitment to inquiring into yourself, the universe does not have to use catastrophes to wake you up."**
> **—Gay Hendricks**

As you commit to listening and honoring your truth, no matter what, life is going to support you in clearing the pathway for more authenticity, presence, and true connection to arise. Prepare to see what no longer serves you or fits with ultra-clear vision and discernment—it's time to let go and be free. So much awaits you on the other side of the familiar patterns and survival mechanisms you've learned to cling to as a safety net. Your true self is here, waiting to play and be fully expressed in an absolutely incredible life designed just for you to learn and grow through and enjoy. *Let's dive in.*

ASCENSION LEXICON: GLOSSARY

As you continue through the pages that follow, you might come across words that feel new to you or seem to take on a different dimension of significance with new context. **As we evolve and expand, usually the words we use to articulate our experiences must also shift to more accurately reflect our new level of consciousness.** Here are some key terms we'll be playing with assembled in a *lexicon* (a cool word I love for *vocabulary*). I'd love to offer my definitions of these terms before we go in deep together. Feel free to add your own definitions as they develop and revise however feels authentic to you.

One of the most powerful practices I've been challenged with is to define the words I use to ensure they are actually my own. **We can sense the truth by the way it feels, and eventually, when we are absolutely grounded in our true voice and expression, ultimately our presence alone communicates far more than words can even attempt to describe.** But for now, with words as our primary mode of relating—I'll do my best to offer up my take on some of our designated terms.

activation: any experience that ignites a greater depth of understanding and therefore makes possible a new way of orienting in consciousness and reality.

Akashic Records: the collective history and wisdom of all souls and all lifetimes across all universes, beyond time and space, stored in the Akashic field (also referred to as the *zero point field* or *known field*); the energetic fiber connecting all living beings.

alchemy: the transformation of matter into a new form; the science of shifting states; a process by which a living being can transform into a completely new state or embodiment.

ascension: a journey all souls travel through while integrating into the body on Earth; an alchemical process of self-actualization in which spirit embodies into form.

attune(ment): to attune (*verb*) something is to welcome it into a
more harmonious resonant state; to offer an example of resonance
by which something or someone else can match or synchronize in
frequency or tone. An attunement (*noun*) is a process or action by
which one attunes someone or something else in a particular way; an
offering of an example to learn from and resonate with in a new way.

awakening: the experience of waking up—coming to—from an
old way of being into more conscious, enlivened, and empowered
awareness; shining the light where it was once dark.

coherence: a state of being in unity or completely integrated within
oneself; a felt experience of consistency, presence, clarity, and assurance in one's innate wholeness.

consciousness: a dimension of human experience that is constantly
evolving, expanding, and illuminating greater awareness of being
within oneself and within the world.

dimension: an energetic octave defined by a range of particular
frequencies; a measure of density that evolves and expands along a
trajectory of universal ascending consciousness.

ego: a part of human consciousness that is self-aware and tends to
oversee aspects of experience related to survival, self-esteem, and
self-image.

embodiment: the process of unfolding or way of becoming actualized;
the act of completely residing within one's body; the evolutionary
process by which spirit materializes into form.

emotion: energy in motion; the brain's translation (communicated
through neurochemical responses) of bodily sensations' meanings,
often based on past experience; a mechanism by which one may
orient and make meaning of reality and its implicit feedback.

empath(ic): an empath (*noun*) is a being with the capacity to experience and feel the multisensory perceptions (such as feelings,
emotions, physical pain, distress, happiness, sadness, etc.) of other
living beings, including humans, animals, the Earth itself, plants,
and etheric spiritual entities. Being empathic (*adjective*) entails
experiencing a highly attuned sensitivity to the sensory perception
and felt experience of other living beings.

energy: a measure of infinite potential; energy can neither be created

nor destroyed for it is the omnipresent source essence encompass-
ing and interconnecting all existence.

feeling: the capacity to consciously discern and interpret emotions; a
mechanism for translating the body's emotional response to reality.

frequency: a measure of vibrational octave, potential, and capacity.
Frequency defines and measures the layers of light and sound that
constitute the fabric of reality's dimensions.

intuition: the gift of sensing what is right and true without requiring
rational evidence. Intuition can be expressed through one's multisensory perception, usually as a feeling, knowing, sensing, seeing, or
hearing.

multidimensional: the capacity to traverse or experience multiple
dimensions of consciousness and reality simultaneously. For
example, a multidimensional being can feel a profound grief for
the loss of a loved one while simultaneously holding the awareness
of peace, ease, and acceptance for the perfect path unfolding. *Also:
a human being having a spiritual experience through their ascension
journey of soul embodiment.*

nervous system: a complex network of circuitry throughout the human body designed to manage all of the body's operative systems
and ultimately the entire system's response to the external world.
A healthy, self-regulating nervous system resides in homeostasis, at
peace in the present moment, grounded and self-contained in one's
own energy.

patterning: the often inherited repetitive mental, emotional, physical,
and spiritual behaviors and orientations (feelings and beliefs) that
one can enact consciously or unconsciously, usually resulting in
familiar, repetitive outcomes and identity structures.

power: a source of energetic influence that generates, amplifies,
illuminates, enlivens, and supports expansion. *Also: the conscious
capacity to choose, discern, invoke, and embody.*

quantum: we live in a quantum reality in which all that we perceive
as matter is simply energy (quanta are the smallest measures of
energy) amassed in particular patterns that appear as form to the
eye, which is conditioned to only perceive physicality.

reality: a totality of existence as our consciousness understands and seeks to perceive it. It is oriented differently through unique personal lenses informed by various aspects of conditioning; reality to one person may be completely different from that of another.

recalibrate: the act of conditioning or transforming oneself or one's orientation to reality in a new or different way. An ability to shift one's way(s) of being and perception(s).

resonance: a measure of relatability that denotes attunement (or lack thereof) with a desired way of being or feeling. Feeling a resonance with someone or something (a person, place, idea or experience) can catalyze a felt sense of pleasurable, magnetic synergy.

shadow: an area or structure (physical, mental, emotional, or spiritual) that blocks light from fully flowing; an unconscious pattern stemming from unresolved trauma that expresses through survival and self-protection strategies.

somatic: a way of referring to any experience or expression relating to the body (soma).

soul: individuated source consciousness seeking to learn, expand, and understand itself.

spirit: eternal source energy that animates all living beings; source connection enlivening the soul into form.

surrender: to completely let go and yield to a higher power; to release control, attachment, and expectation.

transcend: to move beyond what one thought was previously possible; to surpass all limitations.

transmute: to transform or alchemize one form into another usually more true, coherent form.

trauma: memory of highly impactful experience (from this lifetime or others) that is stored in the body until it is consciously metabolized and released.

"Step into the fire of self-discovery. This fire will not burn you, it will only burn what you are not."
—Mooji

1

CONSCIOUSNESS: WHO, ME?

I opened my eyes, startled and blinded by the fluorescent hospital lights, and immediately felt shocked to see my hands restrained to the edges of the hospital bed by thick handcuff-shaped, plastic clasps. How did I even get here? I started to piece together what memory I had access to. I had started the night with friends, pre-gaming for a new acquaintance's birthday party at a new club in Chelsea just around the corner from Union Square. I had been living in New York City for a few months by then, just barely finding my footing. We had a special table reserved and everything felt very VIP—it was going to be a great night, I had a feeling. I drank too much champagne before we even got there, and one of my last memories was using my new camera to snap pictures of our table and all the beautiful people surrounding it, eventually standing on one of the tables with a bottle in my hand, drinking straight out of it like I was the queen of the club.

I loved the feeling of being in my own music video with my own soundtrack—everything was happening for me and I was in Heaven. The anxiety I normally felt spinning around in my mind was silenced by the profuse amounts of alcohol I was downing and the attention I was attracting. Even if people were worried about me for appearing to black out and fall over, it was still attention, and I liked it. In fact, I lived for it. When I woke up restrained in the hospital, instead of feeling concerned about the state of my body or overall health, my first thoughts circulated around where my new camera, my jacket, and my purse were.

I had a tendency of losing my stuff back then, and probably within the first six months of moving to New York from Southern California— for the first time without a boyfriend to babysit me—I had already lost my wallet with IDs and all my cards three times. I screamed to get the doctors' attention to let me go—I had to get home to get ready for work. I had a restaurant gig later that day that I couldn't miss or else it would be the second time I was fired from a restaurant after working there for only a few weeks. I vaguely remember fighting with the doctor to let me go, and it felt like I snuck out somehow without any of my things except my jacket, which luckily had not my camera in it but a totally new, even better camera. So the night wasn't a wash after all.

This is how disassociated I was at the time: when I look back and remember what I was prioritizing or able to garner from reality—the fact that I was so focused on external material items, how I looked instead of how I felt and what next thing I needed to do—it shows me how disconnected I was from my inner being. I had no awareness or consciousness of my emotional state other than it felt so bad I couldn't wait to drink more to turn it all off.

It was 3:00 A.M. and I had found myself more hungover than I'd been in a long while despite having experiences like this a few times a week at least. I got to the diner on the corner and somehow ordered some water and an egg sandwich. I must have dined and dashed because I definitely didn't have my wallet. That's why the hospital was so easy to check out of—and since they didn't have my ID I must not have been charged for the ambulance ride from the club to the hospital. I was a Jane Doe for all they knew.

"Great, I'm the hook," I thought to myself. Another win from a somewhat awkward evening. I wondered what my friends thought of the whole thing. I did, however, need to get back to that club at soon as possible and see if I could find my wallet and anything else I had left behind. I would go later that evening and the shame of what had happened would start to creep in as the doorman recognized me and checked in to see if I was okay. "Of course I'm okay," I thought. "I'm fine, couldn't he see me now? Just give me my stuff so I can get out of here and pretend like nothing ever happened." It would be too painful to process or feel the gravity of what had actually transpired.

I didn't have the capacity to even consider that as an option. It wouldn't be until years later in early recovery from drinking and drugs that I would start to let these repressed feelings flow, which meant that I cried for what felt like a year straight. I had so much pent-up sadness and grief and unthinkable amounts of traumatic memory from so blatantly disregarding my health and well-being. For years from about age fourteen at the beginning of high school, I was so unhappy and anxious I sometimes wondered what it might be like to simply leave. Occasionally I would black out and walk into traffic hoping a car would just hit me—get it over with already. I was too much of a coward to take my own life straight up, but I'd be fine if someone else could do that job for me. A part of me admittedly liked gambling with god and the universe.

I felt so abandoned and disconnected. "If you really exist, god, are you going to let me die? Is there actually anything supporting me? Am I even here for a reason?" These were definitely some of the unconscious currents powering my life at that time. It was a heavy existence indeed, on top of the pressure of looking good and trying to sell myself on the story I was creating: I followed my dream of living in New York City and I was making it work, having fun with my friends, going out to flashy clubs every night, and living the dream. Look at me. Inside I was dying and on the verge of complete collapse. Not enough drugs or alcohol in the world could shut off the unparalleled anxiety and self-hatred I was living with in every moment. I could never do anything right and the voice in my head was only ever reminding me of how I would never be enough no matter what I did. Plus I had to figure it all out alone.

It took many more experiences of rock bottoms like that night in the hospital—more than I might ever be able to even recall, honestly—to finally realize: I need help, I can't do this anymore. The shame became too immense and I had given up trying to make it all work. All my effort was never working no matter how hard I tried to convince myself. I didn't know where else to go until I realized that my parents and numerous therapists over the years (each one I'd stopped seeing the moment they mentioned I might want to reconsider my relationship with alcohol) had recommended I try Alcoholics Anonymous (AA) for support. Finally, I was desperate and willing to try anything, even that.

My first meeting, I cried the entire time, so much so that the scarf I was wearing had to be thrown away because of the snot and tears it was soaked with by the end of the hour-long meeting. As hard as it was to try to relate to people outside of a bar or night club, I tried to let myself be carried. I thought my first sponsor was hitting on me and asking me out on a date when she invited me to start reading the big book of the 12 steps. I just went with it, despite my misgivings and doubts. I even continued doing side hustles a few weeks into sobriety as my emotions started coming back online. I would experience paralyzing fear about financial scarcity and be driven to do a Craigslist hustle for a few hundred bucks. Then I would feel so much shame about it and paranoia that I would see the person I had hustled with or that they would tell others about me and what I had done—that I'd be found out.

Eventually I had to make an agreement with my sponsor that I wouldn't go on Craigslist for at least ninety days, since it was seeming a lot like a placeholder for my relationship to alcohol and drugs: this pattern of seeking quick fixes, attention, and money from strangers on the internet. I had replaced one distraction and means of checking out with another. I learned years later that all of these behaviors were part of the same pattern I had innocently developed from trauma—these were the ways I had learned to try to take care of myself, to soothe myself, to provide support. I did the best I could do with what I had at the time, and knowing my history, it all makes sense, and more so as the journey continues on. I am grateful to have lived to tell the stories now so that perhaps others might not have to go as deep into the darkness as I did to catalyze awakening.

TUNING INTO A NEW INNER CHANNEL

I can almost remember the precise moment in which I realized for the first time that the inner dialogue that had been running in my mind for seemingly my entire life wasn't the only voice I could access. It was a shocking, almost terrifying revelation to receive at that point. For my entire life—perhaps a quarter of a century—I was unconsciously driven in every way by this intense, even rather abusive voice that I had never even been aware of. All along it was setting my entire inner soundtrack and overarching guiding plan for my life. Weird. What was I supposed to do with this information? It felt like a ton of bricks that I didn't even know existed had been walled up around me for my entire life and were finally starting to fall down. It hit hard and hurt. I suppose the world you thought you knew falling apart can feel like that.

It's moments like these that catalyze us into new realities and the practices therein that become our foundations, our lifeboats, our saving graces. We could always choose to give up and let something else happen (i.e., dying, dissolving, disappearing? Are these even real choices?), but we haven't come all this way to just give up completely. So more often than not these sometimes reality-shattering moments that seem like total catastrophes at the time actually help shape us in the deepest sense—they can skyrocket us into entirely new ways of being, sometimes overnight. That's precisely what's happening now, on a global scale—like one we've never seen before. More and more people are waking up—wondering why they're here, what this whole life situation is really about, and how we might be able to find more meaning and purpose in this reality we've agreed to play in.

I only recently learned that not everyone has an inner monologue (or different voices or channels) that they are aware of playing in their inner experience. But I do sense more have this awareness than not; at least for now that seems to be the case. The times we live in now feel like a critical juncture in which we are becoming more aware of ourselves as the operators or perhaps receivers of a much grander spectrum of expression than we had ever previously considered. **This is the essence of ascension and consciousness awakening in simplicity: our unique experiences into sensing and seeing our conceptions of reality and all its inner workings and our own true natures. As we deepen in our unique multisensory experience of reality, we sense more into why we are here and what we are truly capable of experiencing and creating.**

> **"The power of an idea whose time has come is really the power of Spirit at work. When enough of us, along with one or two at visionary consciousness, begin to contemplate these in-Spirit ideas, they can't be stopped."**
> **—Wayne W. Dyer**

As a child I was highly intuitive, very emotional, empathic, and loved to play with my dolls, creating imaginary worlds containing grand civilizations and alternate realities with their own intricate social orders. I was always fascinated with how people were. Not just what they *did* or how they *operated* in life but literally *how they existed*—how they "be'd" if there was such a term. I probably wasn't consciously thinking these thoughts about what it was like to be human, but looking back I can see that this quest to discover what "being" was led my curiosity for much of my life, and this led me down many rabbit holes. One of those is definitely leading to being right here, right now, with you.

I distinctly remember when I was around age nine and my family moved to the middle of San Francisco—I mean, right smack dab in the city center. We had moved from the relatively suburban quietness and homogeneity of a small Massachusetts coastal town to the hustle and bustle of the Lower Haight, with more diversity, chaos, noise, and potential per square foot than I had ever before experienced. I started to feel painfully anxious and insecure. I would be short of breath in public, I would turn red whenever asked to speak in class or when I felt another person was seeing me too up close and personal. I'd stay up for hours and hours each night obsessively circling the clothes and supplies in catalogs I required my parents to buy for me so I could adorn myself in ways that finally would make it feel more comfortable to be in my body. The way I understood how to be in the world depended on a great deal of external validation, plus reliance on my appearance and acknowledgment from others to get love and to feel worthy and ultimately to affirm my entire existence. All of the pressure to look and be a certain way spiraled into a life-long struggle with body dysmorphia—the inability to see true reality, especially when it came to my appearance, which I was mostly sourcing understanding about through the eyes of others.

My embarrassment, dysmorphia, and painful insecurity were often quite paralyzing. In elementary school, it didn't help that even though I was at the top of my class—the first to win spelling bees and geography quizzes, with a great capacity to memorize, digest, and transmit complex information—I had brown stains on my front teeth from a condition known as fluorosis. Despite my innate intelligence and accolades, I always had this underlying feeling that something was wrong with me born out of a physical manifestation of something that was never my fault to begin with. I've grown to understand that this kind of underlying experience early on in life—the emotions and lessons therein, not so much maybe the specifics—is actually quite common. Can you relate?

As far as I can recall, here is where my initial confusion and perhaps even amnesia about who I am and why I am here first took root. Quite early on I learned justification of my physical existence was wholly dependent upon my appearance, which required external validation, approval and acknowledgment from others, hence my obsession with my body and presentation. I learned at some level that if you loved me, liked me, approved of me—and of course I could feel you feeling this because my empathic sensitivity was highly attuned—then perhaps I could feel good about myself, finally.

So the moment in which I suddenly realized I had a choice as to what inner voice channel I was tuning into was rather exciting, maybe even a little liberating. At first it was also quite sad to realize how angry, self-critical, and judgmental I was of myself all that time, like I was speaking to myself as though I were my own worst enemy, in a tone that I would never wish upon my actual worst enemy. I wonder how many of us are living in internal experiences just like this.

For many it can be a jolt when you are caught by the surprise of hearing another voice within you that you have never witnessed before. It can feel like your sense of self is being shattered before your eyes. It can feel ungrounding and dissociating, absolutely. Sometimes this process unfolds quickly, and sometimes it happens slowly. There is no one way to live your life, there is only *your* way. Do you notice if you have other channels or voices you can choose to listen to? Or have you never even considered this being a possibility and the fact that I am mentioning it to you now sounds a tad bit scary, if you're being real?

Perhaps this voice is that of your higher consciousness or higher self, or maybe you resonate more with the term *true self*. The label here doesn't matter so much as the *feeling*, which you'll find is a central theme of our exploration in every step we take. Focus on the feeling and amplify the sensations you want to experience more deeply. Consider again (*consider* is such a powerful term that helps us to open our minds and therefore our hearts and intuitive awareness to new possibilities that inevitably lead us into expansion) that there is a guiding voice and presence, a conscious-ness, within you, or operating through you, perhaps as you, that wants you to be happy, to feel loved, and to know that you are whole and com-plete precisely as you are, right here and now. Wherever you are, however you are feeling and being, right now, is absolutely perfect.

"I find it amusing that we're all pretending to be normal when we could be insanely interesting instead."
—Atlas

In fact the end of every chapter to follow comes full of invitations for you to play and put into practice all we're learning and exploring. What's the point of more concepts without actually exploring the embodiment of your own understanding? But I don't want to leave us hanging or waiting till then, especially with all that was just covered. So when it comes to connecting with yourself and starting to differentiate your higher self-guidance or intuition from any other voices or energies present, one of my favorite practices for this is also the most simple. Lie down on the ground—best to do this on the ground as opposed to a couch or chair so you can really connect with the Earth—and align your spine as straight as possible to the Earth. Set a timer on your phone or watch for a few minutes; three is usually a great start or more if you'd like. Then start to take the deepest breaths you've taken all day—or maybe in all of your life, why not?! Feel your breath travel from the crown of your head down to the ends of your fingertips and toes and even into the earth.

Slow your breath down some more and notice how all your body sys-tems start to relax and rest into more presence. This can be challenging at first, but with practice I promise it becomes such a nourishing feeling to bask in your own energy and feel your system recalibrate with the nour-ishment of new oxygen and energy flow. From this space of presence and attunement to self, explore and play with your intuitive guidance. Do you have a question or something you'd love support with? See how it feels to ask and simply listen. If nothing comes in at first, that's totally fine.

Release expectations and any idea that it should go any particular way. Everyday is different and our bodies and energies are constantly evolving.

We'll get more into intuitive attunement and other ways to support yourself in remembering your higher guidance and unique ways you receive direction soon, I promise. For now, what would it feel like to do a practice like this for a few moments a day, knowing you're building the capacity to support yourself more each time? Congratulations if you've given this a go! It can be the most challenging thing to really sit with ourselves. So much vulnerability and emotions we've never given space to feel can come up. As long as we make a beginning and have a willingness to explore this new territory, there's really no greater gift we can give ourselves than the gift of our own presence and attention.

ASCENDING CONSCIOUSNESS

Here we are with a seemingly unanswerable question before us: what is consciousness? We'll notice this is a welcome trend in our path ahead—more paradoxes and questions that lead to only more questions. In fact, we may find that a core aspect of consciousness awakening, accepting life as it is and showing up as our true selves, isn't so much about finding the right answers to questions as it is about developing a greater capacity to ask better questions. You know that feeling when you understand something in its full depth and then you can explore it with such precise questions that excavate deeper into the truth of the matter at hand? It feels so good. Let's try that.

An inspiring friend once said: "The questions you're conditioned to ask prevent you from receiving the answers you truly seek." With that in mind, it seems that deep down what we're after in this ascension process is the ultra-satisfying sensation of experiencing ourselves as understanding something so fully that our questions penetrate the very nature of reality. Through this way of being, our inquiries can bring about completely new possibilities that we never could have before imagined. What would it be like to become blank slates and consciously practice curiosity and genuine wonder about the nature of the world as we experience it? Imagine what news ways of being and seeing may emerge from this emptiness free of constructs or conditioning that inevitably keep us repeating the same familiar cycles.

This consciousness question seems more like something that gets to be lived by each and every individual on their own path, as it is perhaps unanswerable otherwise. It is an experiential exploration requiring your full presence and participation. It is perhaps the reason we are on Earth, incarnated in human form in the first place: to experience what consciousness is and to develop our own unique conception of reality therein. **What is ascension about for you? Let your life be the answer, let your choices be the journey, unfolding before your eyes.**

From this seemingly simple inquiry, thousands, maybe millions of writings have been created since the dawn of humanity, which is certainly beyond what we're conditioned to believe in as recorded history. From what I've gathered, human history goes back much further than anything we've been taught—we'll venture further on into this potential in our path ahead. Herein lies another opportunity to play in asking better questions as we expand our understanding and remember our innate wisdom.

So what is consciousness and why does it matter to explore it? Still waiting for an answer from me? Instead of quoting other teachers, writings, scientists, and the like who have countless definitions and quotes to offer as to what consciousness is and why the exploration of it matters, I'm going to cut right to the chase and give you what feels true to share for our unique evolution underway. I think that's all that really matters, actually, especially these days, as we see the guru paradigm that's led us for so long falling apart faster than we can keep up.

We are now fast emerging out of the ages of guru-worship, in which seekers followed a supposedly special being residing up high, untouchable, on a spiritual mountaintop. Instead consider this: **You are your own teacher. You are the leader here, creating your reality, leading your life, with every choice you decide to make or not make. You are in charge, can you imagine?** And that is precisely the point of our path, our co-creative exploration into consciousness, at hand: let's uncover what being the guru, the creator, the leader of your own life truly entails, and how to live this powerful invitation in as many moments as possible. From here, *you* decide what ascension and consciousness mean for you. Do we even need a definition to attach ourselves to in order to explain or understand—or, rather, remember—that which we already are and always have been? When we are being who we are, the need for words to explain ourselves and definitions therein altogethers seems to fall away.

"The only way to deal with an unfree world is to become so absolutely free that your very existence is an act of rebellion."
—Albert Camus

Why did you pick up this book in the first place, what drew you in? What are your intentions for learning about ascension, awakening consciousness and learning how you may live with more awareness, greater presence, power, and authenticity? Why is now a crucial moment to be asking precisely these questions? Maybe you are in the perfect place right now to receive your own guidance and to trust yourself more than you ever have. Are you starting to feel some layers of control and contraction fall away already? Great, right on time. Let it all go—everything you thought you knew about yourself, the world, and each other. What if you and I get to be blank slates, completely open and able to begin again so we can learn what life has in store for us?

Let's try it out and explore together, as though we're starting from scratch, what ascension and consciousness have to do with where we are and who we are right now, shall we? Another way we can understand consciousness is as pure awareness. For the purposes of our exploration I would add that it is also this awareness that brings an idea or energy into form. Without consciousness or awareness, nothing exists. It is our awareness of what is that brings the focus of our consciousness into material existence. Can you see how your perception is allowing the reality surrounding you and within you to exist in the first place?

Consciousness, perhaps in its ideal sense, can also be understood as a state of being fully awake, completely present, and therefore capable of clearly observing subtle and overt energetic forces that are at play in constructing reality. Consciousness is the awareness of all that is, as experienced from the vantage point of your inner observer, which some may refer to as the soul, your true self, or your inner being. Consciousness also infers presence, which can be understood as your aliveness and the extent to which you are willing to be completely present within your body, your emotions, your thoughts, and your actions.

"Attempting to understand consciousness with your mind is like trying to illuminate the sun with a candle."
—Mooji

Loving yourself, choosing yourself, and living the kind of life you truly want to live in all possible regards sounds awesome, doesn't it? And isn't that what we all truly want and deserve? I think so, and, considering that countless memes on social media, refrigerator magnets, postcards, and the like are all annoyingly implying how fast and simple it is to self-actualize and embody one's ideal self . . . shouldn't it all be pretty easy? Let's be real though. The path into self-love, awakening, creating your reality, and all the other personal development and spiritual slogans in between is one that must be all your own, designed for you and by you. Choose your own adventure. Enter at your own risk. Sometimes I wish we had been given (or had given ourselves) more warning signs for the actual path ahead.

Ascension, awakening to your true self, and really loving yourself for who you are right now require your full consciousness all the time, all the way here, fully present. That takes devotion, because this path of evolution isn't easy or even fun all the time—sometimes the growth and healing that emerge for us to be with and even alchemize can feel like death as the old layers of our false selves and the old behaviors that don't work anymore (and never really did if we're honest) fall away. It really does feel like we could be dying as our ego itself sheds its protective layers that equate all pain with the threat of actual mortality.

Trust me, you're not alone. We all have traumas and wounds that shape who we are, what we believe, how we show up in the world, and what experiences we avail ourselves to have again and again. It seems to me that we always have two choices: to see how life is happening *for* us (and perhaps even that you've created it precisely like that) or that it's happening *to* us. Are you at this moment choosing to be a creator or a victim? Are you choosing to love and accept yourself and move in the direction of your heart's calling or not? Perhaps ascension and awakening our consciousness can be that simple. Let's see.

"Once you have given up your limited self willingly to the Unlimited, you will rejoice so much in that consciousness that you will not care to be small again."
—Sufi Inayat Khan

AWAKENING IS AN INSIDE JOB

Welcome to Earth! You're a multidimensional human being with an incredible soul that wants to be fully embodied and expressed, and you are here to live an extraordinary life. You're here to know yourself, you're here to meet yourself, to explore and come into deep alignment with what you believe in, to remember why you are here, to understand what gifts you are here to give and to receive (and eventually to understand they are one and the same), and ultimately to know your innate ability to imagine and then create precisely what you want.

We're living on Earth in quite an astonishing time, to say the least, wherein everyday it feels almost as though millions and, yes, imagine billions, of people are waking up. They are waking up to themselves. They are waking up to who they really are and why they are here. They are waking up asking questions like, "What is my purpose? What is my destiny? How do I live a meaningful life? How do I take care of myself? How do I live in alignment with my soul? How do I trust myself? How do I follow my intuition? How do I become truly present? How can I receive more of what life really wants to give me?" Perhaps you've found yourself asking similar questions and maybe some others too. We can dig deeper in our attunements to follow at the end of this chapter, promise.

Waking up is the process of remembering oneself, remembering why you're really here, and remembering that you always have a choice. In every moment you have a choice wherein you can decide to align with your highest calling, what it is that you truly love, what it is that makes you feel most alive, what it is that life is naturally guiding you toward, or conversely you can choose to be in resistance. Did you have to read that again? Choose to be in resistance. It doesn't feel great to hear that reflection, yet in my experience, acknowledging our responsibility in creation of our reality is a key step toward allowing more alignment, ease, and enjoyment in—to everything.

Do you really have a choice? Imagine that your conscious waking state is a series of moment-to-moment opportunities that you are responding to. And each of those moments is giving you a chance to attune more precisely with your true desires. **Waking up, then, is really the process of learning to listen to yourself so that you can actually feel, hear, know, and trust your desires. Waking up is also about becoming the observer of your reality, becoming aware of your capacity to create your reality in great detail.**

Living fully awake and present is a path that each one must trudge individually as each path is completely unique. In this way you can responsibly make the choices that feel best for you to support you in living the kind of life you want to live. The question becomes: what kind of path will you choose to carve out for yourself? Will you choose one in which you're awake and devoted to being fully alive, completely present to make clear decisions that feel aligned with who you really are? Will you devote yourself to knowing your inner being, your deepest desires, your soul calling, and your genius gifts? Will you design your life to support you in sharing and expressing precisely who you truly are? Or not? It's hard to believe this is a choice, but it is one that we are challenged to sit with and consciously align with again and again, especially amid expansive periods when resistance to take the next right step into the unknown may be at an all-time high.

**"Our difficulties launch us into new states of
consciousness where we are inspired to step out of the
reality of our smallest thoughts and step into the limitless
freedom of our biggest dreams."**
—Debbie Ford

The journey from being asleep and unconscious toward ascension, awakening, and consciousness embodied in this human form is one of continuously expanding into more love, truth, integrity, and absolute resilience. It is one of intentionally seeking to go into your shadows and triggers to activate the lessons you are here to learn. These lessons always lead into more wholeness, remembrance, and freedom. It's all an inside job, truly. And you get to dive deep, all the way in and through whatever is seemingly in the way of simply being yourself.

At this moment in time, I believe waking up is inevitable, and we each get to choose how difficult or easy our process is. We might as well learn how to live in this awakened state as our consciousness naturally expands more and more everyday while the Earth's frequency (have you heard of the Schumann Resonance?*) silmultaneously rises more and more each day. We learn how to acclimate to a higher frequency way of being in which energetic sensitivity and higher consciousness are the new norms. We have arrived.

Waking up means you start to see through the ways in which you have been complicit in following an authority or a leader that you never actually really agreed with but that you followed because you felt safe and secure knowing that someone else was responsible for your well-being. Waking up means you awaken to your own innate sense of self-leadership and self-responsibility. Here you take responsibility for creating your life

---

* The Schumann Resonance is a measurement of Earth's electromagnetic field including the scale of frequencies running through it. This measurement shows that Earth's frequency has been rising exponentially over the last few years especially of late. As Earth's frequency elevates, I believe we are all fundamentally supported in elevating our individual frequencies and therefore increasing our individual capacity for consciousness. When we operate in a higher frequency state, we are more in tune with intuition, with the natural flow of life, with the elements, with our body's needs and guidance and we can experience a more full-spectrum range of emotions and energies in a more multidimensional way of being.

as you desire, as you realize that living your purpose and the meanings that you derive from how you show up in every action are up to you.

Ascension is an inner journey deep into your cells, and even into the depths of your energetic blueprint. It means meeting all the parts of your-self that have been hiding beneath insecurity, fear, and all separation-based constructs that you learned to keep you safe from being truly seen. Being seen is revealing, intimate, and at times overwhelming. Why? Because you are actually seeing yourself in your divinity and your infinite power. You are remembering you are capable of creating whatever you want. It can feel so confronting to behold our true capacity and power. It might even feel impossible to grasp it all as the process to embodying more of our selves and our innate potential is an infinite one with no end.

> **"We do not see things as they are, we see them as we are."**
> **—Anaïs Nin**

Ascension can feel like a huge responsibility. We can sometimes be surrounded by people who are not standing in their own power, play-ing small, and it can feel dangerous to stand out and shine too bright. By doing so we might bring up sadness, disappointment, insecurity, and emptiness in others, and no one wants to be complicit in creating more of what we don't want. But it's a backward cycle, isn't it? You might not want to shine too bright because you'll make others uncomfortably sensitive to how they're also not showing up fully or shining? That doesn't make sense, does it? What if we dropped that program once and for all?

It's a lot to take in sometimes, that in any moment you can create whatever you want. In fact, that's why you and I are here on Earth. We are here to remember this infiniteness of our existence—and to no longer be overwhelmed or burdened by it but instead inspired, elated, and ex-panded. How about that? At the end of the day it's not your job to manage anyone else's experience, life, feelings, energy, or reaction. It is, however, your responsibility to continuously seek to embody your power and live completely and fully all the way alive. It's up to you to do what you want, and to free yourself from familial and social conditioning and repression. It's yours to choose again and again to give yourself permission to take up space in this world, then expand even more. You can allow yourself to shine your light. By doing so, you become an example of what's possible. In simply being, the way you are becoming in turn inspires others to attune to their own liberation, should they so choose.

Ascension is a personal choice. What a relief to claim that we are done taking responsibility for others and for the planet as a whole. We aren't even responsible for others waking up, or for influencing others' choices in any particular way. Can we trust ourselves to choose what's right and for others to do the same whenever they are ready? Here is our practice at hand.

On this journey of ascension, you and I embark upon self-realization and self-remembrance of our innate wisdom, truth, and power. We will receive guidance and support in transmuting shame, guilt, fear, and everything else that we feel has been holding us back from living the life we are here to live and to fully enjoy. We will learn how to be authentic, responsible leaders and creators of extraordinary realities that will continue to amaze us by how much more magically our experiences manifest the more we trust, surrender, relax, and allow life to support us precisely as it's designed to. It's time to receive.

"Conscious evolution inspires in us a mysterious and humble awareness that we have been created by this awesome process of evolution and are now being transformed by it."
—Barbara Marx Hubbard

WHAT HAPPENS WHEN YOU WAKE UP

Ascension involves seeing the reality in which you live more holistically, seeing it as an interwoven tapestry. You begin to have a multidimensional experience in which all of your senses are lit up and fully utilized, in which every cell in your being is illuminated with more energy and a greater capacity to receive more information, insight, and inspiration. When you first wake up, oftentimes you might ask yourself, "Why am I here? What is the meaning of my life? What are we all really here for?" You very naturally start to see the ways in which you are out of alignment or out of integrity when it comes to living the kind of life that you feel worthy of living.

When some people first wake up, it can be the most uncomfortable, painful, gut-wrenching, soul-crushing experience imaginable. For many on this path of awakening, it is exactly that. It can feel at times that a part of you is dying. What's really occurring is old identities, old aspects of yourself, are in fact dying. It's interesting to note that your ego doesn't make the distinction between a real-life physical death and the spiritual energetic death of an old self.

When you first wake up, you may start to feel more sensitive to everything. Your senses light up, your perception expands, your ability to feel deepens, your intuitive expression widens and shows up in ways that are sometimes surprising. You may have more recall of your dreams. You may start to sense more of an empathic ability in your conversations and relationships with others, especially with those who you care about most.

"Consciousness is a mystery that faces the mystery of potential and transforms it into actuality. We do that with every choice we make. Our choices determine the destiny of the world. By making a choice, you alter the structure of reality."
—Jordan B. Peterson

You may start to feel a deeper yearning for purpose and meaning in your life. You may start to see through habitual patterns and obligations and structures that feel so familiar in your life. You may start to feel incredibly uncomfortable in situations, dynamics, and relationships that used to be really safe, that used to feel really comfortable for you. You may suddenly start to see the ways in which the things that used to be so familiar are actually no longer aligned. You will start to see through things that feel superficial. You may even start to feel sensitive to advertising, promotions, or people that are trying to sell you on something or coerce you in any way. All in all you become more highly attuned to truth and untruth. You can feel what's real (and unreal) from miles away. This is why cultivating trust in our intuition and clear discernment are some of the greatest tools we can harness in our ascension and embodiment process.

For me there were numerous awakening moments, and there are more to come, surely. The longer you go on your path of awakening and remembering, the more you see how continuous the awakening one undergoes truly is. Ascension is happening in each moment with every activation of our consciousness into deeper presence and greater fulfillment of our purpose, devoid of any externalized goal or attachment. Maybe our purpose becomes as simple as being ourselves and doing what we love. Maybe one's purpose is to embody love, truth, justice, or beauty. Maybe our purpose isn't about what we do but who we are while doing it or, rather, being it. Does that ring true for you too?

My first wake-up call came when I really had no choice but to get sober from drugs and alcohol at the age of twenty-four. The moment struck while I was sitting in my therapist's office, who at the time I thought I was going to see for career counseling. Somehow, though, I started telling her the truth of what I was really doing on the side of my day job. I was masterfully leading a double life at the time. I was living in New York City, working in financial services by day and then secretly working side hustles by night. These side hustles entailed putting myself into grave danger repeatedly and hiding amidst tons of fear and shame underneath it all.

"Everything we do is for the purpose of altering consciousness. We form friendships so that we can feel love and avoid loneliness. . . . We read for the pleasure of thinking another person's thoughts. Every waking moment, and even in our dreams, we struggle to direct the flow of sensation, emotion, and cognition towards states of consciousness that we value."
—Sam Harris

Based on the abridged version of my life that I was sharing with my therapist, she was going to prescribe anti-anxiety medication to me because I was showing all the classic symptoms of manic depression or bipolar disorder, or some mix of the two. I felt immense shock at this potential diagnosis, especially because I sensed that I wouldn't be able to drink alcohol while on that medication. And then what? A huge part of my life and identity—the one who only felt comfortable drinking in a club surrounded by loud people and loud music to drown out my anxiety—would be taken away, and I couldn't have that. No way.

So I started telling her the truth of what I was really up to. I finally told someone—a living human—the truth of what I was involved in. You see, I was stripping at a club two nights a week from 8:00 P.M. to 4:00 A.M. and then going to work from 9:00 A.M. to 5:00 P.M. the next day as though nothing had happened. I was also "assisting" a Wall Street banker in his penthouse apartment to coerce girls from a popular online listing site to do naked photo shoots and sexy video shoots, usually under the influence of copious amounts of alcohol and sometimes drugs (although by then I was usually drinking enough to feel like I was altered beyond any state that drugs could induce). Lastly, I was occasionally going to interviews for various escorting jobs that I obsessively thought could be my ticket to financial freedom. It seemed like a way out of my perilous student loan debt and all the worry I felt about my credit cards and bills that were piling up to a paralyzing degree.

I had gone into that therapist's office to get career counseling. Why? Because I thought if I could just know what my purpose was, I could stop drinking and doing drugs, stop putting myself in danger, and stop worrying about money all the time. But there was something about her that allowed me to open up more deeply. I ended up telling her everything. I told her about the drinking, the drugs, the lack of eating and sleep. I even told her about the dangerous encounters with strangers and the late nights falling asleep on the train by myself still dressed in the costumes from the club. The look on her face was my moment of grace. Her eyes staring back at me communicated more than she'd ever know. I felt like I saw myself in the mirror of her eyes and finally realized the dead-end road I was on if I continued doing what I was doing. My life choice was revealed, clear as day: did I want to live? If I answered *yes* to that question, then I would have to change what I was doing and take a new path.

It was unbearable at the time. I couldn't go forward the way I was going, but I had no idea what to do instead. The shame I felt was paralyzing. The fear was overwhelming beyond belief. I didn't want to die, but I truly didn't know how to live. Awakening is just like this. I had no idea where I was going but I couldn't go back to what was, ever again. For me, the new path started by walking into my first meeting of Alcoholics Anonymous. It was there where I finally let myself be seen and held by others whom I could start practicing being real with. There, everything changed.

Service announcement: please don't let the AA references get in the way of connecting with the underlying surrender and wake-up call I'm conveying and inviting you to consider. AA was a huge part of my life and helped me in so many ways for a few years. Until I naturally evolved out of identifying as someone *with something*, I had to constantly repeat to be a part of a program based on common identifiers. I am endlessly thankful for all I learned there and for the brilliant relationships and support I will always remember. For now, I choose to continue practicing sobriety as long as it feels authentic to me and as long as it feels good for my body. I am admittedly even now still learning to release judgment around the right way or best way to attain spiritual liberation and to embody pure presence. For a time I thought absolute sobriety was required, and yet now I am seeing more and more how everybody is so unique and may ask for different support in various moments of life's waves. We are evolving so quickly, and as we do, so do our unique needs and methods of support. As long as we keep listening and responding with what is truly right for us—I believe we can do no harm.

"You're an infinite soul, a spark of Consciousness, and your perception is a creative decision you're continuously making."
—Yol Swan

There were many other moments of ascension and consciousness awakening that followed—some shocking in their immensity and others (especially lately) more subtle and sometimes even unnoticeable in their simplicity. I'll share more through our pages ahead when it's relevant and helpful to do so. Some entailed seeing and hearing my own intuitive guidance for the first time; some entailed seeming breaks with reality in which I felt new sensations and potentials open up before my eyes; some entailed being able to sit still in actual peace and presence for more than ten minutes, and others have felt like the most unfathomable, miraculous synchronicities and cosmic alignments I could never have imagined happening so perfectly. Some have also left me crying on the floor, processing out an emotion I've repressed since childhood or from another lifetime. In the moment it's arising, even if it feels impossible to fully release, I still do my best to try and simply allow it.

What I've learned most of all is this: can we love and accept this moment, ourselves, and everything in between just as it is, and just as we are? This might be the key to everything we've ever wanted: finding true acceptance and meeting life just as it is without wanting to change or control anything at all. It's okay to try it all on for size—it might feel intense or even impossible to ponder this right now. And that's absolutely perfect if that's the case. Can you be okay with being precisely where you are, as you are? Let this be your practice going forward as you release attachment to any pressure you put on yourself to be anywhere (or anyone) else. **An old saying from recovery comes to mind here, about miracles and what they promise herein: they materialize in our lives when we are ready to receive them, sometimes quickly, sometimes slowly—and they will always arise when we are willing to do the work.**

> **"The two most important days in your life are the day you are born and the day you find out why."**
> **—Mark Twain**

In our journey into ascension and attuning to higher consciousness we entrain within our beings the core transformations, healings, and awakenings we are called to activate at this time of great remembering here on Earth. Take what you need and leave the rest—and also consider how perhaps the more you put into action what's here, the more you may feel like yourself. What kind of world do we get to play in when more of us are choosing to embody our true selves more often than not? I wonder what life will be like when more of us are listening to our inner guidance, trusting our truth, actualizing our purpose, and really remembering who we are and why we are here. Sounds like a lot of fun, doesn't it? Let's see what we're really made of.

> **"Going beyond our ordinary concept of self is what always brings us the greatest sense of joy in life. Going beyond our own boundaries brings us an ecstatic awareness of how we are truly created in connection with all that is."**
> **—Cynthia Sue Larson**

ASCENSION IS A GAME: LET'S PLAY

One way I like to conceptualize reality and our collective experience of life is to look at it like a game. Have you ever felt like relating to life this way? I've also witnessed and felt this vision of life as a game numerous times in sharing energy healing and intuitive guidance from the Akashic Records (a high-frequency field of energy containing all the history of all the souls in all of the multiverse, beyond space and time and all perceived limitations therein). Did I just freak you out? If so, it might not be the last time—but hang in there, we're still getting acquainted. The Akashic Records are just an energy source that we can all attune to when we choose that can be felt and accessed as a space of unconditional love, healing, and pristine clarity. No big deal, just multidimensional humans having fun over here, doing what we do, playing in all the realms we get to weave in, when and how we want.

I want to share some experiences with you from my explorations in Akashic healing and intuitive energy work. But first, some context may be helpful. The Akashic Records are a multidimensional, intuitive energy healing modality I've studied, practiced and taught since 2015. Since beginning my practitioner journey, I've been honored to share sessions with hundreds of people all over the world. As our Ascension Lexicon reminds, the Akashic Records are the collective history and wisdom of all souls and all lifetimes across all universes, beyond time and space, stored in the Akashic field (also referred to as the *zero point field* or *known field*), the energetic fiber connecting all living beings. To me, they are a source of unconditional love and healing that we can always access whenever we choose.

Many times in sharing Akashic Records transmissions, as well as in a past-life regression experience, I've seen the vision of a library or, as some may refer to it, the hall of records. In this library, a higher vibrational realm, there appears to be a collection of all kinds of different games, some of them reminiscent of different board games we may know and love, like Candy Land, Monopoly, and the Game of Life. Imagine an array of every kind of game you could imagine, all of which have different objectives, different kinds of players, different kinds of themes, different ways to win, different obstacles, and different strategies.

Now imagine these games are like placeholders for the kinds of narratives and experiences we choose to live out in each lifetime. Perhaps we each incarnate into Earth to try out different games and different ways to play according to different rules. Then, maybe part of each game, no matter which one we choose, actually unfolds as an invitation: we may have begun in a particular game template but eventually we realize and remember that we can make up new rules, new strategies, and that, in fact, we've actually been creating the game (and chose it from the start) all along.

"Man is the only creature who refuses to be what he is."
—Albert Camus

Imagine this is the lifetime in which you choose that you are going to learn how to master love. So, in this game of mastering love, you're going to choose the perfect family that's designed to imprint the perfect traumas of abandonment, betrayal, and rejection so that you have that contrasting experience of believing that you are not enough and that you need to be more in order to receive love. And maybe you threw in a little bit of addiction, plus some codependency for good measure to really learn what it means to come into sovereignty and interdependence: true intimacy with self and others.

I experienced a lot of sexual shame and trauma from being highly disassociated for much of my life—meaning I felt like I was existing outside of my body largely to avoid feeling the immensity of sensitivity I could access through embodiment. I didn't have the tools to withstand my capacity for feeling and sensing data from the world around me, so my coping strategy was to check out and let my limited mental frame of reality (my intellectual mind) lead the way, unknowingly of course. Yet somehow I still managed to have a lot of sexual experiences and relationships since my mind thought I should, especially by a certain time. But my body wasn't always on board with the experience and oftentimes incurred a sense of violation or unwarranted entry, which was very traumatic in hindsight.

Tying this back into the idea that we choose to come in and play certain games in this life to better know ourselves and to master specific lessons our true being deeply desires understanding, I can see now how I actualized a lot of sexual shame and trauma in this bodily experience in this life to help catalyze my awakening and desire for actual embodiment (which requires healing disassociation). Not only have I realized this pattern in myself, but I have helped countless others through similar experiences as well, all pointing to the possibility that in a way we experienced certain traumatic events to help us specifically learn the unique lesson(s) we wanted to deeply understand and maybe even master in this life. I am aware that what I am offering here can be easily misconstrued as implying that sexual abuse or any trauma one experiences in life is a result of their own choosing. This is not my intention. Plus, to say that would be a vast oversimplification that strategically deters us from exploring new awarenesses and emergent possibilities to further expand our reality and self-concept.

For me, and for so many others I've seen move through their ascension-embodiment process, we inevitably arrive to a moment of truth where we get to accept our reality and what happened to us for what it is and then, choose from here—what we want to create and how we want to orient. I believe that I experienced immense disassociation, dysmorphia, sexual shame and violation, addiction, and other traumas to help me wake up and come more into my bodily form so I could actually listen to what my body had been trying to tell me all along. Otherwise, without accepting these experiences as lessons—what other choice did I have available? Could I have continued as I was living only to eventually die? Or, could I instead choose to wake up, change, evolve, and thrive. Is there really a choice in this case anyway?

Perhaps then one might choose at some level, maybe at a soul level, reinforced by one's higher consciousness, that "Yes, I want to live, I want to actually understand myself, meet myself, and love myself—and despite everything that's happened, I want to know the truth." Here is where the healing journey begins. It's time to learn about all the ways that you uniquely want to receive healing. Here we are invited to learn how we prefer to receive and give ourselves our own best medicine—we start seeing and remembering who we really are and then the journey we thought had already started truly begins. Then someday we'll meet and have a talk, much like the words put forth in this book, about all you learned and all you went through, so that perhaps someday maybe many others might benefit, learn, and heal from your experience. Maybe this is the point.

Evidently, the real game is to figure out what game you are here to play and then decide how you want to play it. How do you want to show up, how do you want to feel, what lessons do you want to learn, what obstacles do you want to transcend, what are you focused on achieving? It's all up to you. You are here to play the extraordinary game meant just for you to learn and remember yourself, and you're creating all the rules. I also love to witness this invitation as a call to action—for us to individually and together create all the things and ways of being in the world that we wish existed. Sound like fun? Let's play.

One piece of our collective game I love to highlight is this: **Being spiritual isn't special, it's simply our true nature.** Being spiritual isn't something that makes you different, important, or even cool, although it does seem like it's quite a trend these days. Maybe that's for the best: the more catalysts for trying new things and expanding one's understanding of reality, the better, right? Being spiritual is actually no different than being human. As humans, we are inherently spiritual beings. It is our nature. We are spirit embodied in human form, and perhaps our life, especially as we awaken into our higher consciousness, becomes about really knowing the spirit that we all carry within us, that we all share.

"The privilege of a lifetime is to become who you truly are."
—Joseph Campbell

How does it feel to relate to ascension as a game? And to realize that at some level we all chose the game (this life) that we most wanted to play (the lessons we wanted to learn and grow from)? I don't know about you, but it feels pretty unifying to me, especially when we consider the collective shift we're all now invited to embark upon out of the victim game into the game of conscious creator. Maybe we can all actually start to see how much of our lives thus far have entailed an evolution out of victim consciousness, away from feeling that we are victim to circumstance.

As we awaken and ascend into higher consciousness awareness, we start to see through the collective conditioning that has been predicated on fear, scarcity, and competition. We also see how these ways of being actually feel quite unnatural to our true selves and the kinds of states we are more familiar with orienting to. When we operate from the space of awakened consciousness, presence, and authenticity, we can really see through these games that are based in control, fear, and duality. From here, we play as conscious co-creators in the game of ascension and embodiment instead of victims to any paradigms that used to run our lives before we woke up to interrupt and repattern it all. Another correlation here is when you wake up, you naturally feel a desire to clear your physical body, to become healthier, and to start taking good care of yourself. You'll start to feel more energetically, emotionally balanced and stable. You very naturally will gravitate toward spiritual tools, emotional support, and community that resonate in a higher vibrational way of being that you feel yourself called to attune to more fully.

Let's take a moment, shall we? Seems like we can tune into some immense compassion right now for the millions and even billions of people who are waking up in this moment, wondering almost overnight how they got here, what it is that they're here to do. Maybe even you, reading these words right now—you're starting to see your life in a completely new way, seeing how you can no longer go along with the motions, can no longer show up to a job you don't love, can no longer show up to relationships that feel draining, can no longer stand for so many obligations in life that aren't truly fulfilling, that don't serve you at the soul level.

> **"All of our suffering in life is from saying we**
> **want one thing and doing another."**
> **—Debbie Ford**

Trust me, we'll get into all of this in the journey ahead—I've been where you are and resonate so much with how overwhelming everything can feel at the beginning of making a new path like the one we're just now exploring. Something we'll be invited into considering again and again is that there is no rush—and maybe we can actually slow down a whole lot, especially since so many of us have been speeding through life wondering when we'll ever get to the finish line. Well, consider that maybe there isn't a finish line and nowhere to get to—only an invitation to be more fully where we already are, as we are.

2

I'M ASCENDING, NOW WHAT?

What would it be like to allow your entire being to be fully here, revealed in your immensity and sheer magnitude? Not holding anything back, not hiding away to please or make anyone else comfortable? What if you were to let the ferocity of your presence and its penetrative effect be felt by those you came here to illuminate and divinely trigger? How much more energy do you have to channel into what feels good for you—your own creativity, desires, and divine callings—when you stop trying and managing and efforting in all the ways you learn to turn off and turn down? I'm willing to explore all of the above with you if you are too.

What happens along the ascension path pretty quickly is that the people who are no longer in resonance with you as you choose to grow and evolve get knocked out of the field (as I like to say) pretty fast. Those who aren't willing to be in their own truth and light will stand out like sore thumbs in your awareness now more than ever. Sometimes we really are moving too fast and becoming too bright for some others to handle. But those who are ready will feel in your presence an oasis of healing and remembering—we can't help but have this effect on one another. It's like a domino effect of truth—one truth activating the next and so on; the resonance is infinitely magnetic. Then life gets even more fun because we find more of our true soul family connections, the people who just get it, who are easy to be with.

"There is almost a sensual longing for communion with others who have a large vision. The immense fulfillment of the friendship between those engaged in furthering the evolution of consciousness has a quality impossible to describe."
—Pierre Teilhard de Chardin

Yes, your entire life may shift or, at least, what you used to think it had to be surely will—instead you open to infinite possibilities and ultra-clear guidance as to your next right steps. Here we get to practice letting go of thinking in general. We are invited to not fill the space revealing itself but instead to watch the show. It's all already happening—an aligned, awakened, purposeful life—through you and for you. Can we receive it all at our full depth? And learn to even enjoy the space in between words? Here we are invited to sink into greater stillness and silence. Here is where more of who we really are is welcomed forth and met. Here is where we feel in our bones all we came here to remember and radiate. Here is where we can truly meet—ourselves and each other—at last.

This sounds all lovely and wonderful until you sit with the potentials and start to maybe feel a little anxiety arise around the how-to part. We want intimacy, we want presence, we want awakening and all the gifts therein to share and celebrate—yes, it all sounds so good. Give it to me now—I want that, yes, like yesterday. But how do we get there? Well, that's what we are venturing into here. A big part of our journey will entail again and again the practice of checking our minds and all their embedded conditioning that's been driving our life ship for far too long. Here we adventure into ending the repetitive unconscious loops we see unfolding in too many familiar ways. How? By tuning into our higher mind or intuition, our bodies, our hearts, and our feelings.

Our minds are incredible instruments indeed and quite genius when it comes to executing certain tasks and creating on many scales. Yes, we love our minds and we're grateful for the capacity to think, to be in inquiry at such great depth, to problem solve, and to carry out complex orders in bringing our dreams to life. However, the reality is our minds up until now have been overly conditioned to operate in default survival mode, ripe with far more fear, anxiety, and scarcity than we require.

We now live in an era in which we've never been more safe, we've never had this much access to technological advancement and resources therein, and we literally have the means to solve nearly all of our global crises in a moment's notice if we could only agree on which course of action to take. You see, we have no scarcity of resources or solutions. We have the more beautiful world we know is possible right here, ready to live into at our fingertips as soon as we decide to change our behavior and conditioning to allow us to finally relax into what's already here and start consciously making the most of it. The biggest global issue at hand right now isn't environmental or sociopolitical; it's not even humanitarian.

What we have on our hands is a crisis in consciousness. We have a mass population of humans on Earth who have been asleep for too long, believing by default that they're victim to the world around them, that the world is even out to get them, that they're alone in figuring it all out, and that there's a scarcity of resources that need to be fought for in a collectively agreed upon every-man-for-himself mentality. The real issue with most of us, however, is really not our fault. It's most often simply a side effect or even a guarantee of the cultures we are conditioned in our entire lives, which teach us to look outside ourselves instead of inside for all our basic needs.

"It's clearly a crisis of two things: of consciousness and conditioning. We have the technological power, the engineering skills to save our planet, to cure disease, to feed the hungry, to end war; but we lack the intellectual vision, the ability to change our minds. We must decondition ourselves from 10,000 years of bad behavior. And, it's not easy."
—Terence McKenna

What if flipping our script is as straightforward as shifting our programming much like we would for one of our phones, smart TVs, or computers? Think about it: isn't it strange that in the lifetime of your iPhone or computer you typically make numerous updates without giving it a second thought? And why? Because making the updates ensures your system runs effectively, can adapt successfully to changes in the ecosystem or environment, and can function at the highest possible level no matter what. So why don't we approach our bodies, our consciousness, and our whole beings with the same awareness and rigor?

Think of your consciousness as the software of your internal operating system that powers all aspects of your supercomputer body. The body actually contains other bodies within it that can be thought of as the emotional body, the mental body, the physical body, and the energetic body. Sometimes these bodies are also referred to as *planes* in which your consciousness can experience itself in different tones or textures. There are also, of course, subsystems at play weaving through your operating system, supporting the super computer in optimally functioning—some of which include your circulatory system, your nervous system, your endocrine systems, your lymphatic system or immune system, your digestive system, your muscles, skin, hair, nails, bones, and your reproductive and respiratory systems.

Consider all the layers in your awareness now that make up your entire being. And now consider the rather limited frame through which we all too likely orient. We are seeing such a small snippet of what's actually here, feeling such a small slice of the overall potential of what is truly available to us. Ascension initiates us into sensing there is so much more than we've ever known, and we get to experience it head on. Our infinite, awakened reality invites us to figuratively jump off cliffs into unknown new possibilities again and again. Eventually, with practice we become comfortable with the sensation—leaping and flying—as we remember that it's not our job to know anything but instead to enjoy the show and even—dare I say it—have fun on this ride called life. This process entails a deep nervous system rewiring that is a large part of the path home to ourselves and each other.

"Vulnerability really means to be strong and secure enough
within yourself that you are able to walk outside without
your armor on. You are able to show up in life as just you.
That is genuine strength and courage."
—Alaric Hutchinson

EARTH SCHOOL: WE CAME TO LEARN CONTRAST

Have you ever considered that we might be here on Earth to be in school?
It sure does seem like we are here to learn a ton and grow, so the school
analogy fits us pretty well, don't you think? What I've come to understand
is that we really do get to choose to see this lifetime as our school within
the greater game of our life if we'd like to. Consider this: Earth School
is a place where we arrive when we are ready to learn about contrast and
polarities, so we can masterfully understand the true nature of reality as
our soul most deeply desires to understand it. What if we come here to
simply learn and understand, period. Maybe with that in mind, we can
stop being so hard on ourselves and others to be perfect, to have life figured out, to be somewhere other than where we are. Maybe we can rest
into the knowing that we are all here to learn and grow and that there
is no end point or destination in the process—just more evolution and
expansion, infinitely.

What I feel to be true at my deepest heart's knowing is that we are all
such infinite beings, we are all spirit. We are all infinite spirits. We are all
aspects of divinity. Each and every one of us is part of the same light. We are
a warrior crew indeed—truly, a ground crew made up of absolutely bright,
powerful, radiant lights here to shift consciousness on mass levels—to architect new realities we've never seen before actualized in the physical plane.
I like to consider how not just any spirit chooses to come down and attend
Earth School. It feels to me that Earth is a place where particularly powerful

spiritual beings choose to come explore a specific calling, yearning, or mission to transcend and transmute particularly dense energies. They do this not just for themselves and for all of the other living beings on Earth but for the collective consciousness of all of the multiverse.

Did I lose you? There we go getting all multidimensional, flying into the ethers. I get it—maybe this is newer-feeling information, but like I said before—can we wear some of these potentials like loose garments and see where they might lead us if we play along? See how it feels. I promise it can't hurt. What I'm getting at is simply this: the universe we've been taught to believe in is actually far more vast than most would care to admit. And we're barely scratching the surface of what's truly possible through our intuitive perception, our multidimensional gifts, the expression of our genius and really our awareness and remembrance of how vast the history of our planet and our multiverse truly is. We are like infants in a spiritual birthing process.

One thing to inquire into—who historically has been in charge (or rather, put themselves in charge) of telling history? History ("his-story") is always recorded and told from the position of the winner and in many cases the oppressor. So, perhaps the history that we've learned in school, the history that we've been conditioned to practice, to study, that's been ingrained in our consciousness, has always been skewed according to what story benefits those in charge. So much history has also been destroyed along the way, especially strategically so if it didn't benefit the ones in power. Here we have an opportunity to clean the slate of what we think we know—and all we've been taught—to instead open up to what else might be possible for us. Perhaps we get to tune in with a new narrative, a new collective story, one that feels better, is more empowering and supports us in living the kinds of lives we want to live.

"Until we heal the root cause of our suffering, and awaken to our true nature, our inherent confusion will continue to manifest itself in the world around us."
—Joseph P. Kauffman

I don't know if we are born remembering where we come from and why we are here—although many children being born nowadays are remembering all of the above as it's seemingly more natural for them to do so. They are bringing in so much light with them and so many new energies. I didn't start tapping into multidimensionality or the potentials that I now speak about pretty matter-of-factly until I was a few years into my meditation practice and started dabbling in energy healing and the Akashic Records. Step by step, year by year, practice by practice, more new worlds and potentials therein started opening up, inviting me in to explore and ask new questions, so I would remember and maybe help others to do the same.

One of the first times I opened the Akashic Records was in my first practitioner training. I was in upstate New York with an intimate group of fellow students, eager to put to practice what we had felt such a resonance with for what seemed like lifetimes. I remember finding out about the training in a very synchronistic, surprising manner. I was scanning the newsletter of one of my favorite Brooklyn healing collectives (Maha Rose), and as I noticed their Akashic Records training I felt a wave of energy shock my system. It surprised me to feel such an immense resonance and familiarity, like I had to do a double take and try to remember where I had heard this term before, although I knew at some level I never had till then (in this life). I felt such a strong pull to attend, so I signed up right away without reading much about it, just knowing I had to be there.

In one of our early attunements in the course, I felt such a profound recall of other lifetimes and dimensions I had lived in and practiced the Akashic Records in. In experiencing this energy for the first time, I was initially overcome with what felt like sadness or immense grief at missing this feeling I had longed for this entire life. Here it was, overtaking my body and consciousness with this incredibly potent wave of unconditional love and healing—the highest-frequency energy I had ever felt up until then—and I was already missing it. I felt like I had arrived. I was home. I knew this place and space, and I remembered in this exploration into deep receiving and attunement that I knew how to do this work, that I had done it many times before. I had even taught others how to access these energies.

So much memory came flooding back to me. I remembered. Sometimes that feeling of coming home to yourself can feel heartbreaking at first. It's that unbearable lightness of purely being. It's a paradox I suppose: we break our own hearts as we really feel the depth of our own presence, power, and potency. But maybe instead of breaking open, like we think our hearts are, they are actually just expanding to hold even more of our true light—our true selves—wanting to move through. This process has been a continual practice over the years: allowing space for more of what's true to show up and radiate throughout this body, these cells, within this consciousness. And it is a process that truly never ends and continually surprises one with new depths, curves, and turns along the way. We are infinitely expanding; this I know is true.

> **"You have to leave the city of your comfort and go into the wilderness of your intuition. What you'll discover will be wonderful. What you'll discover is yourself."**
> **—Alan Alda**

We'll get more into the Akashic Records and some other fun, magical, multidimensional healing protocols and insights in our steps to come, promise. But for now I hope you get why it's important we consider how much more there is to the entire story of what we've been taught. There is so much more outside the box of our supposed history, rules, conditions, and limitations therein. Being open to questioning and considering anew the entire picture of our collective history is one of the first steps in reclaiming your personal power. When we really remember where we come from, who we are, and why we're here, our power feels infinitely accessible and the responsibility that we're gifted to create a beautiful, harmonious, thriving world naturally arises.

Earth School, I've been shown, is a place where spirit comes to learn duality, to learn contrast, because there is nowhere else in the entire multiverse where this is possible. What a fun game we come here to play indeed. Imagine being embodied as pure infinite spirit or light. Imagine existing as pure spirit in a state of pure energetic presence wherein there is no thought, no judgment, no analysis, no need, no obligation, and no yearning. Where there's only pure presence and being, wholeness and completeness.

But somehow, these warrior souls choose to leave the heavenly realms to descend into the physical, because it's only through a human form in the physical plane that we can experience pain, lack, fear, separation, and all the other flavors of duality in between. It's here that we at some level choose to forget everything from before to start again solely for the purpose of learning who we truly are and what we are made of. We choose the game we want to play, the lessons therein we want to learn and grow from, and then we give it our best shot. Isn't it fun to relate to humanity from this lens? It feels like we are all on a big team or maybe even part of a big, weird, magical, wild family.

"It is possible that the next Buddha will not take the form of an individual. The next Buddha may take the form of a community, a community practicing understanding and loving kindness, a community practicing mindful living."
—Thich Nhat Hanh

MEETING YOURSELF FOR THE FIRST TIME

Waking up to who you really are means becoming still enough to actually listen and becoming clear enough to actually see. Can we be willing to look at ourselves in the mirror and see what's really there? It's so intimate and vulnerable, sometimes overwhelmingly so. And often we're programmed to move so fast through life, to be a cog in the wheel, to just keep chasing the next thing outside of us that we think is going to give us happiness in this present moment, that we miss the gift of meeting ourselves because we aren't available to actually receive what's already here.

This is precisely the moment where ascension really kicks in: time to wake up, get present, get connected, and focus on what's been here all along.

I know for many of us, when we first start to awaken and come into the practice of meditation, it can feel overwhelming and terrifying to be alone with ourselves. It is revealing and intimate to finally be still, to actually listen and feel and not be in criticism or escapism. It's wild when we start to realize that something has always been there, wanting to be acknowledged within. When I started practicing it felt like I didn't have a choice—especially shortly after quitting drugs and drinking, my mind felt insane, and my emotions felt overwhelming beyond belief. I found that without a drink in my hand and a night club to go to with loud music playing, I didn't really know how to interact with other people—and definitely not as myself.

I didn't know how to communicate with presence or with attention, and it was hard for me to listen. I was distracted, nervous, anxious, and insecure. My inner monologue would take over my experience, and loudly: How do I look? What are they thinking of me? What do they want from me so they'll like me and I'll feel accepted? What do I need to do to feel safe? Once I cleared more of the fog I had been inhabiting, I could finally see how much anxiety I had avoided by treating it with superficial substances that only gave a temporary relief. What was shocking to see was that all those years as I got clean, when I thought I was medicating my problem, my anxiety actually got worse and worse because I was never taking care of the root of the issue.

> **"Your purpose is to share and embody the gifts**
> **you've always wanted to receive."**
> **—Sydney Campos**

The first time I felt that I had truly met myself was in a healing session that my reiki healer at the time surprised me with. I had no idea what inner child work was and had no concept of how intense it would be for me to experience my inner child at that moment in my path. I had been clean a little over a year, was going to meetings, and working hard at my recovery and spiritual growth. I was taking better care of myself and living more consciously than I had in my entire life. Part of my self-care regimen included weekly reiki energy healing sessions and intuitive coaching with this wonderful woman who was a shining bright light and example for me at the beginning of my journey. Working with her was the biggest investment I had ever made in myself up until then which felt impossibly edgy at first—I wasn't used to spending money on my well-being, which felt so intangible. Welcoming in that level of consistent support was likely the best decision I had ever made in my life.

A bit into the energy healing session, which is really like a meditation, I was guided to meet my inner child for the first time. I felt so much emotion arise, noticeably a profound sadness and grief I had never felt before. It reminded me of the kind of sadness I would sometimes allow myself to feel when I was really drunk, waxing nostalgic about societal injustices like slavery and inequality; the impossible, existential kind of grief that so many of us hold deep within because we never have a space to express it out in a world that seems designed contrary to everything we've felt to be true (and just).

Upon being invited to meet my inner child, I saw her in my inner vision, but I couldn't hold her hand or have her come close to me as the guidance in the meditation suggested. It's hard to put into words the feeling, but it felt like my own heart was breaking because for the first time I was noticing this very real aspect of myself that I had forgotten. Surprisingly, she didn't want to come close to me like I thought she might want to, even though I asked.

I cried one of the deepest cries I had ever cried, and trust me, that's saying a lot. In my early sobriety I cried for about a year straight as all my emotions came online. This moment, however, was an intense one that brought up so many more questions. What was this part of me that felt so familiar but also so far away and so far forgotten? Why did I forget about her? Why didn't she want to come close to me and be my friend? Would we ever be friends? Could I ever make this right? Did I do anything wrong? Was this my fault? So many questions and not a single answer in sight, until I was ready to really do the work in this realm, something that came little by little over the years, piece by piece. And even still the work here continues. Healing abandonment trauma (and all the other trauma programs therein) is quite a tall order, but again I am reminded: we can heal, we can repattern, we can birth ourselves anew. This is why we are here, and we're just getting started. More on all of this to come in the following steps. We'll go deep, all the way in.

> **"The future world will be a world created by adults
> who can see through the eyes of children."**
> **—Richard Rudd**

Usually we find upon really making an effort to meet ourselves as we are now that we are such utterly complex, multifaceted beings emanating so much within us that there aren't enough stories or anecdotes or memes we could share to do adequate justice to our infiniteness. We start to see the layers and masks we've been taught will protect us, help us to survive, fit in, play certain roles and parts, do what is expected of us, and so on and so forth. You get the picture. With so many of us there is a truly painful weight being carried—some might call it the weight of the world—or perhaps it feels like a scared little child within, with so much to say, so many feelings to feel, and so many incredible gifts to give.

Becoming self-aware or self-conscious can likely come with intense sensitivity and perhaps even overwhelming fear, anxiety, and paranoia. Ascension calls us forth into deeper levels of self-compassion, self-love, and acceptance, all themes that we will of course be exploring in our path ahead. It's all here for us to receive. Sometimes awakening to a different inner voice or seeing how you've been making choices that don't actually align with what you truly want in life or with what you tell yourself you're committed to can feel quite jarring. It's like the movie you've been playing and living in suddenly stops with an abrupt reverb and everything you see scrambles before going blank—impossible to make sense of. From here, it's time to start anew. A fresh path awaits. It might feel like trailblazing, but isn't that what we're here for after all?

WE ARE CREATORS, REMEMBER?

We are evolving out of victim consciousness on a mass level—can you feel it? As the Earth's frequency rises, so does that of everyone's individual energy and attunement to subtle signs and resonances guiding them to listen more to their hearts, their bodies and their intuition. But how can we trust? How can we listen? Is it safe? Will we be alright in the process? Now we have a whole body to navigate, complete with feelings, trauma, memories, conditioning, and sometimes even energies that we find upon closer investigation were never ours to carry in the first place.

It's an overwhelming task, truly loving and taking care of ourselves in this multidimensional, multilayered human experience. We are such complex beings; every human is an entire universe of experience, wisdom, language, projection—it's a miracle we're even able to communicate to one another given how incredibly unique our life experiences have conditioned us to be. But we're no longer victims, even to the conditioning we may have been taught defines our entire lives, gifts, limitations, and possibilities. It's time to look within and develop our own intentional rules of engagement for playing an entirely new game. Whatever has been in the way of being, doing, or having what we truly desire *is* the way through to the other side.

In our ascension journey, we are invited to consider seeing ourselves as creator and creation, one and the same. The more we awaken, the more we become connected and unified with all living beings and with all facets of reality. Sometimes it feels like we're dissolving into oneness or pure energy, expanding beyond our conditioned confines of skin or physical limitations. Here we feel our malleability and our innate ability to witness ourselves through it all, which is quite a trip. Perhaps we aren't simply creators—deep down it feels oftentimes that we are artists, here to create beauty. Someone I admire goes further to call us all "heart-ists" which is to say that we are each here to uniquely express something beautiful, straight from our hearts—and this is our gift to the world, shared through the song of our lives. How's that feel?

**"Creativity is the state of consciousness in which you enter
into the treasury of your innermost being and bring
the beauty into manifestation."**
—Torkom Saraydarian

Ascension is an inside job alright, an inner awakening to remember our innate capacity to create our reality in every moment. It is the journey of coming home to ourselves and seeing how maybe, just maybe, we've been creating everything already—just unconsciously—so why not start creating more of what we truly want? Why not be who we really are and live the kinds of lives that are nourishing, loving, beautiful, and wildly empowering—just the way we like it?

The real question we meet on our ascension path, over and over is: are we willing to let all the false aspects of ourselves go, especially those rooted in past trauma and projections, so that more of who we truly are and all we are here to be can simply arise? Maybe the only thing in the way of being, having, and doing precisely what is meant for us to experience is the programming, or ways of being, we've unconsciously learned to live. It depends on the game we are choosing to play of course. Are we victims of circumstance without a hope in sight? Or are we creating the entire path for our highest good so we learn what we came to remember? Perhaps every moment is a new opportunity to choose.

Bigger Contrast, Bigger Lessons

I was on track to being a millionaire in 2017 if only I had stayed the course. This thought arose recently as I was inspired to write about what was transpiring at this time in my life, which felt like ten years in one, including some of the biggest lessons I had ever learned about giving my power away and chasing money as a means of proving my worth and value. It feels meaningful to share more of my story for context. What follows is a firsthand account of how trauma can craft our reality until we consciously integrate it through our bodies so it no longer determines the course of our lives. We must finally feel it to heal it.

At the very beginning of 2017, I landed for the first time in Bali. I had hit rock bottom in financial scarcity, rooted in unresolved abandonment trauma that showed up in my reality as not feeling supported by life or by myself. I had always felt unstable, especially when it came to money, and had difficulty holding on to it. I was exploring the possibility of being a sugar baby for a person I thought was a rich financier based in Jakarta. A sugar baby is a nicer term for a would-be escort-type person who exchanges attention or more with a (usually) rich man who wants to pay to "care for" the expenses or lifestyle of his sugar baby. I had learned about this particular man—allegedly called David—on a website someone mentioned at the goddess retreat I had just attended in New Zealand, of all places. I figured that even though I did similar exploits with stripping and escorting years ago before getting sober, maybe I could do it again from a conscious space. *The truth was I just wanted someone else to take care of me and couldn't admit that I didn't feel worthy of doing that for myself.*

Long story short: my exploration into being David's sugar baby had me leaving a yoga and meditation retreat on a small island next to Bali to take a plane to Jakarta, one of the biggest, most chaotic cities in the world, to meet David in a mysterious luxury hotel for what seemed like would be a weeklong foray. Talk about contrast. I got to the hotel and started unpacking my things—but meanwhile I was incredibly anxious and felt like something was really wrong. Maybe the shame was catching up with me finally—and maybe my intuition was trying to warn me too. I was so disassociated at that time yet doing the best I could to take care of myself. I was a master at ignoring my feelings if they stood in the way of my goal. In this case, becoming David's sugar baby seemed like my ticket out of debt and financial worry. I had told myself I could be his reiki healer and health coach—just like any of my other clients, right? Except he'd pay more for my special attention. I felt validated and I was willing to give it a go.

He called me to arrange a meeting time for the following day. I agreed but then called him back moments later to see if we could reschedule. A coaching client meeting had come up and I realized—maybe by divine intervention—that I needed to show up for my client more than I needed to risk my life to show up for David. When I requested we shift the time, his sweet and caring tone shifted immediately to a cold, direct warning that sent fear rippling through my bones. He said: "As long as you're on my dollar and my watch, you'll do what I say." Then he hung up the phone, and I noticed our WhatsApp message that we'd been communicating in disappeared and that it was encrypted all along with no history shown to reference as proof of our encounter. My life flashed before my eyes in that moment. David was the only person who knew where I was—in his hotel room on his bill. He had my passport and identity info, and all of my travel, I realized, was booked by a third-party intermediary—there was no evidence of his existence to be found anywhere.

I gathered my things as quickly as I could, with my heart racing and my head pounding. I quickly texted a friend to let her know the jist of what was happening so at least someone else knew where I was. Reminds me of the times back in New York when I would hauntingly leave my apartment in Brooklyn and let my roommate know offhandedly: "I'm going to Connecticut and if I don't come home by tomorrow, call the police." Talk about cries for help—but I didn't know any better at the time, and at least I was trying to give people some clues into the dangerous situations I would frequent.

So, there I was—rushing out of the hotel room in the middle of Jakarta to run for my life to the airport to get on the next plane to Bali in fear that I might be kidnapped or worse. I wasn't even sure if I was being watched or followed—if I was safe at all. It felt like having a heart attack for hours on end, but my system was used to suppressing so much anxiety and holding it all in, it must not have even been that bad compared to what I was already used to dealing with. I landed back in Ubud a day or so later and found myself on the floor crying, disappointed that I had risked my life for the fantasy of maybe getting paid a few thousand dollars. How little regard I had for myself. All the meanwhile I was coaching clients and working with startups online, feeling like a complete fraud. The shame was unbearable.

From this space of immense vulnerability a Facebook post from a woman who appeared to be a "high-ticket mentor"—otherwise known as a multimillionaire coach—spoke to me. I didn't realize then that her scripted post was coded with hypnotic verbiage and was part of a pyramid-like scheme of other coaches who all spoke, looked, and felt similarly and preyed upon people in similar circumstances to my own. But I went for it and reached out to her for support—it felt good to be understood and to feel seen. I invested all my capital in two mentors like this—with the promise of building a stable business I could be proud of. But I was trying to build everything from the outside IN. And the funny thing is: it appeared to be working.

I had my first $21,000 day, then $70,000 month and the supposed "quantum leaps" (the term used hypnotically by the mentors) continued. I was quick to share about all the wins on social media as was my mentor at the time—taking credit so that all my supposed results never felt like my own. Maybe they weren't, because I wasn't being me anyway—I was being an avatar copy of my mentor and all the other people she was affiliating with who again all sounded, felt, and looked the same and probably were using the same scripts to attract clients. As soon as I had more money in my bank account than I had ever seen at one time, my mentor was quick to get me on the phone to explain why my $5,000 per month investment in coaching needed to immediately "up-level" to $11,000 per month to reflect my new expansion. It felt gross, but since I had already given her all my power, I had no choice but to agree and abide. Otherwise it seemed I would lose everything I had built—the house of cards would topple. Then a month or so later this mentor, whom I was paying six figures a year to coach me in "quantum leaping," was supporting me through a very intense trauma healing moment.

The thing was—unfortunately—she couldn't hold the space for me in the way I required to move through what was coming up. We can only meet people as deeply as we've met ourselves—which couldn't have been more true in this instance. The gift here was seeing how I was better equipped to hold this kind of healing space than she was as I watched her get triggered by what I was processing, which happened to be about code-pendency and the mother wound. Perhaps she was triggered because what I was expressing touched on the toxic dynamic we were unconsciously playing out in our mentorship. I was playing the role of her daughter, and she was playing the role of my mother, and together we were doing our best to repattern our respective wounding hidden in the shadows: *I'm not enough and I'm not supported.* We had so much in common. We were mirrors in so many ways, which is why I was magnetized to work with her, as I'm sure all the clients I attracted while emanating her energy signature were, as well.

It wasn't all horrible, I suppose. I was attracted to her at first because of how fearlessly she shared her truth about multidimensional experiences and intuitive insights she regularly tapped into. Meanwhile I was still afraid of publicly speaking to the cosmic experiences I was having with clients in the Akashic Records and in my own energy healing journey. The witch wound was echoing strong—the fear of being burned or persecuted if I were to share anything contrary to the popularly accepted understanding of reality.

Ultimately, all I wanted was to learn how to abundantly support myself (which really meant feeling completely safe and secure) through doing what I love, which is teaching and healing to help others remember themselves and create what they're truly here to create in this life. But as long as I sought the answer to this outside myself through external, material results, I would continue giving my power away without fully learning the lesson I was really after. What I really wanted underneath it all, which only became clear years later, wasn't money or fame or accolades of external validation—what I desired most of all was a healed nervous system with the capacity to operate in consistent presence and stability no matter what. From here I would know my value and worth intrinsically, I would trust my intuitive knowing, and I could discern the most aligned next steps in my destined path. From here I could create my desired experience and start to live a life far beyond anything I might have then imagined.

I got a taste of being rich, and it was a wild experience—but it wasn't at all what I wanted, because it wasn't accomplished in my authenticity or with any stability to feel consistent. Most of all, I learned what I never wanted to do again, which can also be a great gift in and of itself. Honestly, I had to take about two years to recover from that experience and all it brought up. The person I thought I was had to die a few times in order for me to feel more deeply the true being that's been seeking and performing, hiding under so many heavy layers of validation. This all stemmed from the "I'm not enough" game.

In the years to follow this experience, I've loved delving deep into practices and explorations intentionally designed to help one further detach from learned conditions and personality aspects that unknowingly shape reality until we consciously interrupt to course correct in our ever desired direction. Most of all I continue to see how all paths lead us into deeper presence—and from this depth of presence, all potentials we could ever desire exploring become more possible and easier to access. What I wanted all along wasn't an outside thing—but in fact a deeper connection with my core essence. I have a strong sense this is what we all eventually come to terms with at the end of the day; the material world is so impermanent after all, but our essence is eternal and attuning with it more deeply yields our highest fulfillment. I don't recognize who I was before—and I'm sure this process of self-forgetting gets more frequent as we continue on the ascension path. We forget all the parts of ourselves that we thought we were or that we were taught to be in order to make way for more presence and attunement to who we actually are being, now.

Remembering Our Power

We are powerful beings, and it's time to take our power back from all the things, people, and institutions outside of ourselves that have conditioned us to believe otherwise. We each carry a potent truth within, and when we are in tune with this inner guidance we are unstoppable. Not just that, but when we are listening to our truth we also work better as a team. In this way we can connect more with ourselves, with each other and with all of life. The best part is that it doesn't even take a critical mass of billions of people to choose to start consciously awakening to their truth. Even a small percentage of humanity ascending into more truth, presence, and power is sufficient to move the dial for the whole collective. We are that powerful.

We've even seen this concept proven in statistics of groups practicing meditation in cities like Baltimore and Washington, D.C., which are notorious for violence and high crime rates. For example, when a group of around 1,500 people practiced meditation in Washington for a prolonged period consistently over four weeks, the crime rate notably dropped by about 23 percent.* It has been proven in other locations that even just 1 percent of a vicinity's population meditating produces a measurable improvement on quality of life for the whole population.** And that's just meditating, which is only one aspect of all multitude of practices and ways to play in ascension as we explore and get to know our true selves more deeply.

I'd take it a level further and say that really only 0.01 percent of our world's population is required at this time to choose ascension and awakening into their higher consciousness in order for the entire planet to really shift in a meaningful way, into more of the ways of being indicative of a thriving society. As our collective chooses to wake up, chooses to fully be present, chooses to live the lives that we are designed to live, and chooses to create and play the game of life according to our own rules, we catalyze a universal shift for all. Our ascension can't help but impact, inspire, and amplify the awakening of the whole.

Heaven on Earth is here in this moment, when we choose to be. Can it be that simple? Maybe it is, if we allow it to be just that. What if choosing to be here, where Heaven on Earth is, begins by making a conscious choice to be here, where it's all happening already? Let's remember who we really are and why we came here. We are powerful, infinite beings born here on Earth at this time to awaken and heal so that our presence itself becomes healing to others who seek to remember. Our presence is healing simply in the light and new potentials we can't help but radiate in the energy we emit. Perhaps we'll never know the full extent of the impact we have here in this life, on the whole. Eventually, when we are so immersed in living our best lives and loving ourselves, our planet, and each other, we won't care so much to measure impact or how we are received, anyway.

---

* "Can Group Meditation Prevent Violent Crime? Surprisingly, the Data Suggests Yes: New Study," EurekAlert!, April 14, 2016, https://www.eurekalert.org/news-releases/671086; "Meditating to Try to Lower Crime Rate," *New York Times*, August 1, 1993, https://www.nytimes.com /1993/08/01/nyregion/meditating-to-try-to-lower-crime-rate.html.

** "Follow-Up Study Suggests Group Meditation Reduced Murder Rates in Large US Cities," EurekAlert!, March 30, 2017, https://www.eurekalert.org/news-releases/511271.

"To be creative means to be in love with life. You can be creative only if you love life enough that you want to enhance its beauty, you want to bring a little more music to it, a little more poetry to it, a little more dance to it."
—Osho

Caring what others think matters less and less as you learn to trust your own truth more fully and let your truth be your guiding directive for all you are and all you do. As we learn to completely love and appreciate ourselves in our whole uniqueness and recalibrate our inner being to the wholeness we have always innately been, we will feel so fulfilled, gratified, and present that the measurements, material manifestations, and all the ways we've been conditioned to substantiate and validate our infinite worth, value, and existence will fall away.

There is no comparison, judgment, jealousy, or hierarchy when we are completely present in our own heart. Instead, we see everything as a reflection of our inner being. We meet every other being as an aspect of ourselves, here to remind us of a part of ourselves that would love to receive more of our own love. What parts of you would love permission to be in the light, completely alive, radiant, wild, and free? What parts of you are dying to be expressed and to be held and received and felt and known? What inner longings have you repressed for this life and so many others that you were taught to feel ashamed of, guilty for, regretful for having in the first place? Why?

Awakening and embodying our deepest longings and desires is the key to unlocking our infinite power and presence. This is the essence of ascension and creating the game we are here to play in this life. We are meant to meet ourselves, each other, and this life in full depth and absolute presence. We are here to experience the magnificent spectrum of feeling and energetic potential that's possible through these bodies, souls, and spirits. We are here to become ourselves, who we are beyond the layers of conditioning, trauma, fear, and projection that have seemed to keep us captive for too long.

"Do whatever brings you to life, then. Follow your own fascinations, obsessions, and compulsions. Trust them. Create whatever causes a revolution in your heart."
—Elizabeth Gilbert

When we shine our blinding light so profoundly, others may stumble in our path, sure. It's understandable how our full presence shocks them out of their sleeping stupor. But maybe this is the point—and one we are meant to become comfortable with as we better know ourselves. Maybe there is no such thing as fear at all, only the feeling of facing one's own innate presence, which is so radiant it can feel overwhelming to behold.

In our journey ahead we are tasked with learning to expand our capacity for love, for joy, for presence, for abundance, for truth, and everything else we hold as sacred. We will see how we expand naturally the more we allow ourselves to let go. It's time to release all that we are gripping on to. There's nothing more to manage or control, only experiencing life on a deeper level to feel, express, trust, and allow. What is meant to be is already here, simply waiting for us to open and reveal. Can we become comfortable expanding into the infinite and dancing in the unknown like it's our job (because maybe we find out it absolutely is)? I'm game to find out if you are. So shall we?

CONSCIOUSNESS AWAKENING ATTUNEMENTS

Silently See the World Around You

Our first activation in consciousness awakening is as simple as this: Observe your reality silently for at least five minutes, without moving, intervening or doing anything at all. See how this feels to practice simply being a witness to what is already happening all around you without you interfering, controlling, or managing anything at all. This practice might be excruciating to try even if just for a few minutes: observe your compulsion to move or distract yourself, and stay committed to your mindful, quiet observation of it all.

Here you are developing your capacity to be a conscious observer of your reality, to be the operator of your consciousness system, right? You can set a timer to create a container of exploration for yourself, and once the timer goes off, reflect on what came up for you and see if this was challenging or if there are new insights to celebrate. Every time you answer these questions your response may be different. This practice gives us so much richness if done on a recurring basis. It's a beautiful way to check in and attune yourself more to being the witness and co-creative participant in what is already aligned and designed in your world without any urge to interfere or initiate. You can simply receive.

When Do You Feel Most Alive?

Our next attunement will help you open up your consciousness and become more awakened to your innate capacity to be a mindful observer rather than a limited manager of your supposed reality. Play with emptying yourself out to receive each moment from a completely new vantage point. Ask yourself what kind of practice or activities support you in feeling empty, present, free, clear, and able to really receive the beauty that is already all around you. It's different for everyone, but for you, what brings a feeling of deep gratitude into your heart? What makes you feel most alive?

These are great questions to explore for yourself by journaling or even by sitting in quiet reflection or meditation. This is also a potent way to start to play with your intuition and higher consciousness guidance, which loves to respond to these types of imaginative inquiries. You may even consider practicing on a daily basis, and take notice of how each day is so different. Inquire and reflect: today, what is calling me forth to express my complete aliveness? What can I commit to today that will support me in feeling my total expansion into new depths of creativity, vitality, play, and joy? What is it you would like to feel like, more often—and what is it like for you to simply choose to practice feeling that feeling right now?

"Your problem is how you are going to spend this one odd and precious life you have been issued. Whether you're going to spend it trying to look good and creating the illusion that you have power over people and circumstances, or whether you are

**going to taste it, enjoy it, and find out the
truth about who you are."**
—Anne Lamott

Soon, you won't require external stimulus to feel the way you want to feel—practice attuning yourself like the frequency shifter you are to feel how you want to feel independent of your external reality. The most powerful way to do this is by thinking, or better yet writing down as quickly as you can (advanced practice is to do this looking at yourself in the mirror and saying the celebrations out loud, looking in your own eyes!), at least seven things you are grateful for or celebrating. It's even more poignant to conduct these celebrations about yourself. What are you celebrating about you right now? Beyond what you do or what you produce, what is special about you, what qualities and ways of being deserve love and acknowledgment right now? How does it feel to give yourself your own love and fully receive it?

Into-Me-I-See

Lastly, we are invited into deep intimacy and a profound vulnerability when we meet ourselves. Stand in front of a mirror and look yourself in the eyes. Can you really be with what shows up? The first time, we often find ourselves startled with how much emotion immediately arises when we actually start to see what's looking back at us. We take some deep breaths and gaze into our own eyes and start to feel whether or not there is love there, whether or not there is compassion and acceptance. What is the first feeling that arises upon doing this practice, upon gifting yourself this moment of your presence? Consider allowing this feeling in a little more, moment by moment. Take it slow, go at your own pace—remembering and reminding yourself you have all the time in the world which maybe now you're dedicating more consciously to the most important person in your life: you.

3

SURRENDER, BUT HOW?

Have you ever felt a bit (or a lot) annoyed by the spiritual memes and jargon out there reminding us all to just surrender, let go, and trust while taking the leap, confident that the net will appear? It feels so often like these messages are conveyed from an assumption that letting go is really second nature and we should already all be able to be there, wherever *there* is (maybe a secret place where everything is easy and effortless, where money rains from the sky and all our human struggles seem to disappear?). For many years these messages always struck a chord in me: if everyone is talking about surrendering and just letting go as the pathway to an easy, fun life, why couldn't someone tell me how to actually do it? Does everyone else already know how? Maybe this was another aspect of the human experience I seemed to have missed the intro training on, but I sensed I wasn't alone in feeling that way. How about you?

About a year into my recovery, I was managing a lot just learning to be a human being again, working in an office environment with other humans. With all the unique complexity, traumas, and conditionings, we are all holding, it's a wonder we can form companies, communicate, and make things at all. At the time I was just trying to get through the day without being paranoid that everyone in the office was talking about me or that every time my managers looked at me they were considering how they could easily validate their plan to fire me. Around this time I signed up for inspirational daily emails from spiritual teacher Abraham Hicks.

On my way to work most mornings, taking the subway from Brooklyn up to Herald Square, I would read Abraham Hicks's emails and feel frustrated that I was missing something. Why did it all sound so easy, but still something wasn't landing? Were other people getting this and simply living according to these principals? Why did it seem so hard to grasp? My mind couldn't wrap itself around the seemingly simple directives like "let go," "be in the vortex," "manifest abundance," and "follow the flow," and quite honestly it annoyed me to consider—how could you give such simple advice but not explain the actual process for following it? I wanted to surrender but I had no idea where to begin. In fact when I thought about the process for how to do it—the operative word being *thought*—I got completely lost and confused. And for many years it seemed like I just stayed stuck in that loop—*surrender, but how?*

> **"Just let go. Let go of how you thought your life should
> be, and embrace the life that is trying to work its way
> into your consciousness."**
> **—Caroline Myss**

I wanted to let go of everything I was continuously stressed out about, I really did. I just had no clue where to begin. Like many of us out there on our awakening journey, before waking up, I had lived an entire life— over two decades—based on the illusion that I was in control of every-thing and that life was up to me to figure out. Sound familiar? I think a lot of us are born into this kind of patterning: an operating system in which we undergo extreme pressure to be perfect, to have everything figured out, to know where we're going and what to do before we even start. Basically, to play god.

I don't know if everyone has this experience, but I've got to admit I do see it as more common than maybe we care to acknowledge. Did you ever learn at a young age in your family dynamic, usually unconsciously and rather automatically, to manage other people's emotions and experiences in order to feel loved and seen? Did you ever learn to shift your own ways of being, actions, and choices based on what you thought would be more ac-ceptable to those around you so they would validate you and even in some cases affirm your existence? Even if you resonate with these strategies just a bit, here we open up a great awareness and inquiry that can empower us more fully to let go, to surrender, and to trust that life really is supporting us. It's one thing to say it—that we trust life and all will be well when we surrender—and it's a wholly different experience to really know it and feel it in our cells. Let's explore the embodiment process.

**"The moment of surrender is not when life is over,
it's when it begins."
—Marianne Williamson**

WHY IT'S SO HARD TO LET GO (BUT WE CAN DO IT)

First things first, let's call it like it is: surrendering isn't an intellectual process. Letting go is not something we think ourselves into. We couldn't even if we tried. What's funny, though, and perhaps you've even experienced this, is that the more you try when it comes to letting go, the more frustrated you may become, until eventually you annoy yourself so intensely that you do actually completely give up and, imagine that, surrender. Have you ever tricked yourself into doing the thing you've sought out to accomplish using the path of self-annoyance? This strategy may work occasionally—and it's fun to have a good laugh at yourself afterward, definitely—but there's got to be a more sustainable way to get this new muscle reflex developed, right?

Trusting the process and having faith that a net will appear or that life will support us when we take a leap into the unknown isn't something we will into being, manage, control, or even have reassuring evidence of before it happens. What I've found, honestly through a lot of trial and error plus huge mistakes where I've fallen on my face repeatedly, is that surrendering is a pretty intense multidimensional workout that's especially challenging at first. It's a full-on marathon, a complete system upgrade and deep deconditioning process that initiates us to build a body that can experience and sustain deeper states of trust, safety, and presence. These are the key ingredients we are after when it comes to truly surrendering.

In other words, surrendering requires building a body that can reside in a space of trust, safety, and presence. Sounds pretty simple, right? How hard can it be? Well, I suppose it's as hard a process as we want to make it, but for most it can be pretty excruciating. It was and even still sometimes continues to be difficult for me. Letting go of control can be akin to healing a lifelong addiction to "knowing." This is usually evolved as an underlying strategy developed in reaction to a very early experience of not feeling safe and then learning to control our environment to assure some form of stability in the midst of inconsistency or chaos. As Dr. Gabor Maté reminds us in *When the Body Says No: The Cost of Hidden Stress*: "For those habituated to high levels of internal stress since early childhood, it is the absence of stress that creates unease, evoking boredom and a sense of meaninglessness. People may become addicted to their own stress hormones, adrenaline and cortisol. To such persons stress feels desirable, while the absence of it feels like something to be avoided."

No wonder it's hard to feel safe and simply let go of control. Not to mention most of our society instills in us certain belief structures and thought patterns that encourage our survival strategies to get ramped up at a young age as opposed to cultivating the operating systems that accentuate trust, presence, safety, and calm. Of course I couldn't get down with Abraham Hicks as I was just getting sober and learning about basic human relating skills outside of a dark, loud night club. My nervous system was shot and overwhelmed with all the sensory information I was already responsible for processing just to get through the day, not to mention the added pressure of having certain dreams and visions to achieve on top of an already full plate of responsibilities.

> **"Courage is not about being fearless; it's about letting fear transform you so you come into right relationship with uncertainty, make peace with impermanence, and wake up to who you really are."**
> **—Lissa Rankin**

One thing at a time. If I've learned anything over this journey—and what I want to invite all of us to consider—is that it's so important to be right where we are and not wish to be anywhere else. Wishing we were further along or regretting the past are distractions that stack up against us on our way to remembering presence and truly letting go of control. It's not our job to know the future or to feel bad about supposed mistakes we made along the way getting to where we are—it all happened to help us get here. What if where we are now is perfect and right where we are supposed to be? What if acceptance around who we are being in this specific moment is the key to the freedom and peace we've been seeking all along? What if in acceptance we actually experience a deep surrender to what is, in all its perfect imperfection?

What happens eventually: the layers of control release and walls of protection start to come down. As we heal our nervous systems and attune to greater calm, peace, and presence, we can feel ourselves more fully and can start to more naturally trust the aligned unfolding of our lives. We start to experience more firsthand evidence of how life is actually always working out. Really ask yourself too: when you look back at your life, did you always have what you needed when you needed it? Did things always work out, even if they turned out differently than you imagined or expected? Did life unfold even better than you could have imagined? Here are some questions to consider that have helped me along the path, especially when fear has arisen about venturing into another unknown.

The antidote to overthinking is presence and feeling. And yet sometimes the experience of actually doing so isn't always positive, and that's okay. When we have a triggered response arise to something that happened in our past that's still catalyzing a fearful projection of what's to come, can we look at this information as a gift that's showing us where we can bring our awareness into healing? The thing is, our intellectual mind—which we are mostly entrained to live by, certainly in our societal and educational programming—isn't a very creative instrument, not anything like our intuition or imagination. Our intellectual mind, wired for safety and survival, really, houses a library of negative and fearful experiences that it can easily source from to project upon future potentials, preventing us from trying anything new. The intellectual mind doesn't like change or the unknown—it is designed to track the past and protect against future unknowns based on prior experience. It finds comfort and safety in familiarity. Even something (or someone) that's not necessarily "good for you" can be comfortable and familiar, and so the mind can latch onto this pattern because at least it's not a scary unknown.

Can we have some major compassion for ourselves, please? It seems it's so easy for us to be hard on ourselves, to think we should be further along than we are, to have it all figured out, to be at the finish line, as if there is one. We are born on day one up against a lot of programming, trauma conditioning, fixed ideas, and energies that aren't even authentically ours. Eventually, we come to and realize we get to unravel it all and meet what's underneath. It's not the tidiest process, this unraveling—no, it can really be quite a mess, and an uncomfortable, sweaty, teary, sometimes gross one, at that.

> **"Depression is your avatar telling you it's tired of being the character you're trying to play."**
> **—Jim Carrey**

I once hosted a retreat in Maui converging around intentions of healing and integrating trauma. Personally it was one of the most challenging groups I ever had the honor of being a part of let alone facilitating for; in moments I felt underqualified to fully support the processing of trauma regarding social injustice, systemic oppression, racial inequality, and religious programming that was ripe within our field. I was continuously humbled by all that was presenting itself—and its immense complexity—for us all to be with, to feel and repattern. Midway through the retreat, someone expressed with seemingly genuine surprise: "I thought this was a healing retreat." I smiled and laughed a little (mostly on the inside) at hearing this and wondered if this person thought that maybe healing meant taking a vacation from one's problems and escaping into a beautiful island paradise to forget about it all. Or perhaps this thought arose as a deflection from feeling and being with the wounding that was arising to meet and heal.

Either way, it made me think of a funny image: a group of people gather to do healing work together. At various times throughout the experience you see one person drowning in a puddle of tears; another one sweating buckets as anxiety and deep wells of grief purge out of their system;

another one coughing up a storm, letting all the energy of repressing their truth for years finally drain out of their body's cellular memory; and another one stuck in the bathroom the whole time, detoxing their digestive system from all the overload of psychic and emotional information they hadn't allowed themselves to fully metabolize over this lifetime. There's another one in the kitchen, emotionally eating, looking for anything and everything filled with sugar, to numb the pain of all the emotions and memories arising from a childhood she tried so hard to forget and shove deep down where no one, especially her, would ever have to feel it again. Quite the party.

Healing doesn't look one way—and it surely doesn't usually look like an escape to an island paradise. Although, now that I think about it, I have posted my fair share of sun-kissed selfies to social media where I am on a beach with a beautiful background with some words about awakening and something else inspiring. So sorry if I've been part of the misleading problem. But truth be told: do any of us really post pictures to social media when we are in the depths of a true healing crisis? It seems it's more typical for us to share after healing has integrated—when we are bright and shiny and able to share our awakened state, which just might move and inspire others to take a dip into the deep, sometimes dark depths of our true nature.

THE LIZARDING LIMBIC SYSTEM

It's hard for us to let go because our entire body and nervous system therein is programmed with multitudes of trauma (sometimes inherited from generations past, which we'll get more into later) as well as protection and survival strategies that make it challenging to simply be and relax into presence. It's a lot to handle, really, this whole being-born-as-a-human thing. Right off the bat, in many cases at the moment of our conception and all the time we are in utero, we are already receiving programming (imprinting) that will catalyze certain emotional patterns and energies to be present throughout our lives. We are already absorbing the experience of our parents, and of our mothers in particular, before we even take our first breath.

If our mothers were under stress, feeling significant repressed emotions, going through any traumatic experiences (isn't being born and all the processes therein pretty traumatizing in itself?) or undergoing major life transitions and transformations (again, having a baby is already ticking off a few of these boxes), just by being in utero while all this is happening, we receive imprints of how to be, how to feel, and energies to orient to upon coming into form. When I learned about this process, also known as the limbic birth imprint, everything changed. And more started to make sense about the wiring I came into this life with. When we become conscious of these imprints, we can bring more conscious awareness to our bodies and beings and start to repattern ourselves to experience the kinds of lives we are here to live.

> **"The emotions, traits, and behaviors we reject in our parents will likely live on in us. It's our unconscious way of loving them, a way to bring them back into our lives."**
> **—Mark Wolynn**

Let's talk about the limbic system—have you heard of it? It's something I wish we had been taught in our early years; I wonder how different the world might be if we had the opportunity to learn about self-care and our nervous systems from day one instead of learning the hard way through trial and error with usually a whole lot of pain in between. Have you heard of the *lizard brain*? That's a part of our conversation at hand too—it's the part of us that is a seriously ancient remnant of our evolutionary biology, left over from a time when our lives were much more about life and death and basic survival; kill or be killed, etc.

Basically we are unlearning in real time the parts of our biology and neurochemistry that have been anchored into place for generations and generations, since the dawn of human existence, that have kept us in a hypervigilant state of fight or flight even though our living conditions are generally safer and healthier now than ever before. What a mission we signed up for indeed—just deprogramming lifetimes of fear and survival instincts out of our cellular memory, no big deal.

So, let's dive into the limbic system, shall we? Here we have a key aspect of our bodily system that actually regulates our nervous system and our survival instincts, plus all the parts of our animal nature, like our instincts to eat and reproduce. Funny that in school and in society in general it seems we hear more broadly about the nervous system than specifics of the limbic system, when really it's the limbic system that is overseeing so much more of the key inner workings that power our existence and experience of reality. We can relate to the limbic system as the central command station for our memory storage and retrieval, emotional regulation and intellect plus our unconscious, autonomic nervous system expression.* This is the most ancient physical aspect of our brain—an artifact inherited from our hunter-gatherer ancestors that's located in the brain stem, responsible for our survival and likewise credited with triggering our fight-or-flight response in the face of danger.

The thing is—our brains haven't evolved as fast as our external circumstances and consciousness on the whole have. We still have a brain wired for fight or flight in the face of any unknown potentials, which the brain labels automatically as threats, whereas our actual realities aren't usually threatening us with life or death. Instead our evolution and consciousness advancement are inviting us more often into new experiences that welcome forth pioneering expressions of creativity and innovation. We are here to create and experience new realities we're meant to enjoy, but our nervous system wiring and lizard brain, which we're so often unaware of, tend to keep us in survival loops that prevent us from moving forward into the unknown territories we are destined to explore and architect.

**"The purposes of a person's heart are deep waters, but
one who has insight draws them out."
—Proverbs 20:5**

---

* V. Rajmohan and E. Mohandas, "The Limbic System," *Indian J Psychiatry* 49, no. 2 (April–June 2007): 132–139, doi: 10.4013/0019–5545.33264.

Overall the highly mental operating system that most of us inherit as a deeply rooted cellular imprint is not designed to bring us into the present moment. It's certainly not helping us out when it comes to surrendering, trusting life to take care of us, or being calm and at peace in stillness and quiet. No, for most of us, learning to be still and quiet with ourselves, without distractions or ways to check out, is excruciating, especially at first. And it's not our fault; we are up against a lot of wiring we inherited and it takes a bit of effort to first become aware of it, forgive ourselves for what we didn't know, and then start exploring our own unique paths in embodying who and how we want to be.

Herein lies the nonlinear path of ascension: a personal journey all your own that truth be told can be summarized with some pretty hilariously on-point memes. One of my favorites is divided into two panels: "before awakening" and "after awakening." "Before awakening" shows a close-up of a shoe pushing a person deep into a puddle. "After awakening" zooms out—The person is actually holding the shoe, crushing themselves down deeper into the puddle.

Maybe the puddle is meant to symbolize all the tears we inevitably cry on this unraveling, awakening journey—we are crying out all the misunder-standings and confusion we've learned to hold in along the way. Maybe this is how we let go. We are really like infinite cosmic onions—I think a friend said this long ago—"The deeper we go into our layers, the more we cry."

So essentially we have a massive invitation here to really get to know ourselves at the cellular level. What is our nervous system and limbic system programming that has set into motion (unconsciously) particular ways of being and strategies that aren't really aligned with the kinds of ex-periences we want to be living? If awakening truly is an inside job, how do we start to unravel the structures of our bodies that may have manifested unbeknownst to us patterns of protection, stagnation, and repression? A powerful inquiry to explore our nervous system wiring and decondition-ing is to get curious about your birth process—sometimes referred to as *sequencing*. What was happening at the time of your conception? What was your gestation like? Was anything happening in your parents' ex-perience that was traumatic or intense that energetically impacted your experience in the womb and imprinted you with certain energetic or emotional undertones?

Furthermore, we can explore a lot about the birth process itself to shine light on many facets of how we are wired to create, lead, and relate in the world. For example, how was your birth process? Long and drawn out, painful, fast, and to the point? Was some kind of interception required? Did you want to come out or did you stall to stay longer in the womb? This experience tells us everything about the creative process we tend to play out in our lives—how we show up in life, in relationships, in our creative ventures, and maybe everything else too. If we were slow to come out into the world and maybe even at some level didn't want to, so labor was long and drawn out and maybe even required some kind of induction, perhaps this experience is imprinted upon how we are slow to move into action when it comes to creative projects or aspects of life that require us to take initiative. If we were quick to come out, how fast are we orienting to life and all its potentials? Perhaps here we might want to remember the importance of integration and slowing down instead of rushing and constantly moving so quickly. How we show up for anything is how we show up for everything—isn't it the truth?

> **"By developing a relationship with the painful parts of ourselves—parts we have often inherited from our family—we have an opportunity to shift them. Qualities like cruelty can become the source of our kindness; our judgments can forge the foundation of our compassion."**
> **—Mark Wolynn**

Some of the answers to these inquiries are areas we get to explore together in the pages ahead, but if anything feels important to mention right now it's that this process of our own unraveling seems to be a life-long one. The moment we seem to get to the point we wanted to get to, we inevitably realize that there's so much more to go. The ascension process, at least for me anyway, is also about learning to be okay with this—every step of the way, being right where you are, as you are. Letting that be enough. And letting it all go too—a perfect opportunity to practice what we're talking so much about here. Can we surrender our identity within awakening and what ascension should supposedly look like and where we should be along the path? How can we bring ourselves back into this present moment? Even just for a second—how do we feel relaxed, calm, at peace, and at ease right here and right now? Breathing deep tends to really help—as do the numerous attunements and activations we'll get into next.

NERVOUS SYSTEM ATTUNEMENT

Maybe the whole journey of ascension can be boiled down to one's path from the head into the heart, or rather from the intellect into intuitive knowing and feeling. I think we hear about the nervous system in middle school biology, but not nearly to the degree that is helpful for us to really understand what we're working with on the individual, psycho-spiritual level. The nervous system is our body's portal into feeling, trusting, sensing, experiencing, and responding within all aspects of life. At this point in my path, all roads seem to always lead me back to myself and how my body and nervous system are developed (or, underresourced) in their capacity to sustain more consistent (and at times more potent) levels of energy, insight, and presence. Have you ever considered how yours is shaping up, or what kinds of imprints or patterning you had infused into your circuitry from day one? These are great starting points that can inform our healing journey.

Attunement is one of my favorite words, and I'm aware that some may read it and wonder, what does that even mean? Well, as always I encourage you to make your own meanings of everything as that's really the best way we understand anything, from our own unique vantage points and authentic translations. For me, attunement is a way of coming into resonance with something or someone, or perhaps a way of harmonizing or integrating with a new state of being. It is a key to embodiment and certainly a helpful instrument along our ascension journey. Think of the way you tune an instrument to be in a certain melody—well, could you imagine that our bodies are similar in the way that they tune to certain energies and that they themselves are actually more like instruments than we might think at first? Just like a guitar is tuned to a certain harmony, we can attune our bodies to certain emotional states, ways of being, thoughts, and, I suppose, anything else we attempt to practice.

So when it comes to our nervous systems, what might we want to attune to? Well, let's start by exploring the question implicit in this invitation: when it comes to living the kind of life you truly want to live, how do you most want to feel? What kinds of states of being do you want to have as your underlying default? What types of energies and expressions feel most nourishing to embody? When do you feel most yourself—how would you describe your character when you are residing in a space of peace, calm and acceptance? When we get clear on how we want to feel and what states of being are most supportive to living the kinds of lives we want to live, we can then explore numerous pathways to attune our nervous systems accordingly.

Before we get into ways we can attune our nervous systems, another thing to consider is how our nervous systems actually house the wiring for our emotional and energetic bodies, which can actually be thought of as one and the same. As we've touched on thus far, we are so much more than our physical beings, and luckily science is finally catching up with what mystics and healers have known for millennia: we are pure energy, as is all of our known existence. Time and space are the basis of all illusion. If we really unpack that, we start to unravel the idea of supposed physicality and the tangible world we've been conditioned to see and orient within.

We'll dive deeper into this later, but what's important to consider now is that our energetic bodies have many layers. Two we'll focus on for this conversation are the emotional body and the etheric, or spiritual, body. Other aspects or layers of our energetic bodies are our physical body and our mental body, which are important to consider in relating to ourselves as energetic beings. When I started understanding this concept more in depth I discovered freedom here—if we are energetic beings, we are more malleable and updateable than I ever imagined before. We can change much more easily than we might think—we are mostly fluid after all.

**"You don't have to control your thoughts, you just have
to stop letting them control you."**
—Dan Millman

Let's also explore one more key distinction when it comes to nervous system attunement and repatterning our bodies for more calm, safety, trust, and presence—the key ingredients for surrendering control and trusting life to take care of us. Just like we have an energetic body, we have a sub-layer of this that is attributed to emotional imprints specifically. When we have trapped emotions or unexpressed/repressed experiences that don't get fully metabolized through our systems, these energies get stored in the body or in a layer of our energy field (in our emotional body). When we have trapped energy in the body or in our field, we can oftentimes unconsciously project the energy into our physical reality to experience events that help us catalyze opportunities to heal (essentially, make conscious) whatever the repressed energy is.

For example, perhaps as a child someone experienced the trauma of feeling abandoned by their parents simply because their mom and dad didn't pay attention to them with the level of presence they really required to feel loved and supported. (By the way, the definition of *trauma* for our purposes is a deeply distressing experience.) This is quite a common experience actually—and the child's healthy response in this case would be to feel sadness and anger that they weren't getting a fundamental need met by the people who were meant to meet it. However, what usually happens in this case is that it wasn't welcome in the family dynamic for the child to safely express sadness or anger because already they tracked within their family field that if they were to express how they really felt, they might make things worse or make Mom and Dad uncomfortable. The child might deduce that their authentic expression and healthy communication of their real emotional state might stifle the potential for love, attention and presence, further lessening the chances of securing the kinds of outcomes the child really wants.

So the anger and sadness get repressed along with feelings of unworthiness. A patterning gets set: the child learns they have to do more to get attention and be loved—they learn to go above and beyond, to be the best they can be, to be perfect, to do anything to make Mom and Dad happy so that maybe, just maybe, they can get the attention and loving presence they've always wanted. Often this kind of patterning, rooted in trauma (of a core abandonment wound), evolves as someone grows up into codependent relationships and various forms of addiction that are based in an underlying desire for control that conveys a temporary solace amidst inconsistency and chaos. As an adult this energy gets projected again and again into someone's relationship dynamics, recreated as the original abandonment trauma or wound of feeling unseen or not enough. It's so familiar to engage in this way, since it's often the only way we learn to be in a relationship if we stay in our unconscious childhood wounding.

It's a wonder how anyone could simply let go and feel safe to surrender when most of us are walking around with immense guards up and wearing masks we don't even know we're wearing; it's all part of an elaborate system we learned at a very young age to protect ourselves from supposed danger. Now, let's remember that danger, according to how our lizard brain categorizes threats, doesn't always mean life or death anymore, but this antiquated and overdeveloped part of our system doesn't register the difference. Our limbic system registers fear and stress, or trauma response, the same way it would as if we were going to lose our lives if this stress or trauma were to happen again. It therefore serves up that memory unconsciously every time a similar situation appears, regardless of whether it's actually life threatening or not. We have a lot we're up against when it comes to reprogramming ourselves for more calm, peace, and presence.

We can start to attune our nervous systems to more of the ways of being we actually want to experience by becoming more aware of our traumas. It sounds simple, maybe even obvious to say so, but I've learned not to assume. We never know where others or even ourselves are really at till the healing path gets real, and by that I mean really uncomfortable. In the moments when our deepest, darkest traumas and pains are revealed—or perhaps feel like they're exposed unwantedly—how do we show up? Do we meet the opportunity with an openness to heal and a capacity to watch ourselves as conscious observers? Or do we react quickly and make snap judgments that can tend to lock us and anyone else we're relating to in boxes (certain projections or belief structures) that are really hard to get out of?

> **"By processing information from the environment through the senses, the nervous system continually evaluates risk. I have coined the term neuroception to describe how neural circuits distinguish whether situations or people are safe, dangerous, or life-threatening. Because of our heritage as a species, neuroception takes place in primitive parts of the brain, without our conscious awareness."**
> **—Stephen W. Porges**

When we get to know who we are, which includes getting to know our core wounds and the traumas that have invited us to grow into more of who we really are here to be, we start to learn the mechanisms and techniques that work best for us to relax, rest, and receive. One day a long time ago I was writing, and this little mantra came through to remind me of the simplicity within our own attunement process:

Trust, Relax, Surrender, Repeat

What if life is a series of following these few steps again and again till they become more of a muscle memory? One day we'll eventually realize that we've been so in the present moment, trusting, relaxing, and receiving what we've always envisioned enjoying, that we didn't even have to think about anything at all. We were already being it.

Our surrender activations at the end of this chapter will give us plenty of ways to play in these new, unfolding energies. At the beginning of the nervous system healing process, what has been most challenging for me and most others that share a similar path in repatterning has been to really allow oneself permission to slow down. And when I say slow down, I mean sloooow down, really, all the way. We don't often take a moment to recognize how our society has programmed us to move so quickly and frankly rush through most moments without taking some breaths for integration in between experiences. It took me forever to learn this about myself—especially when unpacking the limbic birth imprint, which for me meant acknowledging all the aspects of my labor process and delivery that were rushed and entailed high levels of adrenaline and stress, therefore informing most of my strategy in approaching life for the next three decades.

> **"Your genius simply makes you a truly joyous human being.
> That is your higher purpose—to be radiant for no
> reason other than being alive."**
> **—Richard Rudd**

How can we consciously allow room and space for the body and spirit to really genuinely relax and rest? When the body can rest fully, the spirit can settle, and our minds can eventually experience more ease. From here, healing naturally happens. Alignment is an automatic outgrowth. Our reality can reorganize, usually in profoundly beautiful ways we never would have thought of within our intellectual mind frame. When we rest, we allow more of our authenticity to shine through, which means more of our true essence can radiate in all sorts of ways—signaling life to meet us more clearly where we are instead of sending us confusing inputs in response to somewhat dissonant outputs that get transmitted through a sped-up, messily (or not at all) integrated energy system.

Here is a personal creative inquiry for us all to uniquely explore: When do we feel most at ease? How do we love to relax? When, where, and how does our body feel most supported to really let go and simply be? How can we give ourselves more space and opportunities to experience all of the above, more often? Perhaps these ways of being can be woven into the foundation of our entire lives, and from here the practice of simply being will give way to deeper trust, safety, and presence that naturally overflow into ease in letting go and surrendering. At least that's a start.

**"Three mantras you should never say: (1) I don't know.
(2) I'm not ready. (3) I can't do it."**
—Yogi Bhajan

WHAT IF EVERYTHING IS ACTUALLY OKAY?

It might be a tough idea to really sit with, but the further we go on the healing path in our ascension process, the more we inevitably see we are creating every experience in our reality to help ourselves see more of who we really are and what we are capable of. Are we always willing to take a look in the mirror and consider that maybe most or all of our supposed challenges are usually of our own making? Not usually at first—it's hard to admit it, and we usually find many ways to avoid facing this reality at all. But eventually, maybe even inevitably, we come to see that when we take responsibility for being right where we are, as we are, and accept what our reality is showing us about ourselves and our choices, we end up with substantially more freedom (and power) to choose our next steps.

One of the most simple yet profound reminders I've found—and isn't it true that the most profound teachings tend to be the most simple?—is a permission slip for ourselves to admit (especially when life inevitably gets hard) that maybe, just maybe, everything is okay. In fact, whenever we are in a bind or life feels impossible, what if we interrupted the sometimes automatic worry-mode looping with an honest questioning of ourselves: **What if everything is okay, and what if in this moment I am okay too?** What if there is nothing for me to fix, manage, figure out, or even change right now? An advanced, next-level step in a moment like this would be to then consider: if this is what is happening in my present reality, how is this actually okay, just as it is, right now? When we can come into acceptance for what is happening, what we are feeling, and how we are being in that moment, we create space for expansion, and more clarity naturally arises.

I wish someone had taught me this when I was born. Kind of like I wish I had a book like this when I was little—could have saved a lot of years of feeling like I was on the wrong planet, always looking up to the sky wondering if someone could beam me up so I could go back home. Earth certainly always felt like a foreign place that has been extra challenging to adjust to. I sensed an underlying dissonance here as early as I could remember, that things like society and the way people were in general just seemed out of whack. Why couldn't we all just get along—and why are there homeless people, and why are people going hungry, and why are there wars? You know, typical questions an eight-year-old, highly intuitive, empathic child would naturally be asking, the usual. But here we are, right on time, and the world we came here to experience is finally ready for us to fully shine our light and awaken to our true selves—seriously, it's time. Sometimes I feel like whatever we were doing before now was just killing time, because at some level we knew the world wasn't ready for what we had to bring yet.

No matter where we are at in the journey—especially with regards to wrapping our minds around the concept of surrender and healing our nervous system—we still have a lot more to go on the path ahead and many layers to unravel that will support what we've explored. In fact I think as long as we are alive in these bodies there will be more and more layers to experience. Perhaps this is the point of being alive. So can we be okay with being as we are, right where we are? What if everything really is okay? It's such a sweet interruption to ask ourselves this and genuinely ponder it instead of going into worry or control mode, as many of us are traditionally conditioned to operate, especially in the face of potential crisis.

"The real purpose of life is to experience the divinity within."
—Amma (Mata Amritanandamayi)

Cognitive dissonance can be our friend—and when self-imposed in a practice like this (intentionally confusing our minds by introducing a new thought pattern or response), it can lead to some beautiful new insights that invite us into entirely new potentials and maybe even realities. When we start to earnestly ask how everything is actually okay, we can start to collect evidence as to how life has been supporting us, how we have always been taken care of more or less, and how actually maybe everything up until this moment, even if it was hard here and there at times, has eventually worked out pretty alright despite our best efforts to control, manage, fix, and will a particular path into being.

Maybe we start to also see how we've actually been letting go and surrendering more than we ever considered—maybe we were doing it all along without thinking about doing it, without wondering how. Maybe while we were finally allowing ourselves to rest and relax, we were receiving what life was wanting to support us with all along. Maybe it was all so easy we didn't even notice and thought instead we had to figure something out. Maybe the joke was on us—a joke from our higher selves it seems; a giant, infinitely unfolding cosmic joke indeed.

SURRENDER ATTUNEMENTS

Consider this: maybe letting go or surrendering can be as simple as admitting to yourself that you don't know and you'll stop trying to pretend to know or to figure anything out. Can we give ourselves permission to let go of needing to know—where we fit in, who we are, why we are here, if we are enough, all the questions that really don't have a definitive answer? Can we take the pressure off of ourselves to figure it all out, as if that was ever our job to do in the first place? Let's fire ourselves from that role for good. How does it feel to say to yourself: I don't know what I'm supposed to be doing other than what's right here and now? I don't know what things happening around me mean either, and that's okay.

Deconstruct Your Fear

An activation we can explore that assists in attuning to surrender is to practice embodying and personifying whatever it is we are afraid of experiencing if we let go. Can we consider that sometimes the things we are confronted with that can at first feel threatening might usually, eventually reveal themselves as initiations into wholeness and expansion? Could it be that the things that really scare us, especially new experiences that we've never had before, invite us to grow into our full capacity and see ourselves more clearly? Maybe. A great way to find out what might be underneath any fear or self-doubt is to practice writing a letter to yourself as the thing that's feeling scary.

For example: say you're exploring quitting your job to start a new venture or go into a new position (really you can insert any example here of starting something new that you've never done before). Write a letter to yourself as the new job—what will it teach you, what is it wanting to show you about yourself, how will it challenge you to see yourself in new ways? What about this new venture is going to stretch you into new capacities and potentials you never before thought yourself capable of? When we can give voice to the supposed unknown, even through playing a creative, imaginative game like this, we can start to move through the fear and stagnation that wants us to stay stuck in what's familiar instead of growing.

Future Self Letter

Another favorite exercise similar to this is to write a letter to yourself from your future self—the version of you that's looking back at where you are from a few months or even years into the future, where you're achieving your goals, living your dreams, learning the lessons you want to learn, feeling the ways you want to feel. Here is how our minds are really designed to work—using our imaginative visioning power to template how great our futures can be instead of perceiving how scary or limiting they seem when based solely on limited evidence provided by the mind's catalog of past traumatic experiences. Let's create a new experience, a new path forward. Letting go can be a game we learn to play, just like anything else.

"Stop acting so small. You are the universe in ecstatic motion."
—Rumi

Earth Transmutation

A great practice for attuning to letting go and surrendering is something I've come to understand as Earth transmutation—a practice in which we connect consciously with the Earth and send away energy from of our body and consciousness that we no longer want to carry anymore. To try this practice and make it your own, explore how it feels to connect with the Earth in a meditative space or even outside in physical contact with the Earth in a way that feels best for you. You can also consider connecting with your Earth star—an energy center (similar to a chakra, or particular point in your energy field or etheric body) that resides about one to one and a half feet beneath your feet, toward the bottom of your energy field, anchoring you into the Earth. Once contact is made by taking a few deep breaths into this energetic area a bit below your feet, surrender all that no longer serves you through this portal into the Earth to be transmuted back into light. Say aloud or within, "I surrender," as whatever is meant to release comes up to be acknowledged; then, let it go. Into the Earth, into the light.

DOSE Yourself

I can't believe I didn't put this together until recently, but hey, better late than never. Did you know the hormones responsible for happiness and good feelings spell out DOSE—how funny/perfect is that? D for dopamine, O for oxytocin, S for serotonin and E for endorphins. For a little refresher and context: "Hormones are chemicals produced by different glands across your body. They travel through the bloodstream, acting as messengers and playing a part in many bodily processes. One of these important functions? Helping regulate your mood. Certain hormones are known to help promote positive feelings, including happiness and pleasure."*

Dopamine is probably one of the best known happy hormones. It is directly related to pleasure, helping our brains register rewards and memory and ensuring all systems are firing. Oxytocin is sometimes referred to as the love chemical; it gets amplified when you feel yummy feelings from physical connection or while developing an intimate bond. Serotonin can support a balanced mood as well as regulated sleep, appetite, digestion, learning and memory recall. Last but definitely not least, we have endorphins, which act as the body's

* "How to Hack Your Hormones for a Better Mood," Healthline, July 25, 2022, https://www.healthline.com/health/happy-hormone.

built-in pain relief whenever stress or disease arises. Endorphin levels also tend to increase in reward-inducing activities like eating, working out, and sex. So, that's a lot of data—what do we do with all of it? One idea or invitation: tune in with each hormone's purpose and explore how you can self-generate more of all of the above for yourself if that's the support you're presently calling in.

Want to feel more rewarded for taking care of yourself? How do you pump up those endorphins? Perhaps consider a more fun, inspiring workout routine that gets your heart pumping. Want to feel more love and affection? How about asking a loved one or a friend for a cuddle session or even try putting a weighted blanked on yourself to see how compression soothes your system. When was the last time you self-pleasured and gave yourself plenty of time to bask in the beautiful feelings of self-love, turn-on, and celebration you've generated throughout your body, radiating through every cell? Dancing is my absolute favorite way to activate all of these happy chemicals while also shaking free any stuck energies or densities I no longer want to be carrying around. Give it a try and see how much more goodness you can allow in.

Somatic Surrender

Embodying surrender somatically (in our cells) can feel like giving yourself permission and space to move like you, to feel however you're feeling and to let that simply radiate through your authentic expression. From this space of deep connection with your inner being, allow your body to move you in all the ways that feel most expansive and nurturing. Be in moving conversation with your body—allow it to open and vibrate as your authentic self. Another layer of the embodiment of surrender involves consciously tensing up every muscle in your body, from the tip top of your head to your fingertips and toes. Breathe all the way in as much as you can and then tense all your muscles as tightly as you can for as long as you can and then only let go when you absolutely must. You can do this a few times and see what you notice energetically. You can add another layer here by imagining the vision or desire you want to actualize—anything at all (what do you most want to receive, embody, or experience?)—as you tense up, gather all your energy in your center, and inhale as much breath as you can. Then, when you can't stay tense any longer, let everything go and practice visualizing the dream or desire floating away too, perhaps encapsulated in little bubbles of light.

Visionary Divine Union

When we have big visions birthing through us, no matter what they are—the things that make us feel most alive, that inspire us to grow into more of ourselves—we are invited into deep surrender as to how the process for birthing the vision will unfold. One of my favorite games we can play as we dance in this visionary space is something I call visionary divine union. What if our visions that we are called to birth into reality are actually living, breathing beings all their own with souls and everything? We can commune with them, seek guidance from them, and really partner with them in actualizing our desired intentions with a lot of joy and maybe even some grace. Here's how I love to play: come into intimate connection with your vision, whatever it is—maybe the inspiration to move into a new space, start a new job, enter into a new relationship, birth a creative project, anything that's making your heart sing. Imagine this vision is a being all its own. Can you personify it as its own character you can be in conversation with? See how that feels. Some may love to explore this conversation in writing or in meditation—see what works for you. Playing with visual art tools like drawing and paint is also fun and might even be a richer experience when we take out the need to articulate intellectually with words.

> **"Your vision will become clear only when you can look into your own heart. Who looks outside, dreams; who looks inside, awakens."**
> **—Carl Jung**

Then maybe in conversation with your vision, can you explore what commitments and/or new agreements are present to acknowledge or co-create? What are your shared intentions? What does your vision desire from you? What healing is your journey into birthing this vision initiating? How would your vision like to be supported in true partnership/divine union? Where else can you let go of attachment to results, to how the process unfolds and to anything else that feels heavy in this relationship? Where can you open to more presence, authenticity and genuine creativity in this co-creation? Usually when we are in an expression of play that feels authentic to us, we are naturally experiencing a state of surrender—free from thinking, free from control, free from worry. When we are practicing playing in our inspiration while enjoying the present moment, we are spacious and open to receiving support in more ways than we can even imagine, and we allow life to have space to show up and surprise us in pretty miraculous, usually unexpected ways.

My Favorite Practices for Nervous System Healing

I'll leave you with some of my favorite body support practices and tools I play with pretty regularly to nourish, rest, repair, and recalibrate. Tune in with them on your own and see what resonates—leave the rest. Perhaps this list of potentials inspires you to explore creating a new self-care routine of sorts—a body support regimen in which you can feel more supported, at home, at peace—more like you. The more we can receive support in allowing ourselves to truly rest, the more we naturally heal and develop capacity for our essence to come more online. Think of it like creating your own cosmic chiropractor menu of your favorite support tools and techniques—custom curated just for you to choose from whenever it would feel good to receive.

Some of the practices I play in regularly include:

- visiting a sensory deprivation float tank for deep, integrative meditation and energy clearing
- resting under a weighted blanket or covering my body with pillows and blankets so I feel weighted compression (this can help induce deeply relaxed states)
- cupping and acupuncture
- energy healing or hands-on healing from trusted friends
- making myself an intentional healing bath (or a foot bath if you don't have access to a full-size bath) with essential oils and Epsom/Himalayan salts
- craniosacral therapy (body/energy work)
- all kinds of massage
- rebounding on a trampoline (can even be jumping jacks to get the lymphatic system circulating/cleansing)
- a self-massage my therapist calls "cow bites," which entails making big bite-like grips with your hands over your arms and legs—compressing your body in ways that feel good and holding for as long as is comfortable
- giving myself a strong hug—really, try it: it feels so good, and

don't let go for a while as you breathe into your own support here, creating soothing compression
- colonics and enemas: cleansing the gut and colon is such a key practice when it comes to emotional detox as well—we store so much memory in our guts, not to mention all the undigested food and energy that tend to get stored in there no matter how healthy and active we are

Explore on your own if you want to learn more about any of these practices and trust you'll be guided to the perfect place and people if you earnestly seek to receive the support.

4

SHINE LIGHT ON SHADOWS

First up, let me just say that an entire book, maybe a series of books actually, could easily be written about our journey into illuminating and integrating our shadows. Sometimes I look back and laugh at the entire proposition to write a book about ascension and a supposed path within it. It feels like spirit, god, source—whoever you believe in—must be smiling, maybe even giggling a little at us in our attempts to make sense of such immensities. But such is the human experiment, and here we are, doing our best. Maybe everything we go through is for no reason other than to become living, breathing examples of the lessons we've learned in a world that's finally ready to receive our medicine, awaken, and heal.

We hear the word *shadow* tossed around a lot, especially in spiritual and personal development circles—but what does it mean to you? Do you visit this concept frequently in your vocabulary, perhaps when describing challenges and growing edges (aka the edges of the cliffs into new unknowns your personal growth is nudging you toward) that invite you into more authenticity and groundedness in your own presence? One of my favorite sayings—and honestly I forget if I said it first or if I heard it somewhere and then repeated it a few times, so much so that it became my own: *Nearly everyone is trapped inside a closet they don't even know they're in.* This is what it feels like to be stuck in your shadow aspects, wounding, and trauma reactivity that can unknowingly keep you in a prison of your own making until you decide to free yourself (or you're shocked into awakening and have no choice but to start paying attention and maybe, just maybe, venture out on your healing path).

For me it's been helpful to relate to the shadow aspects of ourselves and the world as an essential element of this dualistic experience we've elected to have in this physical realm. It takes some pressure off to do so—

relieving us of any stress around getting out of the shadow to fully im-merse ourselves in the light, or something like that, as if there's only one place we're meant to be all the time and it's all bright and shiny, always. Herein lies another misconception we see rampantly in most spiritual circles and teachings—they often remind us to look toward the light, be the light, shine your light—all the ways of saying the same thing: focus completely on the light, and the light is the best part of ourselves, so let's be that. What seems to get missed in this strategy, often wrought with bypassing and repression, is the importance of meeting our darkness, our wounds, our traumas—maybe collectively understood as our shadow—in order to feel our wholeness. Integration is related to integrity—you can tell they come from the same root meaning just by how they sound, right?

"Our life is shaped by our mind; we become what we think. Joy follows a pure thought like a shadow that never leaves."
—Buddha

As far as I see it, integrity is one of our greatest values that we have the potential to actualize in this human experience. It means being com-pletely integrated across what you feel, think, and say and how you act. It means we are in alignment with how we show up and how we really feel on the inside. When we are in integrity and we are integrated in our wholeness—loving all aspects of ourselves—we are in alignment with our purpose, we are ourselves, and we are beyond any compartmentalization that society or anyone else would project upon us in an attempt to limit, control or even understand our infinite potential.

So let's face it: are we ready to meet our darkness? Are we ready to feel our shadow aspects, see them for what they truly are, and maybe, slowly by slowly, even start to love them and appreciate them for the rich lessons they bear? Maybe we're getting ahead of ourselves, but I figured I'd put all the cards out on the table for a nice heads-up about where we're going. I am a fan of going into the fire and letting it burn away what no longer serves—especially when it comes to burning away illusions and falsities around perfectionism, looking good, performing and keeping it all together in some neat little box that somehow seems easier to make sense of but really deep down has never felt real. Our whole societal conditioning has usually taught us otherwise—and here we get to strip all the masks away and see what's underneath. What do you say, are you up for this adventure?

WOUNDS THAT UNITE US

The beautiful thing about the shadow is that we all have it. It's such a universal aspect of our human experience to share wounds, traumas, misunderstandings, and various tragedies along our evolution that catalyze at times the ideal conditions in which we can better see ourselves and learn to grow and heal in the ways that empower us most. We could go pretty deep into why there's been such a historical tendency to hide from the shadow, to repress our darkness and to shy away from any talk about trauma healing or sensitivities therein.

To keep it simple—I'd say that humanity wasn't ready to wake up and take responsibility for all that it means to be completely empowered, fully alive, all-the-way-turned-on human beings until now. To really wake up means being willing to meet yourself as you are and to love the parts of yourself you learned to shut down or hide in response to various traumas that happened along the way. For whatever reason, and maybe it took quite a while to arrive, we weren't ready—but now we most definitely are.

What I continue to see again and again in my own healing journey and in the mirror of all those I am graced to witness along the way is that no matter how bad, alone, wrong, dirty, gross, ashamed, unlovable, unwanted, or whatever else it might be we think we are, we are never, ever alone in feeling what we are feeling. In fact, what I love seeing is how the things we tend to feel most ashamed of, that we really don't want anyone else to know about us ever, that we think if someone were to ever find out we might even die, are usually almost always the things that everyone is waiting to love us for.

"Integrity is the recognition of the fact that you cannot fake your consciousness, just as honesty is the recognition of the fact that you cannot fake existence."
—Ayn Rand

The things we hide and learn to repress about ourselves, especially when it comes to deeply repressed feelings of shame and guilt, are usually the experiences that we find to be most universal across humanity. Maybe this is another part of the awakening game in which we see the universe has always been playing some cute jokes on us—watching us to see what we'll do if given the opportunity to open up to a new level of connection or vulnerability. Will we take the risk to be seen, to be revealed, to be as we are?

I could tell you a lot of stories about this particular pattern, but there is one thread that really comes up loudly as we start to explore the shadow and the universal wounds that unite us, especially when it comes to repressed shame and diminishing our innate power. For many years I carried immense shame that I repeatedly faked orgasms and truly thought there was something wrong with my body—like it didn't work in the way it was supposed to. What I didn't know until later was that this pattern started much younger than I cared to remember. It started with a core trauma that my body reacted to by shutting down my sexual energy (which is really the root of our authenticity and creativity, which we'll get into more later) when my expression of feeling good made someone I depended upon (my dad in this case) noticeably uncomfortable.

It didn't help that upon losing my virginity at age eighteen, I also was in a relationship dynamic wherein my boyfriend would show me porn and suggest that I "be more like them"—instead of appreciating the ways in which I was already showing up. Years later, it also clicked that being put on prescription birth control at age fourteen had something to do with the inherent disconnect between my mind and body—making it even harder for my mind to let go and trust my body to do its natural authentic expression. Birth control was incredibly dissociative in my experience—I felt disconnected from my intuition and therefore from my true self, so it was nearly impossible to feel safe to simply be or receive.

"Love knows no shame. To be loving is to be open to grief, to be touched by sorrow, even sorrow that is unending. The way we grieve is informed by whether we know love."
—bell hooks

Again, an entire book could probably be written about the female orgasm alone and why we historically learn to repress our sexuality and power as women in a patriarchal society—but it feels important to mention this specific experience, because for many years it was the greatest source of my shame, unworthiness and disempowerment. And I kept it all to myself for years and years, suffering in silence, thinking I was the only one in the world having this experience and that worse than that, something was definitely wrong with me for having this problem. Why couldn't I just be normal and be more like those girls my boyfriend was showing me in the videos? Was that really what I was supposed to be like? It's what he wanted, so maybe that's what was right, and the way I was was wrong.

Long story short, it wasn't until almost a year after getting sober from drugs and alcohol and still feeling a bit emotionally overwhelmed and super anxious that I realized I needed to detox from hormonal birth control, which I had been on for the past decade. Interestingly enough, I had been put on birth control right around the same time I started drinking and doing drugs in the first place, which made me wonder: did I start partying around that time because the birth control made me feel so disassociated from myself and real feelings that I had to seek other means of connection? I think so. And yet such is life and part of the path I chose, which luckily now I've made peace with. Still, it feels important to share since I wonder if many other women are on a similar trajectory without considering the potential harms of disconnecting from one's natural rhythms and intuitive energy cycles, which hormones completely interrupt and in some cases shut down.

The shame I felt about not being able to perform sexually and constantly pretending and playing the part I thought my boyfriends wanted me to play was immense and such a painful weight to carry alone. I was never present for my own enjoyment of intimacy; instead sex felt like a job I had to do to make sure my partner had the experience they were expecting or else I'd be left alone. Eventually this constant repression and pretending manifested as recurring cysts on glands I had never before heard of. I also suffered in silence, trying to heal at emergency urgent care appointments and with various doctors, some telling me that they had never seen anything like this before, which is probably the worst thing you could expect to ever hear from a doctor.

I still suffered in silence, never telling my boyfriends for fear of them finding out that something really was wrong with me—anything to keep them from leaving me. Codependency was a familiar energy for me to play in at the time—it paired nicely with alcoholism and frequent drug use, of course. I was terrified of being left alone to finally just be with myself. Anything but that.

Much later, after finally being on my own for the first time in many years without a boyfriend to babysit me, I found myself in an underground strip club dancing for New York City's crème de la crème of Wall Street and real estate plus experimenting with escorting a bit on the side. I loved having a double life—working in a financial advisory office by day and at the club a few nights a week as a completely different person. I was starting to explore this sexual expression and identity that I had repressed for so many years. Hiding in all these relationships gave me a false sense of safety and security, but really they were prisons of my own making in which I was trapped in playing a character I never actually wanted to be.

"Nothing goes away until it teaches us what we need to know."
—Pema Chödrön

Here I was finally starting to express who I really was and how I wanted to play intimately—but I still didn't feel safe to do so outside of the confines of underground clubs and scenarios that most people weren't even aware existed. I learned so much during this time—especially the realization that so many of the men that would come to these places were really seeking healing and a safe place to simply connect as themselves where they could receive love and presence. Our society is quick to judge our desires and limit our expressions in accordance with what's been deemed acceptable or safe by some arbitrary lens of standards. Who is making the rules anyway? The media, the government, or is it ourselves who are complicit in filtering our own expressions so that we stay in loops of repetition and homogeneity without ever stepping out of the box as examples who pioneer new potentials?

One day I finally was encouraged to share the story of my sexual repression, faking orgasms, and all the insights therein on a livestream video. A mentor I was working with at the time helped me connect the dots between the immense amount of energy I was constantly draining trying to keep all these secrets and manage all the masks I was wearing to a fundamental difficulty I was experiencing in magnetizing (and frankly, stabilizing consistently) more prosperity into my life and business. I was studying sexual energy and the concept of magnetism as connected to core traumas and seeing firsthand how when we repress our shadows and shame in particular, we siphon our creative energy away to constantly manage the identity we've learned to hide behind. And the role we're always playing (and the many masks we're wearing) actually takes a lot of upkeep to maintain, which diminishes our capacity to create, to resonate as ourselves and attract the opportunities meant for us, and to receive prosperity or love when it does inevitably arrive.

Even though it felt like my entire body was shaking and like I was certainly going to die if anyone were to ever know this terrible truth about me, I knew I had to speak the truth and be witnessed by others while doing it if I ever wanted to be free of these stories and structures that were keeping me in a prison of my own making. We make the prison, and we also have the key to unlock the doors whenever we choose—I was ready to see it for myself, so I dove in headfirst. I fired up the livestream, and already I felt so much energy diffusing through my system. Trauma healing can feel like that sometimes—like an off-gassing of energy or a heightened vibration that shakes out of the system as it's on its way out, from deep, dark nooks and crannies of our most intimate parts, which make for great hiding spots.

I told the story of how when I was in first grade, six years old at my birthday party, I was dancing and having a blast and eventually found myself dancing on my dad's lap and maybe, just maybe, rubbing myself just a bit on his leg, just because it felt good to do so. Not that I was in any way sexualizing my movement or thinking about it in any other way than simply listening in the moment to what felt good and doing that. But in that moment my dad's energy said everything about how terrible that choice was—my movement made him noticeably uncomfortable, even to the point where he forcibly took me off his lap and placed me on the ground, saying something like: "No, don't do that."

Beyond his words, I got at a deep level in that moment a cellular imprint that effectively taught me to never listen to what feels good in my body again without really checking out how the other person involved is going to react. Or maybe more simply, what got anchored in was the belief that: when I listen to my body's wisdom about what feels good and express accordingly, the people I love and depend on to support me get uncomfortable and might be mad at me or leave me.

No wonder I carried on for so many years in shame and hiding, repressing my sexual energy, feeling bad for simply following the natural—and by the way healthy—desire and expression of self-pleasure and self-exploration of this beautiful body. Another universal wound that unites us is really the core wound of sexual repression. Parents that are caught in their own sexual repression are most likely going to project that energy onto their children, keeping many of these cycles in motion until one by one we wake up and decide to take our power back and reprogram ourselves according to our authentic energies and desires.

> **"You find that being vulnerable is the only way to allow your heart to feel true pleasure that's so real it scares you."**
> **—Bob Marley**

Back to the livestream. I was sharing the entire timeline of the story with my dad's lap and then the shame of self-pleasuring as a child, wondering if there was something wrong with me for exploring my body so young or maybe too often (who knows, it's not like we have many healthy examples and conversations to reference about topics like this); sharing about being a stripper and working as an escort for a brief stint toward the rock bottom of my addiction; and finally admitting that in all my relationships over many years I had never had a real orgasm despite faking them all the time. I put all my cards out on the table—admitted absolutely everything and set myself free from the immense shame I had been hiding deep within for years and years, maybe even this entire lifetime and even lifetimes past.

I felt such an immense release through the whole experience of sharing followed by a slight terror after it was completed—quickly going into self-criticism and feeling somewhat overexposed. But what I saw completely shocked me—a huge response from friends, clients, and tons of people I didn't even know or hadn't heard from in years. And they weren't putting me down like I thought they might be—no, they were supporting me and sharing loving, celebratory reflections and resonance with how they related to what I shared. In fact, so many women actually responded to me and even messaged me privately, sharing that they were so thankful to hear my journey—through listening and relating they were able to heal some of their own shame and repression they'd been too afraid to unlock too. As the experience had some space to integrate, I felt so much of my energy come back online—so much more of my creativity became available, and I felt like a huge weight, one that I had become used to carrying all the time without a thought, had been lifted off of my shoulders. This new lightness would take some getting used to.

So let's go back to our core universal wounds, shall we? We all have so much more in common when it comes to core wounds than we'd ever think, and what a beautiful gift to share, especially when we start to open ourselves more vulnerably to being seen and receiving support on our healing journey. We are never alone in healing the parts of ourselves we've felt afraid to meet. Let's always try our best to remember that when we feel like we are the only ones going through something, that's usually a sign that we get to ask for help and invite someone in to help. Usually the moment we feel most alone is when we are on the precipice of a breakthrough that's inviting our consciousness to completely shift into a new reality.

The fear-driven thought of "I am alone" is usually coming from the ego or personality-self that at some level is invested in staying the same— even if it means staying in the same familiar wound. At least the familiar wound is safe because we know what happens when we stay in that pattern, even if it hurts. As we awaken and ascend into more of our multi-dimensional consciousness and authenticity, and start to see that we are made up of many different aspects and energies, we get to observe these thoughts more objectively as they arise instead of reacting to them and letting them dictate our lives. Again, acceptance is one of our greatest practices for coming into presence and clarity no matter what situation might be arising. How is what's happening right now absolutely okay? What if the way I am feeling right now is also okay, and there's nothing to fix and there's nothing wrong?

> **"Yet the knowledge of what is possible lives on inside each of us, inextinguishable. Let us trust this knowing, hold each other in it, and organize our lives around it. Do we really have any choice, as the old world falls apart? Shall we settle for anything less than a sacred world?"**
> **—Charles Eisenstein**

In exploring universal wounds and collective traumas, the three common collective ones I've noticed we've all got playing out at some level are the mother wound, the father wound, and the god wound. Again, an entire book could be written about just these or maybe each of them on their own—there's a lot here, but it's important to consider these together for the journey underway. After unpacking these a bit, then we can get more granular and excavate our personal trauma patterning by navigating the specific core wounds of rejection, abandonment, betrayal, guilt, and shame. I look at our collective and personal wounds as inter-woven layers and textures of traumas we each carry at some level to help us learn more about who we really are and why we are here. Maybe all the traumas we share even empower us to eventually convey the teachings and medicine we are here to exemplify through simply being ourselves.

Mother Wound

One of my biggest challenges in this life along the awakening path has involved the multilayered experiment into healing the mother wound. This seems to be a pretty common wound we all collectively share resonance with in some respects, and it can be profound in its sometimes subtle, unconscious impact on our lives. The mother wound entails any experience of feeling abandoned by one's female caretaker during childhood and can even manifest as subtly as feeling like your mother simply wasn't present at the level you required to really feel like she was actually there.

It's common for people to bypass the consideration that they might have trauma informing their relationship strategies and patterning, especially if they think that according to appearances, their family dynamic seemed to be picture perfect. The thing is, trauma doesn't have to be an outright abusive or physical manifestation in the dramatic sense we're used to seeing in TV and movies. It can be subtle and sometimes even invisible to the mind—but the body can be feeling all along that the love and presence that one really requires to feel safe and validated are absent. The body can then create all kinds of subsequent reaction strategies.

Usually we can reverse engineer the path of our trauma from how we are showing up later on in our adult lives, especially in intimate relationships, where everything, eventually, no matter how hard we try to hide it, gets put on blast. If we tend to experience relationships with a flavor of codependency or underlying insecurity or anxiety, it might very well likely be due to the foundational energetic relationship with our mother being rife with uncertainty and inconsistency. Again, trauma doesn't mean that something terrible and outright obvious had to happen to you in order to matter. In fact some of the most stark imprints come from trauma that was instilled before we could even talk or much less make sense intellectually of the world around us. A lot of trauma gets put into play before we can even remember or have words to describe it—but again, our body remembers and records the energetic memories and subsequent reaction patterns that were initially installed simply to keep us safe and ensure we had what we needed to survive.

I learned about the mother wound a few years into my journey into recovery as I was exploring new layers that were ready to heal, especially as I was unpacking all the codependent and toxic relationship patterns I had played out over the years. Awareness of the mother wound arose as I was diving deeper into inner child healing after a rather shocking initial experience I had with an energy healer—I started to mention this briefly a bit earlier. This experience showed me just how far I had to go when it came to feeling at home and connected within myself. I was guided to meet my inner child in a meditation combined into a reiki healing session, and when prompted to acknowledge myself in my own inner experience with my little one—I couldn't say "I love you" to myself. This broke my heart and hurt in ways beyond what words can describe. But it was a major starting point to diving deeper into the pathway of wholeness within. I didn't know it at the time, but everything was about to change, again.

"People have a hard time letting go of their suffering. Out of a fear of the unknown, they prefer suffering that is familiar."
—Thich Nhat Hanh

I've done a lot of inner child work over the years, which I can't recommend enough as a key practice and modality for self-healing along our ascension journey—and we'll explore more about this at the end of this chapter. Eventually this work led into learning about internal family systems and family constellations, therapy practices that blew my mind wide open as to the depths of how intergenerational trauma is passed down, overloading us with inherited patterns and strategies that we get initiated into eventually completing. A saying I love reminds us that "if we carry intergenerational trauma, then we also carry intergenerational wisdom"—and this wisdom resides in our genes and in our DNA. When we complete the lessons of the inherited traumas, we get to cultivate the wisdom and embody it through being ourselves while hopefully enjoying the lives we came here to live.

In my case the mother wound showed up as my mother simply lacking her own attunement to presence due to a long line of women coming before her that never had an attunement to presence either. How can you give something you never had? But still, as children, we don't know this, and we deserve to feel safe, validated, seen, and loved, no matter what. It's just that these support structures aren't always available if the people we are born to depend on as our caretakers aren't equipped to offer the attunement we crave.

Another layer in the mother wound dynamic in my case was alcoholism and addiction in general, all underlaid by immense anxiety, stress, and a drive to control and compartmentalize instead of feel and metabolize the fullness of the feelings that were arising. Again, if you never had an example of someone teaching you the healthy way to feel and process emotions, how do you learn? And how can you give that example to someone else? You can't. And herein lies the intergenerational trauma cycle in which various strategies or repressions like this get passed down until someone, maybe you or me, chooses or is chosen (same difference) to heal the pattern, recode one's system and complete the cycle for good.

The mother wound can entail a variety of experiences depending on your unique situation, but it always boils down to a fundamental absence of the love, presence, and attunement one requires to feel safe, validated, worthy, loved, and seen by one's mother. A multitude of circumstances might have been unfolding at the time, getting in the way, distracting our mothers from being able to be fully present—and we likely learned to get pretty skilled at making excuses if this was, in fact, our experience.

What matters now that we are choosing to repattern these wounds is to give ourselves space to feel the grief and sometimes even layers of anger and other emotions that understandably arise when we admit that we didn't get what we needed and that it wasn't our fault and it wasn't fair. Yes, it's what happened and we accept it as it is, but in order to truly start healing and welcoming in all the parts of ourselves that have been forgotten or repressed along the way, we must give ourselves space to acknowledge the pain and longing that are surely there for missing out on the deserved experience of what it is to be loved, attuned to, held in unconditional loving presence and care, and to truly have our unique needs met.

Those of us with mother wounds, especially before we are conscious of this patterning, tend to find relationships that reflect to us the familiar energies of unavailability, abandonment, and insecurity. It's common to explore experiences of addiction and codependency as well as to constantly doubt one's own intuitive guidance and to usually struggle immensely with hearing and communicating one's authentic truth. People pleasing and validation seeking are typical outgrowths of this patterning, which completely makes sense as we learned to master the art of getting attention and managing others' reactions to us to get the love we never had. It's also common within codependency orienting from a mother wound for people to experience what's known as enmeshment or blending with someone so much that you almost feel like you become them or like you can't be away from them, ever.

"Forgiveness is the highest form of spirituality."
—Nozer Kanga

When you have experienced the mother wound, it's common to develop a tendency to apologize intensely—usually too much—whenever you feel you've done something that could threaten connection, even if what you did is considered pretty normal. You are always on alert as to how your actions are impacting the others involved. Heightened self-criticism is perhaps the biggest outgrowth of this wounded experience—and has certainly been the biggest one for me to work with. Even now it can be the loudest voice in my head, especially when I am venturing into even bigger dreams and callings. It makes sense though—doesn't it?

Of course we developed a loud inner critic that's hypervigilant to perfectionistic tendencies and wants everything to be absolutely manageable and under control. This is how we learned to feel safe in the midst of what was usually complete chaos, inconsistency, and uncertainty when we were little children completely dependent on others to take care of us. And because we didn't receive what we needed to feel safe and secure, which was our birthright, we rightly developed strategies in our own inner realms to make sense of the situation and survive. The other options were slim pickings and really seemed to boil down to allowing oneself to go completely crazy in an understandably crazy situation.

Another aspect of the mother wound is referred to as a *break in the bond.* Mark Wolynn, one of my favorite teachers and facilitators of family constellations and inherited family trauma therapy, reminds us that: "As infants, we perceive our mother as our world. A separation from her is felt as a separation from life. Experiences of emptiness and disconnection, feelings of hopelessness and despair, a belief that something is terribly wrong with us or with life itself—all these can be generated by an early separation." So the mother wound can happen even soon after being born, when we exit our mother's womb—the first separation happens, and perhaps even at that energetic moment in time we make a meaning about that which resides in our cells until we become conscious of it and then start to heal. If there was a break in the bond with the mother, such as not being held enough during infancy, or perhaps even being left in another part of the hospital, isolated from human contact in the first days and weeks of one's human existence, these factors can contribute to imprinting within the mother wound.

Trauma doesn't always mean something bad happened to you as an action conducted by someone else—it can also mean that you experienced something distressing for no other reason than it happened, and your body remembers that it happened and made up a meaning and subsequent survival tactic to protect you from experiencing it again. One last piece I've noticed come up again and again in this healing work, especially in family constellations, is the connection between the mother wound and one's ability to effectively and responsibly steward wealth and abundance (which doesn't just mean money but can mean love, purpose, power, fulfillment, intimacy, pleasure, and more).

For example, and certainly this has been true for me in my path, when someone has money issues, such as the inability to hold money, build savings, or generate sustainable income (always in chaos or going for broke), this patterning is usually correlated to an early break in the bond with their mother. Since there was a lack of stability and safety, usually in infancy, and as our mother represents relationship to life, support, and abundance, if that bond was broken somehow, these energies of fear and insecurity and scarcity (of love or attention or money) show up in our relationship to resources. They can even play out in how we manage or don't manage our own energy effectively. It can be as subtle as Mom not being present or attuned and therefore an insecure-anxious attachment was formed that connects to our own ability to self-regulate in stability and presence.

Father Wound

Similar to the mother wound, you can imagine that the father wound shows up in our lives as reactions and survival strategies developed in the absence of a father's unconditional loving presence, attunement, and protection while we were growing up. Again, this wounding doesn't necessarily source from a dramatic physical sense in which there was abuse or something very specific that would paint a picture of a family dynamic gone wrong. Sometimes the deepest traumas we have to repattern tend to be the most subtle ones, those that happened before we could even use words. Most of our core wounds get set into motion between the ages of zero and four, perhaps even up till age seven. So yes, we're set up pretty young with the lessons we are destined to learn on this embodiment journey, yes indeed.

The father wound can manifest as an overall experience of one's male caretaker being absent—either physically not present while you were growing up, or even emotionally or energetically checked out but still orienting with you physically. Again, the way this trauma shows up can be so subtle. So often we can get stuck in the story that "my family loved me and did the best they could." We have so many beautiful pictures of our family gatherings and trips and the stories we tell about all the great times that we can be distracted from feeling the underlying pain that is often residing deep down, begging for our acknowledgment of all that was unjustly never received. Perhaps your father was there physically and showed up as best he could, but when it came to you receiving the attunement, affirmation, and feeling of safety and protection that you required to feel validated in your existence, worthiness, and enough-ness, your father didn't convey the presence required for you to feel what you needed to feel.

"Listen to your being. It is continuously giving you hints; it is a still, small voice. It does not shout at you, that is true. And if you are a little silent you will start feeling your way. Be the person you are. Never try to be another, and you will become mature. Maturity is accepting the responsibility of being oneself, whatsoever the cost. Risking all to be oneself, that's what maturity is all about."
—Osho

It's okay to feel however you want to feel about this; absolutely any way you are feeling is perfect and meant to be—remember our practice of acceptance? Here's a great moment to give it a go. When I started to do this work, I felt a lot of anger and frustration as to how unfair it was that I had the wrong parents who literally didn't give me a great setup—emotionally, energetically, and physically. I inherited all sorts of traumas rooted in abandonment and addiction, plus notable genetics for crooked teeth and acne-prone skin (if I'm to be honest about some of what really annoyed me).

My path into entrepreneurship catalyzed more healing around sexuality and creativity as I explored new pathways into amplifying abundance and building capacity for true wealth and greater impact. These energies all go hand in hand and underscore the lesson that when we are being ourselves, fully alive and inspired, we are automatically aligned with abundance. In doing so, I discovered some major healing was required around fundamental feelings of unworthiness and not-enough-ness. Without a healthy example in my life to demonstrate how the divine masculine operates, I was struggling in my own wounded masculine expression when it came to embodying integrity, truth, commitment, initiative, and other incredible qualities I was eager to awaken within. Again, we can't give what we never received—but we can learn to repattern and reprogram ourselves into more of what we desire once we become aware enough to start.

I remember too when I really wanted to join a musical theater company in high school. I practiced my audition song, "Somewhere Over the

Rainbow," for weeks and weeks till it was time to give it my best shot in front of the theater company director. My mom was there with me, and I thought I had everything ready to rock—but when it came time to sing I was paralyzed with fear and couldn't let a single sound come out. I loved singing so much and always sang to myself in my room, in the shower, even with my family around, at least as far as I remembered. Why couldn't I sing in the audition? I shut down. I felt so ashamed at not being able to do it, I think I actually blocked out the memory of it for many years. It didn't come full circle till many years later when I was sitting in circle at a breathwork retreat and another bomb got dropped regarding this father wound I had been skirting around healing. In the retreat circle we were all invited to share a creative gift—something we love to do that expresses our creativity.

I thought it would be a stretch to sing, and I expressed how I felt really scared to do it even though I had been speaking on stages and teaching for years at that point. Something about singing and sharing my authentic voice really terrified me, and my body would shut down when I tried. But here was a chance to go into the fire and see if repatterning might be possible. I started to sing anyway. At first my voice cracked and I felt super awkward and scary to behold, but then the song came out and I started crying. There was a somatic release and energy healing simultaneously beyond anything I had ever experienced. My boyfriend at the time, whose nervous system was very linked up with mine, felt all of it processing through—my immense release of trapped energy that had been welled up as protection for far too long, especially all along the throat and chest (heart) areas.

Our retreat guide mentioned casually how lacking a strong protective masculine presence while I was growing up likely led to the feeling of insecurity and lack of self-assurance I experienced when it came to sharing my gifts and authenticity. I didn't feel safe to be who I really was and share my voice or proverbially shine my full light. Maybe I didn't feel safe to feel fully alive. Then again, I did witness from an early age how when I spoke up and shared my truth or expressed what felt uniquely good to me—just listening to my body and following suit—that certainly made other people around me uncomfortable and seemed to potentially threaten my chances of receiving the tidbits of presence, love, and attention that were already lacking. I didn't want to further threaten my chances of securing an already scarce resource, so I probably from quite young learned to shut a lot down and turn a lot of my energy off so as to not trigger anyone into feeling uncomfortable. It makes sense in hindsight—the perfect strategy to manage one's ability to receive what was needed to survive at the time.

When we experience an absent father, especially emotionally and energetically, we tend to have issues with embodying a healthy masculine energy in our lives, which can lead to challenges with integrity, honesty, commitment and initiative, and feeling on the whole secure and supported. When this wounded energy is present in relationships, whether we are male or female (we all have feminine and masculine energetic wounds and expressions), we tend to experience distortions within self-esteem, emotional stability, anxiety, trust, and boundaries.

For example, if we never had an affirming, validating masculine presence to model healthy masculine qualities with us, we might find ourselves later on in relationships that always bring up our insecurities. Lacking self-esteem, we tend to people please and unconsciously do anything we can to seek validation from those we are involved with, at whatever cost. We might also seek to connect with unavailable people because at some level that feels familiar and therefore feels safer for us to explore as opposed to venturing into actual intimacy, which we might find is actually too confronting for our nervous systems to fully experience. Yes, intimacy is another nervous system attunement that we get to rewire as we unlearn the reaction and survival strategies rooted in trauma and replace them with updated programming designed for true connection, empowerment, and something I like to call *thrive-al* (as opposed to survival).

God Wound

Our final adventure into shared collective wounds is what I've come to understand as the god wound, otherwise felt as an abandonment wound or separation from god, source, spirit, or a higher power of your own understanding. I suppose this experience shares some essence in common with the father and mother wound when we dig into it, but what sets this one apart from those other two is the spiritual and somewhat existential nature implied herein. Let's explore: Do you feel connected to a higher power, to source, or to a guiding light of some sort? How do you relate to yourself as a spiritual being?

It's funny—we're taught in a lot of cases that becoming spiritual is something we have to practice and learn or something we have to learn from someone else. As if there is a way to do it right. What if being spiritual isn't special, and it's actually something we already inherently are, without even trying? What if being human is actually the ultimate spiritual experience—and enlightenment is simply being our true selves? I am willing to find out, and maybe this book is actually a series of stepping stones in that particular direction. Maybe in regards to these questions—about our spiritual nature and destiny unfolding—we get to let our lives and all our choices and actions therein be the answers.

So back to the god wound—it basically gets broken down by this one essential question: Do you feel at some level that you've been forgotten or forsaken by god or spirit? Do you feel like you've been left behind and that all of life has been designed to incur suffering so that you are forever struggling to just get by? Usually if we have any aspect of our experience reflecting a god wound, we tend to orient quite a bit in a victim-ridden consciousness in which we feel at some level that the world is against us and all the odds are stacked in everyone else's favor. We seem to be the ones left out of potential and possibility for happiness, success, love, and whatever else it is that we might imagine wanting.

On one hand what I describe here might at first feel a bit dramatic, but when we really tune into the inquiry for ourselves, do we at some level resonate and relate even just the slightest bit? I know I for one definitely did for quite a while—especially when I turned to drugs and alcohol as a way to escape feeling and experiencing my reality, which was simply too painful to be present for. Underneath those choices was definitely a feeling of abandonment by god—like I had been left alone to figure everything out all on my own, by myself, in my own multitudes of distorted self-identities, addictions, and survival strategies. If there was a god, why did he or she leave me to have this family that I always felt like such an alien in? If there was a god, why were there people starving and killing each other everywhere? If there was a god, why were there all these problems in the world that didn't seem to make any sense?

When we have this fundamental lack of trust in a higher power or higher consciousness, it's easy to live driven by fear and all the survival trauma responses therein. It's easy to have walls up to protect ourselves from getting hurt and to play like life is happening in a dog-eat-dog or every-(wo)man-for-themselves world. Seems like a lot of our society has been shaped accordingly, right? With this energy underlying our reality, we can easily tend toward isolation, immense anxiety, loud self-criticism, perfectionism, and all sorts of other shadow patterns and survival mechanisms in between. How do we show up when we put immeasurable pressure on ourselves to act as god, overseeing the perfect unfolding of all of reality? Quite a task to live up to—an impossible one.

> **"Vulnerability is the only authentic state. Being vulnerable means being open, for wounding, but also for pleasure. Being open to the wounds of life means also being open to the bounty and beauty. Don't mask or deny your vulnerability; it is your greatest asset. Be vulnerable: quake and shake in your boots with it. The new goodness that is coming to you, in the form of people, situations, and things, can only come to you when you are vulnerable."**
> **—Stephen Russell**

That's a Lot! What Now?

That's a lot to consider—it can feel overwhelming to process at first. I didn't come to these inquiries lightly or overnight. But let's consider how we might make a beginning at healing the god wound, and the mother and father wounds while we're at it, since they're all interrelated. The first step in any healing process is awareness. Can we acknowledge the part(s) of us that resonate(s) with any or all of what's been shared here thus far? And then we get to congratulate ourselves for being human—and sharing such universal experiences that forever unite us in our evolutionary journeys.

Maybe one of the aforementioned wounds feels a bit more sticky than another—that tends to be the case. For me it was the mother wound that was strongest of all, followed by the father wound. The god one I got to clean up somewhat quickly, comparatively—especially considering how one of the first things I did when I got sober was get right into the 12 steps of Alcoholics Anonymous, which invited me to turn everything over to a higher power. It helped that I had hit such a rock bottom that I didn't really seem to have any other choices available at the time other than to consider the path laid before me. So I went with it and started practicing surrendering to my higher power (which was the ocean at the time, by the way—something bigger than me that I couldn't really explain but I trusted would work and do its thing regardless of me getting in the way; this was something I could believe in) and praying on a daily basis.

Prayer, I learned, can be as simple as asking the universe for support, maybe in the form of meditation or simply listening to nature, and then listening for the direction and guidance that comes. One of the first times I prayed was to the ocean, asking it to wash away all my fears, anxieties, and obsessions. Visualizing the wavy waters cleansing my body, my mind and my energy field seemed to work—I felt relief even if at the time a part of me thought it was all very silly and awkward. But I wanted to change more than I cared to maintain my obsession with looking good—and the relief I felt soon after first attempting this new practice was enough encouragement to continue.

I learned the serenity prayer, one of my favorite prayers, in AA, but I bet it comes from many other older spiritual traditions: god grant me the serenity to accept the things I cannot change, the courage to change the things I can and the wisdom to know the difference. Don't you think we tend to overcomplicate some of these things that more and more reveal themselves to be a part of our fundamental human nature? I know I do, even still. Especially when we remember that being spiritual isn't special and that we are inherently spiritual beings that know how to connect to other energies and support structures beyond the physical realm we've been conditioned to orient to in a rather limited scope.

"Lives fall apart when they need to be rebuilt."
—Iyanla Vanzant

TRANSMUTING AND TRANSFORMING CORE WOUNDS

We are in such a potent moment of rewriting our human stories, aren't we? We are learning to restore and come into right relationship with the sacredness of ourselves, with all things and all other beings—seeing them for the first time maybe in their divine design and imperfect perfection. When we start to accept ourselves as perfectly imperfect and maybe even start to love ourselves just as we are a little more, we see that it becomes a bit easier to start feeling more love for the world around us and accepting what comes, just as it is. Our core wounds that unite us in the human journey are no joke. They are serious initiations with sometimes tragic consequences that awaken us to the sacredness of these bodies, to these precious lives we get to live and maybe even to the magic that's inherent in simply being alive and awake in moments like this.

Our core wounds reveal our strength, our beauty, our capacity for love and healing and point to what lessons and medicine we are here to exemplify through our being. At least this is a helpful way I like to orient to the human experience—when I can remember to do so, it usually proves to be an effective strategy. But when you're in the depths and throes of suffering in a wounded pattern—especially when it gets louder as it's on its way out—it can be hard to remember. That's why it's a requirement these days that we develop reflexes and muscle memory to help remind us, especially when we are seemingly stuck in a rough moment. What are our support structures, how's our inner relationship, that loving voice of reassurance and encouragement? What fail safes do we have set up in our realities that help remind us of who we are beyond any story that might be playing loudly in our experience (or in our inner voice)? We're uncovering and amplifying all sorts of pieces to this precise puzzle—one that you will put together in your own way—in our path infinitely unfolding.

Our other layer of collective trauma we tend to universally share includes the core wounds of rejection, abandonment, betrayal, guilt, and shame. As we ventured deep into the mother, father and god wounds, did you notice essences of these other core wounds interwoven too? As we continue to see in our ascension journey, everything truly is connected, especially when it comes to our core wounds and collective trauma imprints. We might each feel a resonance with all core wounds to some degree, with one or two of them figuring more prominently in our evolutionary story. For me, abandonment rings pretty loudly in my story of trauma healing, connecting directly into my experiences within the mother and god wounds, respectively. How about you? Perhaps one of the core wounds may seem to stand out more than the others. We'll explore what each entails in just a moment.

But first I want to name something that might have been present for you if you've made it this far in our exploration. What if you don't resonate with anything shared here thus far? What if you don't feel clear on your relationship with trauma or any ways in which you may have been impacted? I notice sometimes in writing this it might feel like I am assuming that everyone has elements of trauma in common because this has absolutely been my experience in my own life and in working with hundreds of people over the years in transformational healing. And yet, this I also know for sure: we don't have to go digging or efforting to find the thing we relate to if it's just not clear or present in our awareness yet. If you're in a different place in your path, but still feel a curiosity to learn about this vantage point of the human experience, perhaps that's why you're here now—to simply receive and inquire into some new curiosities and potentials. Again, as with everything here and maybe within all of life, wear the personality, identity, and concepts shared like a loose garment—that's airy, flowing, and easily adaptable depending on how you choose to move and evolve.

Rejection

This one tends to manifest in sneaky ways and can be one of the most painful emotional wounds. It can manifest unknowingly as paralyzing insecurity, embarrassment, difficulty in connecting and creating intimacy, and lack of self-confidence, especially when it comes to going all-in on one's dreams. Rejection could have been imprinted as a core wound very early on in childhood if parents were neglectful of attending to a child's needs or calls for attention. It could have happened in as subtle a moment as a child wanting to show their parent something they made that they felt proud of and in that moment the parent wasn't available to give them the validation they wanted. Because of this, the child learned to repress their own natural sense of pride and self-affirmation, therefore undermining their capacity to feel valued and assured in their creative capacity.

I experienced a bit of this early on, and when I tune in it feels like it occurred at a very subconscious level, which means I must have been very young when this energy was imprinted. I recalled—during a network spinal analysis bodywork session—that I incurred quite a bit of tension all throughout my neck and shoulders from a young age due to not feeling safe to fully let go in my parents' arms when they held me. Already from infancy I was learning to carry my own weight and be self-sufficient so as to not feel disappointed or rejected if support never showed up. Rejection was the meaning I made up about feeling like my parents didn't really want me. I must have felt like I was a burden to them at some level—why else did it seem like they never paid attention to me in the ways I wanted them to?

This realization actually came to me years into recovery when I was visiting my parents after attending my first Burning Man festival. I had an insight that at a deep level within I felt like my mom actually didn't like me. I knew it was her job to love me, but regardless of that I wasn't really sure if she liked me as a person. This was a core rejection wound I had been carrying within for nearly thirty years, until finally I decided to bring it up with my parents to discuss head on. The truth is I didn't decide to tell them intentionally. I was getting into a triggered state with my mom, arguing about something that didn't even matter as a way to express the underlying frustrated energy that was coming up due to something else happening we probably weren't fully conscious of at the time.

Instead of going into a fight from this triggered state, I remembered the insight and simply interrupted the ordinary trauma response pattern of getting angry and storming out of the room by instead pausing and asking if we could talk. I remember a huge release of energy followed by lots of tears upon admitting to both of my parents this insight—that I wasn't sure they liked me. I know they had to love me, but did they like who I was as a person? Somehow, someway, I had felt unsure since I was very young, maybe since I was born. What unfolded was an hours-long talk and more tears unpacking this feeling and insight and all the times and ways it might have arisen in my life and in our relationship thus far. It was a big moment to be that vulnerable with them, and that was proof to me of how conversations can be truly life changing when we are willing to show up as we are—authentic, vulnerable, and open to shifting our perspectives around judgments we've been holding in place for an entire lifetime.

After that experience I can't say my relationship with my parents dramatically changed in a permanent way, but I can say that I felt more connected to them and myself in a way I hadn't before. I felt some deep layers of tension or control—energetic layers that were in the way of us truly seeing each other for who we are—definitely dissipate. Most of all from this encounter I saw how valuable it is to give ourselves permission to not know. How often do we stop ourselves from having healing conversations where we can feel seen and heard and met because we're too afraid to start or even try?

Just because we don't have a sense immediately of how the conversation will go and what to expect, we stop ourselves before we even open to a new possibility. Why are we so afraid of surprise? Well, we've established that—the lizard-survival brain hates surprises, especially when massive transformational healing and awakening could be on the menu. What if we gave ourselves permission to not know—to even admit it out loud— but then proceed anyway to authentically express what's on our heart as best we can in the moment? I wonder how our relationships and experiences of life in general would shift forever just from us making this simple step and being an example of a new way.

> **"Yesterday I was clever, so I wanted to change the world.**
> **Today I am wise, so I am changing myself."**
> **—Rumi**

Abandonment

Oh, lovely abandonment wounds, feels just like home.

Too soon? I smile writing these words, because it reminds me how healing the really intense parts of ourselves—especially the aspects we used to have a lot of shame and overall heaviness around—eventually can become lighter and even something we can poke fun at just a bit. A real sign of healing and recovery in motion is when you can be playful with yourself in a loving way that signifies a certain healthy acceptance and detachment have taken form, you know what I mean? Abandonment for me is a very familiar core wounding, probably the one that figures most prominently in my journey—so I'm allowed to make fun of it!

Abandonment can happen in a multitude of ways—maybe infinite ways when we really start to explore. What matters most in determining if you have this wound too is to really ask yourself if you ever felt like you were left behind by people you depended on for love, care, and affirmation. Did you ever feel purposefully overlooked or unnoticed, like you were invisible? Were you literally left alone or abandoned at any time growing up and felt fearful that you would be left alone that way forever? In that moment when you felt left behind or forgotten, did you make that mean something about you at a deep, unconscious level? And how did that meaning take shape later on, perhaps as various protection mechanisms and survival strategies, especially in your relationships (to prevent the same experiences from happening again)?

For me abandonment was a felt experience of my parents simply not being energetically available for me to attune to. They were there physically and loved me as best they could with what they had (both didn't really have the most loving, nurturing examples of parents themselves to model after or attune with), but energetically and emotionally they weren't present with me in the ways I really required to develop a nervous system that could feel safe, loved, trusting, and like I could really relax into being. To this day this is something I am working on and can share more about later as we delve deeper into the body's role in ascension and how important it is for us to cultivate an intimate relationship with our physical vessel, especially as we energetically integrate so much new information and insight literally at the speed of light. Abandonment is my greatest wound, and I am grateful for it more and more every day. Through these experiences of working through these imprints and patterns I am learning about true unconditional love, connection, intimacy, and presence in ways I might not have otherwise ever imagined being able to understand.

Betrayal

Have you ever had your trust broken by your parents or someone close to you that you relied upon to take care of you at a young age? Betrayal can happen very subtly but can nonetheless imprint on our consciousness (and bodies) profoundly, catalyzing numerous protection strategies that can follow us for lifetimes if we don't actively choose to break the cycle by repairing and repatterning. Having our trust broken can happen in a multitude of ways.

Maybe there are infinite expressions of each of the core wounds we're exploring, and the names or labels of the wounds are just here to help us wrap our minds around them so we can navigate different access points on our healing path. As with everything shared in our journey thus far, take what resonates and leave the rest—and make up your own language if something resonates but doesn't land in the way I am perhaps reflecting here.

Betrayal can feel like watching someone you love, like a parent, disappoint you. Perhaps you put your parents on a pedestal and thought they were invincible, perfect humans—gods even—until they showed you otherwise and broke your reality in the process. Maybe this happens for all of us at some point early on, what do you think? Betrayal can feel like your parents being ripped off the pedestal you placed them on. It can happen when they disappointed you in how they behaved, made you feel like you couldn't trust them or feel totally safe with them, or when they acted in any other way in which they appeared to threaten your confidence in their capacity to be effective caretakers.

For me betrayal is a strong undertone of the abandonment wound and showed up as my mom's tendency to drink a few nights a week to the point of being pretty unconscious. I think from a young age I felt betrayed by her decision to seem to choose alcohol over me and then I made that mean all sorts of things about my value and worth as a person. This wound certainly contributed to my development as a master performer and people pleaser—I learned to excel at doing what I thought my mom or anyone else I depended upon might want or be impressed by so I could get their attention and love.

Guilt

Here's a big one that many of us have in common, and before we go deeper into it, let's clear up a distinction that I find really helpful to consider: the difference between guilt and shame. Guilt and shame are two sides of the same coin and often go hand in hand but are expressed, or rather repressed, in slightly different ways. The core wound of guilt would say: "I feel bad for the bad thing I did," whereas shame would say: "I am bad for what I did." In this way guilt feels closely related to regretting what you perceive to be your past mistakes and oftentimes taking on way too much responsibility for outcomes and experiences that were never yours to hold in the first place. As children, we often don't know any better and simply personalize many of our experiences, and unfortunately guilt tends to start accumulating pretty early on in this regard.

The burden of guilt when carried on through life tends to manifest as immense unworthiness and low self-esteem. When someone feels so bad about what they allegedly did, how could they feel themselves worthy of being happy, free, supported? Guilt can speak to us as an inner voice that's constantly reminding us of how we aren't enough, we can't have what we want, we aren't lovable or deserving of love and affection, and maybe we don't even deserve to take up space by existing. Guilt might have been sequestered away as a core wound early on when we experienced something bad happen and made it mean that the situation was our fault even if it had nothing to do with us.

A common scenario I've seen in many people with this kind of patterning: when the child is very young, parents get divorced and the child internalizes guilt for the parents separating, making it mean that it was their fault. Of course this isn't the reality of the situation, but from a young child's vantage point, especially between ages zero and seven, the child's understanding of the world is so insular that they can't help but personalize everything that they are experiencing in their microcosmic reality. When guilt is repressed as a core wound, protection strategies later emerge in the form of blocking oneself from opportunities to succeed, to prosper, to bond intimately, and to be emotionally available for genuine connection and fulfillment.

This wound also manifests as a hyper-focused intellectualized way of operating in the world that gives way to a great difficulty oftentimes in listening to one's feelings and body signals, or intuition, for that matter. We see a similar pattern within all core wounds, actually, in which the wounds translate as repressed energy hidden in the body that stimulates the development of certain avoidance patterns, all designed to turn off or cut off our access to key signals and systems that are meant to harness intuitive and emotional guidance. It takes so much energy to keep our wounds repressed within—sometimes it can feel like an entire dam being held up all through our waking lives that we're not even aware of until we become aware of our healing work. When we start to let go of the energy spent on repressing the wounds to instead let them come into the light, we start to feel so much of our energy come back online so we can use it in more effective, supportive and nourishing ways.

> **"In every single moment we've always done the best we can—if we could have done better we would have."**
> **—Cambria Moss**

Shame

Again, shame is similar to guilt and often goes hand in hand with the aforementioned experiences. However, it has a key distinguishing element: its personalization into "I am" instead of guilt's "I feel." Shame can really feel like a sense of disgust or dirtiness within oneself—a feeling of not wanting to be with yourself, as yourself. Shame is perhaps the sneakiest of all the core wounds in my experience, and maybe the most universally pervasive at that. It can get anchored into one's being so early on in a myriad of ways—all dependent upon how a child makes meaning of a situation. Perhaps when a parent unintentionally sounds like they are putting the child down for doing something bad or wrong, then the child translates that or hears it/feels it as "I am bad."

Similar to abandonment wounding, shame too can manifest in the absence of loving presence and attunement when a child makes up a meaning about their perceived experience of neglect (even emotional and energetic, not just physical) as being their fault. They might develop the idea and patterning underlying that: "My parents don't want to be around me because I am bad." Again, these core wounds get programmed into us oftentimes before we can even talk, let alone before we are making sense of the world and all the complexities therein.

The biggest outgrowth of shame when repressed for a long time is a loud inner critic. It makes sense that we would develop this as a defense mechanism though, doesn't it? It took me a long time to get that—and to let go of even beating myself up for being aware that I had an inner critic. It was like I had an inner critic of my inner critic—such a shame spiral indeed, I'm grateful to laugh about it now. When we learn to repress shame and even toxic shame, which grows with us as we mature, our inner critic gets kicked into hyperdrive to protect us from ever making the supposed same mistakes again, to keep us safe from ever feeling that horrible feeling of neglect and unworthiness that started that first moment in which we were "bad."

There can also be this phenomenon in those harboring deep shame in which we constantly see where we could be and how much better we could be while criticizing ourselves for never being enough and never being where we should be now. In other words, shame tends to lead to immense perfectionism, which can also have outgrowths of obsessive-compulsive tendencies, substance abuse, addictions, and other ways we learn to be in control and "keep things together" so as to never make mistakes again. Quite a tall order, but so many live that way for a long, long time, and it's wild to imagine how many more people out there are still playing the game even though it's definitely one where everyone loses. Shame is such a universal experience that our whole next chapter is dedicated to unpacking it some more, so hold tight. Deep breaths, we're going in.

"Religion is for people who are afraid to go to hell. Spirituality is for those who've already been there."
—Ralph Smart

ILLUMINATING AND INTEGRATING THE SHADOW

Enlightenment is remembering who you truly are and being relentlessly devoted to being precisely that. In all moments. How's that for a life extraordinarily lived?

Can you rest easy—no, easier—into the unknown emptiness that naturally unfolds in the absence of action? How does it feel to be, with you, as you? What story would you choose if you knew you were creating this and every moment thereafter? The story about your family in particular? What gifts have they given you to alchemize? How have they helped you to grow and evolve and become the powerful, resilient being you are?

Now is the moment to go all the way in and face what's there to be met, uprooted, and alchemized once and for all. There is immense completion available to us right now regarding deeply conditioned patterns and ways of being we've played in for lifetimes that may have informed our whole reality up until now. What's especially highlighted are ways in which we make sense of our value and worth conditional upon externals, productivity, doing in general, and anything else outside of us.

We are the ones that determine our value. **No one else has that power unless we are at some level consciously or unconsciously giving it to them.** We each have a unique journey when it comes to this moment of truth—but perhaps it can be this simple: make the conscious choice to commit to a new way of being. Take this initiation, staring you in the face, urging you to choose yourself at last. We don't have to wait any longer before we can choose to chart a new path forward.

Here's a reminder again: pain will travel through families until someone is brave enough to feel it. This is our work at hand. Let's also consider how our traumas and core wounds are quite possibly the activators of our genius and even the gifts we came into this life uniquely to share. For those of us who are empathic and intuitive by nature, or even those who are awakening into more of these capacities day by day, would we have learned to feel everything and everyone if we hadn't first learned that we had to in order to survive? Even if our parents had the best intentions, still we didn't get the love we wanted and that made us believe we're unlovable and unworthy, catalyzing challenging relationship paradigms for years to come. But from these challenges we are destined to learn the true meaning of unconditional love and owning our intrinsic value—by first understanding the absolute contrasts.

Until we wake up from the dream which is this story and inherited identity and all the trauma responses therein, we are slaves to repeating the past again and again, passing these traumas and protection strategies on to future generations. What does it take to finally feel the feelings and memories at their depth so we can release the energy and allow these imprints to heal and restore? We can decide when the patterns complete their cycle. When the trauma heals, it's up to us when the repressed energy in motion—emotion—is felt and finally set free. We've had the keys all along to unlock ourselves from the cages we didn't know we were in—and fly.

WHOLENESS ATTUNEMENTS

We are ready to cultivate ourselves anew. We are ready to honor and let go of the past and the stories that we thought made us who we are. We are ready to receive ourselves now as who we are in this moment, beyond our conditioning, beyond our trauma. We are ready to feel and receive ourselves as perfectly imperfect and wholly complete. We are ready to practice acceptance of where we are now and who we are being in this moment. We are ready to consider how this—and we, just as we are— might already be enough.

Who You Are Being Is All That's Required

One of my favorite reminders reflects: who you are being is all that's required. It's a simple yet profound invitation to consider how in any moment *who you are truly being* is all that's required to help you get to the next step along your aligned path to wherever it is you are desiring to go. Here are some of my favorite ways to bring ourselves into presence, feel more acceptance, let go of the past, and welcome ourselves to walk with a little more levity.

We've churned up a lot of energy in the journey thus far. Do you feel a heightened awareness of memories and patterning you'd love to let go of or relate to in new ways percolating in your awareness? Imagine yourself as making a new beginning into an entirely clear path. What are you letting go of before you venture forth on this new journey so you can fully enjoy it as your present-moment self? To do this practice, it might be powerful to go out into nature somewhere and really connect with the Earth. The Earth has a way of bringing us into more harmonic resonance with our hearts and with elements of our true selves we can't always access as easily if we are in environments that tend to encourage a more mental and intellectual state of awareness.

Life Is a Ceremony. You Are the Ritual.

Have you ever created your own ceremony before? We are such ritualistic beings by nature, and ceremony is simply a practice of creating sacred space to honor a particular ritual that feels good for you to experience and receive. Just for fun, create your own ceremony with yourself, preferably in nature, and burn away all that you are leaving behind in the old reality-paradigm you are evolving out of at the speed of light. Write the old beliefs and energies and behaviors down or speak them aloud—or express them in any other way that feels authentic to you. You can even try writing as the old belief or pattern that you are releasing. Share from its perspective how it helped you to grow, what you learned, and what you are now committing to.

You may feel called to dance, to move, or to emote in another way—your body and spirit know how to release what no longer serves when simply given the space to do so. Feel the feelings and memories that come up in the process and let them go—anger, resentment, fear, and anxiety may be particularly amplified as they usually are when we are getting ready to step into a new unknown. As the energies arise, feel them shake out of your cells; see them float up into little bubbles of light and then get composted back into the Earth (or sent back into source above) as seeds from which new life will grow.

Get Curious

Another part of recognizing and embodying more of our innate wholeness is to become a frequent practitioner of self-inquiry. There are so many ways we can inquire into our nature and into the nature of reality—doing meditation, dance, and creative expression; receiving bodywork; adventuring to new inspiring sites around the world or in our own backyards; connecting with the Earth in ways that feel most nourishing; and so much more. Some of our inquiries might include really getting curious with ourselves and asking: How did we choose the perfect parents to evolve with in this lifetime? What lessons have been gifted therein? What is it we want now and never feel like we received back then? How is the absence of this said desire still present and continuing to drive aspects of our realities?

Re-Mother Yourself

When it comes to healing the mother wound, for example, how can we commit to more downtime, relaxation, rejuvenation, nourishment, and rest? Often when we have an absent example of a healthy feminine role model growing up, we can learn to overwork and be addicted to control and management of our external circumstances as a way to create a temporary sense of inner satisfaction. We didn't learn how to rest and simply receive and trust that life would support us. Some wonderful ways to practice: schedule a solo date or take some time off work to really practice being with yourself. What about dedicating alone time every day to allow your muse to be activated (unplanned, unscheduled flow time)? Allow yourself time and space each day to tap into your creative muse—painting, singing, moving, dancing—in any ways that feel good for you. Create simply for the sake of creating, enjoying every moment without an end or objective in mind. Simply because it feels good.

Turn on Receiving

Another healing practice when it comes to our core wounds is to consciously exercise and develop our capacities to receive. Practice conscious communication to ask for what you need and empower others in your life to support you. Drop out of the need to make up a reason or justification before doing so—trust in others' sovereign ability to make decisions for themselves and to align accordingly with the highest good. We can also practice self-soothing: what feels best for you to receive in terms of nurturance and soothing of your physical being? Self-massage; self–energy healing; deep, slow stretching. Aromatherapy. What does your inner muse desire to feel nourished and nurtured? Listen and receive.

Re-Father Yourself

When it comes to healing the father wound and elements of the god wound, we are invited to calibrate our understanding and embodiment of boundaries, initiative, personal power, truth, and integrity in major ways. How can we create clearer boundaries in our lives, in how we allow ourselves to be available, especially in how we commit to having downtime and rest? Drop any commitments or obligations that don't feel fun or that feel draining in any way; do so without a justification or story.

Turn Truth All the Way On (and Up)

Another aspect of healing into more wholeness is to get curious about where in our lives we are being asked to show up in more truth and integrity. What truth wants to be expressed and how can you support yourself in expressing precisely that? Are there any loose ends in relationships or in life overall that feel like open energy drains—in which a question has been left unanswered, or a conversation has been left feeling murky and unresolved? Is there any ensuring commitment on your end that arises in your awareness now—that would feel good to take on in order to create clarity and stability in these situations?

Become Your Own Permissionary

One of my favorite questions ever asks us to consider: What if I gave myself permission in this moment to celebrate myself and the world around me as perfect, whole, and complete? A massive anecdote for all the trauma healing and integration processing underway is to simply remind ourselves to return to gratitude again and again. Even when we are in tough, sometimes even painful moments, we can interrupt ourselves from going into a suffering cycle and instead remind ourselves to celebrate that we are aware, we are growing, and we are committed to being ourselves no matter what. What if every pain point along the journey is giving us an opportunity to better know ourselves and what we are truly capable of? Can we celebrate our friends and family too for moments in which they are going through a hard time—asking them what they are celebrating and what they are learning about themselves in the process?

What would life feel like if we knew that we are infinitely supported, no matter what, just because we are alive? How does it feel to receive this support from yourself? No matter where you are on your path, it's absolutely perfect. Healing unfolds for each of us uniquely, in our own time, at our own pace—let's listen and honor what is emerging and practice high levels of patience, compassion, and unconditional love and understanding with ourselves.

Embodiment is radiating complete presence in every aspect of your being while meeting all that is arising with love, kindness, and compassion, no matter how messy, confusing, exhausting, confronting, disorienting, or humiliating your deaths, rebirths, enlightenment, supposed regressions, and destined expansions always are. Sometimes the most powerful messages we can ever convey are communicated through our authentic presence embodied in silence. As we'll understand more and more on our journey ahead, our energy communicates the truth of who we are more precisely than words can usually ever attempt to decipher.

"Trauma compromises our ability to engage with others by replacing patterns of connection with patterns of protection."
—Stephen Porges

I'll leave us with this beautiful story detailing a practice shared within an old African tribal tradition. In this tribe's particular practice, when someone does something wrong, the community members take the person to the center of the village, where the tribe surrounds them and for two days says all the good they have done. The tribe believes each person is good but sometimes people make mistakes, which are really a cry for help. They unite to reconnect them with their good nature.

What a beautiful example. How can we hold ourselves in this kind of love and acceptance and also maybe even do the same for others? What if we lived our lives based on the knowing that when we do what is best for us, we are automatically serving the whole? Whatever is in the way is the way forward—whatever is coming up is here for us to feel and heal. We got this.

5

TRANSFORM SHAME INTO VULNERABILITY

Could we imagine that shame is actually a gateway into the super-power of vulnerability? Could we consider that the darkest depths of the various aspects of ourselves and our experiences are coming up now in our awareness to be fully felt, and even acknowledge that they play a crucial part in teaching us true love? It might not completely make sense at first, and trust me, I totally get it. The further I go on this path, the more accustomed I get to "breaking my brain"—that feeling when something resonates but doesn't quite make sense yet. When our brains feel like they're breaking, I've learned this is a great sign that we are rewiring our programming and belief structures at a deep level, opening space for new potentials to anchor into our consciousness, and therefore throughout our reality.

It feels like another *leap . . . and trust the net will appear* meme again—except that this time it's appearing more like that famous one about how the cracks in our wounds are where the light gets in. I actually love that quote, it's a good one, but at first when we hear something like that and we're not quite at the *feel it to heal it* stage in our path, it can sound a bit condescending. It's another one of those *surrender, but how?* paradoxes we find ourselves in. Let's dig in and see what's waiting to be revealed.

A friend told me recently of an amazing acronym for shame I hadn't heard before: *should have already mastered everything*. I love this so much because it speaks directly to the underlying energy of shame, which often translates to feeling that one is inherently bad, not enough, or fundamentally broken in some indescribable way.

If we are carrying immense shame, we usually don't think too highly of ourselves. And on top of that, we might also have a highly skilled inner critic that's masterful at reminding us of just how behind we are. We never do seem to get to the finish line or end point—the *there* we're supposed to be at by now, wherever *there* is or if it even exists.

Shame seems to be one of the most common universal wounds we share as humans. Literally everyone I've ever worked with seems to have an aspect of shame present in their patterning, holding them back from feeling how they want to feel and being how they want to be.

On top of that, can we imagine that shame is actually the lowest vibration or most dense energy we have accessible to us in this life on Earth? It's the heaviest, deepest, darkest energy we've got to work with, and it typically gets stuck deep in the body, coincidentally in the deep, dark wells of our lower chakras—from the root of the spine to the sacral and solar plexus. It gets stored usually quite early on in life, before we can even remember logically what happened to trigger it into being taken on. This trauma memory gives way to countless protection strategies, emotional patterns, thought forms, and belief structures that end up being a lot to manage. The energy we end up harnessing to keep all these protection programs in motion eventually feels incredibly draining and can result in all sorts of physical ailments and even various states of disease, which usually pop up simply to get our attention so we can heal the underlying emotional or psycho-spiritual issue at hand.

> **"If you allow someone to be who they are and they allow you to be who you are, then that's love. Anything else is torture."**
> **—Ra Uru Hu**

As we explored a bit earlier, shame usually emerges very early on in childhood and can become a natural response to energetically sensing that a parent or caregiver doesn't show the love or appreciation we are desiring in a moment of vulnerability. Shame can come up when the response we expected doesn't meet our needs or wasn't even shared in the first place— the ways we make meanings about these moments can be so subtle and yet so complex and follow us for lifetimes. In an instant where a response we thought we wanted wasn't shared in the way we needed it at the time, we can easily make up meaning that we didn't get what we needed because we were bad, we did something wrong, or whatever was negatively unfolding was our fault. Then a shame pattern gets set into motion, filled with all sorts of familiar pain points, refined survival mechanisms, and strategies to prevent that original wound from being repeated again.

I love shame so much—really, at this point in the journey, I do. It's shown me again and again that when we choose to meet it head on, in ourselves and especially with others as our witnesses, we stand to harvest the most beautiful seeds of healing, connection, intimacy, and true presence we can ever imagine. And that's not a hyperbole—the connection and new depths of authenticity we can experience can literally blow us away when we are willing to set ourselves and each other free from these imaginary prisons. We lock ourselves in, sometimes for our entire lives, in jails that we finally see we made up to begin with. Shame is a portal into our greatest gifts, which we are here to share and ultimately enjoy in this human experience: vulnerability being the first, which naturally overflows into intimacy, authenticity and immense personal power, and magnetism.

If anything feels more clear after traveling this far together, ascension is an inner journey that takes us deep into meeting our darkest shadows to illuminate our brightest light, inevitably remembering the wholeness that we are and always have been all along. As they say, our shadows and wounds surely do lead us again and again into revealing our greatest gifts and capacities—our superpowers even. It's all part of how the game is designed, remember? We choose to come into this life to play a certain game consisting of specific lessons we wanted to learn so we could awaken and remember our true selves and carry out the purpose we wanted to experience and maybe even enjoy. And what a relief—we get to do it over and over again, learning new things each time, oftentimes repeating the same lessons across lifetimes—why? Maybe because we love to experience different angles of the same stories. We love to learn and grow; it's who we are.

I wonder if shame is the wound we most universally share because collectively at this point in our human evolution we decided on some level to experience this one most intensely so we could heal it most powerfully—at the root. Shame tends to also be an endemic layer in all other core wounds and within our collective trauma patterning. Think of how much of our society—and I suppose when I say that I am assuming a bit of a context of Western capitalistic society and all its trappings and implications therein—is designed in an unconscious response to shame and the repression seemingly required to hide it deep down. The holy trinity (as I love to call them) of money, sex, and power come up in this part of the conversation—how are core aspects of our reality, our livelihood, our life force, and capacity to create so often experienced as the greatest sources of our shame? Let's dive in.

WHAT IS SHAME AND WHY DO WE HAVE IT?

Shame is a state of being that arises when you are disconnected from yourself and your true nature—when you're lost in identifying with what you should be, who you should be, what you should have done instead, and are feeling perhaps others' disappointment with how you don't match up. One of my favorite reflections about shame and the other shadows we build our whole lives and identities around avoiding comes from the visionary philosopher Bayo Akomolafe, who reminds that: "Trying to escape the prison is what gives it form." I had chills all over the first time I heard this and wanted to repeat it to everyone I met for days after because it moved such a deep chord within me.

Maybe it takes reading it a few times to let it sink in. So here we have the proverbial prison of our own creation—the shame we are hiding deep down so no one finds out how bad or dirty or wrong we are. We build our entire lives around repressing these feelings and experiences so that no one will ever find us out, but in doing so, we are validating the prison's existence in the first place. Can we see the house of cards, which can actually fall down once we admit the prison wasn't something that existed before we made it up? Maybe we're getting closer.

Shame is also one of our biggest blockers to manifesting and magnetizing the kinds of experiences and realities we desire. One of my favorite books of all time is *Conscious Loving* by Gay Hendricks and Kathlyn Hendricks. It's all about intimacy and conscious relating, and it naturally explores core wounds and trauma that get in the way of true connection.

It reminds us that: "Most bad luck is not luck at all. It is the direct out-growth of internalized feelings of shame, guilt, and self-hate." In other words, it takes so much of our creative energy to repress the shame we carry deep down within—constantly we drain our life force to hide away what we are afraid to reveal instead of freeing that energy to create and resonate as our true selves.

Let's imagine ourselves as energy fields (or bubbles of light if you will), here to broadcast a unique frequency that only we can transmit, that's pro-grammed to resonate with and attract the specific experiences and oppor-tunities that are designed for us to receive and enact. I've seen it countless times in various healing sessions (sometimes I call these containers) where someone feels like they are out of alignment with the path they sense they are meant to be living. They feel mismatched within their relationships, their career, and energetically they just don't seem to be flowing with ease. Usually this means there's a cosmic invitation to explore how shame might be playing a part in this person's life to give them a wake-up call to claim their power back from the story they've been letting run their reality. Perhaps it's the moment of reckoning to liberate themselves from the self-imposed prison of *shoulds* and *have to*s they've felt they had to settle for in their shame-ridden sense of self.

My biggest source of shame has always manifested in sexuality, which really is another word for creativity. Our society conditions us with all kinds of beliefs about sex and sexuality, but what I've come to find is that sexuality simply means authenticity—it is the authentic, unique way in which we express our creative capacity. We naturally are born with unique things that turn us on or inspire us about being alive, right? This is our sexual energy speaking to us and through us, guiding us to feel resonance with the kinds of experiences and opportunities we are meant to have in this life. This is a completely natural force we are wired with as human beings, but so much of our society and culture seems to have an agenda built on making this energy wrong, or bad or even evil. I wonder if it's because of how threatening it is to the status quo to imagine more and more people turned on by life, listening to their intuitive guidance, trust-ing their bodies' wisdom, and sharing incredible creative genius. Perhaps it's terrifying to ponder.

When we have sexual shame instilled in us from a young age, we tend to have all sorts of distortions that take shape later on in our creativity, authenticity, intimacy, sense of alignment with our purpose, and ability to simply receive. It's common when this energy gets shut down early on to start learning to externalize one's worth outside of oneself—seeking validation from others to prove that you are enough and that you are worthy of love or simply being alive. It's also common to learn to unconsciously give one's power away to others, to depend on them to help give you the answer to what you should do, what you should want, who you should be, and where you should go, ad infinitum.

When we turn off our sexual energy, we lose our sense of aliveness, our core sense of self. We feel disassociated from who we really are and why we are here and energetically go through life like some kind of being with its head cut off, practically running around in circles, not knowing any better. I definitely did this for many years until later on in my ascension process when I started to put the pieces together around sexuality and how so much of my deepest repressed power and creative capacity was hidden in my shut-down sexual energy circuits. I probably learned to turn off my sexuality the first time I expressed my truth and felt someone else's negative reaction. This again feels to be a somewhat universal experience, especially in those of us who as children were highly intuitive and empathic and loved to call adults out for what we sensed was dishonesty. In situations where we were simply speaking up when we knew something was wrong, we were usually put down or even punished for doing so and learned right away to numb our senses and sensitivities—which later we remember as our superpowers—to be safe and survive within a family or societal dynamic that really wasn't built to support us.

> **"Denial, the act of not being aware of inner feelings and**
> **fears and motivations, is the opposite of mindfulness."**
> **—Brian Weiss**

So essentially, when shame is coming up on our path to become intimate with, it usually means that we are ready to deepen our connections,

intimacy, and authenticity within ourselves and with all of life. Perhaps we take on shame in the first place to experience what it feels like to withhold love and connection from ourselves, so that when we start to experience our own love and learn how to authentically, intimately relate, we really appreciate it more and never take it for granted. I frequently hear messages like this, especially in various energy healing and Akashic Records guidance experiences, but our human consciousness doesn't always like this message at first; especially since with this kind of guidance we are invited into greater self-responsibility, neutrality, emotional maturity, and acceptance.

Somehow most of humanity at this time chose to learn the lessons of repressing shame, maybe so we could all collectively play out the story of healing the roots of shame to remember the true meaning of unconditional love, our own inherent value, our innate worthiness, and our infinite capacity within to create literally anything we can imagine. When we are in the pain of the wound and identifying so closely with it, the last thing we want to hear is that we chose this or that this is all happening for a reason.

"Intimacy is the key to manifesting equilibrium in the world. Intimacy in this context refers to honesty in interaction with others. The vital role of honesty is to create a clean group aura in which all hidden agendas are laid on the table. Without this, no true equilibrium can ever be reached."
—Richard Rudd

Yet the higher perspectives I hear again and again—usually when I take a moment to feel the love underlying the messages that truly hit home and sometimes even break the heart open just a little more—really do want us to consider how we choose hard lessons for the joy and even for the fun of it, because as souls we simply love nothing more than to grow and expand and remember our true essence. I love what Brian Weiss reminds us of in his prolific accounts in *Messages from the Masters*: "Sometimes a soul learns to love by becoming what it most despised."

THE DIFFERENT SHADES OF SHAME

The things we are ashamed of—or whatever it is we've convinced our-selves needs to be hidden in order to ensure our survival amidst the tribe or to coerce love or attention from the beings we most want to receive love from—are actually *the precise elements of us, our lives, our stories, and our experiences that everyone connected to us craves to know and love.* I feel like these days, all of us are leaders—all of humanity is here to lead, each in their own way, that's who we are and how we are called to show up, especially now that all hierarchies are dissolving. Why, then, is it such a common experience that it feels challenging to be *seen* or that a deep fear of being seen emerges upon taking a powerful step onto our purpose-aligned path?

We all have a desire to be of service here on Earth; we wouldn't be alive at this time otherwise. And maybe the purpose of our lives is to discover our unique gifts, give them to ourselves, and then share with the world fully and completely—could it be that simple? The fear of being seen along the way comes down to an aversion to vulnerability. What if we aren't good enough, what if we are rejected, what if people don't understand or won't love us anymore if we show who we really are? This is precisely the game we are here to play and maybe even win. The beautiful part is that this game really is a team effort, and everyone's invited to the party to bring this baby home to the finish line. I think in this case there actually is a finish line, although we continue evolving and expanding infinitely in our ascension—our finish line is more and more people awakening to their authenticity, sharing their creativity, and living meaningful lives built on fulfilling contributions that absolutely light them up.

Shame can actually be a really helpful tool for uncovering and under-standing our gifts and genius because usually it leads us right into our vulnerability and authenticity, where our true selves love to hide out. This has certainly been the case for me. Sexual shame was imprinted at such a young age, and I learned to shut my energy down to appease my parents and not make anyone else uncomfortable for fear that I might get even less attention and love than I already felt like I was receiving. There was no more I could risk wasting, so I did what I had to do to survive within my context at that time—but doing so led me down some pretty interesting pathways later on, to say the least. My sexual shame manifested as all kinds of distortions and even addictions ranging from codependent relationships, alcoholism, and drug abuse, as well as sourcing sex as a means to define my value, risking my life repeatedly for the thrill of it, escorting, stripping, and even getting fired from a foot fetish party I felt really fortunate at the time to be invited to work at. All of these experiences, in hindsight of course, were on my path to show me more of who I really am, what I am here for, what I am capable of and what my greatest gifts authentically manifest as when wholeheartedly shared. Ready for story time?

It was close to 4:00 A.M. and I had already been ready to leave for hours. In fact I consciously started getting even more wasted, letting new guys buy me drinks at the bar—forgetting I was there to make money—to help pass the time. It was about 8:00 or 9:00 P.M. when my night had started in this members-only Manhattan strip club and I was there with the full intention of making at least a few hundred dollars; maybe if it was a good night I could make my rent over the eight-hour period, just $700 would do it. That minus the $60 I owed in dues to the house mom (the girl manning the check-in area in the locker room downstairs).

I told myself I would stop as soon as I got a real job, whatever that was supposed to mean. For some reason at the age of twenty-three, I was overly concerned with getting health insurance and a 401(k), both of which I had yet to experience but seemed like the holy grail of security. When I had those two things covered I would be good—right? Then I could feel safe enough to finally connect to my real purpose and maybe then, only then, could I start to feel fulfilled. That was my plan and I'd do anything to see it through.

Ever since I was little I had a deep desire within me to help make the world a better place. I had always wanted to help others feel happy and have fun, which I knew even before I could speak was the whole point of this life thing. I even got held back in kindergarten a year for being "socially underdeveloped," which really meant I was bossing around all the kids, trying to get them to play the most fun game of all. I just wanted everyone to have the most fun, couldn't my teacher see my clear intentions?

But instead from an early age I heard again and again from the full spectrum of surrounding adults: *don't be so precocious, stop being so bossy,* and especially, *don't talk back.* I later came to unravel that these early commands deeply impacted me, leaving within me an impression I would come to abide by for the next few decades.

You see, all along I was subconsciously being taught to not be a leader, to not speak my truth, to not trust my intuition, and to not stand up for what I truly believe in and desire. I learned that to fit in I had to play by the rules, be the same as everyone else and listen to whatever adults in supposed authority were saying, never to question or doubt their directives.

Suppressing my own truth started early and eventually became as natural as any other deeply embedded survival instinct I had within me. But my longtime suppression took quite a toll, like I was a pressure cooker waiting to burst at any moment—resulting in a looming state of intense anxiety, at times feeling like I couldn't even breathe.

But the first time I got drunk was like finally, for once in my life, being able to breathe. I had arrived. Suddenly my never-ending thoughts and overwhelming analysis of everyone else's feelings and thoughts and what they were thinking of me turned quiet. I could finally just be. I felt free. I felt like I could do whatever I wanted, finally, and say everything I had been holding in for so long. I could be me.

The same saga would play on repeat for years and years, until nearly a decade later when I finally hit rock bottom, losing track of all the identities I had mustered up to simply get through my daily life. Alcohol and drugs (including relationships, an addiction in and of themselves fueled by the drug known as codependency) followed me through high school, college, and afterward to the point where I found myself in New York City living more double lives than I could even keep track of. I was finished. Exhausted. Depleted. I couldn't keep up the act anymore. It was too much.

But you never would have known that was the case, even if you had known me for years, if you worked with me (at any of my multitude of jobs at the time), if you were my roommate, my boss, my parents, my brother, any of my family, really. No one knew what was really going on. Just like hardly anyone knew what was going on all those years where I felt like I could barely breathe.

I was going through all the motions of normalcy on the outside, that's for sure—I knew how to play a great game and put up a solid front. I had always been a chameleon after all. Empaths are like that: since we know how you feel, we can be whoever you want us to be in order for us to know you will approve of us, love us, and simply give us what we want (which is usually almost always, underlying all else, love).

I had become addicted to the freedom that working at the underground strip club offered me. Of course I could get as intoxicated as I wanted to, which made me a pretty horrible stripper who regularly lost money and often made the mistake of being too genuine with supposed clients, forgetting that I was there to work. But underneath it all, I felt like I could finally be me. And I could be bad. I could be sexy. I felt appreciated and rewarded even for simply being myself.

Since my partying days started I had always made a point to do well in school—if I worked hard enough there then I deserved to have fun and let loose on the weekends (and eventually the weekdays too). I deserved to do whatever I wanted to do, especially since I was carrying the weight of the entire world on my shoulders all along. I deserved a break. That's what I kept telling myself. A decade-plus break.

My break ended when I hit rock bottom—which might as well have meant when I just chose to stop digging—and started my recovery. Like many other things in my life, my career continued along an upward trajectory as I stayed sober. In just a few years I moved from agency to agency, even having a stint as a solo-entrepreneur strategy consultant in between. All the meanwhile I was delving deeper into spirituality, meditation, and various other forms of transformation and healing. When I removed the substances from my system that had been blocking off my ability to feel and sense what was really going on, I finally had no choice but to start listening. And eventually listening started to feel pleasurable instead of like a burden—once I learned how to do so in my own way.

With the help of guides, mentors, and trusted friends, I started to see myself in perhaps the most truth I had ever before experienced. I learned about the roots of my pain and self-induced suffering. I started to feel again, and not only that, I started to trust my intuition and learn to discern between my own feelings and everyone else's.

But nearly six years into my sobriety, working as a transformational mentor, operating my own business for over half a year and living out my dream of relocating to Bali, my looming shadow of scarcity came knocking once more. The truth is, even though I had overcome huge obstacles and experienced firsthand incredible transformation and healing, I still reverted to some very old behavior resulting from deeply repressed shame, scarcity, and insecurity I hadn't yet met or integrated. This of course was the foray into the sugar-baby adventure with the elusive character known as David I mentioned earlier, in Jakarta. Funny to think I'll never know if there even was a real person behind that encrypted WhatsApp account.

I was an example that many people looked up to and even came to for advice and guidance, but all the meanwhile I was repeating an ancient pattern I thought I had left behind years prior, before I got sober, in the darkest days of my addiction. Even though I appeared to have everything going for me, I was still operating with the deep-set belief that the universe wasn't going to take care of me.

And the paradox was that I knew deep down everyone else was taken care of, and I could even convince others to trust and have faith in their own divine guidance. In fact I had a gift for guiding others back to themselves and their own innate trust in the universe and its infinite source of abundance rather easily. But I couldn't do the same for myself, no way. This lack of trust and deep-set fear that I was alone—and not only that, that I wasn't going to ever feel safe, especially financially—manifested as this dangerous old behavior coming to life one last time.

> **"Real health is only found when your inner being is completely at ease with life's inherent uncertainty."**
> **—Richard Rudd**

And everything that happened, just as it did, is absolutely okay. And I love and accept myself for all of it and celebrate the lessons therein. I did what I knew how to do at the time, and I did the best I could to take care of myself with what I had. I learned so much about who I really am through the process and got to really see what I am capable of when I put my mind to something. I am strong, resilient, and capable of anything I set my focus on—which is pretty fun nowadays, especially since I am no longer risking my life.

So with that out of the way—let's delve into the different kinds of shame and explore how they all interplay within one another and within each of us. From my story above we have a lot of examples to reference too, which is helpful in discerning which aspects of shame might resonate more for you in your own path. Here we get to consider what fits and simply leave the rest, always reminding ourselves to ask: is this true for me? And if not, then leave it be.

I get curious about what the world might be like if more of us really understood the different shades of shame we carry and how these tend to uniquely inform our various relationship strategies and coping mechanisms. When we understand ourselves and our wounding more fully, we automatically invite more compassion and understanding into all our relationships—giving others permission to see in our reflection more of who they really are and what new potentials they might want to live into. I love the ripple effect we infinitely set off when we start to heal. There's no better feeling—and so much of it happens automatically without even trying. Just being.

Unlovable

A common side effect of shame is feeling unlovable, and as sad as it is to consider, I sense many more are experiencing this feeling, albeit usually at an unconscious level, than we care to admit. I felt unlovable as I was from a very early age, especially as soon as I learned that in order to get attention from my parents I had to perform and be good enough to get them to look at me. Shame and abandonment tend to go hand in hand in many instances, and this was certainly the case for me and many others. Which came first—the shame or the abandonment? Usually the abandonment wound sets in and can happen even close to the time we are born, then shame follows as the imprinting we incur to make sense of our reality. If we were abandoned, there had to be a reason why. Maybe it's that we were unlovable as we were—and in order to "fix" this supposed problem, we devised all sorts of strategies to create connection and security where there probably was none to begin with. We started taking it all upon ourselves to figure it out and get what we need no matter what, at whatever cost.

The anecdote to this particular flavor of shame tends to entail a rigorous commitment to consistent practices of self-love, self-celebration, gratitude, and self-soothing and really a combination of all of the above, often. When we have this expression of shame deeply rooted into our being, self-care and self-soothing can be the last thing on Earth we want to do, especially if they require us to be alone with ourselves. That might be the scariest thing ever, especially early on in the awakening path, since usually the thought of being alone is terrifying. It means we actually have to be with ourselves without distraction—finally processing all the energies and emotions we typically shut down as we go about our waking lives externally focused on what we can get to fill the alleged void we feel inside.

As part of our self-healing process, we start to inquire into whether or not there really is a void at all. And additionally, we start to ask ourselves questions like: What is loveable about me? What is beautiful about me? What do I celebrate about myself today? What am I appreciating about myself in this moment? Maybe the lovable question feels like a stretch, totally understandable. Be where you are and explore—starting with gratitude about yourself and how you are being in this moment (not what you've done before or what you are showing externally to the world as a marker of productivity or something else you get attention for). When we start to take time to appreciate ourselves for how we are being now—especially in the moments when no one else is looking—we can really start to connect with our true selves more intimately and see what really is lovable about us. Here is where our major repatterning begins as we start to practice and prepare ourselves for owning our value while co-creating genuine connection and authenticity in all our relationships from here on out.

Unworthy

Another layer of shame usually involves an immense feeling of unworthiness or even overall worthlessness. The two terms sound the same but have distinctly different meanings. Feeling unworthy translates to feeling undeserving of happiness, peace, love, and fulfillment—or really feeling unworthy of anything that you could imagine truly desiring. Feeling worthless signifies a fundamental disbelief in one's own inherent value and worth as a being. If we feel ashamed of who we are at some level, we usually feel unworthy most prominently and also could feel a dimension of worthlessness too. Usually you can feel which state resonates with you more by inquiring within as to whether you feel you deserve to be happy simply for being who you are—or do you feel like you need to work hard, be better, or be different to feel happy?

If you find yourself over-working, over-performing, and overall trying really hard, so much so that most of life is feeling like an exhausting struggle, usually an energy of unworthiness is showing up to pay attention to and learn from. Feeling unworthy can teach us a lot about working hard to get what we think we want—but our lives can easily be fueled by the belief system that says it's all up to us, and us alone, to decipher and follow the perfect plan and path to the future we are meant to arrive in. It's a huge weight to bear—walking through life with such an immense pressure to figure everything out as though it's our job to play god. But when unworthiness is at play, we can feel we are all alone and have to do whatever it takes to support ourselves. Receiving support or asking for help are often out of the question—especially if we are already working with abandonment, betrayal, or rejection trauma that makes us shy away from even asking in the first place for fear that when we ask the help won't show up or it won't come in the way we need. It's better—and safer—to not even ask so as to not be disappointed.

One of my favorite ways to start working with healing unworthiness and worthlessness energies is to become focused on ways you can cultivate positive self-esteem. When we have more esteem for ourselves, we can start to build a foundation upon which worthiness and feeling our own innate value can actually become sustainable states of being in our everyday lives. It's important that these self-esteem building components are actions or energy put into form, not just thoughts or affirmations. In other words, what kinds of activities and commitments do you feel bring you joy, grat-itude, and inspiration about being alive?

Two of my favorite questions to consider: When do you feel most alive and how can you allow more space in your life for you to practice precisely this, and often? It's important we make the commitment to action simple at first so as to not become overwhelmed. Often we can take on too much, and it ends up being a recipe to fail because we overload our systems with too much information we aren't yet built with the capacity to handle. So start small—and consider committing to one action you can take consistently for an agreed-upon amount of time, like a few days or a week or two (a good commitment is not much more than this at first, again, small wins are great to build momentum).

A great example might be committing to take a walk around your neighborhood for at least ten minutes each day for the next five days. When you complete this commitment, celebrate yourself for showing up in this new way and building your self-esteem and sense of value. Then do another commitment for maybe a little bit longer of a time frame and maybe add in one or two new activities that inspire you to feel your aliveness. Celebrate yourself every step of the way for committing to make the changes required to build an entirely new way of being for the rest of your life.

> **"If you really want to get along with**
> **someone, let them be themselves."**
> **—Willie Nelson**

Overexposed

When we feel like we've been caught in the act of doing something others think is bad that provokes a negative response, usually from someone we depend on to take care of us, we feel overexposed—another common texture of how shame manifests. This one can be particularly tricky, however, in that overexposure can happen so early on that we can tend to overlook its key originating moments, even later on in our healing path after we've shed a few layers and gotten to know ourselves a bit better. Overexposure can feel like an internalized sense of being bad, or dirty, or wrong, or broken due to someone else's alleged reaction to what you were doing *or, more subtly, how you were feeling* in a moment when you were simply being yourself.

This can especially happen when we are younger, before a ton of social conditioning has set in and influenced our beliefs and behaviors. Oftentimes we are simply playing and exploring and having fun, listening to our intuition and our body's messages, which are naturally designed to guide us in usually beautiful ways meant to bring out our purpose and gifts. It may be a moment when, say, you were simply exploring your body and sensing new feelings regarding what was enjoyable and pleasurable for you, before any context of sexuality or all the social meanings and constructs of body image and so on and so forth set in, and someone like a parent or significant role model in your life stumbles upon you and reacts with any form of discomfort (usually due to their own sexual repression and social conditioning). You may in that moment learn that trusting how you feel or doing what feels good for you is bad.

This is a common wound many share. Its origin can even take the form of being put down or distanced energetically for simply speaking up when you felt the honest desire to share your truth. Perhaps there was a time when you listened to a creative impulse to play or perform in a certain way that agitated or activated adults around you, but you were simply sharing your authentic desire and creative drive in a way you loved to express. But because of the response you were met with—a form of rejection, perhaps—you then learned to shut off your natural impulses to share in the ways you love to. What we often unravel later on in the healing journey—maybe like now—is that the moment when you agitated those around you was actually most likely a great expression of your uniqueness, gifts, and purpose.

When you were being you, you agitated those around you to perhaps consider shifting their view of reality. Their conditioned social norms were challenged simply by your existence providing a new example of what's possible, and this, my friends, can be real confronting, especially when the challenge comes from a child. So, overexposure is a complex wound we get to work with—and it's connected to a stark invitation we have upon us to innovate the ways we parent and interact with youth (especially our own inner child aspects) in general from the get-go. How do we allow safe space for children to practice being themselves? If we can do that, they won't have to repress and pretend and forget who they are, or later on find themselves in a crisis that catalyzes their remembrance. Maybe now we can pave an easier, softer way.

Some of the best medicine for healing overexposure has to do with self-esteem building and self-love practices mentioned already, but with an added focus on discovering and reawakening one's creative, intuitive gifts. Befriending the body and learning to listen to its messages and guidance is another critical aspect of healing this dimension of shame, but we get more into that a few steps along the way—since it's such a big one and there's so much more to say on this particular piece within our embodied ascension path. To make a beginning at healing overexposure right now, the best practice you might consider is making an effort to learn about your creative impulses and ways in which you love to express your unique view and experience of the world.

Do you love to make art? Do you love to dance? How do you love to create and experience beauty? Maybe you don't want to make anything, but instead you find that you love to indulge in the simple pleasures of life in other ways. Find what those ways are for you—through play, discovery, and exploration—and dedicate yourself to experiencing more of what brings you pleasure, joy, and inspiration as a regular part of your daily practices. Here is where you get to remember how you love to feel most alive, especially when it comes to the sense-pleasures of life and how you prefer to enjoy, create, and amplify beauty in whatever forms you desire. When we allow ourselves space in our lives to enjoy beauty and really take it in—in the ways we most enjoy receiving and experiencing pleasure—we heal our hyperactive nervous systems, allowing (retraining) them to slow down and smell the roses (try it: smell some roses!). We learn to relax more fully into presence, we build self-worth and esteem, and we naturally cultivate more love, gratitude, and positivity within so we can therefore radiate it out.

Abandoned

Oh yes, my familiar favorite flavor of shame—oh, sweet abandonment, the gifts you keep giving me to work on and grow from are so immense, maybe infinite even. I've come to love this core wound because it really is my deepest one of them all; it's taught me the most about who I really am and why I am here: to be a bridge from Heaven into Earth and a radiant, embodied example of authenticity, presence, and unconditional love. Pretty cool, right? I don't think I would have had access to those possibilities or to my divine purpose had I not first experienced lacking all of the above for most of my life and, even worse, feeling like I didn't even deserve to have any of them, ever. Abandonment has so much to teach us in the context of shame, and as we start to unravel the lessons, maybe we can find a bit of gratitude in the process.

This particular thread of shame stemming from abandonment trauma, which we already discussed as we explored the universal core wounds that unite us, runs real deep alright, through the core of our human history. We are meaning-making machines, especially as children before we are completely conditioned and imprinted with all our operating system structures, beliefs, and programs. And it's completely understandable how we make it our fault that someone forgot about us, left us, didn't pay attention to us, or didn't seem to want us around. In the moment that original trauma happened, it hurt and we needed a reason to make sense of why that would happen in our reality, mostly so we could register the formula in our lizard brain, which wants to prevent that pain from ever happening again.

Then we get equipped with that memory via an easy-access Rolodex that alerts us immediately whenever a similar energy in our lives arises that we might subsequently need protection from. It can even mean that if someone looks like, feels like, or sounds like the person that was a part of this original wounding, we get the signal to be on high alert: danger, danger, this person seems like that person who hurt us before and we never want to experience that again. Protection shields, survival strategies, coping mechanisms, masks: activate! This is the cycle we usually follow before we make the trauma and its source conscious and start our paths of integration, healing, and resolution.

Shame from feeling abandoned, unwanted, forgotten, or simply not paid attention to in the ways you uniquely needed to feel validated, loved, affirmed, and secure takes shape in so many subtle and not-so-subtle ways in our lives—most notably in our relationship strategies, which tend to mirror the heightened insecurity and unavailability we were imprinted with from the start. But first, to become available for the relationships we say we want, we get to really tune in with healing our relationship to ourselves. When we start to heal this particular aspect of our shame, we are invited to consider practices that help connect us back to ourselves in whatever ways feel warm, loving, nourishing, and integrative. How would it feel to be in a loving, secure, present relationship with you?

Usually when we have this imprint of abandonment and shame, we grow up to repeat this pattern of treatment to ourselves. Where are we abandoning ourselves now as adults? How do we put ourselves last on the list of people to consider and care about, usually without fail? How are we putting other people's needs before our own, again and again, and usually serving others without giving much attention to ourselves? How are we hyper-focused on the external world around us and how everyone else is doing and feeling as opposed to tuning into our own inner experience and prioritizing our own well-being? Big questions, I know, and perhaps not so easy to really take in at first, but can you see how these might be great indicators into how certain patterns of behavior and habits get to change?

When we start to take responsibility for our trauma and healing, we get to become very honest with ourselves about what in our lives is not working. What's incongruent in our actions and habits and what we say we want to be feeling and experiencing? So to start in this particular thread of healing, a great practice to begin with is to make an inventory of commitments or obligations you have made to other people and entities outside of you that feel draining, imbalanced, or out of integrity in any way—can you give yourself permission to lighten the load of responsibility here or cancel it altogether? Now is the time to focus on yourself and your own repatterning, which at first might mean really cleaning your slate so you can dedicate more time and energy to taking care of yourself and learning what that actually means for you. How do you want to be taken care of? How do you want to receive your own love? **How do you love to be nourished? Ask. Listen. Receive. Commit. Follow through. Here is where we begin.**

TRANSMUTE TRAUMA INTO YOUR GIFTS

The long-followed stress-struggle-addiction train stops here, beloved. The rate at which we're evolving won't allow us to subside in low vibrations of suffering, worry, addiction, or any other forms of bypassing what wants to be fully felt. Our wounds and our addictive behaviors, mostly our addiction to suffering, are being healed at a mass level in this moment of revolutionary consciousness awakening.

As such, we are being invited to feel our depths and finally ask: what is it that I really need in this moment to feel supported and how can I give that to myself now? Advanced practice is to know your needs and clearly articulate them and request they be met by the people in your life who you know are resourced to be able to support you in those specific ways. The veil is so thin, and masks are dismantling faster than we can keep track of the identities we learned to maintain for survival's sake up until now. We are remembering we are not alone. We are here to thrive, which invites us to support ourselves and each other to shed our former selves with grace.

We learned to seek perfection to be loved and accepted and seen, to feel validated in our existence, to feel worthy, to matter. But this codependency only exists when we believe in the illusion that we require another to validate our existence in the first place. If you've always been looking outside for the mirror to reassure you, you'll always be left wanting more, and this sets off the insatiable chase for filling the unfillable void within.

Because there is no void, herein lies the paradox we're being called to fully acknowledge and embody. Our mind and trauma conditioning may have taught us to believe we're not enough, we're incomplete, we're not worthy, we need X to feel Y, we need others to validate our enough-ness and prove we're really here, wanted, loved, and even needed.

But when we realize the supposed void we're feeling is a learned construct developed to substantiate a particular conditioning we took on to fit into a family system and then later into societal systems, we allow the whole show to unravel. That's what it is really—the multilayered strategies and conditioning we took on to protect ourselves and play whatever role was most safe, secure, and accepted for a time: a show, a channel, a resonance we've been tuning into until finally we realize we can change the channel. Just like that.

Your not-enough-ness and fear of not existing arose to teach you sovereignty and wholeness and to embody divinity. Your abandonment trauma has helped you to master love, beginning with self-love first and foremost. Your shame of being dirty or bad or wrong has taught you self-acceptance and compassion in ways you never otherwise would have learned. Codependency and victimization in the face of intimacy and invitations to fully embody your power have initiated you into greater discernment, boundaries, right use of power, and attunement to your deepest desires.

Would you now know what it is you truly want and love and what you're here for—what gift and genius you're here to share—had you not first lived so long chasing all of the opposites? Forgive yourself for being an infinite expansive soul inside this gorgeous, decadent, multidimensional body with so much inheritance to sort through and integrate.

"Our whole spiritual transformation brings us to the point where we realize that in our own being: we are enough."
—Ram Dass

Shame is the lowest vibration or most dense energy we have accessible to us in this life on Earth—and shame typically gets stuck deep in the body as trauma memory that then blocks us off from being our most powerful, magnetic, loving selves. Our bodies are mainly energy fields, which has been scientifically proven with field theory and neuroscience, and beautifully articulated in the work of Dr. Joe Dispenza and other thought leaders bridging the timeless wisdom of yogis and mystics with modern science. In *Becoming Supernatural,* Dispenza reminds us: "The only way we can change our lives is to change our energy—to change the electromagnetic field we are constantly broadcasting. In other words, to change our state of being, we have to change how we think and how we feel." Precisely. Consider how any dense emotions or energies that are not allowed to be fully processed or felt that then get stuck in the body's cellular memory which then broadcasts through the field as obstructions and distortions of one's manifestation potential.

If you are carrying dense energy that blocks your power, life force, vitality, and full aliveness from flowing as it's designed, you are more likely to attract situations, people, relationships, and reflections that mirror the lesson that caused the density or shame to be imprinted in the first place; until, of course, you choose to release the energy and emotion around the shame so that you can free yourself of the repetitive cycle once and for all. The longer I go on this path, the more I am reminded of its inherent simplicity: feel your feelings completely, until they can be completely metabolized; aim to hold on to nothing—no stuck stuff—in the body or energy field (make energetic hygiene a priority); allow life force to flow freely so it can guide your destined path of aligned purpose; continue returning to the present moment to discern your next right step. And trust, when we are present, our next right step is always clear. If it's not, then we most likely aren't actually being present with what is arising. Aha—the cosmic joke—life is always sending us back to ourselves; to meet what longs to be loved and accepted.

Shame can first imprint when the response you, as a child, expected simply didn't meet your needs and you made that mean something about you—that it was your fault. Most of our early trauma tends to set in before we have the words or processing capacity online to understand how we are making meaning in the world—we are like sponges instantaneously responding to all the feedback in our environment. In doing so we set into motion patterns and protective strategies that can last a lifetime if we stay stuck in the same cycle of response which started at the specific age when a core wound was first etched into our experience.

Maybe you've experienced that in yourself or another—when a trauma is unconsciously touched later in life and it can feel like you or the other reverts to a younger self, perhaps the specific age when the triggering traumatic experience first happened. Even if you're thirty, forty, fifty years old—you can instantly revert to four, five, or six when the first experience of shame or wounding arose in your experience that someone decades later is now reminding you of so you can finally fully feel it and integrate what you choose to learn.

TRANSCENDENCE ATTUNEMENTS

It's funny, we go on retreats to remember who we are and why we are here, but what about creating a life that we don't ever feel the need to retreat from? How can our life become a continuous transformational immersion (with integration, rest, and rejuvenation too, of course), how can we always be in practice, how can we always be open to healing? This is a curiosity of mine, especially as I tune more closely into where it seems we are evolving collectively. We are learning to be more resourced in the ways we support ourselves (and then—each other). We are inviting more intimacy and authenticity into our lives in every aspect—in all relations. We are creating new contexts in which healing can happen in the moment it's called for, not hours or days or years later when we find ourselves craving a solution in a therapy session, away at rehab or amid yet another breakup from an all-too-familiar relationship dynamic gone wrong.

We are learning what it feels like to be supported in being ourselves, completely in alignment with our truth, feeling safe to be seen, as we are, here and now. Practicing opening up to receiving our own love and receiving all that wants to come through us at times can feel immensely overwhelming and even terrifying at first. After lifetimes of conditioning in which we learned we couldn't trust, couldn't be magical, couldn't dance in the unknown mystery unfolding, couldn't play, couldn't feel the way we were feeling—our ascension journey can be a lot to take in, especially when sometimes it feels like everything is hitting us all at once. Luckily we have numerous practices and integration support to play with as we venture forth, carving our own way into being ourselves beyond the noise of any conditioning and unconscious patterning.

Redirect the Movie of Your Life

One of the most powerful ways I've come across to heal shame, even the deepest, darkest respites of it trapped in our cells and hidden caves of consciousness, is something I've come to know as timeline healing. I love to do this process by first identifying an energetic pattern or even a behavior or survival strategy that we are ready to release. This practice invites us to really feel it to heal it—all the stuff we've been carrying around without even knowing it—and let it go. From here we can repattern our understanding of history and identities therein and instead start to create new realities and future potentials . . . and it feels so good.

To start this practice, I suggest laying down in a comfortable position so you feel nice and cozy and supported to really relax and let go. Your consciousness and body are going to really guide the way here—it's amazing how much healing happens when we simply create the conditions for it to occur, which usually simply means just slowing down, breathing, and going more at our own pace of processing. Once you are comfortable in your meditative space (sometimes I like to play healing frequencies like 741, 432 or 528hz—if it feels supportive, give it a try), bring the earliest memory to mind of when you first felt shame.

If you feel comfortable, you can even ask your higher self to show you the movie of memories connected to this energy and visualize yourself as though you're watching a show of your life. Then simply let the tape or movie play of all the various shameful imprints shown in chronological order. In each experience that comes into your awareness, feel anything that wants to be felt that wasn't allowed to be expressed at that particular moment long ago. Is there anything that wants to be said or shared now that your loving presence is willing and available to receive it? Next, see if you can observe what was being learned at that time. You can even ask yourself—or ask your higher self to illuminate for you—what was I learning in that experience? How was I growing?

One thing to consider: it can be useful to set a timer for this experience so you don't feel like you're taking on too much at once. Even starting with ten or fifteen minutes can be such a powerful practice. You may also feel supported sharing space with a trusted friend or support while first doing this too in case it feels like a lot of emotion is ready to come up to release. I know for me, even still, it's important to call in support and coregulatory touch when I feel big emotional waves ready to release and integrate. It can be so healing to ask for help in this way, especially if you've been more familiar with trying to go it alone and keep everything in. Trust that your body will never give you more than you can handle resource-wise in any moment and that taking it slow can be the best medicine. If you feel a calling to explore this practice, make it your own (as with everything here) and see what pacing feels natural (and even nourishing, perhaps) to you. You are your own best guide and here is where you can deeply show up for yourself and hold space for your true self to come closer to home, to you.

After you've dabbled in this practice, seeing what you see now from perhaps a new perspective, what commitments or new understandings are you taking away to inform your present-moment experience? So much subtle energetic movement and healing can happen in this practice. Trust you'll find your own way—there's no wrong way to do this, only your own way to navigate that's perfect for you. Follow the practice for as long as feels comfortable. If you doze off or go into a bit of a trance, that usually means a deep subconscious clearing is underway, which is fantastic news—the body is releasing a lot of stored memory that it no longer needs for powering survival or protection protocols.

Alchemize Shame

Another great attunement for transmuting and transcending energies of shame that can appear unconsciously in our lives is to take an inventory of anything and everything in your life that feels draining, discouraging or dense when you feel this aspect in your awareness. This can include people, places, things, responsibilities, really anything. Where in your life are you showing up in any ways that don't feel fulfilling, that don't feel creative, that don't support you in embodying your values?

When you make your inventory, write everything down in a list by hand so you can really see it all—and in doing so make a note of what particularly feels heavy or comes with a sense of dread as you take note of it. In this exercise we see how when we allow our energy to be drained or exhausted, we may be operating from unworthiness rooted in shame and a sense that we don't deserve better. By becoming aware of the specific drains, we acknowledge the feelings associated with them and start to see clearly what new possibilities and paths may arise instead.

Once you have a full inventory of the energy drains and exhaustive points of life, take it all in and try your best, without judgment or criticism, to notice the feeling associated with each of these aspects of life and see if you can simply give yourself permission to let any heavy feelings arise, be fully felt and process through. After moving this energy for a bit—however long it takes to start to feel a bit more spacious, at your own pace—perhaps you'll start to notice naturally that a new commitment or direction wants to arise. Knowing what you know now about how these habits were formed (reactively from a belief about yourself that you don't want to empower any longer)—does any new commitment or action arise that feels more in alignment with the ways of being you want to live into from now on? How can you lighten your load even more—can any of these old habits or behaviors be let go of for good, even one at a time?

Dismantling the Ego

One of the most powerful ways I've practiced healing shame and transmuting it to reveal my gifts hiding underneath is to continually be in practice of asking and answering this question: What is it I am most afraid of anyone knowing about me, and what would be the most revealing way I could share this—in a way that feels like it would destroy my reputation? Now, this approach isn't for everyone, but for those of us who see the world we are here to create and can tap into the future timelines of the more beautiful world we know is possible, one that is becoming closer and closer with each breath we take, releasing the ego through this kind of questioning has been ultra-effective at healing shame.

I mean to posit this question as an inquiring exploration—you can try journaling about it or meditating on it to see what else comes up—and less so as a prescriptive action since even just the inquiry can bring to light a lot in our awareness we may have not otherwise been ready to name or feel. However, if it comes naturally to you to follow suit with action arising from your inquiry—trust what feels true for you. When we listen to our truth and go at own own pace with discernment from presence and stability, anchored in wholeness, we are usually right on track.

Inner Child Alchemy

In transcending shame inner child work is a key modality here to support our higher consciousness awakening. This has certainly been the case in my journey of transcending addiction, codependency, and distortions around sexuality, money, and power, and it continues to be a foundational element in becoming sovereign leaders and creators of our extraordinary lives.

Here's one of the best practices we can start with, and it's simple enough to be done in five minutes a day. At least once throughout your day, or perhaps more often if you find this supportive: close your eyes, put your hands on your heart, and take a few deep cleansing breaths. Call into your awareness a vision of yourself at a younger age, any age that feels relevant to you in that moment, which might be different from day to day. The perfect age will arise immediately as the timeline that requires your attention now.

Envision yourself at that age and notice what comes up. What emotions arise? It's okay if it feels like a lot at first—many in my experience can't even visualize themselves as their inner child or as a younger self because they experienced so much trauma that they've just blocked out the entire segment of their memory right across their life. This is more normal than we might imagine—it happened for me at first too. It's important we give time and really go at our own pace to truly allow ourselves to heal. Eventually we come to see that any energy that's being drained by suppressing emotion, memory, or experience is energy that could be more battery power to your life, to your creativity, to your relationships, to your joy. So it's imperative we make a beginning with this practice to start to bring into awareness the parts of ourselves that we cannot stand to repress and ignore any longer.

Sacred Self-Celebration

Lastly, a beautiful practice to heal shame involves dialing into self-celebration and gratitude, on a consistent basis if we can. At first it might feel so impossible to genuinely celebrate ourselves. God knows we've spent a lifetime practicing being hard on ourselves and criticizing ourselves for just not getting anything right—sometimes the shift in our perspective to noticing the positive aspects of ourselves can be a huge stretch, and that's okay. First we get to accept where we are as ourselves and let that be enough. Are we willing to make the change and try on a new perspective?

If so, then you can make a beginning by creating a sacred space for yourself in your home—somewhere you meditate or maybe somewhere you associate with self-care and connecting inward. If this is new for you to think about, that's perfect too—might it feel good to have a space dedicated to your well-being and happiness? In this space, however it shows up for you, you're invited to create an altar that honors whatever it is you feel is sacred for you, about you, and about anything else in your life that you want to celebrate and practice gratitude for. At a certain point you may feel called to add pictures of your family and ancestors to the altar as a way to honor where you come from too.

You may put a picture of yourself at a young age, as well as sacred items or other pictures of things that remind you of celebratory moments on your journey here. Something that really helped me recently was adding pictures of my parents and grandparents to my altar alongside my child self—the entire lineage being celebrated here together helped me ground into more appreciation for my whole family's journey and all they went through to simply live. This is where we come from—such a long line of beings who went through so much, for us to be brought into existence.

When we have an altar set up physically, it helps to program our subconscious mind, which speaks in symbols and feelings, with the energy of gratitude more often—even when we aren't necessarily focusing on gratitude as a practice. Just by having this sacred space set up, we are moving leaps and bounds in shifting our perspective about our past and all that's made us who we are. Remember, the things we're most afraid for anyone to know about us are usually the things everyone is waiting to love us for. Can we give ourselves permission to be who we really are? Can we let all the love in—all the way—and receive ourselves in our perfect imperfection?

6

FORGIVE YOURSELF; THEN FORGIVE YOURSELF SOME MORE

Forgiving ourselves can be the hardest thing we ever do. Plus, what does it actually mean to forgive? *Forgive yourself* seems like a phrase we hear often, especially in religious contexts that imply that it means freedom—in forgiving ourselves and each other we somehow free ourselves from the burdens of guilt, shame, and regret that we too often carry along with us through life. I used to always think forgiveness was something I needed from other people—kind of like I needed their approval to feel valuable or worthy of not just love but of existing in general. I thought forgiveness was dependent on others and that there was something I had to do to get it. What I found, however, was almost a reverse-engineered concept of what I had thought to be forgiveness—we don't need anyone else to achieve the freedom we desire. Such is the paradox of life, I suppose—we withhold from ourselves what we want most, often thinking we need someone else to approve of us first to have it, when really we've had the power all along to give ourselves what we need.

Now I define forgiveness as letting the past and all perceived mistakes or regrets go so that you can see yourself with a clean slate, free of all burdens and with acceptance of the past as perfect. What happened is what was meant to happen, or else it would have happened differently. And however you showed up in the moment was also what was meant to happen, otherwise you would have done differently. When we accept the past as it was—as perfect without regret—we can forgive ourselves for any perceived mistakes or regrets we might be holding, which usually stem from a desire to have simply done things differently. Usually always in hindsight, right?

Sure, we can see how some situations could have been better if handled in a different way—but how much suffering do we avail ourselves to by constantly hanging these regrets over our heads, walking through life with a heaviness, wishing things were different than they are? Acceptance is really our master key when it comes to forgiveness, and the two together work in concert to initiate us into a deeper experience of the present moment. When we can be at peace with the past and accept it as it was meant to happen, we can be at peace in the present moment, which is where life is truly happening. From presence we see clearly and make better decisions that we feel good about—ultimately giving ourselves less fodder for regret as we walk our path.

I learned about forgiveness, like many other lessons, I suppose, the hard way—or maybe just the intense way. Somehow my soul seems to enjoy learning the hard way in this life—or maybe I've just been stubborn up until a point and the lessons had to be loud to really get my attention and integrate all the way through. I was about a year and a half sober, regularly going to AA meetings, working in advertising in New York City, and my life was really feeling like it was flowing. I was happier and more connected than I'd ever felt before—I had a great community, a sense of purpose, I was thriving at my job, I was receiving support, and I was doing my spiritual work in the 12 steps of AA, which was catalyzing huge growth and awakening.

> **"Holding on to anger is like drinking poison and expekting the other person to die."**
> **—Buddha**

At one point I got to step 9 in the 12 steps. Number 9 is the one about making amends, which I had heard a lot about over the course of my recovery. But it wasn't turning out how I thought it would. Instead of making a list of all the people I felt guilty toward or afraid of ever seeing again because of the harm I'd caused in the past through my addictive behavior, I was sneakily instructed to take out the list of resentments I'd already made during my fourth and fifth steps and then look over all those names of people I had held grudges toward or worked through resentments with. These were going to be the same people I would make amends to—the ones who initially bothered me so much I held memory of them in my consciousness sometimes for years later. I didn't understand at first—it seemed backward: that the people I was angry at or holding something against were actually the ones I needed to make amends with. So much for making a fresh list of people I could call up and show how well I was doing now—no, there would be no ego stroking in this process, much to my disappointment. In fact, a massive deflationary process was about to start, one in which a big bubble of stories and identities wrapped in regret and shame was about to pop for good. I was about to experience true forgiveness, and not in the way I thought it was supposed to happen.

I reviewed my list of all the people I'd had resentments toward and added a few new ones that I had done noticeable harm to, the people that weighed heavily on my consciousness, those who, if I ran into them out in public somewhere, I'd be terrified to face. I had made up so many stories about the horrible things I had done. Usually back when I was drinking and causing all the damage, my M.O. was to run and detach whenever something got hard in a relationship, rather than face it and come to a new understanding, which I was not equipped for at all. It was easier to delete (as I liked to call it) people from my life and pretend I never knew them in the first place.

But with this detachment pattern came a lot of dramatic, frankly exaggerated storytelling to support my case to completely delete someone from my life. I didn't necessarily have an accurate view of what really happened, so making amends was as much about cleaning up my side of the street, owning my part, taking responsibility, and facing my fears as it was about right-sizing reality and coming to a clearer understanding of the truth.

My greatest lesson from making hundreds of amends over the years—from facing people I had stolen from, people I had gotten into fights with, friends whose homes I had trashed when blacked out, people who I had embarrassed by drinking and getting arrested or taken to the hospital, to friends I had just stopped talking to because I was too embarrassed to ever face them after they had seen what I had done—is that I don't require anyone else's approval or even presence to receive forgiveness.

Forgiveness, and the freedom and permission that come from it, is something I allow myself to have simply by deciding *I deserve this, I set myself free, I have permission to let this go forever and accept the past and learn from it.* Then I move on. I had thought all those years that I needed someone else to validate me in order to be truly forgiven—but it's just not the case. In a way forgiveness can be a one-way street after all; it doesn't require anyone else or even an agreement with someone in order to let yourself be free. I learned through facing hundreds of people I was often terrified to see that in most cases I was the one holding myself hostage with guilt, shame, regret, and oftentimes a story of how badly everything had unfolded that was far worse than what the other person remembered.

In fact, in a lot of amends experiences, the person I was afraid to see, who I harbored so much shame around, usually gratefully received my amends and also wondered what had happened to me—they would say: "You were actually a great friend and when you disappeared I missed you and wondered where you had gone." Talk about rewriting reality. In my mind I had been a horrible friend and was ashamed to ever see the person again.

I was really afraid of how I remembered myself in that person's presence, of the shame and guilt I felt that was brought up every time I thought of them, which made it easier to effectively cancel them from my life rather than simply face the truth and try to come into acceptance and learn from it. The second option sounds so much easier now but probably only because of the repatterning that I chose to undergo through facing all those people I had been terrified to see. Now when given the opportunity to make amends to take responsibility for a supposed misstep, I usually don't wait so long as the pain of living in a misunderstanding that could easily be right-sized or clarified with a bit of communication or reflection just isn't worth sacrificing my peace.

I wonder how much of reality we remember incorrectly when we hold ourselves in these stories of shame, guilt, regret, and the other burdens we can carry for a whole lifetime simply because we are afraid of facing reality and the supposed reflection of who we truly are. We learn to invest so much in protecting our identity. We learn to put so much energy into maintaining a familiar story line, even if it's one that says *I am bad* or *I don't deserve love* or *I deserve to suffer,* instead of facing the truth, usually in a relationship that wants to invite us into a new potential and path forward. Why is it so impossible sometimes—the invitation to completely change our identity and construct of who we think we are, simply by asking someone else for feedback, asking them how they experienced a situation and overall being willing to be more flexible and understanding within how we relate to ourselves and reality?

When did we become so rigid? Well, as we've seen thus far, the first few years of life are when everything gets set into motion, including much of our identity structure and core traumas that inform our personality and ideas about reality and how we are designed to show up in it. One of my favorite definitions I learned in recovery explains what a miracle truly is, especially as it relates to sobriety: a miracle is a personality change sufficient to bring about recovery from a seemingly hopeless state of mind and body. This definition might have been more specific to alcoholism, a term I don't identify with anymore since knowing that alcoholism, or really any -ism, is a symptom of a deeper-rooted core wound; but I love the implications here for all of life. What if a miracle is simply a gift of personality change in any way we are requiring one—that when embodied helps to welcome us home to our true selves, restored as our original blueprint?

> **"If you want to know where to find your contribution to the world, look at your wounds. When you learn how to heal them, teach others."**
> **—Emily Maroutian**

A miracle is a personality change sufficient to bring about recovery from a seemingly hopeless state. Yes, please. I would add to this—that a layer of forgiveness is required in actualizing this personality change:

forgiveness is a conscious decision to unburden oneself of any regret, resentment, shame, guilt, or other heavy emotional energy regarding a past experience in order to come into acceptance of oneself as perfectly imperfect, whole, complete, and free in this present moment. Forgiveness is the way we let ourselves off the hook for anything heavy about the past. We let ourselves detach from our past experiences and accept them as perfect lessons that brought us to this moment, as we are meant to be, right where we are meant to be. Forgiveness invites us into more maturity—and responsibility for ourselves and the way we relate to the world.

We exit victim consciousness when we choose to forgive ourselves and step more fully into the role of conscious creators that we are here to embody. In forgiving ourselves we acknowledge: I am responsible for my own happiness and freedom, for these are gifts I choose to give myself and receive at will, again and again. No one else is in charge of my happiness or sense of freedom. I am responsible for accepting the past, learning from it, and being a clear vessel for new experiences to emerge in this present moment.

FORGIVENESS IS A REVOLUTIONARY ACT

Could we imagine that everything you've been through, no matter how hard, how painful, how intense, how seemingly shameful, has been the perfect initiation or lesson that you've at some level chosen to teach you what you've always wanted to learn and master? When we practice forgiveness, we give ourselves permission to attune to more peace, ease, and happiness no matter what's transpired. **Forgive yourself for what happened before you remembered who you are.**

It might feel triggering at first to consider this invitation, as of course it implies a completely new way of viewing your life and reality as a whole—but let's face it: Are you the creator of your reality and actualized destiny or not? Are you a victim or are you a leader? Are you choosing expansion and light and happiness or not? It's up to you, and right now you are offered a simple choice that can redefine the entire way you view life now and forever. When you forgive yourself, you are saying to yourself that you understand everything you've been through, even the supposed mistakes and wrongdoings or regrets, were absolutely required to bring you right here to this moment. You wouldn't be reading these words right now if you weren't ready to resonate in this new paradigm.

It's okay to feel depleted; remember you've been running a spiritual marathon recovering countless dimensions of your true self, integrating aspects long forgotten and repressed, all while navigating the most massive shifts in our material reality that any human has ever seen. No one before us has experienced life in a body on Earth with energy moving through us like this; this fast, this potent, this complex. We are integrating lifetimes in dreamtime, processing centuries of ancestral trauma in a day, cutting cords with all the outdated systems and thought forms inherited by this body but foreign to our soul.

We are remembering our infinite beingness. What is it to be truly here and now in all moments without a reason or thought? To simply be in silence and stillness, watching the dream unfold before our eyes? Which is more real and who's to say: the dream while you supposedly sleep or this waking moment? I can't tell anymore. So many dimensions are blurring together but always pointing me back to the body—you're here to be completely human, remember?

What's it like to be in the body, completely? To feel at home? To feel safe? To feel held, like you have a stable support structure within and upon which to infinitely expand? What's it like to devote yourself fully— even though you thought you already had long ago—to unconditionally loving yourself as your own divine mother and your own divine father, in sacred union, married within, with the sole purpose of honoring-loving-nurturing you? Just because.

Forgive yourself quickly. You are developing and integrating a whole/ holy new operating system. You are pioneering and anchoring entirely new templates for all of humanity—each aspect of density-distortion you transmute within your being, you transmute for all who are willing to receive your gift of attunement to a new way. Your healing is no small feat. It is not selfish. It is not something to judge or be embarrassed by. You are on a divine assignment of transmutation and alchemical embodiment—here to architect Heaven on Earth through your presence, perfectly prepared for this moment.

Go at your own pace. To do so is revolutionary in a culture that has ingrained in us so deeply hierarchy, comparison and competition. This is a long game. We are emerging into timelessness, remembering grace-patience-allowing-receiving. This is who we are.

We are pioneering entirely new templates for all of humanity—each aspect of density or distortion you transmute within your being, you transmute for all who are willing to receive your gift of attunement to a new way. Not only is forgiving ourselves and each other a revolutionary act, it is actually a miraculous one at that. When we can truly experience the freedom of forgiveness, miracles seem to naturally abound. I say this to myself as a reminder of something I know that's true from the higher-self perspective, a truth my human self doesn't always tune into by default, especially when life gets challenging.

Sometimes our body memory, our somatic imprinting, sets into motion at such a young age, and can spout such loud messages and thoughts that it can feel like forgiving ourselves is the last strategy we'd consider exploring. Usually when I am in pain or working through a particular trauma—or resisting it at first—my tendency, at least, which has been wired in pretty deeply, is to fix it, to change it, to transform it—to no longer feel the pain. Turn it off, turn it down, anything to make it stop. How is forgiveness supposed to help me out of the discomfort? This option doesn't at first make sense to the mind that wants immediate relief.

After all we've covered thus far, let's take another look at what forgiveness means, shall we? What does it mean for you, how is it landing now? It's definitely one of those terms we readily throw around and mention often, especially in personal development and healing circles, but do we ever stop to really consider how we uniquely define and perhaps redefine it (upon coming into new understandings) for ourselves? Sometimes when we don't define something's meaning for ourselves, we can more easily overlook its true power and potential for assisting us on our paths. For me, forgiveness can also be an intentional practice of balancing energy exchange with anyone or anything we've either given our power to or taken power away from.

Whenever there feels to be an imbalanced exchange of some kind that leaves a feeling of discomfort, there's likely something between you and another that remains to be resolved. Sometimes the exchange can feel imbalanced in ways that are unconscious to us but can present emotionally as resentment, anger, sadness. It's like we're walking through the world with an open wound at some level, just waiting to get triggered by another familiar situation that brings our awareness back onto the original happening, hopefully with an intention to finally heal.

There's learning about forgiveness on the surface level—the kind you learn about when you're little and start to explore the concept of manners, maybe around the time of kindergarten or first grade. Around the time we start socializing with people outside our immediate families we usually start learning about proper conduct and forgiveness as a practice therein—isn't that funny? Right away when we start learning to relate to others, we learn to say *I'm sorry* and *please* and *thank you*, but never was I taught anything about owning my power or not giving my power away to things or people outside of me to define my feelings, my value, my sense of safety. Interesting to think about what kind of world we'd live in if we started to consider these concepts earlier on in our lives.

Maybe we'd have less to unwind and repattern later on if we were allowed or encouraged to simply be ourselves in the first place. The other level of forgiveness that feels more authentic to explore here is one wholly contingent upon the relationship we have with ourselves. We might think at first that forgiveness has to do with someone or something else—and that we are responsible for setting that other entity free from any traps of anger or resentment or otherwise negative energy we're holding them in for a supposed wrong they committed against us.

Maybe instead forgiveness has everything to do with our relationship to ourselves and ensuring we are in integrity with how we are managing our own emotions, our power, and unconscious attachments therein. **Maybe forgiveness has never actually been about anyone else but ourselves.** Maybe forgiveness is simply the way in which we set ourselves free from anything we've been holding on to, especially from the past that keeps us stuck and stagnant or outside of presence. Above all else, hopefully by now we've established: forgiveness is a revolutionary act and practice of self-healing that can deliver us home to ourselves and into the relationships that we've always desired.

CULTIVATING RADICAL SELF-COMPASSION

I alluded to this a bit already, but there are more layers to reveal. I first learned about forgiveness—the real one, not the superficial *I'm sorry* one we learn pretty young—around the first time I started to process the fourth and fifth steps in the 12-step recovery program of Alcoholics Anonymous.

The fourth step involves making an inventory of resentments you have with everything and everyone in life, plus you start to take responsibility for where you set the ball in motion for each situation (usually through unclear expectations and unbalanced energy exchanges). The fifth step is where you read the fourth step out loud and in doing so start to see the patterns of how most resentments you hold are actually the same scenario over and over, rooted in a similar wound or core reaction. My first fifth-step experience was a spiritual milestone on my journey in which I saw for the first time how the world wasn't actually out to get me but that I was, in fact, catalyzing many repetitive events and experiences through unexpressed expectations that would usually always end in disappointment and more suffering.

Going through the 12 steps is a process that has its benefits for any human on their evolutionary path—it is a tried-and-true process for understanding one's core patterns and traumas, reconnecting with spiritual guidance and resources and becoming empowered to alleviate immense suffering. In fact, this book was born out of the exploration and curiosity: what are the 12 steps of ascension and what is the process for recovering one's true self? How can we awaken to our core sense of self and start living the kinds of lives we know we are destined to enjoy and share? Even after you have put down harmful substances or addictive behaviors to a degree—there always seems to be more depth to explore in touching our true selves and how we want to express in our chosen reality. And the journey never ends, as long as we are alive—we can always go deeper. This is what we are templating together, now.

Back to when I first learned about true forgiveness. I had a few months sober and was very much still in a deep process of emotional recovery into more stability and calm—my nervous system had been so fried after all the drugs and drinking for so many years. I was shot in a lot of ways, unable to rest and relax, let alone be present or breathe in all the way. I look back on how I was then and feel so much compassion as well as empathy within the universal human experience. I think most people are still walking around terrified to relax, to let go, to simply be. They are unknowingly moving through life with so much protection, masks on and survival strategies ready to launch at our beck and call. What a whole lot of energy to always be managing these multiple arrays of protection all the time, right? Phew, it's certainly a lot.

I completed step one which meant I had admitted my powerlessness over alcohol and that my life had certainly become unmanageable—that was easy to see. I had surrendered (to the best of my ability) my life over to a higher power; something greater than me—*me* being the ego identity that had gotten me into so much trouble in the first place. I trusted that this higher power would take care of me and guide me on a new path. I didn't need to know the instruction manual and all the inner workings in order to just let it carry me; I was learning to let go and finally surrender. I think sometimes my whole relationship with alcohol and drugs wasn't so much that I was actually chemically addicted. I think I just found a way to self-medicate and turn off my overactive mind that was so intent on controlling every aspect of my life—blacking out drunk or being taken over by certain drugs was the only way I could let go, to rest into faith, to actually live and maybe even just breathe. Sometimes I would even call drinking *time traveling*—when I didn't have to worry, I didn't feel overwhelmed, I didn't feel like I had anything to hold back so tightly, I could just let everything go. I could be free. I wonder if others have had this experience.

**"Are you paralyzed with fear? That's a good sign. Fear is good.
Like self-doubt, fear is an indicator. Fear tells us what we
have to do. Remember one rule of thumb: the more scared
we are of a work or calling, the more sure we can be
that we have to do it."**
—Steven Pressfield

Once I got to step 4, my sponsor cleverly instructed me to write a long
list of all the people, places, and ways of being (especially social constructs)
that irritated me at some level or that specifically I felt resentful toward. I
loved this idea—finally, a chance to complain about everyone and everything that's ever bothered me, and trust me, I had a long, long list I'd been
keeping track of for my entire life, just waiting for the chance to eagerly
share my sob story with a sympathetic soul who could validate my suffering. I completed my list, which was a full notebook at least, and then
I got the next instruction for the process. To my surprise, for each one, I
had to write where I had "set the ball rolling" to initiate the situation in
the first place and then, knowing this, I got to reflect on and write out
what I would have done differently instead. These were the people that
I ultimately would owe an amends to; whomever I felt resentful toward
was almost always someone I was invited to forgive. At some level—and
I would see this over hundreds of cases to come—they were reflecting a
part of myself I wasn't willing to fully accept or integrate yet.

It was hard at first to really be honest—you mean I'm to see how this
person I've hated and been annoyed with for all these years was actually
impacting me on levels deeper than simply bothering me or disrupting
my life? That they actually had a key piece in my healing journey to share
with me in the reflection they were offering? And that I might have been
complicit in setting up the entire annoying situation on top of all that?
That was a hard sell. But ultimately this was the start in seeing where I
was responsible for certain aspects of my experience of reality. And from
here I could finally start to make better choices to cultivate more of the
experiences I actually wanted as opposed to those meant to trigger me

into new consciousness (usually through a lesson painful enough to wake me up!). Can we become willing to harvest the gold beneath the surface of supposed irritation and resentment to instead give way to deeper awareness, clarity, and most of all, a return to more of our true selves?

Consider for yourself: how many tumultuous lessons have been garnered from perceived failures, mistakes, and at times dangerous moments that have actually led you into forgiveness and ultimately more self-love and acceptance plus strength to move forward? Nowadays we move through so many (infinite) waves in our multidimensional life experiences—with continual purging of old ways of being. We are getting more accustomed to shedding new skin more quickly now as we are being challenged to face our depths, even deeper. The outdated survival programs, protection, and self-preservation protocols can't come with us where we're going. And it can hurt to feel these layers. The not-enough voice and conditional self-love tactics can be so loud; they're coming up heightened in awareness to meet in new ways. Can we interrupt them from taking over like they're accustomed to? The healing underway isn't about turning those energies off completely but instead welcoming them to integrate in new ways.

"A failure is only a step on the way to your success."
—Yogi Bhajan

Sometimes it feels like nothing is real, like I am not real, like nothing I have done is real. I feel incongruent with how others relate to me and how I see myself now. Sometimes it feels I am learning to see and be with myself, for the first time, like this. It hurts to feel how for so long I wasn't sure if I even existed because no one was there early on to validate and attune with my being in the ways I needed then. Learning to love oneself like this, now, is definitely like shooting in the dark. Even after so many years of doing the work and transcending so many layers and identities, there is still infinitely more to welcome forth.

As much as I want to run away from the pain sometimes, even

still, the practice is instead to reach out in connection instead of hiding in isolation—sharing truthfully instead of donning a mask of self-deception—letting the layers of protection, fear, and contraction melt away as we let others truly see, be with, and support us as we are. The practice is to welcome the parts that feel hard to feel—to make space for them, to speak to them lovingly, to go back to basics—pausing to ask your little one: "How are you, darling? What might you need to be supported right now? How can I help?"

This can be a paralyzingly challenging practice, even for me to this day. The deeper we go, the more we feel—and it can feel like making it all up when it comes to learning how to best self-soothe and resolve the immense energies that come up to process. Even while finishing writing this book you're reading now, over the summer solstice in June 2022, I had some very tender layers of early childhood trauma arise to feel, and it was incredibly humbling to be with. I was shown even more clearly my patterns of hyper-vigilance and how this patterning has been so successful in underlying my drive to achieve, create, and most of all be ultra self-sufficient. I had to be as a child, and those skills, developed far too young, have served me well in our culture that celebrates productivity and initiative indeed. But when it comes to asking for support and letting love in, it can still feel so challenging to really show up for myself in these ways.

I wonder if I easily stay so busy with so much responsibility and things going on as a way to stay closed off from others and keep myself *safe* from true vulnerability and intimacy. It can still feel so scary to let people, even my closest friends, see that I am not perfect. If they saw the real me and all I am carrying and how much I am still growing—that I'm really not perfect at all—will they still love me? My heart knows the truth here, but my wounded aspects still sometimes don't want to hear the answer—the pain of rejection would be far too great, so I might as well not risk any potentials for my fears to be proven right.

My inner dialogue will still sometimes say: it's better to heal in silence and solitude. Better to only let others in or share about experiences when they're more integrated and I have a valuable lesson to teach that others will feel like they're getting something from. All of these patterns are rooted in my core wound of *I am not enough.* To what extent is everything I've created or been drawn to create an outgrowth of a deep desire to prove

my worth to myself and to the world? I am open to continuing to explore the reflections that come in this inquiry, knowing that there is no
right or wrong answer, just more clarity and consciousness to arrive into.
Here is where we can meet ourselves and our most tender spots—with
curiosity and compassion for all we have grown through and continue to
grow through.

It's astounding to see how our core wounds truly can power so much
of our existence and operating patterns until we make them conscious.
Even when we do become conscious of them, there still appears to be
endless territory to explore, heal, and just be with (and maybe, just maybe,
forgive)—without any final destination in mind. Maybe we are always
learning and growing through these new evolutions and awareness as long
as we are alive. Maybe this journey of growth and expansion is the entire
point behind this human experience.

Rebuilding trust after such a long life of self-abandonment and breaking trust again and again to instead prioritize others over oneself takes
time to repair. This is the reconstruction underway. This seems like the
path to embodying integrity. From here we experience our own radiance.
From here there is more ease, allowing, receiving. Maybe. I don't know.
I am hoping. I am learning. I am seeing pieces start to come together. I
am showing up the best I can. I have never been like this before. It's like
meeting myself for the first time, again. *I love you, keep going.*

Holding all the parts of this sacred human experience and all its complexity, with all the aspects of our multidimensional beings and divine
blueprint that knows who we truly are, why we are here, and the loving
intentions steering this ship called life. Surrendering some more. Crying
some more. Releasing. Cleansing. Breathing deeper. Expanding to welcome more in and all the way through. Loving ourselves anyway. Let's
meet here.

FORGIVENESS LEADS TO LIBERATION

Can you see everything you've moved through so far in life that might
have been a source of regret instead as a seed of growth and fuel to the fire
of your expansion and evolution?

I had already made probably thirty or so amends, maybe more, a year into my sobriety, and I was starting to feel more free as every amends lightened the load of guilt and shame (and associated identities therein) I was carrying, in some cases for many years. However, around my second year in AA and next round of amends, coming up on step 9, I was strongly advised to not contact my ex-boyfriends because, although I definitely owed them amends for harm caused, I wasn't yet mature enough to be able to do so with a clear conscience, without seeking validation or wanting to prove myself to them and show off how much better I was since we were last together. I proceeded on through my healing and evolution, but a year later I was getting a loud message in my meditations to revisit the potential of making amends to my exes. Could I do it in a clear, non-triggered way that earnestly sought to clear my side of the street and not anything else?

I was also starting to explore dating and relationships at the time—I was ready for a new potential partnership but felt strongly that I couldn't venture into that territory without first clearing my past relationships, which were weighing very heavy on my heart and in the stories I told about myself. The guilt and shame I held for how I showed up in those relationships were so painful—I felt so bad about how I had acted and how unfairly I had treated the people that I shared such intimate experiences with, who loved me as best they could with what they had at the time. I met with my sponsor about it and decided, yes; it was time to make amends to all my exes and forgive myself so I could fully move on into a new paradigm for all relationships.

I started with my ex in San Francisco, my first boyfriend, whom I lost my virginity to. I still carried so much shame around all the times I was partying blacked out and he had to babysit me or rescue me from a party where I was embarrassing myself. Seeing him for the first time in many years was incredibly nerve-wracking, but just restoring physical contact allowed for so much energy to clear—the new beings we were since we saw each other last were allowed to reconvene in a new context and circumstance. I said my piece and took responsibility for my parts as best I could—and he accepted my amends and simply requested that I keep taking care of myself as I was.

That's the thing about an amends—it's not an apology. An amends is a clearly written script wherein we take responsibility precisely for how we caused harm, without triggers or personalized attempts to get validation or otherwise. Writing the amends in and of itself, even if it's never shared with the person you're writing to, is such a healing practice. Can you write about a painful circumstance you feel guilt or shame about without trigger and really take responsibility for harm you caused in an honest and authentic way without seeking anything in return? If you can, this is a huge step in your own self-forgiveness and healing path.

At the end of an amends it's advised to ask the person receiving the amends if there's anything we can do to make it right. Over the hundreds of amends I've made now, I've usually received very similar responses from most people no matter what kind of relationship we had: "I'm so glad you're okay, I hope you continue taking care of yourself, I hope we can be in contact and be friends again, I missed you and it's so good to see you doing well."

In the past when I caused harm and felt shame or guilt about some-thing I had done, I had a tendency of cutting someone off and out of my life completely—it was easier to delete them than to face what I had done. Many of my amends were about reconnecting with those people and taking responsibility for what harm I had caused and also hearing their version of what had happened, which was often different from mine. So often they expressed confusion as to why I had dropped off the face of the Earth and they had never heard from me again. They missed me. But to me I had caused irreparable damage and didn't deserve to be in their lives—by exiting out of their reality, I was protecting them from more disappointment. I thought I was doing them a favor. This is the story shame and guilt love to replay in our minds to keep us hostage to these self-sabotaging, separative identities—preventing connection and repair with those who actually want to love us.

When I was living in New York, I remember being on my lunch break one day at my ad agency job and getting guidance to text Tom and Car-son, exes who were next on my amends list, to see if we might be able to meet. I had no idea if they would even respond to my message as our breakups were tumultuous, and we hadn't spoken for years since I cut off contact.

Carson had in fact called me once about a year prior, and I got his missed call in the bathroom while I was at a huge AA meeting in midtown Manhattan, of all places. Even though I had deleted his number, I recognized it from memory and wondered—why on Earth would he be calling me after all this time? It had been many years since we last saw each other in Brazil, when he came to visit me on my study abroad program, and I ultimately broke up with him afterward in the most terrible way. I sat with the possibility of calling him back and went through all kinds of horrible premonitions about why he might have called me in the first place.

A few days after I got his missed call while I was in the meeting, I was sitting in Bryant Partk, anxiously looking at Carson's number, wondering if I was going to press the button to call. I hit it before I could think too much more about it. I heard his voice, and it scared me how it felt like no time had passed at all. I was surprised to learn how he hadn't tried calling me before for any of the reasons I had thought up; instead he was just seeking to connect about a hard time he was going through with his parents. We had connected about shared challenges in our families and their histories throughout our relationship, and he was reaching out for support the best way he knew how, even if I wasn't the ideal person to be reaching for by any means. There was more to the story that he wasn't yet giving away, though, which I would only find out a few years later when it finally came time for me to make my amends to him in person.

Later on, when it was finally time, I finally texted both exes who were next on my list—terrified about whether I'd even hear from them and if I did, what they'd say or how they'd meet my message. Funny thing was: I heard back from both of them relatively quickly and it happened that both of them were living in close proximity to each other in Southern California, hilarious! They were practically neighbors, hopefully without knowing it. To my surprise they were also both open to meeting me and hearing what I had to say. So I booked my cross-country flight and also confirmed that I would meet them over the same weekend in two meetings close to one another—funny enough at two different Mexican restaurants. How perfect—just like the old days when we used to get California burritos after going to the beach all day. I was terrified still about the journey ahead and had no idea what would happen. But I knew I had to go find out—that facing the truth was key to forgiving myself and seeing what new potentials might become possible in my relationships. I was ready to be free.

I definitely wasn't holding as much heaviness with Tom as with Carson, so that felt like a better meeting to start with. Lighten the load there first and then save the most intense one for last. Something like that. My body was overcome with anxiety upon first seeing Tom in person. So many years had passed since our intense fights and screaming matches that ultimately led to me kicking him out of the apartment we shared in downtown Santa Barbara. We had met in Brazil, and it was actually Tom who factored into how I broke up with Carson, as sad as I was to admit it.

Tom was waiting for me at the Mexican restaurant in Encinitas, a beautiful part of San Diego where he grew up and where we used to spend time when we dated. He was shorter than I remembered and at the same time it felt bizarre seeing someone I had spent so much intimate time with seem so familiar but also completely different through my new eyes that could now see reality more clearly. I got right to the point and recited the amends I had prepared to take responsibility for my actions that were out of integrity, including my drunken outbursts, the way I ended our relationship rather violently, and any other ways I had caused harm through putting myself in danger, causing him to worry about my safety, and being disrespectful around his friends and colleagues. Lastly, I asked him if there was anything else I was leaving out and if there was anything I could do to right my wrongs.

He, much like my high school boyfriend, accepted my acknowledgment and thanked me for my insightfulness and willingness to take responsibility, reminding me that we were both young and wild back then, as though the way I saw it all wasn't so bad in his eyes. He even made his own kind of amends too for any ways in which he met me in the dramatic games I at times initiated, smiling as he seemed to say *it takes two to tango*. He, like so many others I had met in this way, simply wanted me to keep taking care of myself and to keep on my path that seemed to be doing me a lot of good. We hugged goodbye after the brief lunch and encounter we shared on that sunny day in a place we used to adventure around together when we were in love—and I felt more weight I didn't even know I had been carrying all those years lift off and out of me forever.

Carson was one of my longest relationships, which included living together at UC Santa Cruz in a tiny studio apartment for a year. I really loved him, and he cared for me in so many beautiful ways that I had never experienced before. We both also loved to party and drink and be wild. It was a perfect match in many ways, and I could have seen myself marrying him and spending the rest of our lives like that together. He was a year older than me, and when my senior year at UC arrived, I was feeling antsy to travel abroad and go on an adventure to Brazil. He would come visit of course—I couldn't be away from him for too long. We were so attached.

But as soon as I was on the plane with the other students in my program (all from other UCs) on the way to Brazil, Tom immediately caught my eye, and I almost surely made up my mind right then and there that I would be with him. He had an undeniable swagger and intelligence about him, plus charisma that Carson didn't embody in the way I thought I wanted. These were the stories I told myself, then at least. Long story short—Carson came to visit me in Brazil, but already I had been there for months, developing a friendship and masking the immense attraction I had toward Tom. I wanted to be with him, but I was too afraid to tell Carson it was over and far too comfortable being in his familiar arms with all the attention I could muster for days on end. He was filling an immense void, and being with him did feel like a drug I didn't want to give up. Letting him go would mean having to feel all the feelings I was avoiding by distracting myself in our connection. The way I remembered history for a long time was that after he came to visit me for a honeymoon-like adventure in paradise, I broke up with him on a Skype call, letting him know that long distance just wasn't working for me anymore and I wanted to move on.

At least that was my chosen way of remembering history until he told me otherwise on the phone that day in the park. He corrected history by letting me know how the infamous Skype breakup call was actually catalyzed in the first place: When he got home from his long trip back to SoCal, he saw on Facebook of all places that my relationship status had changed from being in a relationship with him to being in one with Tom—someone he barely had heard any mention of. He was hurt and confused beyond words. But in my version of reality I developed to suit my desires, I made up a whole other story—it worked quite well to validate my choices.

I was in shock hearing his version of the story. I couldn't believe I had been so selfish, but then again, yes, I could. It made sense that I would do something like that—just like I deleted people out of my life for years to remove any lingering shame or guilt I felt about how I had done wrong by them. The shame and guilt were still there festering, they just weren't in my face as constant reminders when I had to see them again and again. Here was another opportunity to right-size reality—the truth of what really happened was sinking in deeply, and I felt the gravity of my actions and who I was at that time, doing as best I could to take care of myself within the level of consciousness and resources I had available then. Here was an opportunity to have compassion and forgive. I didn't know any better then. But knowing what I know now, I could do my part to make it right and at least take responsibility.

So there I was, parking my rental car on a dark street near the restaurant I was supposed to meet Carson at. I was fueled with some motivation after a really positive conversation with Tom just the other day. Upon hearing him receive my amends, I felt an enormous release of shame and guilt, and he just asked that I continue on my path and keep taking care of myself so as to not repeat these patterns with others. But Carson felt heavier on my heart—I had really done some major damage with him, maybe in the worst ways I had ever done to anyone before. However, I knew what I had to do and I was ready. Now was the time. I walked up to the restaurant and saw him standing there—but he looked so at ease and at peace. I immediately made up the story that he must have been stoned, since how else would he appear so calm while I was a nervous wreck? We went to go order food, and I felt so awkward the entire time—then to make things even worse, the restaurant was cash only and I didn't have any cash so he had to pay! *Great, what's next?* I thought.

We finally got to a table and I wanted to rush into sharing my amends. But before I could complete the sentence, "I have something to share with you," he met me with: "Are you going to make an amends to me?" I was shocked—how could he possibly know why I was there? There's no way he could have known. He then went on to tell me that he had been trying to get sober for a long time and was finally working the steps in recovery—largely thanks to the immense bottom I sent him off to upon breaking up with him in such a hurtful way. We both started tearing up, and I couldn't believe what I was hearing and seeing. He wasn't stoned—he was sober and radiating the peaceful, graceful ease that comes when we start to practice spiritual principles like taking care of ourselves.

This was a miracle, and I was living it in that very moment. Immense shame, guilt, and grief lifted from my being immediately. I saw how every step in our story was meant to be—how even my poor behavior served a higher purpose to help someone else awaken to more of their own truth. I see how we both served a purpose in helping each other heal. I eventually shared my amends even though the healing had already started landing deeply into my system (I imagine for both of us, although I can't fully speak for him). We spent at least another hour or more sharing about our updates, our families, our experiences in sobriety and just catching up. It was so healing to reconnect with this person I had loved and shared so much with. I saw why I had loved him and why he had loved me, and I accepted our story for what it had been and the higher purpose all of our actions inevitably served. I forgave myself for all the wrongs I had done. I could see a whole new reality for my relationships opening up.

Let's Set Ourselves Free

What I learned through making amends was that the story I was holding myself in—usually one of regret, embarrassment, and criticism—actually allowed me to keep repeating the same pattern that led to regret in the first place. This story was revealed to be distorted or exaggerated once I took measures to right-size my view of reality and the story of myself through the eyes of the person I was giving so much energy to by avoiding. We often think that avoidance or escapism is a way toward self-preservation, but really avoidance is the ultimate energy drain and diffusion of our power.

Even the people we are avoiding receive a lot of our energy by nature of how we keep track of hiding from them psychically, let alone on social media, in physical presence or otherwise. The things you try to avoid thinking about are still taking up your energy—right? So continuing to avoid what's inevitably asking you to pay attention to it is quite an illogical loop to stay stuck in when you know you are here to be happy, joyous, free, and thriving.

Sometimes, the most powerful thing that we could ever do for ourselves and for one another is simply be fully present without filling the space with words, without needing to fix anything. This was most clearly exemplified in my life when I initiated a major healing with my parents in which I revealed to them how I had felt for a long time. I unburdened to my mom some of my deepest fears, such as the thought that she didn't like me, even though I knew rationally that she had to love me. I wanted this deep core wound to be resolved; I wanted to let the heaviness go, and I wanted to experience deeper connection and presence with my parents. I wanted to see them beyond the projections I was unknowingly holding them in, based in wounds I wasn't fully aware I was still harboring. The path toward my goal wasn't clear, but I sensed that through pausing and sitting with what feelings were coming up instead of trying to explain or rationalize anything, resolution would emerge.

By being present with my desire while detaching from my agenda of how I thought everything needed to play out—allowing my parents to surprise me in what they had to share—we got to experience a huge healing and return to love together. Even though the opportunity to engage in a trigger with my mom wanted to arise (which, if followed, would give way to arguing and more unresolved tension), I instead chose to take a breath and pause. I stayed with my desire to explore real presence with my parents and from here I got to see them as completely different people. I felt like I saw them as they truly are for the first time. They are simply humans learning and growing—just like me, trying their best. I got to forgive them and have genuine compassion for how they gave me everything they could in raising me even amidst all the density and trauma they've experienced in their lives. And I loved them more for it.

> **"Sometimes a soul learns to love by becoming**
> **what it most despised."**
> **—Brian Weiss**

SELF-LOVE AND FORGIVENESS ATTUNEMENTS

**"Forgiveness is the only energy that travels back in time so
we can let go of the past. All other energy travels to
the present or into the future."
—Dr. Kristopher Martin**

As we explored earlier, what if everything is actually okay? What if there's nothing wrong, and everything you have ever experienced to get right here in this moment as yourself was perfectly part of the plan all along? It's hard to admit it at first, but I get it. Fully accepting the most painful, terrible things that have happened to us over this lifetime is perhaps one of the hardest initiations we'll ever face, and it surely continues as we grow too. As we expand and evolve on our paths into becoming more of who we truly are, our capacity for forgiveness must expand too. We still fall down, but with practice we get up faster and don't get down on ourselves as much about it—or maybe even at all, eventually.

As with everything we've ventured into thus far, forgiveness is indeed a practice that invites us again and again to meet ourselves in depth and authenticity. No matter how big of a supposed mistake that we made, can we love ourselves anyway and completely forgive ourselves for not knowing before what we know now? Can we love our inner child, our little one that feels so bad for letting us down? Can we soothe ourselves with the most compassion and love, trusting ourselves when we say: it's okay, I forgive you and I love you more.

Here are some of my favorite practices for anchoring into self-love and forgiveness, ranging from energetic, inner work to tangible actions that help us shift our entire realities, sometimes overnight. Hopefully when practiced consistently we develop more default muscles and reflexes to forgive ourselves even more quickly and easily, especially as the leaps and risks we take into the great unknown get bigger and bigger. Cultivating forgiveness and unconditional self-love, especially in moments wherein immense regret or shame arise, can ultimately become one of our greater superpowers. We are on a pioneering path to create a future that doesn't exist yet—forgiveness is crucial so we can keep our forward momentum and resilience intact.

Unburdening

Before we do any practices that involve venturing out into the world and making amends or cleaning up our side of the street, I highly suggest spending some intimate time with ourselves and tending to the parts of ourselves that might be feeling overwhelmed with regret, shame, guilt, or other burdens we're carrying from the past. I can't tell you how many times I've encountered in others and in myself this immense heaviness that seems to go infinitely deep, with new layers revealing themselves every so often when we are ready—like a dam waiting to well up and overflow when simply given the opportunity to release. I wonder how many people are walking around the world holding back immense tears and sadness, full of regret for something they are thinking is all their fault, holding themselves in a past story—when all they're waiting for is permission to set themselves free. Here is a practice I love for unburdening ourselves so we can see clearly, make more effective choices and take more aligned actions from here on out.

I refer to this practice as *unburdening* and we love to do this one in our Akashic facilitator training program when we work with multi-dimensional aspects of ourselves through even other lifetimes. This practice is perfect for what we are exploring now too. Whenever you're ready to explore, just know it can be applied to even more complex emotions and experiences that maybe feel more karmic in nature. For this practice (and it might feel familiar to what we reviewed together in timeline healing on page 153 since it is similar), we get into a comfortable position where we can really let go—I like to lay down for this so my body can fully relax and be at complete ease to receive the benefits of the process unfolding. Then in this intentional moment, decide to summon forth in your inner vision a movie-type reel of your life. You can choose to focus on a particular theme (i.e., you can ask to be shown the theme of resentment or regret and all the events in your life where you are still holding this energy), or you can just watch the movie of your life and see how that goes for you—perhaps asking to be shown opportunities wherein you would like to forgive yourself for any regret or burden you're holding from the past. Either way is perfect and you can always try it again to see if focusing in more specifically is more helpful for what you're calling in now.

Then allow the movie of your life to play before your eyes with the intention to be shown opportunities where you can re-experience the past through the lenses of forgiveness and acceptance, unburdening yourself of responsibility that wasn't actually ever yours to hold. Here is your chance to repattern by learning a lesson and completing any energy that's perhaps been hanging on in limbo till now. You'll be shown anything your consciousness has been keeping track of all this time—and you can choose consciously to interact in these particular moments from your present-moment awareness, knowing what you know now, perhaps better equipped to handle these experiences: What can you see clearly now that wasn't accessible then, knowing what you now know in hindsight? What can you surrender that was never yours to hold in the first place? What can you truly forgive yourself (or another) for and let go of that's been held on to till now? Lighten your load and unburden yourself of any weight that's no longer yours to carry, it's time. You might even see yourself or feel yourself carrying a backpack or bag of sorts holding all the burdens you've at some level agreed to hold. Each one you let go of might feel like taking a stone out of the backpack, allowing it to feel lighter and lighter.

You'll be given opportunities to acknowledge and accept yourself for doing the best you could have at that time (or else you would have done differently). How do you forgive yourself for that experience? Do you vocalize an affirmation to yourself—*I understand why you made that choice and it's okay, I accept you, I forgive you, I love and appreciate you. Thanks for taking the chance to learn that difficult lesson. I see how I've grown from that experience and I see how that experience was perfectly designed to teach me what I at the soul level wanted to learn?* It might be as simple as making eye contact with yourself like you're looking in the mirror, conveying energetically: *I love you. I accept you. I forgive you. It's okay.*

You'll know what to do in the moment—see what happens and trust your consciousness to guide you perfectly. If emotions arise, that's perfect—here is the opportunity to allow some stuck stuff to finally move out of your system and integrate accordingly so you can access new sensations and perceptions of yourself and reality. Another invitation into a deeper presence is here. This practice can be energetically intense, so it's good to hydrate after and allow yourself plenty of space to integrate following the process—be mindful of heightened sensitivity and openness and perhaps be discerning of what kinds of inputs you expose yourself to. Feel free to revisit this practice as often as you are called, perhaps exploring working with particular themes in greater specificity as you become more comfortable in this process. There is such rich healing available here—and it's all self-guided. Every time you give yourself this gift of your own presence, healing happens, allowing yourself to feel even more of your own love and building great esteem and heightened sense of worth and value along the way. You deserve your own love more than anyone or anything else. Time to give yourself your own best medicine in just the perfect way you love to receive. What a beautiful gift to give yourself.

Make an Amends, First to Yourself

I shared a few of my experiences with making amends, which is one of the most powerful practices I can imagine actualizing when it comes to building one's innate capacity for self-love, acceptance, and forgiveness. I at first used to think that making amends was all about creating space for others to forgive me, but ultimately what I found was that the entire process of initiating the amends conversation was opening a space for me to completely forgive myself. Now that's not to say I recommend going on an amends-making rampage, contacting everyone you hold some kind of regret with and apologizing profusely. A lot of our process here in embodied ascension has to do with healing extreme reaction patterns and sinking into more presence, which often means becoming more still and moving more slowly and intentionally. Here's a great moment to practice.

Amends can take so many forms—maybe infinite ones at that. A great way to make a beginning in this practice is to begin with yourself: do you feel like you owe an amends to yourself, for a particular wrongdoing perhaps, for something you're deeply regretting doing to yourself (or not doing enough of), or for something you've been holding over your head as a giant mistake, maybe even for years?

If there's something heavy that you realize you've been holding in your awareness, might it be time to let it go? What would it feel like to forgive yourself for the thing you've deemed as a terrible mistake? One of the first amends I made was to myself for not spending enough time alone to really get to know myself and what I enjoyed in life, what I wanted, and how I really preferred to move through and experience life. I had learned to fill all my time with busy-ness and social appointments to the point where I had no time to rest or relax or be alone. I was terrified of being alone, I suppose, which makes sense because at that time it was scary being alone with such loud thoughts playing nonstop in my mind. Anything to avoid the stress of finally listening to the thoughts and feelings play out, please.

So my first amends was to consciously acknowledge this pattern within myself by writing an amends letter in which I took responsibility for not spending time with myself to really connect and heal. I took responsibility for how I was neglecting my self-care and how I sensed that pattern was negatively impacting my overall well-being. I then made a commitment to resolve my behavior and course correct by spending more time in my own space without plans and giving myself more time to rest, plus a few other promises to take better care of myself and really listen to and honor my needs. This is a great place to start. After your new commitments have been put into practice for a while, you can consider tuning in to see if there are other people that you feel a heaviness, regret, or sorrow around when you bring them to mind.

Usually the people we might owe an amends to are reflecting to us a certain pattern or way of being that we have been unconsciously playing out, and it's time to take responsibility, end the pattern, and begin healing (or rather, begin showing up as more of our fully conscious, true selves). To begin this process, write a list of people, ideas, institutions, states of being in the world, and memories that come up when you explore what you feel shame, guilt, sadness, or heaviness around. Then, from your list, focus on one person, place, or thing at a time—and consider giving yourself only about five minutes for this exercise.

Focusing on one aspect, choose to observe yourself in relationship to this person, place, or thing from a distance—like you're looking down at both of you from a bird's-eye view. See your two energy fields meeting and notice what comes up in the process—what other ideas, emotions, energies do you become aware of? What do you wish you could say or express to this person or this thing that would share your heart's desires and any yearning for forgiveness or other acknowledgments? A lot of energy can move in this process, especially when we simply allow ourselves to authentically communicate while being a loving, honest witness without judgment to whatever unfolds.

To close up the practice, you can take a minute or two to reflect: what did you learn from this experience that stimulated the initial heavy feelings? In hindsight, how did this experience help you grow and transform? What do you now know that you didn't before that can support you on your path? Honor yourself for all you've moved through. And most important, forgive yourself. Welcome forth any new commitments that naturally arise from these reflections and make a promise to yourself to honor them in a way that feels authentic (and maybe even fun!).

Discern Your Highest Alignment

A common mistake I see when it comes to making commitments is the habit of over-committing, which can keep us from doing anything at all because the commitment becomes bigger than we are—an insurmountable, impossible task. So, I recommend creating a feasible commitment that might even feel really simple at first but allows in the long run for consistency and momentum, the keys to sustainable transformation.

For example, say you want to support yourself in being more present and clear in your communications across all relationships, so a commitment to meditate every day arises. Instead of saying that you'll meditate every day for twenty minutes forever (which might be an impossible ask), explore how it feels to commit to meditating for five minutes each day for the next five days. See how it goes, and if you honor your commitment fully, celebrate yourself for showing up and then from there, build on a bit more—maybe a few more minutes and a few more days, and slowly by slowly you'll get to where you're going, but sustainably and with more staying power.

What and/or who in your life is presently feeling draining, discouraging, or dense when you feel this aspect in your awareness? Make a note of what appears as heavy or comes with a sense of dread. Given what you've noticed in your awareness, without judgment or criticism, simply notice the heavy feeling associated with this aspect of life and see if you can simply give yourself permission to let the heavy feeling go.

After uncovering this awareness and bringing it into the light, is there any commitment or new way of being you want to hold yourself accountable to? How can you lighten your load even more? How can you shift your behavior or habits to better support your continued feeling of lightness and expansion? As densities are identified in certain parts of the body during this practice, I love to tap lightly on these areas with fingertips or even with a light fist to help move the energy out of the body, while also directing breath into these spaces. It's wonderful what can happen when we allow more space in the body for more of our authentic presence to flow.

Ho'oponopono: I'm Sorry, Please Forgive Me, Thank You, I Love You

A potent practice for embodying the energy of forgiveness comes from the sacred cultural tradition of ancient Hawaii, a land I am blessed to call home. The term Ho'oponopono translates loosely to "cause things to move back into balance" or "make things right." It entails a four-part phrase recitation of: *I'm sorry. Please forgive me. Thank you. I love you.* I love reciting this prayer while focusing attention on myself, on my own heart. After a few minutes of practicing this either silently or out loud with yourself, you can also practice saying it to someone else by picturing them in your mind's eye or by holding them in your heart.

It's amazing how this practice works to dissipate density and literally shift our energy in relationships too—miraculous shifts can occur when this is utilized consistently. Use it with yourself. With others. With institutions. With ways of being and social constructs. You can even use it with different aspects of yourself—such as with yourself at different ages. This practice feels like a way of allowing us to show up more as ourselves without any projections distorting our perception. As with everything—see how it feels for you and if it works, work it and let whatever healing that's meant to happen, happen.

Metta Meditation: Receiving Our Own Love and Radiating It Out

Lastly, I must share a practice that comes back up on my path year after year as one of the simplest yet profound keys to cultivate self-love, forgiveness, and peace. I first learned Metta meditation (which means *love and kindness*) on a silent retreat practicing with teachers from a Buddhist lineage. I'll never forget the sensation of peace and joy anchoring through my entire being during the eight-day silent retreat wherein the main practice was to internally recite the mantra: *May you be peaceful, may you be happy, may you be well, may you be loved.* Sometimes I would even shorten the recitation to simply state, *May you be peaceful,* focusing in depth on each part of the mantra. To recite the mantra for yourself, repeat for a few minutes: *May I be peaceful, may I be happy, may I be well, may I be loved.* For others, change out *I* for *you,* and notice how the two styles are one and the same. When we increase our own flow of self-love and inner peace, we radiate it out to all beings and to the entirety of consciousness. We are one.

7

BEFRIEND THE BODY

Ascension is an inner journey into the body—inviting us, or rather initiating us, to fully inhabit our cells. Perhaps in the past we heard ascension was a path out into the faraway realms, beyond Earth, beyond the body—somewhere far, far away, in another galaxy. What I've heard again and again these last few years is the reminder to recontextualize our Earth journey as one of embodied ascension. This time around we came here to be fully alive, and fully here, and now, as ourselves.

We can no longer proceed through life led solely by the intellect or mental constructs of what we think—key word being *think*—we should be doing (don't *should* on yourself) and what path we think we should be taking (there it is again). The inevitable path back into presence we are all guided to return to now requires us to come into harmonious union—friendship perhaps lands a bit easier—with our bodies. This doesn't happen overnight. For many of us there is significant reparation and healing in this process before we can even consider friendship or harmonious union—that might seem truly like a quantum leap and perhaps it is from where we now stand.

If we were to really feel our bodies, it would be so overwhelming to behold the miracle we are, it seems we would implode to truly take ourselves in at full capacity. At least this has definitely been my experience again and again. The deeper I go into embodiment and the more I see others do the same, the more our senses turn on, the more heightened absolutely every element of our human existence becomes. The miracle of our bodies and their capacities to breathe, feel, move, transmit, love, and live—we can't make sense of it logically. The brain almost seems to break in attempting to conceptualize the magnitude of their power. Do we have the capacity to be ourselves no matter what? Are we in touch with our true, inherent nature? Are we in contact with our soul essence—our inner guidance and knowing that's here to assist us in navigating our choices and best path forward? Part of the answer to all these aforementioned inquiries has everything to do with becoming friends—maybe even best friends—with our bodies. Let's dive in.

OUT OF THE MIND, INTO THE HEART

I don't think I wanted to be here, in a body, for most of my life, without knowing it consciously, of course. How about you? Did you ever have a conscious awareness of your choice to be fully inhabiting your body—or that you are in a relationship with your body at all, to any degree? It seems more common for the average human to be accustomed to living in the mind most of the time, disconnected and really disassociated from what's happening beneath our neck on the whole.

Once we go deeper down in our body awareness, it can get really weird. There's lots of feelings, stuck energy and sensation going on there—so much perception can open up, so much truth can be revealed. There is almost too much to bear if we don't have the capacity to be with it all— the immensity of simply being completely alive. It can feel overwhelming at first to even consider this potential. I get it, I've been there. And even still it can come up—this pattern that's so deeply ingrained in me, that wants to pop out of the body: *Anywhere but here, anything but this feeling, anywhere but this planetary experience. Take me home.*

Hopefully no longer to our dismay, we remember it's time to leave our disassociative tendencies at the door. They served us for a time and yet where we are going, we won't need them anymore. Now, we are here to be deep in the body—to fully inhabit ourselves (our cells). We are here to tune with our emotions, our feelings, our traumas, our sensitivities, our full breadth of perceptions—all of our capacity. We are here to make peace with being infinite spiritual beings in a finite physicality and density. It is here, upon our acceptance of our present fate, that we can truly start to play as the multidimensional beings we are. It is here where our true authentic essence has permission to fully take shape, beyond conditioning, assumed identities or strategies of protection or survival.

Here we drop all trying and effort and simply return to being who we've always been—before we learned to be something else to get something we thought we needed.

"Choice begins the moment you disidentify from the mind and its conditioned patterns, the moment you become present. . . . Until you reach that point, you are unconscious."
—Gabor Maté

Something that comes up for me, even relatively recently, is the feeling of being grossed out at being in a body. The deeper I go into embodiment, into this form, the deeper the layers of unconscious shame, guilt, anger, repression—all the stuck stuff I've hidden away deep down since childhood, or even ancestrally if we want to include that dimension of experience—are residing, waiting to be acknowledged and released. My parents reminded me once that even as a baby, they would find my poops on the ground, hidden around my room because I would climb out of my crib to go to relieve myself instead of having to poop in my diaper and then sit in it. Even as a child I was grossed out by my body's natural functions and felt like its natural expression was something I had to hide and maybe even feel ashamed of. And never mind sexuality—that's a whole other can of worms we'll get into more in our exploration into authenticity, which is our capacity for expression of our sexual and life force energy.

What I've come to settle more into recently is the awareness that as multidimensional beings, it can feel extremely unsettling to be back in a body after what seems to be a long while. It's awkward being contained in a form after existing as our pure energetic essence for what feels like infinity. Of course we're going to have some awkward growing and remembering to do being back in Earth School in these sacred vessels—they take some getting used to. And it's okay to be awkward and stumble along the way. We think being in the body is uncomfortable until we actually learn, practice, and commit to being in it. The moment being in the body becomes comfortable, being in the mind actually becomes uncomfortable.

Secret's out: No one really knows what they're doing here on Earth (we're like angels—just winging it), and if they claim to then you know to really pay attention to how their presence resounds in your being. Does it feel good to listen to them or does something about the way they are feel off? Always trust what feels right to you—your body is a barometer for truth, remember? You know what is true by the way it feels for you. The more attuned we become to ourselves and our desires, wants, and needs—and the more we give ourselves all we require to feel safe and supported, the more easily we can discern truth in the world around us.

THE BODY TALKS, HERE'S HOW TO LISTEN

I only came into considering my body as its own being—one that I was here to get to know and even become intimately acquainted with—over the last few years. Something shifted around 2018, toward the end of the year, that felt like a collective invitation to drop into the body even deeper. I had been practicing yoga for over a decade and even teaching for a few years. I'd done numerous meditation retreats, had been a practicing intuitive energy healer, and thought I knew a thing or two about embodiment. I had even written a book about empaths and emotional-energetic mastery. But there was so much more I wasn't seeing. Not sure what came first here—the realization of what was missing or a deeper awakening into how much further the embodiment process goes. Trick question, perhaps: as I travel along the path, the embodiment process seems to reveal itself as a truly infinite journey unique to each and every one of us.

One thing I notice to be universal though—it seems, for where we are going in our ascension process, we must come to terms with our bodies as their own sovereign beings that require our support and nurturance in unique ways. Becoming intimate with our bodies and learning to listen to what they are communicating to us in every moment is perhaps one of the greatest skills one can develop on our ascension path. Our body has so much untapped wisdom that we've learned strategically to tune out in order to follow the status quo, to fit into our families, to turn our light down so as to not upset anyone or make them uncomfortable, or for a multitude of other reasons we can all relate to.

Here we consider a bit of a paradox—but isn't everything in our human existence somewhat paradoxical when we really start to explore it more deeply? Seems to be the nature of the universe's way of playing with us, always reminding us to tread lightly on our paths—enjoy the show, perhaps it's all just a dream. Yet we are creating it all, so we might as well make it good. Is ascension actually more of a descension process inherently? Instead of ascending up and out of the body into a faraway celestial realm free from Earth and the densities of human existence at last, perhaps we find ourselves now invited to sink deeper into the body, into the cells, into our core, even into the Earth. Here we create space in our physical form for our spirits, souls, essence-divinity-consciousness to come into form and express ourselves in the material plane. Here is the point from which we descend out of the mind and its limited capacities to weave in reality and into the heart—which holds a truly infinite capacity to feel, love, express, transmit, and radiate desires, imagination, creativity, life force, all of who we are.

There is a Sioux Indian parable that reminds us: the longest journey you will make in your life is from your head to your heart. Even our ancient ancestor brothers and sisters knew the same fate we still face here on our Earth—which feels reassuring, I suppose. They were surrounded by nature and much more connected with the elemental world and spirit, yet they still faced a similar challenge. So how do we make a beginning in listening to the heart, especially if we've been entrapped in the mind and its survival programming for so long?

First, we start by acknowledging that we have a mind, and a body, and a heart—and a spirit. We can consider that these elements of our beings (like many bodies in one) want to operate in more coherence and unity. We consider what embodiment means for us and if it is something we truly want to take on. We consider—do I want to live in my heart? Do I want to open myself to more feeling, intuition, and life led more by my creative essence? Here we venture forth into more intimacy with our inner being and authenticity of our true selves shining through.

How Trapped Energy Expresses Itself Physically

Working as an energy healer and intuitive over the years has shown me again and again the universal commonality we all share regardless of background or context or conditioning—we are all conduits for energy, and if we don't allow our energy to flow, it gets stuck and manifests as physical ailments that simply want us to pay attention.

You might be aware of the chakra system, a reference from Eastern healing tradition and spirituality that symbolizes the energy centers of our body. This system is referenced in more traditions than I can mention, but it first came into my awareness through yoga, as the chakra system is a guiding light inspiring the shapes, movement, and intention of all asanas and pranayama throughout all yogic practices. There are actually more chakras that we can count—some would say upward of hundreds of thousands, and another reference I am familiar with says 144,000 chakras exist throughout the entire body and energetic field. For our purposes here we can keep it simple and stick to the central seven, which are located along the central channel of our spine, also known as the *sushumna* in Sanskrit.

Let's start at the base of the spine, known as the root. This energy center is associated with the color red and connects us with emotions and energetics surrounding home, safety, security, and a sense of rootedness in our own beings. This energy center also has to do with existence itself—and how embodied or fully in our bodies we allow ourselves to be. In our modern world it's common for many people to be heavily oriented in the mind which articulates most prominently within the upper chakras, spanning the throat, third eye, and crown.

Often in coming into awakening it can be a jarring experience to become aware that you are in an entire body and not just your mind. Not to mention, you have new feelings and emotions accessible to you from these deeper layers of your being, and your breath can go much deeper than you ever thought possible. The fun part of this is that when you start learning—and yes, it's a practice indeed—to breathe all the way in, you can miraculously begin to heal and release trauma sometimes effortlessly. Breathing deeply signals the body's autonomic nervous system to go into healing and restoration mode, during which cleansing and detoxing from heaviness and density is a natural by-product.

There are entire books that focus on the chakra system, so I won't go into immense depth on all the chakras here, but I do feel it's important to contextualize our energetic body more clearly so you can see the connection between the mind-body-spirit-intuitive and energetic planes we reference in literally each step in our awakening path. In case you want to go deeper in your study of chakras, check out two of my favorite references: Anodea Judith's *The Wheels of Life: The Classic Guide to the Chakra System,* which we studied in yoga training, and Echo Bodine's *Hands that Heal,* which was a core text of my reiki energy healing training.

Energetic imbalances can manifest as physical ailments to get our attention to feel an emotion fully and release it. The body is genius in the way it communicates the precise signals required to catalyze our highest potential healing and integration. A common example of this would be the issue of back problems which is a pain that most people have experienced at some level. With this symptom in particular, the pain and discomfort usually energetically correlate to a deeply felt fear that you'll fail or that you're not supported by life or by the universe, giving way to an overwhelming energetic sensation that you're carrying a heavy load all by yourself (weighing down your back and body).

Another common pain I see often orients in the chest as tightness, pressure, or sensitivity that literally feels like a heavy heart, usually most often being weighed down by insurmountable grief or guilt. I wonder how many people go to the doctor thinking they have a heart problem that Western medicine can somehow treat with a prescription pill when really underlying their pain is emotional baggage yearning to be felt and released. It's so incredible what happens when we start to feel these feelings we've been unknowingly holding on to when we let them go and actually release.

Our bodies tend to change astronomically, following suit. Suddenly, our entire posture can be different, the way we walk can change, and even our voice can start to emanate a different intonation. I'm celebrating all the changes I've witnessed firsthand in myself and others—people being born before my eyes—when we allow ourselves to feel the burdens that are no longer ours to carry.

What Your Emotions Are Really Saying

"Studies show that most emotions last no longer than ninety seconds unless we attach stories to them. You have a feeling of being lonely—and this will pass through you quickly unless

you make up a story about how you're lonely because you're unlovable and worthless and nobody will ever love you and you're going to be alone forever. When you attach to the story, you suffer needlessly and the suffering can linger for years. But you don't have to choose to suffer this way. Your soul can find peace, comfort, and stillness even in the most difficult times if you're able to view your negative emotions from this witness position."
—Lissa Rankin

Our emotions are always guiding us to come more into the present moment. Especially negative, charged emotions—these are showing us what to tend to in our immediate state of being regarding energies, experiences, and beliefs we're still holding on to, effectively keeping ourselves in the past or future instead of right here and now.

Remembering what the Buddha said in similar terms (one of my favorites because it's so simple and true to the point): "Holding on to anger is like drinking poison and expecting the other person to die." Similarly, I've come to learn that anger is actually closely connected to creativity and desire—whatever you're angry about is a gateway to passion and to unlocking more creative desire and expression that wants to be shared. What about life lights you up the most—that whenever you come into contact with this element or concept of reality, you feel an immediate fervor and ignited fire within? Whatever you feel most passionate about is a key to healing your anger and transmuting it into creative vital energy. Following a resonant thread, whenever you feel guilty, you are still holding yourself accountable to living up to other people's expectations of you instead of living on your own terms. Your anxiety is guiding you to awaken more fully into this present moment, because anxiety only happens when you're regretting the past or worrying about the future unknown.

Another common example I've seen in myself and others is jaw tension, teeth, and gum problems. I've actually been in a healing process of my own when it comes to these particular aspects of the physical and energetic bodies, and the emotional healing process has certainly been humbling. The wounding of a deeply felt injustice seems to be at play here: stress, back problems, digestion problems, worry about things not working out, and an inability to relax without feeling guilty all impact throat and third eye chakras. Inflammation and skin problems, especially in teeth and gums, have to do with worthiness and worrying about how you're seen in the world and how you can digest reality. Do you relate?

Some other examples of how our core wounds and repressed traumas play out in the body to get our attention to attune to deeper emotional and underlying spiritual healing are as follows: Betrayal can manifest in the body as stomach issues, liver issues, and inflammation as a result of high stress and an agitated immune system response. Abandonment can be witnessed as poor posture or a protective stance, and one can even physically move in a childlike way that feels disorienting. Abandonment wounds, until resolved, can also materialize as being vulnerable to viruses, migraines, storing excess fat, and infections; anything to get attention, to be seen, to be cared for—to have a purpose to heal and tend to oneself. Rejection embodied can tend to result in the body having a thinner stature, signaling how a person finds it a challenge to be completely here, to feel like they completely exist or that they can be completely embodied. This one also tends to manifest as skin problems, which can also be a manifestation of anger and resentment—the heat underlying those emotions is not fully able to leave the body and results in acne or inflammation usually with a reddish, firey tone. I know these all too well since I myself have experienced them and have learned through all these years of healing that the root of all disease in the body, no matter how it presents superficially, almost always has an underlying energetic or psycho-spiritual root cause.

Could we imagine that all disease, all illness and mental maladies are simply perhaps spiritual wounds wanting to be healed? Could you imagine cancer is a manifestation of anger and resentment begging your forgiveness and inevitable transmutation therein? That depression and mania and even addiction are all advents of repressed energy and brilliant creativity not being channeled in alignment with your soul's desires? Consider how, as Lissa Rankin explains in *The Fear Cure,* "The body is equipped with a fight-or-flight response, a survival mechanism that gets flipped on when your brain perceives a threat. When this hormonal cascade is triggered by a thought or emotion in the mind, such as fear, the hypothalamic-pituitary-adrenocortical (HPA) axis activates, thereby stimulating the sympathetic nervous system to race into overdrive, pumping up the body's cortisol and adrenaline levels. Filling the body with these stress hormones can manifest as physical symptoms, predisposing the body to disease over time."

Autoimmune diseases and viruses are usually rooted in self-hatred, wherein the body attacks itself—but why? The reasons may be innumerable, yet when you honestly face the truth of who you are and what meaning you're making about you and your life, can you see how you've had the power to heal all along? Can you see how aches and pains in the body are simply signs to get your attention? When you tune into the underlying message your body is signaling to you, what can you hear? You are not a symptom.

Society and the entirety of particular institutions dependent on you believing otherwise have conditioned us en masse to focus on such superficiality and diagnoses instead of going to the root of true healing and liberation. Perhaps society is dependent upon sickness; after all, if everyone was fully alive and thriving, how different would our world be? One of my favorite teachers on intuition and healing, Carolyn Myss, reminds us in *Anatomy of the Spirit* how: "Our emotions reside physically in our bodies and interact with our cells and tissues. . . . Energy is power, and transmitting energy into the past by dwelling on painful events drains power from your present-day body and can lead to illness. The requirements to heal any illness are essentially the same. Think of the illness as a power disorder—almost like a technical malfunction. Once you identify which sacred truth applies to your situation, organize your internal healing process around learning from that truth. That which serves our spirits enhances our bodies. That which diminishes our spirits diminishes our bodies."

Diagnoses prevent inquiry that can give way to true root cause resolution. Diagnoses and quick conclusions based on superficial symptoms prevent us from being curious and therefore open to divine intervention and genius when it comes to excavating the truth of what underlying root cause wants to naturally be revealed, made conscious, and integrated so you can be free. Instead of thinking you're sick or that you have a symptom, what's it like to go a few levels deeper and ask: What message is my body attempting to communicate? What deeper truth is wanting to be revealed? What in me wants to be seen and heard and finally felt all the way to heal? How can I hold myself in such reverence as the divine being I am, knowing I am perfect, whole, and complete now and in every moment?

I understand that what I am sharing here may feel confronting or controversial especially given all we are taught about Western medicine, pharmaceuticals, and the massive advertising and marketing agendas therein that infiltrate deeply into every facet of our society. Plus, being taught we can just take a pill to make our problems simply go away sure sounds a lot more appealing than sitting in discomfort or immense pain and taking full responsibility for unconscious material we may be invited to reconcile within ourselves (for ourselves or for our ancestral line, or even some combination of the two). It's a lot to take on, and it can feel scary and overwhelming to consider, especially if we still feel confronted by our own power, our own aliveness, our own full potential to be fully thriving in optimal well-being. What kind of life would we be living, what choices would we make, if our health was thriving at optimal capacity? If we were more present to tend to our true passions and callings, how would our entire reality be different?

Lastly, I am sharing my own experience from my healing path and from what I've seen work for hundreds of others I've had the honor of walking alongside through similar inquiries and transformations. When we are willing to look beneath the surface of what others say, of what society says, of what any stories outside of ourselves say, and instead listen to what we know to be true, even if it feels like a faint whisper coming from within at first, there is hope for radical change at the cellular and DNA level. There have been times, admittedly, where I still go to the doctor for an antibiotic or a medicine if absolutely needed, even if it's usually my last stop on the block to do so. Sometimes it isn't useful to spend hours exploring why the recurring yeast infection, UTI, or surprising case of strep throat may be rooted in an unconscious trauma that is trying to get my attention to heal—sometimes I just need to take the antibiotic that will kick the unwanted material out of my system and give me a chance to recalibrate amid greater clarity.

This is where our discernment is called for—we know our best medicine and what will work best for our bodies as long as we are listening and re-sponding accurately to what's being asked of us. As with everything, herein lies another inherent paradox, and an opportunity to surf in the space between right and wrong, black and white. Maybe just be in the gray for now and stay curious, stay present: What's my body telling me now? How can I support myself now? What would optimal health and well-being feel like and how can I tap into that state more fully, with what I have at my disposal now? What's something I would love to receive that would support me to feel more nourished, cared for, loved, seen, and affirmed in my existence? Keep listening.

There's so much more that could be said about this can of worms I am offering up for us to explore here—especially given the health crises and global consciousness around medicine of the last few years. Maybe we don't need more answers but really better questions that instead guide us into new, more expansive potentials that can actually support our con-sciousness and bodies to thrive in the ways they are designed to move in this reality. One of the biggest practices and lessons of this time here on Earth (to me at least) seems to be about attuning to deeper respect and reverence for what others choose to do with their bodies—to honor each individual's truth and choices as to how their actions express their truth.

The body is such a vunerable topic—it taps us into our inherent mor-tality and understandably brings up all kinds of edges of our intimacy with life: Are we truly living? Are we truly in the body? Why does it matter what other people do with their bodies—does that actually affect me or why would it appear that it does? What would it be like to live in a world where we can each and all feel safe and supported to have and share unique worldviews and opinions and enact choices that express those views authentically—without fear of judgment or an expectation that we'd ever need to prove ourselves as right or wrong? What if our evolution is inviting us into such presence that all truths are different, and inherently unique, but coexist in such a complementary way that we support and inspire each other to continue evolving and expanding into even greater authenticity—beyond any binary limitations of supposed past constructs of right or wrong? I wonder what kind of world we'd enjoy when we are operating at this level of emotional maturity, self-understanding, and groundedness in our own unique knowingness.

"Intuition is a spiritual faculty and does not explain, but simply points the way. As man becomes spiritually awakened he recognizes that any external inharmony is the correspondence of mental inharmony. If he stumbles or falls, he may know he is stumbling or falling in consciousness. All power is given to man (through right thinking) to bring his heaven upon his earth, and this is the goal of the Game of Life."
—Florence Scovel Shinn

OUR MULTIDIMENSIONAL BODY

To understand how the body is a portal, we must consider the different layers of our bodies we get to play with in this life—yes, that's right: there's much more going on here than most of us were ever taught to even consider. A framework I love orienting in is the idea that our bodies are made up of various layers that make up the whole: a mental body, a physical body, an emotional body, and an etheric or spiritual body. Most of us are immediately conditioned upon arrival to Earth to orient within the mental and physical bodies. We see the world through the mind's eye and we know we can move and function generally to get through life and survive using our bodies' basic features and capacities. But what about when it comes to thriving—creating depth in relationships, establishing emotional intimacy within ourselves and with each other, attuning to our intuition and inner guidance, building a body that feels safe and holds a high discernment of trust and truth, and so much more?

Our ascension journey invites us to become more intimate with the aspects of ourselves that society and most of our cultures at large have left out. The emotional and etheric bodies hold so many keys for us to connect with our true selves, our incredible creative capacities, our spiritual abilities and incredible support when it comes to living our aligned purpose and mission and expressing the unique gifts we came here in this life to experience and share. An entire book could be written about this subject

alone, and actually there already are a few great ones that I'll recommend
in our resources section for you to explore if you're called—I don't want
to repeat or recreate the wheel of great works that already are templating
these awarenesses so beautifully and with such precise articulation. Instead I'll offer my perhaps somewhat unique perspective on embodiment
and integration of our multiple body layers woven into how we make the
move from the head to the heart.

The key I've found again and again in this path is to connect with
our inner child. Can we imagine that the body is actually an energetic
representation of our inner child or that the body could be considered
as a child in and of itself? When we start to befriend the body, in our
unique way, we come into relationship with it as a vulnerable, usually
more infantile-feeling being that is requesting our assistance to support
its journey on Earth. The body is asking for our help—the help of our
higher selves, our spirit, the version of us that knows all is well and trusts
our intuitive guidance that always knows our destiny is bound to unfold
with grace, ease, and efficiency.

Sound a bit out there? I know, it did for me at first too, which was
just my resistance showing up to block deeper layers of intimacy and
self-actualization from taking form. My ego knew that if I was to truly
befriend my body and step into this new dimension of responsibility, my
life and path ahead would never be the same. But now we know—we are
here to change and grow, inevitably, and more than anything, we are here
to become more comfortable and familiar with this very fact. We learn
to expect it—we inevitably resist change and then we welcome our true
selves to interject and give ourselves a pep talk about why transformation
is invited. We walk through the door into another new reality, each time
making it a bit more fun than the last.

The Body Is a Portal to Our Unconscious
Mind and Inner Child

What comes to mind when you think of yourself at a particular age as
you summon forth your inner child? Feel into your heart that energy
of beingness, the loving, innocent, divine child that is you, that is the
essence of who you are, that is the seed of your soul, that is your genius

embodied. That is the part of you that knows no illusion; that knows no scarcity, no fear, no separation; that knows no trauma; that is complete and utter innocence, and complete pure presence.

Think of the way children play. Think of the way children express themselves. Think of the way children tell the truth, unadulterated, unconditioned, free, liberated, divinity embodied: that is you. Connect with that part of you that you know is inside of you now. Trust me, it gets easier with practice. This part of us exists in a different dimension. It's transcendent of our intellectual mind and it really speaks to us through feeling, through intuition, and especially through good feelings.

Oftentimes we are operating on autopilot with various core wound imprints, fueled by unresolved traumatic memories that likely occurred between the ages of zero and seven, determining the course of our lives. During that time in our childhood we are in a hypnotic trance and are literally like sponges; information and data are downloading into us from every dimension of our reality. Even a seemingly subtle experience in your family—for example, you make an exchange mean something about you that then gets programmed at a deep level in your brain—cements you into a survival pattern. You get programmed into letting that meaning validate a belief that could last you your whole life as a survival mechanism to protect yourself—until you become aware of the wound and consciously choose to restore your capacity to exit autopilot, come into presence, and discern what next right step you want to take.

We have this part of our brain that's very connected to our limbic system and therefore all body systems. Remember when we dove deep into understanding the limbic system and lizard brain a few chapters back? Here we are again—still dealing with this remnant part of our bodies inherited from millions of years ago. So, why do we have this part of our brain that's still looming from so long ago? Why have we not evolved out of it? I've come to terms with this reality by simply reminding myself that we have something to learn from it still—otherwise it wouldn't be showing up in our experience so prominently. For me, the lizard brain is connected to our ego-self as well—the aspect that wants to protect, survive, avoid change, and stay secure in known, controllable facts no matter that. The lizard brain, like our ego, wants us to be safe—even if it means staying in the same pattern just because it's familiar and our brain knows what to do and feels like it has control. Let's just say, our lizard brain isn't wired for conscious evolution and expansion.

By now we've established that we're dealing with a lot of unacknowledged (or stuck) stuff (emotional energy, beliefs, memories) in our physical bodies. And it almost seems like the whole system is rigged for our bodies (and our realities) to develop certain ways to get our attention so we can heal ourselves at the root. The lizard brain however isn't necessarily part of the solution when it comes to processing our unconsciousness from presence as an empowered observer and self-healer. No, the truth is we have a reptilian brain from a hundred million years ago that's had lifetimes of practice in refining its keen ability to keep us alive in the very literal sense—from life or death situations where it was kill or be killed, eat or be eaten. This aspect of our wiring even still to this day works very intently to keep us alive in many ways we don't actually need to worry about surviving since we've never been more safe or more resourced than now. So, what do we do with that?

First of all, let's acknowledge how we've all experienced trauma, like being born in a physical body, especially if we were born in an American hospital with bright fluorescent lights, metallic, industrial sharp-edged furniture, and stress everywhere you look. That's the ultimate trauma: Where am I? This light is too bright! Why is someone smacking me? What is this body, these feelings, these smells and sounds? So much gets set into place pattern-wise in these early moments, before we even take our first breath of air.

The entire gestation process, sometimes referred to in somatic experiencing and pre- and perinatal therapy as *sequencing* (which we explored a bit earlier on), can inform the pacing and ordering of how we approach the creative process within and throughout our entire lives. As we start to come into deeper awareness of our physical bodies and all the wisdom and guidance they hold for us, we understand more about how we are wired to create and move through life as the unique expressions we were meant to be.

Let's consider some helpful wisdom and more clear context expertly provided by Gabor Maté in one of my favorite books on understanding trauma and the body, *When the Body Says No*:

> Emotional competence requires the capacity to feel our emotions, so
> that we are aware when we are experiencing stress; the ability to express

our emotions effectively and thereby to assert our needs and to maintain the integrity of our emotional boundaries; the facility to distinguish between psychological reactions that are pertinent to the present situation and those that represent residue from the past.

What we want and demand from the world needs to conform to our present needs, not to unconscious, unsatisfied needs from childhood. If distinctions between past and present blur, we will perceive loss or the threat of loss where none exists; and the awareness of those genuine needs that do require satisfaction, rather than their repression for the sake of gaining the acceptance or approval of others.

Stress occurs in the absence of these criteria, and it leads to the disruption of homeostasis. Chronic disruption results in ill health. In each of the individual histories of illness in this book, one or more aspects of emotional competence was significantly compromised, usually in ways entirely unknown to the person involved.

Emotional competence is what we need to develop if we are to protect ourselves from the hidden stresses that create a risk to health, and it is what we need to regain if we are to heal. We need to foster emotional competence in our children, as the best preventive medicine.

A PORTAL INTO HEAVEN ON EARTH

Here we explore what embodiment really means and why now we are invited to seriously become best friends with our bodies, probably in a way we never have before. So what does it mean? Well, it's spelled out in the way it sounds—in-body-ment. From here we wonder and consider from multiple angles: what does it feel like to be fully in the body, and why do we want to be here, all the way, anyway? It might seem like a weird concept, completely understandable if it does. We'll get more into this throughout this chapter and in those following.

When we are so accustomed to orienting to reality from a linear, intellectual perspective, it can feel odd at first to start feeling more into other parts of the body and cells that we've never before given much attention to. We can start to consider that perhaps we've been so intellectually oriented to protect ourselves from feeling and processing fully the

trauma and painful memories that are stored in the body. When we allow ourselves to befriend the body and provide a safe space for feelings to be felt, true freedom emerges.

We consider how our entire lives have conditioned us to orient to the world from an externalized mind-centered space, so turning inward and really feeling and sensing in new ways can bring a whole new set of challenges along our ascension process. But we are continuously reminded along our path how ascension truly is an inside job. We also entertain how the body represents the subconscious mind and the archetype of the inner child. When we can be loving and supportive to our body and provide a safe, nourishing space for it to thrive, we start to see—oftentimes quickly—how our reality shifts in beautiful, sometimes surprisingly expansive ways.

In our awakening process it is inevitable that we start to allow our spirit and consciousness to descend more into the body so more of our senses and perceptual capacities turn on. We learn how our intuition is accessed through the body and how as we develop a deeper connection to our physical form and senses therein we naturally attune more powerfully to our magnetism, higher guidance, and alignment with purpose and our path.

I heard recently: "You are the ancestor that rewrites your family's cellular blueprint," and it resonated so deeply in my heart as the truth we are all invited to consider in this moment—perhaps a key into why we are truly here and what our path ahead initiates us even further into. On this same note, one of my favorite visionaries, creator of *The Gene Keys,* Richard Rudd, reminds us so powerfully that:

What most people don't realize is that as a salt, DNA is a natural conductor of electricity. It is extremely sensitive to electromagnetic waves. Even a slight shift in your mood will create enough of an environmental signal to trigger a response from your DNA. Likewise a negative or a positive thought will generate a subtle electromagnetic current throughout your body that will stir your DNA into some form of biological response. Most of us are completely unaware of how our moods, thoughts, beliefs, and general attitude literally mold our bodies. What all of this means is that you can never be a victim of your DNA. Neither can you be a victim of fate. You can only be a victim of your attitude. Every thought you think, every feeling you have, every word you utter, and every action you take directly programs your genes and therefore your reality. Consequently, at a quantum level, you create the environment that programs your genes. No matter how positive you try to be in life, if you do not become fully aware of your own Shadow frequency patterns—your so-called dark side—you will never be able to unlock the higher frequencies. . . . This also means that as your frequency becomes higher and higher, you have to process deeper and deeper Shadow patterns that come from our collective ancestral past.

Energy is moving faster than we've ever experienced before on Earth in bodies like this. A whole new operating system is landing. It is the system supporting the divine human blueprint to actualize into embodiment. It is the preparation for our multidimensional capacities, perceptions, and mastery to come fully online—in ways we never before imagined. We are becoming clear conduits for light that can create literally anything. Ideas are flowing faster too—we are receiving more pieces to the puzzle of the vision we are here to build into form.

Our world—its social structure, economy, governance, health care, education, everything it's made of—is ready for redesign, and we are here in this incarnation to sow the seeds of this new architecture, setting the stage for the next few thousands of years. We are no small feat, we humans. Many of us have struggled with addiction, depression, thoughts of suicide, disassociation, and worse plus immense childhood trauma, all to prepare us to cultivate the resiliency to lead in the way we are now invited to lead.

We have learned through contrast what true unconditional love is and what presence and authenticity actually feel like. In a way we have learned universal law from an embodied perspective by way of the extremes we've experienced. From our pain arises a deep knowing that cannot be taught. Many higher dimensional beings are taking on human form and many of us are receiving our own additional higher dimensional aspects now. We are remembering other languages, symbols, technologies, ways of being and seeing, and so much more.

There is an immense integration process in this embodiment in most cases. I have prepared many lifetimes for this and am ready to be of assistance to those called in to resonance. We were already destined to co-create, I am simply affirming the call and knowing here and now. I am prepared to assist with energetic integration and attunement, memory recalibration, purpose alignment, and vision execution. I am here, I am grateful you are here too. Let's build it and be it—Heaven on Earth. It's time.

> **"The mind is the place the soul goes to hide from the heart."**
> **—Michael Singer**

EMBODIMENT ATTUNEMENTS

The most important element of embodiment practice is finding a practice you love and making it your own. We can even easily do our practices on autopilot—so what are practices, or rituals rather, that you love, look forward to, and welcome in to enrich your life on a daily basis? My first daily practices consisted of trying as hard as I could to sit still for even a few minutes of mindfulness. My mind went crazy at the time and I couldn't shut it off, which is what I thought I was supposed to do based on everything I had heard about meditation. What I learned eventually was that my preferred style of meditation was actually movement-based, what a revelation.

My mind was so active, it took really getting into my body, breathing heavily, and moving so much that my full focus was required in presence to feel into a meditative state. Yoga, running, high intensity workouts, and dancing were all my favorite ways to meditate, and committing to these expressions on a regular basis helped me so much, especially early on in my recovery, when I was just starting to come online in my consciousness and embodiment. Never mind everything else you've heard about what meditation is—it's simply a way of practicing presence in the moment no matter what you are doing. So why not choose to intentionally practice activities or rituals you love that encourage you naturally to cultivate more presence and therefore embodiment within your true self?

In, Back, and Down

I'll never forget the moment when I met my somatic therapist (she's also a lot like my cosmic mom) for the first time and felt the most profound level of presence held by another (even palpable through a remote Zoom meeting on the computer). I could feel my own disassociation more clearly than ever before. I had already been teaching about consciousness and embodiment for years and thought I had some wisdom codes to share—but it wasn't until starting our work together that my true nervous system healing path and repatterning really began to take shape. My whole reality would go on to shift every step of the way as I learned to develop the capacity to feel all the layers I was unconsciously repressing for my entire life.

Slowly I began to let them go and feel the trapped energies—with loving supportive presence held, I could slowly move through the sometimes tumultuous layers that no words could describe while the tears flowed for what felt like eternity. I had spent—exhausted, really—so much energy holding certain feelings in, and it was time to "off-gas" them, as I described. That's what the energy felt like as it released, like valves opening up and finally letting out the pressurized steam that was trapped in my body from what seemed like since birth. Maybe some of it wasn't even mine, but I took it on at such a young age from those around that it became part of my structure and subsequent identities and reactionary patterns throughout my life. Letting go of the fear, shame, guilt, grief, and anger means letting the survival, trauma body finally settle and release. So that the underlying true essence of your being can come more into form, become more accessible in the forefront of your consciousness.

The practice I can share for supporting this process of letting go into deeper embodiment, however simple it sounds, is profound and entails just a few steps. Try this for a few moments and see how it feels. First we will explore coming intentionally INto the body: bring your awareness all the way into your body—with your breath, by sensing your essence in your fingers and toes, all the way at the base of your spine. Pause here: What's it all feel like? How's energy flowing through your system? If it's difficult to sense so far, that's okay. See if you're open to continue practicing and celebrate any new awareness that comes online as you continue—even if over days, weeks, or longer. You're on your own timeline and there's no mistakes—just more learning and exploration of your body and the unique way energy wants to flow through you.

After exploring the IN directive and calling yourself all the way in, what's it like to bring your awareness of your energy field all the way back? Oftentimes we project our energy out to the front of our body to protect and track the environment around us while also putting our energy out into the world through doing and lots of action. But we can consciously call our energy back—all the way to the back of our body—and feel our energy field evening out along the back part of us, providing that support and more balanced circulation of energy. This can at first feel like such a game changer. Can you rest into the containment of your own energy field, supporting you like a chair or a comfy, padded, cloudlike body of light holding you up? Can you settle more into this knowing that your energy field is containing your entire being and it can feel like a protective bubble made just for you? Explore and see how this feels.

The final step may feel a bit repetitive with the IN directive, but give it a try anyway after following IN and BACK steps. What's it like to call yourself even further DOWN into your body and energy field? Can you feel yourself again in your fingertips, toes, and at the base of your spine? Does anything feel different trying this now after first practicing calling yourself in and back? Continue exploring and seeing how your energy can move in different ways when you bring conscious awareness to it. Let the process be gentle and as slow as you need to go— your pace is perfect, and remember, there's nowhere to get to except deeper into now: this present moment, as you. I've been amazed at how helpful this practice is when done consistently. Now whenever I feel my energy getting pulled in a certain direction; before an important meeting, presentation, or call, especially; or simply whenever I want to feel more embodied and connected into my own sense of grounded center and stability—I can take a few minutes or seconds and follow the IN, BACK, and DOWN steps to bring my energy all the way home. It's wonderful how different reality can feel when we orient from this center point of our true selves.

Higher Self Embodiment

One of my favorite activations for cultivating our embodiment and feeling of being truly at home in the body as our authentic selves is to inquire within ourselves: what is the physiology and posturing of your higher self? Visualize your higher self, your true self, your divinity— whatever avatar of your being you want to embody more qualities of in this present moment. How do you stand, how do you walk, how do you speak, how does your energy feel? What details do you notice about how this being shows up in the world? What is their expression? Notice what details come to mind—are they firmly grounded, calm, standing up straight, and breathing deeply? Is their heart open, face relaxed, and are their eyes wide? See what it feels like to practice embodying these qualities now, almost like you are playing dress-up or donning the costume of another character you want to explore. Remember, it's all a game anyway—we can't mess it up so might as well make it fun.

Inner Child Embodiment

Similarly, you can do a practice like this with your inner child to strengthen the connection with your little one, who fuels so much fire in your creative, authentic spirit. How does your inner child present themselves when you connect—what is their energy like, what is their posture, how are they dressed, what is their facial expression, what is their speech like? The magic of this practice is that in moments of threat or fear, we can actually supersede the mind's automatic, trauma-based reactions by tuning in with our bodies and activating the posture and energy of our higher selves or inner child selves (or both at the same time if that's accessible) to feel immediately more present, safe, and established in our own center, no matter what's happening around us. The mind catches up eventually with the energy the body is holding, and just like this we can bypass the mind's conditioned reactions, which often keep us in looping cycles of trauma response when really, we're ready for something new. With practice in becoming more attuned to our body's conditioned responses to life, we can interrupt the autopilot reactions and start making more clear, discerning choices with full conscious awareness.

Bodywork and Energy Work

In our ascension journey while we are integrating so much energy on a regular basis and healing our cellular memory, I can't recommend receiving some form of bodywork or energy work on a regular basis enough. I myself have amassed a bit of a reputation for having a team of support in this dimension. Since I am giving so much, it's absolutely essential I am allowing myself adequate space to receive as well. One of the most powerful healing experiences one can have is working with a trusted practitioner who can hold space for your body to feel relaxed enough to deeply let go and surrender—especially when it comes to nervous system healing and attunement to deeper states of trust and safety within. I personally regularly receive acupuncture, deep tissue massages (super helpful for cleansing trauma and cellular memory to allow for more space for presence and authenticity), craniosacral therapy (great for nervous system healing and attuning for deeper states of relaxation and calm), and colon hydrotherapy (to cleanse the gut and balance out the body's flora and capacity to digest and metabolize in a healthy, easeful way). I also love to receive facials and spend time in infrared saunas and cold plunges as well as hot tubs when available.

Some people are afraid to receive bodywork. My parents, for example, never let me get them massage gift certificates, I think because they don't really enjoy being touched, perhaps because they weren't lovingly touched enough by their parents growing up. This brings up a larger issue in humanity right now: how many people are living with an extreme lack of nourishing, loving, healing, safe touch? Don't get me started on the over-sexualization of touch and how that gets in the way of creating safe, loving, healing space to simply receive and regulate and co-regulate our nervous systems. We'll get more into that in our forthcoming chapters, promise. But really—so much of our lives we're conditioned to live in the mind and walk through life hyperactive and hypervigilant. Our bodies are literally buzzing with anxiety and adrenaline, and it's not our fault because this is largely what's displayed in most examples of other people we are seeing around us.

Receive Loving Touch (and Give It to Yourself)

It's a dominant template for society—the alpha, get-it-done, hustle-harder mentality that's uber-strong and in many ways isolated from the softer, feminine, receptive way of being that so many of us are awakening in order to find more balance within. So here's a challenge—do you feel a desire to receive more loving, nourishing, healing touch? What way would feel best to receive? Would you love to gift yourself a massage with a great practitioner? Would you be open to trying acupuncture to see how it can support you? Could you treat yourself to even an at-home facial or pedicure to simply give your body some of the care it deserves to feel appreciated, beautiful, loved up? Don't wait too long before you commit and make it happen. Enjoy the process and receive—you deserve to feel good, to feel supported, to feel taken care of.

So many times I've felt anxious or like I am going into a trauma spiral, and what I really need in those moments is a hug or for someone to simply squeeze me and let me know it's alright. For my abandonment trauma and the way my nervous system is wired, touch is such a potent medicine, especially when expressed in a non-sexual way where I can feel connected to my innocence and divine self, free of any expectations or conditioning. Is there someone in your life you can trust to practice making these kinds of requests with? It can even be as simple as creating space in your friendships and/or in-timate relationships to ask for this kind of support—you can say: "Hey, sometimes when I feel anxious or my body is feeling overwhelmed, it really helps me to ask for a hug or to simply be held. Would you be open to sharing this kind of support with me when I ask you, or could you check in with me to ask if I would like to receive this the next time you notice me feeling anxious?" With some friends I've even set up accountability to do this remotely—if we can't be together physically we can make the requests via phone or text and ask that we are sent healing and loving support in whatever ways are available, sometimes even in a simple acknowledgment, which can be a game changer to receive in the midst of a shame spiral or self-criticism marathon.

Mirror, Mirror

I love visioning so much, and when it comes to the body, we find our-selves inhabiting quite a manifestation portal indeed. But are we using it to its full capacity? Usually not at all. A practice I love for getting back into our manifestation potential and syncing up the body, mind, and spirit on all levels requires us to get really raw and real with ourselves. Are we truly living our purpose in this moment? Do we feel fully alive? Do we feel fulfilled? Do we feel like our full creative capacity and vi-brancy is flowing at full effect? Trick questions, because we can always infinitely grow in all these areas, but the key is to get clear on how we want to grow and evolve and then place our order to the universe using our body as the portal of actualization. Envision your true self or higher self—the version of you that is a few steps ahead of where you are now, that has guidance and wisdom to share with you regarding where you are on your path. This could be you in a month, a year, a decade—perhaps a specific date arises to play with depending on what timelines you're considering growing along.

Picture yourself like you're looking in the mirror—only this time at the version of you that resides in the timeline you are ready to step into. How does this being feel energetically, emotionally, physi-cally, psychically, or otherwise? How do they feel in their body? What vision are they actualizing? What gifts are they celebrating, sharing, and receiving? What is going well in their life at this future-now mo-ment? What help has shown up along the way to assist their success? How are they radiating such vibrant health and well-being? You can ask this version of you like you're in an interview—all of the above questions or any other specific ones that come to mind—to help you feel the literal experience of how their body and cells resonate in this future timeline you are so close to embodying. What does it feel like to embody a more potent state of safety and trust? To walk with profound confidence and trust in oneself? To be fearless in the face of the unknown? This is a great practice to do with a timer for ten to fifteen minutes, or longer if you prefer, and you may also feel called to practice in an actual mirror, looking at your physical face and body, tracking the changes that happen as you allow your present being to embody more of the attunements your future self is sharing with you.

Shake Like You Mean It

A powerful practice for releasing stored energy and emotion, clearing our energy field and detoxing our cells is referred to as *shaking* or in some cases *bioenergetic shaking*. Animals do it intuitively—if you've ever seen a dog shake after getting scared, it's simply intuitively listening to its body's guidance to release energy (of fear and anxiety in this case) that it has no need to carry any longer. Practice your own version of shaking, ideally as soon as you awaken to start your day and even right before bed—think of it as taking an energetic shower after a night full of dreams or a day full of daydreams. Try to stick to the practice of rigorously shaking your entire body and all extremities for at least five minutes (or more if you're supercharged by this practice and want to stretch!). Release all the energy that's wanting to be let go, allow trauma stored in your cells to simply melt away and open yourself up to heightened levels of receiving all that you truly desire in this now (and for the rest of your day ahead).

Bliss Mode

A powerful way to attune your being for bliss and good feelings is to simply practice remembering moments in which you've experienced powerful moments of love and joy. Play with programming those feelings into your physical presence now. Can you simply call those feelings into your being? When was a time you felt completely at ease, held and supported, loved, and/or full of joy and inspiring infinite possibility? If it's not easy to recall: imagine what it'd feel like and envision how your reality is designed around you to to support those sustained experiences. Does envisioning your future self having all that you desire help inspire you to feel how you want to feel? Let it be light, let it be fun—like painting the blank canvas of your life—simply for the joy of exploring something new and maybe, more true.

Oftentimes we are so conditioned to want outside, future-oriented results to happen in a certain way that will activate a particular feeling in us—but we want the feeling now. We just learned that the result has to happen first in order to feel like we are allowed to feel how we want to feel. Why not reverse engineer this equation and choose to feel how you want to feel now? What if feeling good now isn't conditional upon external factors like we may have thought?

Practical application: take ten minutes a day at least—or more—and program in your desired ways of being: love, joy, bliss, ecstasy, anything else you want a more second-nature attunement with. A great time for this is after your gratitude practice and future visioning—simply practice deepening into your desired feelings, practicing how it feels to deepen into love, gratitude, and joy. What does it feel like in your body? Can you go deeper into the feeling and let it fully saturate your being? What would it feel like to let love overflow? To let gratitude expand through every single cell? What does bliss actually feel like in your being? What do you notice about your heart, its beat and rhythm or perhaps overall quality of energy flow in this practice? Does a certain memory help trigger your embodiment experience more fully? Play and keep practicing. We are strengthening new muscle memory that will support in cultivating better discernment of truth, intuition, desires, and ultimately your divinely guided vision.

"The future world will be a world created by adults who can see through the eyes of children."
—Richard Rudd

Be Like a Child

It's adventure time—go play. Do something you've never done before. Make a commitment to do this frequently from here on out. Recognize how playing is such an important medicine when it comes to dropping out of your mind and into your soul. What's your favorite way to play? What's an epic adventure you can go on this week, even if you have to cancel something to allow yourself the freedom to experience it? Stretch—what would be a huge treat to give to yourself? A journey or experience you've been dreaming of taking for who knows how long? Why not do it now?

As much as you can, be mindful of not being on the internet or technology during your adventure; connect intimately with you and your beautiful soul, asking how you can give yourself what you truly desire.

Ask and receive. Stretch yourself and ask for help or support in something you truly want to delegate or remove from your plate altogether. Practice asking for something you really desire in a relationship—can you deepen your intimacy by giving an invitation for honest, conscious communication around honoring your desires? Where do you desire feeling more supported in your life? How? How can you ask for what you need and create a clear invitation to receive it from precisely the entity/entities you have in mind? The bolder your ask, the more powerfully this exercise will impact your ability to receive—you will be guided to expand in your receptivity and embody a heightened level of trust in yourself and in the divine to deliver exactly what you need when you need it.

Given what's now been shared—and hopefully more clearly integrated in terms of how you understand all the different aspects of your operating system powering your consciousness and physical experience in reality—what do we do now with all we've received? That's quite a lot of information and knowledge, which is great, but ultimately what we always really want underneath more information is understanding and felt-embodied wisdom. The most powerful reminder I can think of pertaining to our work ahead is as simple as this: the issues are in your tissues. Healing is not an intellectual process. Awakening to your true self and tuning into your heart and living life accordingly are not linear, they aren't logical and they aren't even sensical at times— but at the same time they represent the most practical, intelligent path we could ever hope to choose. Trust that the steps to follow will take you through more of the intimate journey in realigning your entire operating system and all facets therein to feel authentically expressed as the fully conscious, powerful, radiant being you are surely here to be.

Lastly: Can we stop getting in the way of what's already happening perfectly? *But how?* the mind asks. *Breathe,* the body says (and acts accordingly). There you are. The soul celebrates. Your job as always is to be fully embodied as the infinite spirit you are. Divinity in human-angel form, exploring and embodying: When do I feel most connected to my spirit? How does my spirit love to express itself? How do I feel my soul move through my being? What is the song I am here to sing, the dance I am designed to dance? How do I allow this breath to breathe me, all the way in? Let your life and the way you live it be your unique answer to these questions. It's all a ceremony—this life—and you are the ritual, we are the medicine, after all.

8

ATTUNE TO PRESENCE

What is presence? Presence is a state of being. It is a state in which you can easily feel sense and know yourself. It is the moment in which all of you is here and now in one place, whole and complete. Your presence is also an effect that has the impact of communicating far more than any words can convey. Your presence is communicating your emotional state of being, your energetic alignment, your integrity, and your magnetism.

What is it about our presence that we want to really pay attention to in the journey of ascension? Perhaps it is as simple as: we are remembering and learning again how to be. How to become comfortable without being busy, without having so much to do, without feeling that we have to put forth effort, perhaps, ever again. We are unlearning lifetimes of conditioning that have taught us that being is not enough. That being is not something to be valued and that being is not worthy of any currency that we can intellectually understand or measure or quantify.

However, in awakening to our multidimensional selves, we find that presence and our being is exactly what we value most. It is the presence of others that we desire most of all, and it is our own presence that is required in order to be met at the levels of depth and intimacy that we desire in all of our relationships and with all of life.

So, the journey of becoming present with yourself is the journey of this life. It is indeed the journey of a lifetime alright—perhaps with no end, and we have the opportunity right now in this moment to choose that we attune our focus and all of our energy toward becoming present with ourselves. We are here to really know ourselves. To get intimate with our feelings, with our inner weavings, with our inspiration, with the unique way in which we transmit and communicate and express energy.

"Each person has an ideal, an aspiration for something
higher. It takes one form or another, but what matters is
the call to this ideal, the call of his being. Listening
to the call is the state of prayer."
—Madame Jeanne De Salzmann

As one of my favorite exercises on forgiveness reminds us: presence is the antidote to all confusion. When we can bring presence to all our relationships, especially the one with ourselves, the truth of what we want to experience can be revealed and all healing naturally happens. Here we are welcomed to see clearly and tune back into our true selves, which we inevitably remember and deeply feel as love.

Feeling yourself in your own presence is so much more than words can describe accurately. It's a feeling of unconditional love and acceptance and acknowledgment that you are so much vaster than anything that you've constructed within your mental, intellectual framework regarding your different identities and the characters that you play. When you sink in your own presence of unconditional love and acceptance for who you truly are, you feel the infinite nature of your being. You feel at home. And suddenly, you feel such a great distance away from the stories, anxiety, worry, fear, and noise that you see as automatically generated from an aspect of you—not your true self but an aspect of your being that has been overly empowered to take the lead in life, rather ineffectively.

I wish for all of us to have these moments where we can meet ourselves and see ourselves and appreciate and know our infinite being. The practice of looking ourselves in the mirror can bring so much up. Even the simple practice of celebrating yourself in your own reflection and saying the words you've always wished someone else would say to you—can be a lot to take in. Tears usually start streaming pretty easily from here. What is it you always wish one of your parents would acknowledge you for? What is it you wish you would be celebrated for? What's it like to say those words to yourself and really mean them and receive your own love?

From this intimacy and presence within ourselves, we then meet everyone else, especially those we care most about in our relationships, with greater depth, with greater receptivity, with a clearer reflection in which we not only see each other but in which each and every one of us can see ourselves more fully because it is in each others' reflection that we do see ourselves. Here we see the opportunities for healing. Here we see the opportunities for making our unconscious, conscious. Here is where life gets really real.

SEE YOUR TRIGGERS AS TEACHERS

A core aspect of practicing presence is to become radically honest about anything that triggers you. Anything that upsets you. Anything that bothers you, because anything or anyone that bothers you, that takes you out of yourself, is taking you out of the present moment and is something that is actually teaching you, is reflecting to you an aspect of yourself that is wanting to be acknowledged and loved and brought into wholeness. It is said that the people that trigger us are our greatest teachers. They're reflecting to us aspects of ourselves that we are not yet ready to love.

So, until we are ready to really come into full unconditional love of ourselves, the world around us will continue to reflect unconscious aspects of ourselves that we are not fully feeling, seeing, or taking responsibility for. The same thing with jealousy. If we feel jealous of someone else who's achieving in their life what we feel we should be achieving, we're simply acknowledging that person as an aspect of ourselves we really desire to embody more fully. But the intellectual mind will run the old, outdated programs of jealousy and judgment instead of coming into authentic responsibility that would instead love to suggest to us: when jealousy arises that's a sign for me to get into action and commitment to bring about the desired results that I am now ready to embody in my life. When we are showing up in full integrity and presence, turned on by ourselves and how we're showing up in life, we're enlivened in the ways that we express our creative energy and feel completely utilized. Our attention and awareness is not focused on anything outside of ourselves. Our full energetic focus is called forth toward actualizing our dreams, our visions, our creative outlets.

"To live without awareness is to live as the deaf, blind, and dumb in a world of vibrant light and sound."
—Belsebuub

ARE WE THERE YET?

Being present sounds simple, but really it's been one of the most challenging initiations on my path, which is continually inviting me into greater love, true compassion, and empathy. Some might recall that intimacy is also understood as into-me-I-see or the reminder from Yogi Bhajan that we must "realize the other person is you." For me this has absolutely been the case. Intimacy and connection, of which presence is the absolute requirement, has always been my greatest desire in life. However, of course, it's been my biggest growing edge in transcending trauma and negative self-belief that has in the past told me, *I'm not enough, I'm not worthy of love*, or *I don't exist if you [another person] don't acknowledge, validate, or love me.*

Being present is a core aspect of living a conscious life and in fact is essentially the state of being that becomes more embodied as you raise your consciousness. Perhaps presence and consciousness can actually be thought of as one and the same. However, for our purpose at hand, let's consider: presence is an embodied state of being in which you feel at peace and ease completely with who you are. In presence you're attuned to your desires while being masterfully observant over your thoughts, beliefs and emotions so you can make clear decisions. In presence we can discern to act in total integrity and responsibility as life sends us infinite opportunities to expand and grow into more of who we truly are. Presence is what we all truly want at our core, because it's who we are when we drop out of thought, out of stress, out of worry, and out of anything that's not really serving us to be the happy, loving, leaders of our best possible—or even legendary—lives.

What does it feel like, to truly feel: the whole energetic field emanating from your heart center, completely activated, awakened, and all energy circuits open and online, completely present, really utilizing the full range of perception that you have available through this sacred body? Here is our practice—a practice that has no end. We can infinitely continue expanding into the depths of our embodiment. Presence is the essential ingredient in allowing old ways of being to naturally dismantle. In presence the truth is revealed.

In presence we are our true selves. In presence we are naturally receptive. There is nothing in the way of what's already here. Practicing presence goes against most of our collective and family conditioning—maybe all of it. Perhaps presence is the antidote to conditioning altogether. It's confronting for a world that's taught us to be busy, to overly think with our intellect and source value from productivity, to consider that perhaps it's time to allow ourselves permission to simply be. Funny we would ever take training and courses—or even read books like this—on how to simply be, as we are. But it's not our fault that we came in to experience certain lessons and programs that were designed quite perfectly to teach us what we came to learn, right? Remember, we chose this and maybe even designed it all quite well. Very creative indeed.

TRUE PRESENCE BREAKS REALITY (AND TIME)

As we become more awake and aware we can't help but naturally practice more presence. Presence is a deconditioning of speed—the idea that time is running out or that time even exists. Practicing presence invites us into timelessness and deep enjoyment of the moment, allowing us to notice and appreciate the perfection of what is occurring now. We experience our reality as what is deeply felt in the body instead of what we *think* happened or what will happen, which are limited projections only based on past experience. Practicing presence invites us into deep enjoyment of the senses and refinement of all our senses on many levels.

Imagine yourself as a vibrational instrument, a channel, a tuning fork if you will, whose main job it is to attune to frequencies that you find most agreeable. Just like you're a human radio dial. It is your job to select only the vibrations, frequencies, or channels that feel best for you from the whole wide spectrum of all that are available. From this space of presence you eventually attune to your desired vibration, your desired state, much more easily and from a calm and grounded vantage point. It is in our presence that we can see clearly. When we are truly present we can really allow life to support us more directly. Here and now we are available to receive all the gifts and opportunities that are naturally flowing to us as long as we are open in setting out a clear frequency, a beacon through which we are communicating our desires.

The more present we are, the more clearly we can make decisions that support us in aligning with our highest good and our destiny. The more comfortable we become with being, the more easily we can become ourselves, the more easily we come into acceptance of who we are and the more confidently we are able to share our gifts and our unique transmission of the energy that we are here to express.

Presence is not an intellectual process. It is not simply by thinking that we change and become that which we think. No, we are here for a deeply somatic experience, a nervous system reprogramming that requires transmutation of trauma and stagnant energy that has been in some cases held in the body for lifetimes. Now, our evolution hasn't always worked in our favor, at least when we look at it through the lens of survival of the fittest. Yes, we are grateful for our ancestors, who've been good fighters and warriors and who have survived the test of time, the test of environment, the test of having numerous enemies and threats to life. There was a time and a place over the many centuries of our human history when we were required to be in survival mode, when we never knew if we were going to be eaten or attacked, and when we did need to be on constant alert. As such, our nervous systems evolved to have a strong attunement to survival reaction mechanisms—the coping mechanisms that kept us safe in moments of danger.

Yet, if we look at our society, our culture most of our lives, certainly in this moment and definitely over the last century or so, we've never had more support, more technological advancement, and more safety surrounding us. We've never been so safe. We've never had more resources at our disposal. We've never been more situated than now to finally start relaxing. Yet, why is it so difficult to be present? Why is it so difficult to let go? Why is it so challenging to actually relax and just be?

We have a certain wiring in our nervous system, which has been passed down to us by our ancestors, that has encoded our DNA with a survival mentality. But we are so ready to break free because we see more clearly than ever that we no longer need it. We are here to thrive, not simply survive. And what we need instead is a return to center. A return to peace and ease. A return to calm. An innate knowing in each and every one of our cells that we are safe and whole and complete. That there's nothing outside of us that we require to feel safe or to feel happy. That our happiness is not a conditional state of being that is acquired at a future point. It is something that we attune to right now; we have the capacity in our presence, in our being, right now, to achieve the desired state of being that we most want to embody.

"Hardships often prepare ordinary people for
extraordinary destiny."
—C. S. Lewis

All that we crave, more than anything, is attention, connection and intimacy. What I didn't know at that time was as long as I was looking to what everyone else was thinking, saying, and doing, I really wasn't being intimate with myself. And because I wasn't seeing myself or feeling myself fully, I wasn't available to actually connect with others that I so badly wanted to feel connected to. I wasn't allowing myself to be seen by the people whom I was probably most meant to connect to and whom I would've connected to quite naturally had I actually been available for life to guide us together, effortlessly.

See, the thing is, when you focus on cultivating your own presence and intimacy with yourself, you naturally make the kind of choices and decisions that lead you into alignment with the path you're meant to follow. You naturally fall into alignment with the people you are meant to meet. You naturally align to the opportunities you're meant to receive that elevate you on your path. When we're intimate with ourselves, we can't help but listen to that calling of our soul and our heart that's guiding us to the right places at the right times and to the right people in the right moments.

Alignment is our natural state when we listen to our inner being. Listening to our inner being requires us to cultivate presence and a deep self-awareness and attunement, which is the basis of intimacy, which all starts within.

That One Time at Summer Camp in the "Intimacy Workshop"

Imagine all the fixings of an amazing summer camp experience, but instead of children running around, it was about a hundred recovering alcoholics who were, in many respects, really healing our inner children by being in this camp together. One of the workshops I felt called to attend was called the Intimacy Workshop, and of course I signed up, not really knowing what to expect. But I knew at some level that this was exactly the medicine that I required at this time, because even into my sobriety, I was dealing with an enormous amount of social anxiety, paranoia, and fear, and all-around emotional instability, still learning to hear my intuition and discern my truth from the truth that I'd been conditioned to believe in and follow. There was still a lot of traumatic energy that I was in the midst of healing.

> **"I stopped explaining myself when I realized people only understand from their level of perception."**
> **—Jim Carrey**

In this intimacy workshop, one of the key exercises toward the end was to sit in front of a partner. There was a group of about forty of us, men and women. I found myself seated across from a man whom I didn't know very well but whom I recognized from meetings around New York at that time. In this exercise, we were to breathe together and to make eye contact for what felt like infinity. We also shared a few guided exchanges in what felt to be an authentic-relating-type style of call and response, echoing each other's answer in an empathic listening exercise. But before any of the exercises began, just being in silence with this man and making eye contact and breathing together was so uncomfortable. It was paralyzingly uncomfortable for me to simply be when I was by myself, let alone in front of this other person and with an audience at that.

I was so afraid of what might be revealed. I was so afraid of what this person might be immediately seeing on my face. I was so insecure, and I was so uncomfortable in this exchange. My face was twitching. It was hard for me to breathe. I just noticed my mind speaking so loudly, full of so much anxiety and fear, saying things like, *I wonder what he's looking at on my face. I have a pimple. I wonder what he's seeing. What's wrong with me? I wonder what he sees.* I was so caught up in the experience of what I thought this other person was seeing, feeling, and processing in my presence that I became completely disconnected from myself. Or at least— more so than I already was. I lost all sense of any center I had a grasp on, and I allowed myself to be overcome with painful anxiety and insecurity.

I couldn't wait for this to be over. I felt humiliated. I felt so embarrassed; the way that I showed up in that exchange must have made the other person so unsettled too. So, I felt embarrassed for him to ever see me again. For the rest of the weekend retreat, I made it a point to avoid running into that person because I was so embarrassed about how our exchange had unfolded. I felt sure that he didn't want to see me again; in fact, he must have thought something was wrong with me. He must have hated me. I felt so disappointed by my inability to sit there like the exercise invited us to do—how hard was it supposed to be? It seemed like everyone else was able to do it just fine. I don't know exactly what I did wrong but I knew it was big—and I just felt ashamed, like something was wrong with me.

I spent that whole next year avoiding this person, upholding the story that they must have thought something was wrong with me and that they didn't want to be reminded of the humiliating exchange that we had. So, anytime that I would run into him at a meeting, I would avoid him. I would try not to make eye contact, and I would really wish that

I was invisible in those moments so that none of that painful, shameful memory could surface.

But even still, despite avoiding him, I was attentively holding on to the story that something was wrong with me. That I made him uncomfortable and that I was awkward and that I was incapable. Who knows if I had any positive thoughts at the time, especially about myself; the point is, as you can tell, my inner monologue and concept of reality was overwhelmed by the criticism, judgment, and self-flagellation that was, at that time, my normal state of being. It was the natural way that I was speaking to myself, more often than not, which was incredibly painful and something I felt ashamed to have witnessed by this other person. I felt a deep shame about the way that I behaved in my inner experience, and I never wanted anyone to know about that. I didn't want that to be revealed.

I returned to camp a year later. One more year sober after having done a lot more work, having worked with the 12 steps, having had a lot of incredible celebrations. I decided to attend the intimacy workshop again. It was hosted by the same woman, and there were some familiar faces. And, of course, the same partner that I had last year was back in the workshop again.

But there was no way I was going to allow that traumatic experience to play out on repeat. So, I made sure throughout all of our exercises that I was on the opposite side of the room and that I was always far away from him, as far away as possible, to ensure that I would never be partners with this person and we'd never relive the horrifying experience we had shared the year before.

Now, this is how the universe works in very mysterious ways when it comes to creating the perfect experiences for healing. Much to my dismay, despite my best efforts, the entire workshop group was guided to stand in two lines facing each other. The room separated twenty by twenty, with two lines of people. Through a series of facilitations by the guide, we were directed to reorient ourselves in the room with our eyes closed so that we could eventually find ourselves in front of another person to go into the partner exercise with.

Now, you better believe I did everything I could to ensure I was as far away from this person as possible to prevent any probability we would be partnered. As I blindly arrived at a seemingly random point where I was facing someone, I was so happy to know that there was no way I could be with this person again. Surely, I was going to have a new experience, I was going to have a fresh slate in which to practice presence and intimacy. Maybe everything would finally be different.

Upon opening our eyes at the same time, we were both overcome by shock and also a bit of laughter: Here he was, standing right in front of me. The person I had been avoiding all year was right here, and we were about to do the same set of practices, more or less, again. And yet this time, everything actually did seem different. The initial fear crossed to my consciousness that *Oh my god! We're going to repeat the same travesty again and it's going to feel horrible*, but instead I did the exercises, I showed up in a different way, and I was shocked at my capacity to actually hold and experience more presence.

I had more of a grip on my own sense of center and my breath, which is really the determining mechanism of our presence. When we can breathe all the way into our body we can relax and be at rest. We are in full presence and we can see the world around us more clearly. We can see those in front of us more clearly. We can be in our own energy without the energetic feedback and confusion of reading ourselves through the eyes of another.

So, we carried through the same exercises, and at a certain point I started crying because I was amazed to see how differently my experience was unfolding. I was witnessing myself in presence. I was witnessing myself connecting with this person in a way I never thought was possible, and I felt all these stories that I had created simply fall away. At a certain point, I even felt us dissolve into energetic beings: our physical faces melted and I just started to feel this presence that existed between us beyond words, beyond anything we were able to describe. I felt so much energy released from my system. I felt so much shame released from my body. I felt my mind come into stillness and quiet. I felt myself sink into being in a way I never had before.

After the workshop concluded, I gave my partner a hug, told him that I had made up all these stories about our experience the year prior, and apologized for being so avoidant. To which he simply responded with something to the effect of, "Oh, I never noticed anything. I thought you were really a cool person and I would have loved to get to know you better. I wondered why you would always make a quick escape whenever I saw you around at meetings. I'm grateful that we got to share this experience together and I can tell that you're more present and more centered within yourself." But his acknowledgment felt almost overwhelming to receive, because I saw in that moment a whole reality I had constructed and identity therein—all based on a fearful, shameful projection—fall away.

I felt a part of my heart open in a way that it never had before. I really felt in that moment that I truly saw myself, I truly felt myself. I felt my own presence in a way that I never thought was possible, never thought was accessible. Everything was different indeed.

> **"As you evolve, so all beings will evolve with you. When you raise the frequency in one area of your life, you will also be raising it in all the others. You are a DNA molecule within the body of humanity, and you are fully awake."**
> **—Richard Rudd**

ALIGN YOUR MIND TO SERVE YOUR SOUL

How is now the most perfect moment? This question is such a quick way into presence—in fact, if you think too hard about it, you've already missed the point. We are recovering from an overly developed intellectual capacity driven by emotions that have been programmed to feel exorbitant fear to protect us from perceived dangers or threats, always keeping us in the past or future, out of the present. To repattern this ancient reflex, we must come back to renewing emotion—a way to do that is through our actions and our physiology. As they say: act your way into right feeling or right thinking. Don't think more—instead: move a muscle. Shift your state. Awakening to higher consciousness is all about believing and then seeing versus the outside-in approach of *I'll believe it when I see it*. How about this instead: I'll see it when I believe it. And when I see it because I believe it, I usually realize that I am it—whatever it is I am seeking, is always in some regard—way into more of my true self.

Attuning the body to presence is a journey that can begin as soon as you choose to practice. In this practice of cultivating presence, we must start with the breath. The breath is the central mechanism through which we regulate all of our bodies' systems. And literally, the most powerful tool that we have at our disposal at this time in our evolution is our capacity to entrain our breath to more deep and full expressions in which we fill our entire body with healing breath. Each and every inhale and exhale brings forth a deeper patterning for nervous system rest and restoration.

> **"When I am sharply judgmental of any other person, it's because I sense or see reflected in them some aspect of myself that I don't want to acknowledge."**
> **—Gabor Maté**

The most powerful thing you can do right now to support yourself in cultivating more presence and being is to practice deep breathing. Practice passive breathing, which is simply the practice of emptying all of the air out of your system completely. You'll be surprised how much air is there once you intentionally breathe it all out.

Then, slowly, only when you absolutely must, inhale—start to breathe in slowly through a little straw, as slowly as you possibly can, savoring each and every aspect of the sweet breath filling you up until you fill up to your fullest capacity. Breathing all the way throughout your entire body, holding the breath for just a moment at the top, and then exhaling again through that small, little straw as slowly as you can. Stay empty again and repeat this cycle a few times. If you can, do this practice a few minutes throughout your day and make it a daily habit.

You'll start to see quite quickly that your entire nervous system becomes reprogrammed to a deeper state of calm, to a deeper state of clarity, to more presence. That allows you to make decisions more clearly. That allows you to respond to life from a more grounded, powerful space. That, most of all, empowers your body to feel more vital life force energy channeled into healing and restoration so you feel your best.

Another powerful way to cultivate presence with yourself is mirror work, which is done by simply gazing at yourself in the mirror, maybe setting a timer for a few minutes, and enjoying some deep breaths as you behold yourself in your own eyes. You might feel called to be in dialogue with yourself about what you notice, about what's arising, about what you're celebrating about yourself. This may be, in many cases, the first moment of intimacy that you really have with yourself, in which you truly appreciate and revere yourself. And, it might bring up a lot of emotions. It might bring up a lot of density or even pain if this is one of the first times that you're holding space for yourself to become truly present with you.

For me, one of the most confronting, awkward, painful lessons in cultivating presence came unexpectedly. How could I have ever imagined showing up at the same workshop two years in a row and having such wildly different experiences? And it was so perfect in its design—all of it. I needed that precise contrast of the same people and context as different versions of myself to see how much I had really changed—and what new potentials were now possible. In hindsight I truly saw how we always call in the perfect learning intentions we need at that time to bring us to that state, or that way, we are ready to embody. I wanted connection more than anything—I wanted to feel comfortable in my skin and confident with others around me. I wanted true intimacy but I had so much work to do before I could really receive that which I thought I wanted. I didn't know what I didn't know. The thing about intimacy is we all want it, but very few of us actually put in the practice and commitment to cultivating it within ourselves first.

"You are what you think I am."
—A mantra on one of my favorite shirts that always inspires
people to give me a double-take, especially in airports

Intimacy is not experienced through relationship with another. It is a state of being that we first embody within ourselves that then is reflected in any and all relationships that we choose to show up in, consciously, with full presence.

Intimacy is also expressed as "into-me-I-see," which is a powerful reflection and invitation for us all to seek ourselves more fully and more deeply. When was the last time you really saw yourself? Can you see yourself when you look into the mirror, in your own eyes? What do you see? What do you notice? What emerges?

Whether you like it or not, the masks have come off—all the masks we didn't even know we were wearing are falling away. So, you might as well devote yourself to the practice of intimacy and presence with yourself, because the New Earth is inviting us all into deep connection with the present moment, with our own source connections, with our infinite selves. Everything that you desire is here and now, waiting for you to reveal yourself so that you can be blessed with all the gifts that are here for you to receive.

PURE PRESENCE ATTUNEMENTS

The fastest way to attune to presence is to become like a child. Think about it—how present are babies? They are the ultimate example of presence, and we can learn so much from their ways of being. They don't hold emotions in, they don't repress themselves, they communicate their needs as best they can, they don't judge or criticize themselves—they are who they are and they expect life to support them fully. They embody trust. This is who we all are, how we all started before other stories, traumas, experiences got in the way, got stuck in our bodies and clouded our vision of reality. Maybe we can remember through playing.

Be Like a Child

We covered this a bit earlier, yes—but it's worth revisiting as inner child healing and integration are potent keys into embodying our true selves. **Who were we before we were taught who we should be?** Let's find out.

Go play. Do something you've never done before. Make a commitment to do this frequently from here on out. Recognize how playing is such an important medicine when it comes to dropping out of your mind and into your soul. What's your favorite way to play? What's your favorite way to belly laugh so hard it hurts? What's a dream you've been dreaming to birth into being or to explore, even just a little bit? Why not do it now? When you are on your dream exploration adventure, can you be offline completely and turn off all technology and distractions that bring you out of presence? How are you inspired to fully be in your body?

Inner Compass

An even easier exercise, a mini version of the above, if you will, which you can do right now or in any moment no matter where you are, is to place your hand on your heart and take at least three deep breaths, if not more, into your heart. Sometimes we realize, especially upon slowing down, how good it feels to consciously nourish ourselves with breath and attune ourselves to even more of our own life force energy. Then consider saying to yourself: "I release all that I have known and all that I have claimed to know and now receive and remember that which I truly am." Recently in a cacao song circle (a singing circle where we chant sacred songs and enjoy a medicinal raw chocolate potion made with cacao beans and other herbal tonic elements) here on the Big Island in Hawaii, a wizard friend reminded us all, so quickly that we smiled at how close we came to missing it, to "remember your breath, the greatest medicine in plain sight."

"My experience is what I agree to attend to."
—William James

See Our Beings Instead of Our Doings

Here's another fun exercise—instead of automatically asking each other, "Hey, how ya doing?" can we instead start to play with exploring (with ourselves and each other), "How are you being?" This is such a great question to be living into—even in each moment. Can we ask ourselves and really listen? Can we give ourselves what we truly require to feel secure, safe, supported? Here we are in the midst of the great practice (ascended mastery, that is). Becoming fully self-sourced. Embodying our sovereign divinity. Reclaiming our innocence. Remembering we are creating it all. This is quite a fun hologram to play in.

Resting into Being

"If you want to find your calling in life, you have to make room in your life to hear the call."
—a reminder from my friend, prolific thinker and writer Paul Weinfield

With cultivated presence, we can make room for our purpose and callings to emerge more naturally. We can clean out whatever noise is in the way of simply being ourselves. And we can see more clearly the ways in which triggers or distractions arise in our life to simply point us back to center, to wholeness. Another incredible way to practice presence is to practice acceptance. You can do this very simply by focusing on any person or anything in your life, even an idea that agitates you in some way, that brings you out of the present moment, that attaches to a story or identity that you've made up about yourself, perhaps in avoidance to taking responsibility. Then, commit to what you know is required. To being who you really are. To doing what you're meant to do here on Earth. To being fully alive and aligned.

You can do this practice very simply by allocating a few moments to explore. You might set a timer, if that's supportive. Don't spend too long. Just focus your attention, much like a meditation, on a person, place or even an idea that bothers you. And simply choose within these few minutes to fully receive this thing or person in loving presence and simply see where you can accept it/them as a reflection, as a teacher, as an invitation for you to come into greater wholeness. Perhaps here you may see, love, and accept more of yourself.

You may be surprised to find what happens upon first beginning this practice. You might find great resistance emerges, which is totally natural—after all we are deprogramming a strongly held survival mechanism. Breathe through resistance that emerges and choose to take a minute and be with it. Stay committed, and see what you can accept as the perfect message and guidance to support you on your path.

A Practice for Presence: How Are You Being?

Ask yourself and attune to your present feeling, not what you're doing or how you're looking. How are you being, now? Sink into the quality. If it's delightful, expand further into your depth. If it sucks, expand into that and see how far the illusion of suffering wants to take you. Deepen in this practice by sharing within yourself (by journaling, speaking aloud, or—better yet—connecting with yourself in the mirror) or with a trusted friend or ally. Here's a totally normal example of how my inner being might be speaking if I feel under-resourced or lacking in a crucial core need:

Me right now? I feel shitty. I feel annoyed. I feel like I have nothing to offer. I feel irritated by how many people are so asleep and basic and how most things I write and create can't even resonate with them, so why try. There I go again, trying to share for attention and resonance, and there's the validation seeking, and there I am, trying, trying, trying, it's so effing exhausting, I'm over it. Maybe I should just get a real job, whatever that means. It would be easier than trying to start new visions and companies and rallying people to join and selling stuff and marketing and being an example and being put on a pedestal all the time. It's never enough anyway. Exhausted.

After tuning into a speech like that, I might forget why I started trying to shift or heal in the first place. This negative space is such an old, familiar and hence crazily safe (according to my ego) way of being. Underneath the surface of what's being said, here are some of the deeper inquiries yearning to be explored:

Will I ever fully forgive myself?
Will my heart ever stop hurting?
Will my inner critic ever be silenced?
Will I ever be simply enough, as I am?
Will I ever stop being so afraid?
Will I ever stop pretending?
Will I ever feel free?
Will I ever accept myself?
Will I ever feel like I belong?
Will I ever be truly happy and fulfilled?
Will the world ever actually wake up?

When we consider questions like this—what actually comes up in our reflection? For me: so much anger, so much fear and shame purging from my cells. Underneath it so much grief. Some hopelessness too if I'm honest. But all of those descriptions I just shared are projections and judgments—not actual present-moment feelings. You see, I am not practicing my own practice. But this is the loop that we tend to take, unconsciously of course, even when *practicing presence*, am I right? How can we actually bring ourselves into the true present moment—into acknowledgment of what we are feeling here and now, no matter how challenging it might feel to be with it all?

Here's what I mean. Instead of telling you that I feel anger and sadness, fear, and shame—concepts and words—what I am actually feeling in this moment is tightness in my heart/chest, fire in my belly/womb, and heat running through my body. What's it saying? Breathe, move, relax, allow, receive. In moments of immense intensity and emotional overwhelm—we might have a tendency to go into the mind as a protection strategy that helps us avoid feeling the fullness of intensity that wants to resolve. The mind wants to intellectualize and name the concepts we must be experiencing—instead of actually being present with what's going on in the body, our now-moment barometer of how we are truly being.

It's hard to hear ourselves—or our bodies—in the moment when emotions, judgments, and chaos are running high, but eventually, after the initial tantrum/screaming/crying fit (if needed), let's try our best to return to the practice: how am I being? And it might be helpful to remember the body as a child that needs our love, our support, our affirmation. How are we actually positioned to be a loving, nurturing, supportive parent—as the highly evolved spiritual being we are—to this new baby of a body that's learning to process so much on so many levels? Let's check in:

Oh, there you are, body-soul—what do you need?
How can I support you?
What would feel good to receive in this moment?
How can I nourish you?
How can I love on you?
How can I remember, celebrate, embody beauty here and now?

Sometimes it sucks to be growing; it feels awkward and you feel like a cranky, annoyed baby. I think we really are in spiritual infancy when it comes to being embodied in our multidimensionality in such high-frequency states while still on Earth. So I remember: how do I take care of a baby who is learning to walk, to communicate, to move, feel, and BE in new ways?

Take it slow. Allow. Rest. Breathe. Receive.

Some days require more attentiveness, love, and patience than others. For example, yesterday I enjoyed an expansive, high-vibe day—definitely enjoying and basking in epic energy. But maybe today feels like a bit of a contraction, which almost always signals a quantum leap expansion just around the corner. That's how this evolution ebbs and flows, remember? We continue doing our best. And we remind ourselves and each other, always, that this is, and has always been, enough.

Inhale, Exhale, Slower and Deeper

Breathing can be one of the most challenging, confronting things to practice, because when we breathe all the way in, we really get to be with ourselves. We get to be in the here and now; there's nothing to do and there's nowhere to go. So, our mind's reaction to cultivating this state of presence might be to begin worrying, thinking about all the things that need to be done or regretting what hasn't been done yet or simply thinking and creating data points to strategize around or even create challenges around. But as you continue to breathe and choose to stay with the practice, you may begin to see yourself as the observer of the mind, as the observer of the dialogue that is running, that is wanting to solve problems, that is wanting to create challenges that weren't there in the first place, that maybe don't exist.

As you continue the practice of cultivating presence, it might feel uncomfortable to stay still and be calm when every aspect of your being has been programmed to be overthinking and to be worrying. It might feel like if there's nothing to worry about, something's wrong. But you can know that that's simply the result of a nervous system that's been programmed to become addicted to some hormones, to some chemical responses in the body that are only fired off in the presence of anxiety, worry, and fear. We are undergoing, as a collective, a mass deconditioning from fear, a mass deconditioning from worry and anxiety as we emerge to greater presence, which is really our innate state of being.

Reorientation to trusting one's self and deeply listening to the body's wisdom is the invitation on offer. Listening without judgment and holding space for yourself requires spiritual and emotional maturity, which so many of us haven't been welcomed to fully rise into until now, and yet—here we are, right on time.

What do you need right now to feel your best? What do you cel-ebrate about you right now simply for being alive in your essence? What's the most nourishing, loving way you can be for you right now in this moment? Everything you want starts with you loving yourself, forgiving yourself completely, and accepting that everything in this perfect existence has always been here all along to help you thrive, grow, and evolve into even greater truth.

**"No problem can be solved from the same
level of consciousness that created it."
—Albert Einstein**

Self-care and attuning to one's innermost needs are not selfish acts, contrary to what much of our societal conditioning dictates. When we source our needs from within as best we can and no longer depend on others to unconsciously provide the support we deserve, we show up in authentic presence as who we really are and feel the deep, loving connection required to thrive. Intimacy as we understand it can now take many different forms—not just in relationship with other people or with ourselves, but with all of life and its infinite di-mensions of experience.

When we start showing up authentically within ourselves, we start to engage with life in a totally new way wherein life becomes more like a living meditation. We notice more ease and flow consistently in all aspects of life, we become masterful at creating immediate shifts when we desire to and we notice how the more we trust ourselves to listen from presence, the more life supports us. Here we start to touch into greater depths of our personal power and potential.

9

TAKE BACK YOUR POWER

**"True power never needs to prove itself to others or the world.
True power is only concerned with the job at hand."
—Richard Rudd**

Power is an energetic state of being. Our natural state of being is to be powerful, totally alive, turned on. It's a feeling. It's not something that is intellectually rationalized through. It's not just a concept to grasp—it is an intimate state of being in our selves into which we can infinitely deepen through embodiment. The more that we can cultivate this feeling, this state of being, this presence and clarity, the more we naturally allow our power to radiate and exude.

There's not a lot we have to do or figure out or even release to allow this energy to move through us. It wants to. It's the ways in which we are conditioned to give our power away or disempower ourselves that block the natural flow from unfolding. These are learned ways of being that are very counterintuitive to our natural state, which is to be fully radiant, fully alive, turned on and present.

It's funny we would ever want to learn how to take our power back—I mean, who took it away in the first place? Or did we give it away? Wait, you mean I gave something away that I wasn't even consciously aware was mine to give away in the first place? Welcome to humanity, welcome to Earth School. Here we meet again, this time to explore the different vestiges of power so we can better understand the subtle and not-so-subtle ways we divert our life force energy away and allow ourselves to be drained or weighed down instead of turned all the way on. Buckle up—we're about to dive into the deep end.

So, what does it mean to take your power back? This statement seems to resurface often as a hot topic, especially in personal development realms, and within social movements and activist campaigns, implying that there is something to fight for and reclaim and also that there is an oppressor or victimizer at play. Let's shine light on this far too common dance we can subtly and sometimes not so subtly take part in—and see what truth is here, ready to assist us in our inevitable evolution.

WHY (AND HOW) WE GIVE OUR POWER AWAY

First, we've got to consider how our unconscious mind is orchestrating 90 percent of our physical reality even though we may think we're living as conscious and awakened beings. Till we start really waking up to our trauma and the healing we get to do on our embodied ascension journey, we're asleep in a trance. In this trance we're hypnotized into allowing our core wounds and patterns derived from unresolved trauma to orchestrate our lives until we make them conscious. And we'll keep attracting similar traumatic experiences to trigger us into awakening until we're finally willing to become conscious and heal.

Can you imagine: your energetic field, your sovereign soul self that is your essence, is intentionally designed to magnetize the precise people, places, situations, opportunities that will trigger your trauma, your wounds—whatever is required to make the unconscious conscious and heal? In our awakening process we must become ready to become conscious of patterns and programs running our lives on autopilot and face it all full on. This is part of how we take our power back. We stop skirting around the superficial plane of existence and get to the root of the thing that happened that's still manifesting as obstacles or challenges in the way of experiencing what we truly desire. Allow it to land deep in your being that you deserve to be happy, that you deserve to feel good. These changes all start with fully honoring yourself as the sovereign adult soul that you are, and with cultivating observance of this trauma, and any survival games that are continuing to determine the course of your life and its extraordinary potentials.

We are trained to give our power away early on and in many subtle and not-so-subtle ways. Every addiction we have is a way of giving our power away to something outside of ourselves. An addiction is a pattern in which we depend on an external entity (which can be anything or anyone) to impact our internal state; when we give our power away to something external that we deem capable of changing our experience. This might hurt to hear, but coffee (and I love coffee—even if my relationship with it comes and goes in waves!) can be something we give our power away to when we depend on it to wake us up or to feel energized, happy, alive—insert state of being you are dependent on coffee to shift in you. In what other ways do we go on autopilot to play out addictions—especially the most subtle or socially acceptable ones? These can be so hard to admit to ourselves, and shame can arise in the process. Remember: it's okay, whatever is coming up is so welcome. All of you is welcome here.

One of my biggest addictions has to do with externalized validation seeking, based on my core trauma of abandonment. Because I never felt the attunement and presence from my parents I required as a child to feel differentiated, regulated in myself, and affirmed in my existence, I grew up unconsciously sourcing love and attention (really, any energy) from others as a way to validate my own worth, value, existence, permission to breathe. Our core traumas pretty clearly inform the ways we learn to give our power away—which is the way we've learned to resource ourselves amidst whatever needs were not met at a young age.

Another common example I see is the pattern of giving power away to love and relationships—even sex—in a way we'd call codependent. Usually people (like myself) who didn't have stable, secure attunement in their parents growing up and didn't learn to resource and regulate their own nervous systems easily fall into codependent relationships. In this kind of dynamic, the other person, their energy and love, becomes the partner's life force, meaning for living and seemingly in many ways the most important thing in their lives.

"This human tendency to look for outer causes for our moods is the greatest addiction on our planet. Is there anything you cannot say no to in life? If there is, no matter what it may be, you remain at some level its victim."
—Richard Rudd

Someone dear to me once reminded us that: whenever we are equating something to mean something other than what it is, we are usually giving power away to it. An example of this is the belief system that money equals love, or money equals success, or money equals happiness. Until we can see that money only equals money, we are destined to give our power away to money as an addictive source that we depend on to give us some supposed resolution. As long as we continue to avoid giving that resolution to ourselves, we will beget the endless cycle of attempting to fulfill an unfillable void.

The funny truth of it all—this giving our power away game—is that we aren't really chasing the external thing we think we are. We are after the inside feeling, the embodiment, the knowing—that we are loved, that we are enough, that we are not alone, and that we matter. And we all have this in common, which is another beautiful part of our unified human family—we all pretty much have the same needs and desires when it comes down to it: to be loved, to matter, to belong, and to feel safe. Until we can affirm these ways of being ourselves, without superficially sourcing them from things or people outside of us, we will forever be on the wild goose chase into infinity, kind of like a chicken running around with its head cut off—disassociated from the body, trying to fix something that was never really broken in the first place.

So, how can we heal? How can we make the unconscious, conscious? How can we start to feel free? How can you start to catalyze a sense of liberation in yourself now? One of the best anecdotes is to consider how you, right now, in this moment, are actually the parents that you always wished you had. You, right now, in this moment as your sovereign adult self, have the opportunity to embody the divine masculine and the divine feminine within you as the sovereign mother and father that you never had but always wished you had. Who you are, here and now, in this moment, can give you everything that you've ever wanted.

Your inner loving parents are here now in this moment to tell you every single word that you've ever wanted to hear. They are here now in this moment to give you the assurance, safety, security, acknowledgment, nurturance that you, at the soul level as your inner child, divine in itself, are deeply deserving of receiving. So, I encourage you to consider what it would be like to personify your own inner loving mother and your own inner loving father. In this way we also can start to forgive our actual parents, our family, and our lineage by taking full responsibility for where we are right now and accessing our power to heal. How are you showing up presently as your adult self, as the sovereign soul you are? Are you in integrity? Do you trust yourself?

Are you responsible? Are you taking care of yourself? How do you show up? Do you do what you say you're going to do? If you're carrying the state of your soul's divine inner essence, inner child, how do you talk to yourself? How do you speak to yourself in your own mind? How is your voice programmed, and in what tone and with what energy and resonance do you speak to yourself all day long? How are you talking to yourself all day long? What does that tape say? How are you communicating to yourself and do you want to change the channel? There is this part of me that is a scared little girl who only wants love and acknowledgment, especially from those whom I perceive to be strong, powerful reflections of my true essence. Can you touch into any of your aspects that might be similarly yearning for a special kind of nurturance and care?

We only come into understanding of our true power by giving it away. Seeking validation, feeling jealous or even resentful in comparing oneself to others who seem to be doing better, being better, feeling better, having more success, receiving more love, shining more light—embodying the aspects of you that you're not fully in alignment with, that you're not fully accepting, that you're not embodying to the extent that your being knows you're here to experience—hurts. The hurt is guiding you to realize that you are ready to break the lifetimes-long cycle of making your present-moment love, acceptance, and celebration of yourself (the key ingredients for expansion) conditional upon a future result that you've been accustomed to believing you can control if only you are more X and do more X. It's a simple mental framework most humans have been overly conditioned with in this day and age, and ever since the dawn of industrial capitalism of course it's been highlighted to an extreme.

"Risk everything to be yourself."
—Osho

Remember: you are your own best healer, and you know your best medicine. Your path of mastery now initiates you to become your own shaman, your own antidote, your own divine loving parents and inner children (yes, multiple ages of you experienced and are still carrying trauma and trapped coping mechanisms and old identities). Are you up for the task? Of course you are. You wouldn't be alive on Earth at this time of ascension if you hadn't signed up for these lessons long before your arrival.

What if destiny is already decided; and it's up to you to tune in, listen, and follow your map? Everything and everyone has taught you that you need XYZ outside of you to be XYZ more than who and how you are right now. But there is no future nor any past. There is only here and now and the invitation to decide over and over again to choose yourself, accept yourself, love yourself, and celebrate precisely how and who you are right now. This is all that is true. Everything else is an illusion that's been hardwired into mass consciousness for far too long, and this timeline ends now.

HOW TO RECLAIM OUR POWER
(AND OUR TRUE SELVES)

Healing our inner child wounds and coming into integrated union with our inner being is the key to reclaiming our power and authenticity. Childhood is when most if not all of our unconscious behaviors, patterns, and lower vibrational energies can be taken on unconsciously. Then they just run for twenty years, thirty years, forty years. This work is one of our most potent gateways for completely shifting our realities. It's a life-long journey. It's not like you listen to a meditation once and everything's different—although, everything might be different. Continually practicing and developing a relationship with this inner divine essence that doesn't exist in the paradigm of giving power away is an incredible task. As we attune more deeply to our essence we see how it IS (and we are) power—it is (we are) divinity, pure desire, is fully alive, fully feeling it all, expressing it all.

This is where we learn power dynamics. Power can easily be equated with having a lot of control. I've seen this definition play out in my life, and we see that in our society the people who have power have control of resources and even power over whole populations. Unfortunately, in mainstream society right now, there's a prevalent paradigm of *power over* instead of a dynamic in which everyone is welcome to exude their power together. What might be more beneficial in the current world dynamic is to practice the type of power wherein: I'm powerful and you're powerful, we're both powerful. I don't have power over you, you don't have power over me, but we can still both be powerful. It actually feels good that way too. In the more familiar paradigm of power, I have power over you so therefore you want the same—power over me. It's all about control and domination—usually requiring force and fear.

Another aspect of how we express our power (and potency—a palpable, powerful presence you can tangibly feel when someone embodies it) comes down to integrity. This is really a fascinating phenomenon, maybe some of you can relate. Have you ever noticed that sometimes it's easier to keep a commitment or stay accountable to someone else rather than to yourself? Such as in making plans you set the tone: "Hey, I'm going to meet you there at 8:00 P.M., I'll be there no matter what," and then you keep that date. And yet when it's just us, just me, like when I make a commitment to myself to meditate for thirty minutes at 7:00 A.M., sometimes it's not as easy to keep when it's just me and myself. This is where our willpower—and our practice of being in integrity with ourselves—must kick in. Especially when no one else is looking.

Willpower is about honoring integrity and accountability with yourself and it is the foundation of what builds our capacity for personal power. We are developing more of our willpower right now by being a part of this experience together and going through these practices. Every time you commit to loving yourself, to forgiving yourself, to doing something good for you just because—especially when no one else is there to see—you are building trust. With greater self-trust, you are strengthening your integrity—and self-belief and confidence that you will do the right thing in the right time. You are trusting yourself to be in greater alignment across what you say, what you think, and how you act. What's more powerful than that?

Here we see our upward spiral into greater integrity and willpower, giving way to more palpable personal power. From here we become more radiant and more magnetic too. We've all experienced this before at some point; being captivated by someone's magnetic glow. Usually underlying their allure you'll find an unmistakable sense of goodness, of integrity and alignment across their values, their beliefs, their ways of being and actions in the world. Integrity feels so good to be around. It feels safe and like it's easy to trust and rest into presence with. Our personal power, anchored in integrity and authenticity, shines a light of magnetic radiance. This felt power is an illumination that glows and flows from within yet is simultaneously palpable, inviting, and inspiring to all who catch a glimpse.

The most potent activator of our personal power and inherent magnetism is truth. If you want to expand in quantum leaps within any area of your life—even in love, financial abundance, any degree of success that you can imagine, creativity, intuition, and anything else you desire—seek to embody more truth. Seek to release lower vibrational energies that you are holding in any part of your body: physical, spiritual, mental, or emotional. Lower vibrational energies include guilt, resentment, and anger, with shame being the lowest of all. These are the energetic obstructions that act as hindrances to your natural magnetic state.

We are designed to be magnetic—to summon into our experience that which we desire, with ease and grace and great efficiency at that. Even the experiences we don't consciously think we want to be having are magnetically summoned into our reality because we are that powerful—we are always creating the perfect experiences to help us make conscious whatever is in the way of embodying greater integrity, authenticity, and presence. Who you are is a magnet, who you are is god, who you are is love. All of the other stuff stuck in the way is noise. It's been learned. It's been picked up along the way. Some of it is not even yours.

Let's unpack the *not even yours* part. What did you learn about power from your mother? What did you learn about power from your father? What was their relationship dynamic like in terms of who was in charge, who was dependable, who was responsible, who was in integrity, who was trustworthy, who was reliable? By earnestly exploring these inquiries you will likely soon recognize in yourself a mirror (of your parents) regarding how your own energy is being expressed and embodied through your own masculine and through your own feminine aspects. It can be astounding to see how we allow our power to be drained unconsciously by inherited patterns that we play out from our parents through a kind of unconscious loyalty. Here we can interrupt and even end an oftentimes multigenerational cycle and choose a different path forward. Here is where we can take our power back from our lineage programming.

We get to do it every day if we so choose. What else can we reclaim our power back from here and now? Even still to this day I am amazed—when I take my power back from people or ideas I didn't even realize I was siphoning energy to until finally I feel my own life force come fully back to myself. Perhaps there is infinite power we can reclaim—and infinite power we can experience flowing through us as our capacity to ground and channel it expands. I am not an expert in power by any means—if anything I have mastered giving my power away more than most, so in a way I am an expert in what it is to lose one's power. But this is where I, and maybe you too, can make a beginning towards becoming experts in reclaiming that which we might have never even realized was ours in the first place. What is it like to be truly alive—fully in our power? Welcome to the grand experiment we are exploring in real time for the first time ever, in these magnificent forms, on this wild ride here on Earth.

Let us awaken to remember what our innermost needs truly are and see how we are the ones responsible for listening, knowing, and attending to what is required to feel our very best. Our energy and experience of reality therein are no one else's responsibility, and when we wake up to see that we really are in charge of choosing how we respond to life and what our subsequent experience is, there's no going back. There's no pretending we can ever be victims again. We see that we've had the power all along.

Once you've seen that you are a creator, and witnessed your power therein to architect or rather invite in your ideal experience, you can only realistically choose to expand in your consciousness and self-awareness of the clearing and realignment that your being on all levels (mind, body, spirit, and soul) yearns to embody. Your natural state is perfect, whole and complete and in optimal health and balance. The fact is, our bodies know how to heal rather miraculously when given space to actually rest and regenerate. We are so intuitive that we usually know what we need, and we know how to give it to ourselves when given permission to do so.

Herein lies the paradox—we are so often simply waiting for permission to give ourselves precisely what we need to thrive. And why is that? It almost doesn't make sense. But when we look at the underlying unconscious thought forms, energetic imprints, and cellular memory that we inherit and develop early on from various traumatic experiences and wounds, that we can even inherit simply from the cultural context we are born into, the blocks to permission start to become illuminated.

BEING FULLY ALIVE IS A CHOICE
WE MAKE EVERY DAY

Really meeting yourself for the first time can be one of the most painful, intimate awakening experiences imaginable. I know for me, one of my conscious moments of meeting myself came when I was about seventeen years old and my best friend at that time, whom I had grown up with, told me that she couldn't be around me anymore because of how I was when I was drinking. It was too painful for her to witness my behavior. She gave me an ultimatum: she said that she couldn't be around me anymore if I continued the way that I was going.

It was at that moment that I really woke up to myself and saw what I was choosing. And really, my harsh awakening got kicked into gear with this experience of feeling heartbroken, feeling like I was about to lose my first love. This friendship, this sisterhood, really was a deep love, much like you might feel in a romantic partnership but without any sexualization or romantic intimacy. There was this deep love and sense of family that I felt

like I was giving up on by choosing, at that time, my other love: alcohol
and the freedom of expression and relaxation that came with it.

**"Yesterday I was clever, so I wanted to change the world.
Today I am wise, so I am changing myself."**
—Rumi

When I first started drinking at the age of fourteen, I felt like I could
finally breathe. The first time I got drunk, I finally felt all my worry and
the weight of the world that I was carrying melt away. So, of course alcohol became my love, of course it became the priority relationship in my
life. Yet when my best friend, my sister, the closest person to me at that
time, gave me this ultimatum that she could no longer be around me if I
continued behaving like this, it was enough to shock me into a new state
of awareness and consciousness in which I really had to get honest with
myself about the choices that I was making.

I had to get honest with myself about the life that I was creating. I had
to get honest about what it was I really wanted. I couldn't allow myself to
continue to be in denial or asleep in avoidance of what reality was clearly
guiding me to look more closely at. So, it was at this moment that I decided
to explore receiving support. I was terrified about what my life would be
like without drinking, but I was more terrified of what my life would
be like without my best friend. And that was enough to get me to my first
AA meeting.

I looked up an AA meeting online and saw that there was one happening that afternoon close to my house. And so I was waiting for the bus on
Fillmore Street in San Francisco's Lower Haight neighborhood, right in
front of my parents' house, when, like clockwork, a car full of my friends
whom I had been partying with for years pulled over to say hi. It was
such a funny divine moment of synchronicity. I remember proudly telling
them, "I'm going to an AA meeting," smiling, laughing a little bit, maybe
not believing myself as to what I was really embarking upon.

I don't remember their response, but just seeing them there was a re-minder of how life is always working in divine timing. It was as though a reflection or an echo of my past life (or really my present life at that time) was rearing its head to show how it was still there, even though part of my consciousness was wanting to change and make a significant shift.

But that brief moment of surrender, that brief open window that I had to really change my circumstance, quickly closed as I arrived at the meet-ing and I let my judgment and projection take over instead of trusting and listening to my higher consciousness that got me to the meeting in the first place. Hearing people talk at the meeting, I superficially judged everyone as being way worse than me, and I immediately rationalized that I wasn't that bad. I hadn't lost everything yet, I shouldn't be there. I wanted to go to college and continue having fun, which definitely en-tailed drinking. I had this all under control. So in that moment I chose to see all of the differences. I chose to see everything that I didn't have in common with these people. I chose to see them, actually, as justifications for why my circumstances weren't bad enough yet and hence why I could keep on as I was.

I would continue like that for seven more years, until the age of twenty-four, when I finally did get sober, when things did get bad enough. When I finally couldn't avoid any longer the sad truth, which was that if I continued behaving the way I was behaving, I was surely going to die. Nonetheless, that was one of the conscious recollections I have in which I really met myself and had this window of opportunity, as we all do at times in our lives, to really make a choice to change my reality. In order to step into a new way of being—I first had to let go of my entire identity as I knew it. I had to take a leap into a massive unknown, and completely surrender. I had to give up on what I thought I had control over, realizing I had none at all.

The path of awakening to higher consciousness is one of letting go of old identities and old ways of being that are not in alignment with the truth of who you really are. Drinking, for me, was an escape mechanism. It was an excuse. It was a self-sabotaging strategy that always kept me distracted, putting out fires and playing small. Life wanted to welcome me forth into greater responsibility and greater leadership but as long as I was giving my power away to alcohol, partying, and other ways of numbing out my actual feelings and awareness—there was no way I could show up in the ways I thought I wanted to. I wanted to make a difference in the world and help people but I couldn't help anyone until I helped myself first.

I wanted to be in integrity. I wanted to be in truth. But as long as I was distracted putting out all the fires of the parties that happened night after night and feeling my body suffering and feeling all of the fogginess from being hungover and putting chemicals in my body, I couldn't show up. I couldn't get patient and clear to see the purpose of my life and the greater meaning arise. I wasn't capable of receiving any of that until I was willing to get sober and cleanse my system of all that had been keeping me asleep in so many ways. I had to start from scratch and return to basics which meant learning to really start taking care of myself for the first time. Oftentimes taking our power back—from things, people, and identities we didn't even know we'd given so much away to—begins with committing to taking care of ourselves so we can truly start to hear our inner voice and discernment of what is most true to us.

OWN YOUR POWER: LIVE YOUR PURPOSE

What would it be like to allow your entire being to be fully here, revealed in your immensity and sheer magnitude, without holding anything back, without hiding away to please anyone or make anyone else comfortable? What if you were to let the ferocity of your presence and its penetrative effect be felt by those you came here to illuminate and divinely trigger?

How much more energy do you have to channel into what feels good for you—your own creativity, desires, and divine callings—when you stop trying, managing, and efforting in all the ways you learn to turn off and turn down? Let's see what we are really made of and what shifts are ready to happen to allow more of the real—and truly powerful—you to emerge.

Let us become radically aware of the ways we've given our power away that have led to exhaustion, energy drain, or confusion in regards to what we really desire. Remember, you are the only one in the way of having-being-doing-receiving-living precisely all that you desire.

"Exhaustion is one of the most sincere forms of prayer."
—Lorin Roche

You can be the parents you never had. Consider in fact how this perfect moment is your opportunity to choose being exactly that. Could this be the embodiment of your innate inner sovereignty across all timelines, space and dimensions? Taking our power back means welcoming our inner masculine and inner feminine to integrate into divine union so we can rest into an unshakable foundation of profound inner resource and support. Here is how we truly learn to self-source our needs and yearnings for the love, care, and affirmation we might have not yet received in the ways we truly wanted. Here is where we can become our own inner loving mother and father, and repattern the aspects of ourselves that feel lacking or incomplete—to remember instead our wholeness and perfection. We soon see from here so many new choice points begin to emerge.

How do we make a beginning? Here are the most effective steps and aligned committed actions I've found useful in embodying our true power and taking back all of that which we've given away to anything and anyone outside of you (without knowing it or not).

When we actually become aware and awake and start to intentionally listen to our own individual impulse—our inherent magnetism and intuitive pull toward certain people, places, and things—always in precise timing, we see we are part of a bigger universal puzzle pretty geniously architected to empower perfect unfoldings beyond our imagination. And we also see how we as humans each on our unique paths somehow work together really harmoniously too, just like nature. Somehow, when we are each following our unique flow and calling, there's a job—a place and a purpose—for everyone. There's a unique place in which every single person belongs.

What's been in the way of this natural order from taking full effect in our mass reality experience though is something I refer to as a phenomeneon of too many cooks in the kitchen. Too many people are trying to do the same thing—trying to be like other people who are socially appreciated, valued, and accepted—and with fewer people doing their unique thing, their authentic calling, well. This has created so much chaos in the collective field—it's rare to feel someone doing their unique soul/sole purpose and instead we have far too many examples of people pretending to be like so many others; it can be hard to feel true uniqueness and authenticity even when it's staring us in the face. So, cultivating mastery within what it is that you love most, what it is that turns you on most about life, is where we must focus.

Everyone around you can usually name and see your unique purpose before you can. But the issue again is those of us who feel like we're not in alignment yet. It's like we're still looking for someone else to give us the answer. For someone else to give us permission to do the thing that we actually already know we want when we follow our impulses. It's so simple. It's so easy. Just get out of the way of being who you truly are. Or so we would think—but really, seeing ourselves and trusting ourselves to take the next right step into actualizing our aligned soul/sole purpose can be the journey of a lifetime. It doesn't have to take forever—but it can feel like the most arduous task when we start waking up, and even still it can feel like we're never there—wherever *there* is supposed to be—yet. I still feel this way sometimes. I don't even know where *there* would be at this point on my path—but it can feel like a fun dream to chase at times, usually amid impatience or resistance to doing the next right thing. And it's okay to acknowledge this and accept it as part of the path in learning and unlearning all we are here to uncover.

Get out of the way of being who you already are. We must be willing to look at whatever is in the way—as THE way—as it comes up, in the moment it arises, while it's fresh. Whatever pops up in our way as resistance or trepidation in stepping into greater authenticity, a sense of alignment with our true purpose and potency, or doing what we know our heart is calling us to explore—we must meet this material and welcome it home. These aspects of ourselves that learned to protect us from danger, that learned to keep us safe in the familiar loops of repetition that never change—they want what's best for us but are operating from an incredibly outdated operating system. We, as the evolving spiritual beings awakening into more of our own presence and true reality, must interrupt the cycle and confront our resistances as great gifts and markers of our growth and potential. In the moment meeting these layers can feel scary, confronting and humiliating and sometimes can seem never-ending. But can we be willing to let those false, protective, survival-oriented aspects of ourselves go (or rather, come home)? So that more of who we already are, who we really are, can simply arise?

Turn Yourself All the Way On

Step into your power: we hear this invitation and term all the time, but what does it really mean? For me, it means to be fully alive, be fully turned on. Fully alive in every single moment, completely present in your body. Receptive to the intuitive superpowers that are guiding you through your body in this present moment to live in alignment with your desires, to have an incredible multisensory, multidimensional experience here on Earth.

I love the analogy of plugging into the wall. We have cell phones, which we plug into the wall to charge up. We have computers, which we plug into the wall to charge up too. So why not look at our human operating system, our body, even our consciousness, as technology, as computing systems, multiple systems online at once, simultaneously operating in concert. Just like a computer or cell phone, we need to be plugged in so that our battery is fully charged and we're fully on.

I love the analogy of being turned on when we talk about pleasure and even sexuality. Being turned on doesn't have to imply a sexual impulse. However, why not? Why aren't we completely turned on by being alive and having a purpose? Be turned on by your passion, your creativity. Be so turned on by life that you're just in total, ecstatic, passionate bliss. I believe that's available to all of us, and perhaps that's what our fullest expression of power is guiding us to experience every moment. Turn on passion and infinite energy. Embody your complete energetic expression. How about in every moment? When you're in the flow, doing what you love, feeling amazing, it's like time ceases to exist because time doesn't really exist in this quantum reality.

You've had that experience of transcending time and space before. We all have, and this is what happens when you're in such a dynamic, passionate, embodiment of your powerful expression. You transcend time.

You transcend any limitations. You get to play in a new dimension of possibility. And yet, to be operating in that level of energetic mastery, we must make sure we're charged up.

Let's explore a few more definitions and understandings of power and its many forms. I'd also encourage you to investigate what power means to you and how you relate with your own power, with the concept of giving power away or even with the idea of taking ones power back from anything outside of yourself. In the most simple sense, power can be thought of as the ability to get what you want—and not just get what you want but magnetize and create what you want. Power is the ability to have your needs and your desires fully met at all times.

There's a few different types of power, and as was alluded to a bit before, it can be helpful to orient within masculine and feminine distinctions of power so we can see how our unique operating system might be ripe for greater integration and embodiment. I should preface this with a bit of a disclaimer—I don't actually subscribe to the differentiation of masculine and feminine energy as much as I once did earlier on my path. For a time it was very helpful to understand these archteypes as a way to better see my own shadows and unconscious aspects, especially those being repeated from inherited family trauma via my mother's or father's lineages. At a certain point, though, I must wonder—does harping in on the masculine and feminine aspects of ourselves serve to empower continued separation and perhaps even disassociation instead of deepening into more fully integrated, embodied experiences of our uniqueness that transcend gender, identity, or any box we could ever think to fit in?

So, throughout what we explore next—see if it's helpful for you where you are at on your path to consider these distinctions of masculine and feminine as we come to learn where we can support greater balance within and without. Yet if you also feel naturally the urge to question this approach because a more integrated, embodied understanding of yourself outside of specific aspects already makes more sense to you—then please continue discerning what is most authentic. Please share, in your own way, in your own words, what is arising as the best guidance on your path. I (and I'm sure many others too) would love to explore new ways of seeing and understanding our embodiment processes from those who see through the traditionally taught paradigms of personal growth and transformation into new systems and modalities that can better serve us to consider from now on.

Back to our exploration of the masculine and feminine aspects of our collective humanity and how power can express through each of them. Consider the notion of soft power which equates with feminine energy. Soft power involves seduction, captivation, persuasion, and magnetism—this idea that everything is just coming to you when you're in this magnetic, ecstatic, blissful state. You're so turned on in sharing your passion, sharing your gifts, that you're summoning everything that you're meant to receive to support you and bring your vision into reality, into manifestation. We can also talk about the implicit sexual energy of soft power. I would say that the divine expression of that energy is our creative life force, which is our aliveness. When we are channeling our passion and fervor for whatever it is we love most—or for whatever we are most turned on or charged up by—we are magnetic and more easily attract whatever is required for us to fulfill our purpose at hand. When we are fully alive and awake, we are inherently guided and supported in being our true selves and contributing our uniqueness.

> **"The deepest secret is that life is not a process of discovery, but a process of creation. You are not discovering yourself, but creating yourself anew. Seek therefore, not to find out Who You Are, but seek to determine Who You Want to Be."**
> **—Neale Donald Walsch**

We see soft power especially in advertising. Consider the seduction of certain advertising, the suggestiveness, the persuasion—one example that comes to mind is amazing sales copy. When it just feels like a tease or even like you're being flirted with, when it feels like you're being captivated and it's almost hypnotic in its effect. When you think, *I don't even know what this person is talking about, but this energy is so captivating, I want it. I desire it.* I can think of video advertising especially or even still photography that might have nothing to do with the product being sold but the overall feeling and look of what's being transmitted is captivating in such a way that you feel the energy of the invitation—you taste what it's like to be in the experience of whatever that product is promising, and the allure, the potential on offer—is more potent than even a direct showcase of the product itself might be.

In fact, it's the mystery or understated-ness that actually draws us in more—we want to taste the unknown. Here we tap into an unmistakable aspect of our human experience—the part that is afraid of the unknown but also wants it more than anything at all—we want to explore the void, the mystery of the unknowable, the unachievable, the impossible. We are built to be curious and step into the curiosity of what could be—if only we just took one step further into the new. Soft power, or feminine power, exudes this kind of invitation, inspiration, and muse. It can be intoxicating. This intoxicating, ungrounded effect can also be a shadow aspect of feminine power if left unchecked—a way in which feminine temptation and muse energy can distract and lead to disassociation or confusion away from the purpose at hand.

Hard power, which we can equate more with masculine power, is forceful and at times demanding. *Coercive* is a really good word for understanding hard power. We could affiliate coercive, hard power with militaristic, political operations that would involve more force, such as invasions or war activities. Coercive power can also exhibit commonly in business, for example, or even in any of your relationships. If you're having an argument and you just want someone to agree with you because you're fighting and aggressive energy is present—so you hold your stance and convince the other to get on your side, this is a show of hard power. You might say something threatening or forewarning like: "If you don't see my point of view here and come into agreement with the terms I am outlining, I will have no choice but to withdraw my offer and close the window of opportunity for collaboration, for good." A suggestive, soft power, feminine approach might mean asking instead—in a more curious, suggestive, inspiring, inviting tone: "Wouldn't it be nice if we could do this? Wouldn't it be beautiful if we did this? Wouldn't it feel good? What kind of collaboration would feel most enjoyable for you? How can we create terms in which we both feel balanced and supported?" The hard power, coercive, more masculine approach would more likely make a command, make a directive, make an ultimatum, even.

Coercive energy can sometimes turn into manipulation or threatening aggression if left unchecked—which can mean a masculine shadow or wound is emerging to be felt and healed. When we experience someone being coercive to the point of feeling manipulated or controlled, can we see underneath the superficial game and remember—the hurt child within who's acting out? Perhaps they're simply trying to control their experience and environment to feel safe and supported, because deep within they feel painfully unstable and insecure. Honestly sometimes I wonder if all the world's supposed political conflicts are actually simply the result of hurt children living within adult bodies who are still not getting what they need when it comes to basic levels of safety, love, affirmation, and attunement. Hurt people hurt people, after all—until someone wakes up and chooses to break the cycle by healing themselves and putting a stop to the pain.

Let's dive deeper into the shadows—all the way in. It's fun to give voice to these unconscious aspects so many of us can play out that are also very rampant in our society and external experiences of reality and in our relationships. So we've established partially that there is the masculine shadow, which can express as aggressive, even violent, coercive, and manipulative. The divine expression of healthy masculine energy is truth, trust, and absolute integrity—whereas its shadow is anything counter-acting those states usually from a wound of not feeling worthy, stable, or secure sufficiently to withstand the power of these natural gifts. And then, there's the shadow of the feminine, which we could call the wounded feminine which feels murky or swampy, meaning there's no clear sense of energetic boundaries or differentiation. Wounded feminine energy can feel foggy, it's not clear—altogether lacking boundaries, clarity, and integrity, which then translates to a yucky feeling. It's hard to give words to, but we've all experienced it.

Instead of being captivating and inviting as the muse which is the healthy feminine expression of energy, the shadow of feminine energy can translate into very repulsive energy because neediness and over-attachment are rooted in distrust and all around discomfort. We've felt this before whenever we are in the presence of someone who feels to be leaking out their energy as a means of trying to control a particular result or outcome to suit their needs—even at the expense of others present in the experience with them. It can come across as commanding too much attention, trying too hard to be seen, trying to capture or captivate others' attention or energy—to fill a void, to be completed, to be validated. Naturally we feel repelled by this energy because it goes against the laws of nature to engage with it—we want to meet instead in trust, in clarity, in sovereignty, in truth. Anything not in alignment with our core values will feel repulsive and sticky—like we are being drawn into playing a game we don't want to play. When your truth radar goes off in these cases—and you know something or someone is trying to reel you in with a wounded feminine energy that feels leaky and unsettling, trust your discernment and center more into your own core self and redirect your energy to you instead of to them.

It's more common than we know to be energetically repelled by people that feel too needy. You may see it in text messaging or in how people interact on social media. You may know someone who is too attached, who's grasping at you and in a way perhaps unknowingly trying to siphon your energy to complete or settle a part of themselves they feel unstable in. What's important for us to remember as we all evolve and practice more sovereignty, healthy boundaries, and clear expressions of our personal energy is to trust our discernment at all times, as best we can. We are all learning—sometimes through throwing shots in the dark, as we've covered thus far; pioneering presence for the first time in a body like this can feel like that—how to trust our truth.

Keep experimenting but consciously reminding yourself to check in whenever you come into contact with new inputs—new people, ideas, invitations, potentials—how does this feel for you to be in energetic exchange with? Do you feel balanced, do you feel clear, do you feel invited to make your own choice of how you want to engage? We all have such beauty and wisdom to share deep down—and the most empowering way we can share it with others is to allow them their own choice in how they wish to engage (or not). When we are free to make our own choices according to our own discernment, we are liberated, powerful beings capable of carving out truly unique paths into new potentials and possibilities. Here is how we create the future.

What kind of world do we live in when we are all more integrated in our uniqueness—our full expressions of masculine, feminine, aliveness and all the creative energy we are here to exude? Who are we when we expand even further beyond the boxes of identity, categories, and names that are so limiting to the infinite spiritual beings we are here to embody? Men and women and everyone in between or beyond all have masculine and feminine energetics that we're working with. These archteypes are ancient inheritances from so many generations passed that have played out the extremes of gendered expression across a wide spectrum—and we are taking our power back from history to now redefine our own for the kind of world we want to live into moving forward. What if we no longer have to choose one, of anything, to be—and we can be, instead, both—and all. Or maybe we're none—and we just are. Perhaps I am just me, and you are just you, and all the rest beyond that are names and boxes we've designed to try to understand the indefinable. Divinity can't exist in a box after all. I love that song by Cat Stevens—from one of my favorite movies *Harold and Maude*—that says: "If you want to be her, be her. And if you want to be you, be you. 'Cause there's a million things to do, you know that there are."

Teamwork Makes the Dream Work: Integrated Divine Union

An empowered divine masculine is all about embodying total truth and simplicity in that truth. This energy, in its healthy expression, exudes incredible integrity and a strong commitment to deliverance of authentic desires, aligned action, and pristine clarity in all thoughts, words, and deeds, especially when it comes to supporting the divine feminine. The empowered divine masculine is tapped into divine timing—this energy knows what to do and when to do it and is willing to go to any lengths to do what exactly is required, to deliver the desires that are inspired by the divine feminine muse (emerging from within oneself or from another). The divine, empowered masculine and feminine work as a team. A dream team, in fact.

The divine masculine wants to be of service to the feminine, wants to feel so inspired, so turned on and so alive that from here its purpose is clear. The empowered masculine says: I'm willing to go to any lengths to do what is required to bring my desired reality into being, and the subsequent aligned actions become illuminated when I'm operating in my essence, embodying an activated, powerful state. When we embody our masculine power and potency, we are skilled in moving through life and all relations with directness, clarity, truth, high integrity, clear boundaries, and overflowing embodied presence.

> **"Love is not an intellectual process but rather a dynamic energy flowing into and through us at all times, whether we are aware of it or not. We must learn to receive love as well as to give. Only in community, only in relationships, only in service can we truly understand the all-encompassing energy of love."**
> **—Brian Weiss**

The wounded masculine can manifest in so many ways. One I see most commonly is to overwork, usually stemming from a fear or worry that what we truly desire isn't happening yet—so we must force it into being. The wounded masculine feels impatient, distrustful, and unsure of whether or not the universe is supporting one's desires fully—hence the urge arises to do too much, to try to make something happen all the while being worried, anxious, and noncommittal. As the divine masculine is about aligned, committed action, the wounded expression or shadow here expresses as lack of commitment, uncertainty, and indecision. The wounded masculine forgets its power—forgets knowing that you have the power to decide (and create) exactly what you want. What you want is exactly what you deserve to receive and this discernment is not defined by anything or anyone outside of you. You always have the power to choose.

When the wounded masculine forgets itself and its true power, the feminine is left hanging in the balance—alone, abandoned, free flowing without the support and structure she requires to feel safe and secure to fully expand into her infinite potential. Without the masculine to take the lead in providing a clear container and healthy boundaries through which the feminine can flow and dance—both are inherently lost to their purpose and full possibility. The feminine requires the masculine for support and grounding into Earth the cosmic muses she is so naturally able to tap into and bring in from heavenly realms. The feminine requires the support of safety and reassurance—exuding from truth and integrity and radical commitment to what's good and right—to feel safe to let go and allow a higher-consciousness intelligence to move through her infinite channels.

It's such an interesting balance these elements strike in their divine dance—both requiring specific calls to duty from one another in specific ways. The masculine wants to be inspired and reminded of magic by the feminine—he wants to have a purpose to align with in service to the highest good of all which naturally comes through the feminine when she is in her power. What would it be like to marry these two energies within? What would it be like to experience such deep commitment to honoring these aspects within ourselves that we are living from an unshakable foundation of trust, integrity, and stability that allows infinite wisdom, creativity, and unfathomable muse to endlessly pour through us? *What then shall we co-create?*

Another distinction between masculine and feminine to consider is the mind—our genius mental body and all its wonderous capacities to know, to understand, to conceptualize. The masculine is more oriented in the mind, the intellect, rational thinking, structure, and in focused, clear, organized logic whereas the feminine is more energetic, ethereal, emotional, and anchored in the body and all its expressions of feeling, sensitivity, and sensuality. Right- and left-brain understandings of our operational structures come up here as well—wheras the right hemisphere of our brain is understood to be more intuitive, perceptual, and sensory oriented (which can be felt as a more feminine aspect) and the left is more rational, logistical, and intellectual (masculine oriented).

I believe that now we are evolving into more utilization of our whole brain—along with greater heart-mind coherence in general—that's ushering in a new expression of our divine human blueprint. We are reawakening many dormant abilities and gifts—our multi-dimensional sensory perception that sees, feels, and knows that so much lies beyond what we've been conditioned to *see*. Who are we when we are so integrated in our uniqueness that we can bridge between the intuitive soul self and the rational, structural, logical self in the same moment—what kind of new worlds shall we architect then? What about when feeling and sensitivity are thoughtfully woven into our most rational, structured creations—wherein we place people and purpose ahead of traditional motivators of profit and power? I'm excited to find out and be a part of pioneering this new path, together.

Creativity and inspiration know no time, no space; they know no structure and yet silmultaneously desire structure to truly thrive. How can we become empty channels through which infinite source can flow through? Throughout which more of our true selves can simply imbue? This is how interdependence and divine union originate—the masculine is the grounded container and support required for the feminine infinite flow to anchor into reality. The feminine requires the masculine's structure, clarity and groundedness in order to anchor in her divine inspiration into the Earth plane—here is how we bridge Heaven into Earth. It is through our own bodies first—and then we actualize this more in the world around us through all we choose to create from this integrated uniqueness we can't help but embody. This is the recipe for manifestation. When we merge inspiration, desire, good feelings, gratitude, and excitement for our desires with clear structures, aligned committed action, and high integrity values and standards (like healthy boundaries and clear focus on our purpose), we allow effortlessness and ease in our manifestations. This is how we love to see the feminine and masculine collaborating.

We can envision the masculine as a patriarch and, especially in our current society, the wounded patriarch, which can tend to take on the shape of an inner critic. How would it feel to have instead of that inner critic a healed divine masculine energy embodied in your most powerful expression of self that provides, protects, and serves, and, as an agent of truth, is really here to serve your soul? Similarly, if we imagine the empowered feminine as a royal queen or another powerful muse leader that resonates, what kind of masculine king or counterpart would she most love to call in for her key support team, for her inner sanctum and sanctuary? It can be fun and extremely helpful to play in imagining the physical personifications of these energies to solidify your awareness and integrate more fully what's on offer here. Give it a try. I love imagining my inner masculine as a sexy, tall, handsome king-like leader that I can rely on to support me, to hold me, and whom I trust to always show up in absolute truth and integrity no matter what—there's nothing sexier than that. My inner feminine is a righteous queen, radiating the most beautiful light and charisma—she is beyond magnetic and lights up any space she moves through. She trusts completely in all of life and embodies her purpose of allowing the divine muse to flow through her and color her desires perfectly so she can dream awake the world she wish existed. My personification of these energies has matured as my needs and awareness have evolved—which has been fun to feel and notice over the years. How about yours?

I love this passage in Sara Avant Stover's *The Way of the Happy Woman*: "The divine healed masculine communicates clearly, sets boundaries not barriers, and exerts the will that's rooted in the soul's deepest desires. He does not force, push, manipulate, or control. He's in touch with his heart and with the divine feminine without collapsing into his feelings or agenda of others. He must penetrate the world with his truth and will never turn away from it. He never ever gives up on his service to his higher purpose and from this magic manifests."

This is a beautiful vision of the divine masculine. How does that resonate for you? If you have a desire to speak your truth more fully and live your purpose, that's your divine masculine wanting to be embodied. How do you do that? Start listening to your desires in every single moment. Lean on the feminine's support for empowering your intuition and your soul to guide you based on your desires, based on what feels good, to guide you in aligned, committed action toward bringing your purpose into manifestation. Maybe it's that simple. Let's find out for ourselves.

"Asking ourselves who we are means reckoning with who we were. This can be terrifying, because it also requires us to examine how we've changed. But by not asking, we're not serving ourselves, we're serving others."
—Lindsay Goldwert

Divine Feminine Power

The divine feminine is sensuous and trusting and simply requires feeling safe and supported to actualize as her full potential which is a highly intuitive, inspirational muse. I like to think about the divine feminine as a muse, or even as a goddess. And we all have access to this energy regardless of our physical body or identities. Think of this beautiful, inspired goddess, this conduit that you have within you that's literally just wanting to channel magic through good feelings, through beauty, through love, through nurturance. Do you want to know this energy more deeply and see how it wants to play in your life—to bring more color and depth to your experience and expression? The words *yummy* and *juicy* come to mind—which in the past would annoy me if I ever heard someone over-using them in explaining an energetic or relational concept—but now, further along in my own sensual awakening and embodiment process—I get it. **Words in our current language often can't even come close to doing justice to the meanings we strive to express regarding the felt sense experiences we now have access to.**

Personify divine, empowered feminine energy as your own internal mother or goddess self—think of your divine mother, the mother you've always wanted, the mother that you wished you had. Maybe you had an amazing mom in this life—that's beautiful! Even still—what is your dream mother like, the mom that you wished you had who is just so loving, so nurturing, so kind, so beautiful? Your fairy godmother, maybe; who is she? How does she conduct herself? What about her feels loving, kind, radiant, and just captivating, magnetic? Here is your opportunity to design the support team you wish you had—in just the right ways meant for you to receive.

Here is the empowered, inspired divine feminine energy within all of us that's wanting to bring through muse, your inspiration, divine purpose, and guide life to feel the best it can in every single moment. But how does she become wounded? How does the wounded feminine express itself when this part of us we all share so naturally wants to play in receptivity, beauty, trust, flow, and in magnificent creative inspiration?

The magic of the divine feminine is trusting the unknown, and trusting that anything that we could ever plan is so limited compared to what the universe aims to deliver. She is inspired and embodied in her own infinite wisdom that she trusts that the divine plan unfolding is always infinitely better than anything we could ever try to control or force. The divine feminine believes in magic and embodies complete trust and receptivity. Her job is to receive. She receives support, love, protection, action, and service from the masculine. She receives support and infinite abundance from life. She knows that as we continue to trust ourselves and our innate inspiration arising through our desires, we are always taken care of.

The wounded shadow of the feminine can come up when she is ignored, when the muse isn't allowed to flow and inspiration isn't allowed (or supported with stability and structure) to happen. When she is not feeling nurtured, taken care of or well rested, the values that she's meant to embody can be undermined. When this happens, many people lack a sense of wholeness or a sense of self; they experience self-abandonment. They may think, *I'm not living my purpose, I'm not doing what I'm here to do, my energy isn't flowing freely. I don't feel like myself.* So many people are experiencing that at this moment. Can you feel that? Here is where we can repair any ruptures within ourselves that are begging for our attention attunement, love, and care. We have the medicine and it can be as simple as tending to our needs with our own loving presence—and listening to what's arising.

Any imbalance within the feminine expression of our energy gives way to an imbalance in the masculine too—and vice versa. The two are interdependent, remember? How do we equalize and come into balance between both expressions in the most healthy authentic, feeling ways that work for us to thrive? When the feminine is disempowered and not living her purpose to be the muse in total surrender, the masculine will overcompensate for this lack of inspiration and lack of nurturance. The over-responsible masculine can manifest as leaking energy out through trying to do too much, through exhaustion, and impatience, anxiety, and even an addiction to worry and fear. It can feel like being so afraid—you simply can't do enough to create the result that you think you need to feel okay, to feel safe, to feel supported, to feel loved. And if the masculine is imbalanced with lacking boundaries, broken commitments, vague values, or poor discernment of what's most true—the feminine muse will surely stop flowing, will feel stagnant and other insecurities will emerge to get one's attention kickstarted back into integrity and presence. Not standing up for one's true beliefs and instead letting another's principles overshadow your own and therefore determine your choices to follow is a perfect example of how we undermine our masculine and in doing so also stagnate our feminine power.

Another shadow of the feminine manifests as distrust. Distrust in life and distrust in self. We can also call this unworthiness. Wounded feminine energy usually manifests as unworthiness and a deep, deep feeling of not deserving that which you desire, not being empowered in your desire, not being empowered in your intuitive inspiration, not feeling worthy of receiving the guidance that is always available to you, to all of us. It feels like an ultimate fragmentation from our true selves—when we are cut off from our intuitive compass that is seeding within the perfect steps, the perfect plans we're called to follow, to bring our purpose, our full expression of power, to life. One of my favorite paradoxes of being human comes down to power and how we all want it but to fully embody it—can be terrifying. Just like how we are usually always the only ones in the way of having what we say we want. We keep from ourselves that which we say we desire most because at some level we are overwhelmed by the feeling of our own power. Do we have capacity to hold all of this aliveness? Or will we short-circuit if we allow more abundance, love, presence in? Here is our practice.

So, how do you empower the divine feminine? How do you start to activate more of the sense of innate wholeness you are that naturally knows how to trust, how to receive, how to surrender and simply be a channel for the muse? How do we turn our listening and our receptivity potentials all the way on? The answers to our questions herein reside in embodying our understanding—and living it fully—of integrity, responsibility, and sovereignty.

Integrity is a state of being in which what you feel, how you act, and what you believe are all completely aligned. There is no confusion among any of the three; you are completely integrated in your truth no matter how you feel, think, or show up. Full-power integration across mind, body, spirit, and soul. Responsibility is your ability to respond to life through right action and discernment in all relationships of what is right for you based on what feels best and what feels true for you, regardless of external conditioning. Sovereignty is another key that means you are embodying your power of sourcing your own truth and defining yourself on your own terms. These are the ingredients for living in excellence, integrated in your true self, with higher consciousness leading the way, empowered to pioneer and create your most authentic, desired reality.

If integrity is the state of being whole and complete, integrated within all aspects of your being—your mind, body, spirit, and soul—sovereignty means being self-sourced and self-reliant, trusting and affirming of your innate creator power within all facets of your life. You are embodying your sovereignty when nothing and no one outside of you defines you. When you are embodied in your sovereignty you know you are whole and complete no matter what. You completely own your power, and rest into knowing your infinite creative capacity.

Your purpose is to share and embody the gift you've always most wanted to receive. The path of living your purpose demands discipline and mastery. I wish someone had told me this a long time ago. Discipline is attuning yourself through consistent practice to being grounded, stable, and present. Here is where you can truly listen—where your energy, your power is contained in your sense of center. Here you receive clear guidance and know what is right for you, and you know how and when you're meant to show up. This is alignment. Discipline also entails becoming a conscious disciple of something you want to devote yourself to. What are you in reverence to—perhaps something sacred you are in devotion to in this beautiful life? Become a disciple of this—just for you, no one else even needs to know. Practice reverence and faith with fervor as you walk your path with disciplined commitment. What a gift to give ourselves.

"The meaning of life is to find your gift.
The purpose of life is to give it away."
—Pablo Picasso

You might have heard this before: we're each born as unique as a snowflake, as a unique transmission of a being. No one is the same, by design. We each have this unique soul, a unique body, a unique expression—and a special gift to give through our embodiment that only we can give. There's no competition. There's no comparison. It's funny to think we would ever compare ourselves to anyone else or seek to be like another when inherently our designs prevent exactly that. And yet so much of our society is obsessed with certain images and trends and styles we are somehow encouraged to emulate and copy as a way to fit in, to be understood, to belong. What if instead we fully owned our uniqueness—all out—fly the freak flag high, as they say? We are all pretty weird when we get down to it—aren't we? And by weird, I mean it in the original sense of the word which means carrying great wisdom and insight.

When we are being ourselves—as our uniqueness, simply letting it flow—there's no thinking. When we allow ourselves to follow the creative impulse that naturally flows through in the moment it's meant to, we see how we are naturally guided to be of service in unique ways only we can fulfill. This is how our purpose emerges, without even trying. Our purpose is always naturally guiding us to help and contribute in unique ways—that also usually tend to feel like a lot of fun. Remember what we said before: *who are we when we stop trying?*

Know that you are infinitely supported—by yourself first and foremost and by all the dimensional aspects of you that are always here helping you align with your highest good in all moments. You embodying your highest good is always inherently in service to all. Whatever is in the way, is the way. Trust yourself to know the path that's calling you forward into the most extraordinary version of you that you know in your heart you came here to be.

**"To have anything we want, we need only raise our
level of consciousness to the level of consciousness
where what we want exists."
—Wu Wei**

PERSONAL POWER ATTUNEMENTS

Release Power Leaks

In what ways have you given your power away? To whom? To what? And how? To beliefs, to others' expectations (or your own), to societal conditioning, to fear? What are the cords of energy draining you, latching on to you, holding you back from moving forward on your desired path? Pick at least one person, idea, expectation, or belief, anything you feel is maintaining a powerful energetic pull on you that's holding you back. Prepare to write a letter to this entity in order to release it. Write a letter to your selected entity. In the letter explain how you are ready to release this entity from your field now and forever.

You can trust your intuition to guide whatever else you need to write—what needs to be said to bring closure to this connection? Do you need to express an unexpressed emotion? Tell this entity something you've always wanted to say? Apologize? Make your negative experience known, if there is one? Say what you wish would have happened instead? Let it all out. Once you have the letter completed, knowing it contains everything you need to communicate once and for all, read it out loud and, depending on how you feel about it, decide how to destroy it in a demonstration of complete release.

You can burn it, beat it up (this is healing for somatic release at the cellular level if you feel angry, upset, or have unexpressed tension to let out), fly it away on a kite, anything your heart truly desires. It's up to you. Your intentions will create the space you truly need. Be a conscious observer of any resistance that comes up along the way. If you can, share with someone you love and trust who can support you. A lot can come up in this process. This is an incredibly powerful exercise/tool that will surely be drawn upon going forward—take it easy with yourself in this practice as it can bring up a lot of intensity and unfelt emotions that are ready to be felt and released.

Reclaim What Is Yours

Keep choosing to stand in your power. Another potent writing-reflection exercise that can help us to get back into our power is to freewrite your response to the following question: In order to create all that I desire, what do I now give myself permission to do, be, and have that previously I was unwilling to acknowledge? I love this as a daily exercise of reclaiming what we truly want for ourselves, coming home to our intentions even more clearly and grounding in any specific commitments required to actualize our desired shifts.

"Hold the Field" Practice

This is one of my favorite practices an old friend shared with me a few years back, sourced from Ron Young (you can learn more on his website at healingwisdom.com). It goes like this:

Bring someone to mind that feels sticky or murky—like you've given power to them or perhaps crossed some other kind of uncomfortable boundary to the point where they feel to be looming in your consciousness or field. Bring them into your mind's eye and you can even imagine them as though they're standing or sitting across from you—maybe a few feet away, or closer or farther—depending on what feels best for you. You decide. Then, repeat out loud as though you're saying these words to them:

"I am here, you are there."
"That is your story, not my story."
"When I cannot affect change, I withdraw my energy and attention and place it where I can. In this way, I honor the higher movement and guidance of the Soul."

Try repeating this silently or aloud for three to five minutes once per day for twenty-one days in a row. Notice what shifts after doing so—even on a daily basis you might feel your relationship with the person you are doing this practice on completely change as you change. This practice enables me to catch very early in the process when my body-mind wants to give my power away to someone or something else—what a blessing to interrupt the pattern and reclaim more of our own presence.

Don't Diminish Your Power When You Speak

It's fascinating that when we speak we are conditioned to say *sorry* and *I don't know* to diminish ourselves and not own or trust what we say. Women get conditioned with this in mind particularly strong in our society—don't speak up too loud or question authority or be too demanding, sound familiar? It can also be common to be conditioned to conceal or diminish our raw emotion when we speak, perhaps because we've been taught to think that to do so is too intimate and might make others uncomfortable.

When you use the terms *I don't know, sorry* and *if that makes sense* often, especially before beginning a powerful statement or before making a request, notice if you are diminishing your right to confidently claim that which you absolutely do know. Especially to my ladies out there ready to embody more of your fierce power and directness—stop playing miss little nice girl. The world needs more powerful women who aren't afraid to speak their truth and be seen standing out of the crowd—true leaders. Let's play.

We developed these coping mechanisms to diminish our power when we grew up with people who didn't understand us or didn't validate us. Being powerful necessitates building a strong nervous system that can contain your presence fully and effectively transmit the energy that you are here to hold in and through your body. We are here to co-create and collaborate, and our language must follow suit in embodying our collective intentions.

No one can ever take your power away from you; you are always in charge of who you give it to whether unconsciously or consciously. So how shall you practice? For me when I started becoming aware of my own tendencies to diminish my potency through language, I noticed how often I overstated *I don't know but*, usually before I would say something I did know quite clearly. But I didn't want to seem like a know-it-all or like I was more intelligent (and therefore isolated) from the person I wanted to connect with—so I diminished my power and played small to fit in or belong. I would reroute this pattern at first by catching myself in the autopilot response and interrupt out loud as soon as I said *I'm sorry* or *I don't know* with—*Wait, I do know this*, or *I'm actually not sorry, I know this to be true*. Then—say what you want to say, directly, with ferocity, as clear as ever.

You know what you want and your communication emulates this knowing one million percent. Next time you make a request—ask for what you want as directly as possible, without any permission or diminishment. Try it when you are at a restaurant, just for fun: next time you order, ask specifically to be given the precise order you want even if it requires a bit of customization—take your time in placing the exact order you want. Just like with all of life—the universe is here to serve you, so how are you placing your order?

It would be a little awkward at first—sure, growing pains are sometimes. But eventually I stopped responding this way on autopilot and got more comfortable being direct and forthright, even to the point where others' discomfort at my directness stopped bothering me. I came to realize that others' discomfort is a good thing—they're being faced with truth that's confronting them to speak their own truth more fervently and directly too in moments like this. They're being reminded of their own power too and it's up to them whether or not they choose to reclaim what is theirs and become the leader of their own lives. We are paving the way for a whole new paradigm of relating—and it's pretty badass honestly—this world of leaders leading together.

"Our prime purpose in this life is to help others."
—Dalai Lama

Empower Your Divine Feminine

Entire books could be written on energetic empowerment, masculine and feminine archetypes and divine union—in fact there are probably many out there that dive a whole lot deeper than we have started to here. I smile knowing this. For right here and now though, here are some of my favorite practices for anchoring into more empowerment and reclamation of your divine feminine and masculine energy—explore what resonates and try it on for size:

- Commit to more downtime, relaxation, rejuvenation, nourishment, and rest. Can you schedule a solo date? Time off? Alone time (unplanned, unscheduled flow time) everyday to allow your muse to be activated?
- Practice creative expression: allow yourself time and space each day to tap into your creative muse—painting, singing, moving, dancing—in any ways that feel good for you. Create simply for the sake of creating, enjoying every moment—without an end or objective in mind. Simply because it feels good.
- Practice receiving by asking for help: practice conscious communication to ask for what you need and empower others in your life to support you. Drop out of story or justification—trust in others' sovereign ability to make decisions for themselves and to align accordingly with the highest good. Empower them to empower you.
- Self-soothe: how would you love to receive nurturance and soothing of your physical being? Self-massage; self–energy healing; deep, slow stretching? Aromatherapy? How does your feminine muse desire nourishment? Listen and receive.

- Spend time in nature to recalibrate your energetic system: take a day trip somewhere new, explore your inspiration and muse, see what happens when you interrupt your daily routines and take yourself into a new environment, tapping into your intuition to guide you moment by moment.

Empower Your Divine Masculine

- Maintain clear boundaries: Create more boundaries in your schedule regarding your availability. Commit to having down-time, alone time and time to simply recharge.
- Drop any commitments or obligations that don't feel fun or that feel draining in any way; do so without a justification/story.
- Show up with truth and integrity: Where in your life are you being asked to show up in more authenticity and in alignment with what you truly value? What truth wants to be expressed and how can you support yourself in letting it out?
- Cultivate healthy boundaries in relationships: Are there any relationships in which you'd like to create a better boundary to take care of yourself, to feel more in alignment, and to experience greater reciprocity? What do you require to feel more met and balanced—reflect and get clear for yourself, then share in your desired dynamics. Set the tone for the kinds of relationships you dream of being possible.
- Initiate: What in your life are you being called to initiate? The masculine loves to take initiative on behalf of the feminine muse—what inspiration are you receiving that wants to be enacted via a powerful commitment or aligned action?
- Honor organization, clarity, and structure: Where in your life do you require more structural support? A very common area is finances. Is there any area of your life that could benefit from improved structure and clarity? Commit to at least one action, no matter how small, aimed at improving your structures and supporting your visions in taking shape. Even the small commitment of saving a particular amount of money on a recurring basis can work wonders to instill more grounded presence and integrity.

10

EXPRESS YOUR AUTHENTICITY

Authenticity isn't at all what I thought it was at first. For many years I even taught about it as something else—more like it was a concept of being true to yourself or living in accordance with one's essence. What does authenticity mean to you? Over the years of my own healing journey—notably over the last few years in particular—I've done a deep dive along with many dark nights of the soul getting schooled in the true nature of authenticity.

It's so important to come up with our own definitions and understandings of the concepts and words we use all the time without a second thought—especially if we're ever called to teach them to others. To me authenticity means: the state of being real, as we are, embodied in truth. What does it mean to you? Maybe your words will be better for your own understanding. I couldn't have defined this for you until I came into my own understanding of it by walking my own path. I think the same goes for all of us—we must seek more of our own meanings and authentic words to describe our experiences. This way we can communicate more clearly and in doing so, invite space for more authentic, intimate connection.

Authenticity is also a capacity we can develop—perhaps infinitely, if we are committed to the journey of really meeting ourselves and seeing what we are truly made of underneath all the stories, the programming, the projections and traumas. Something else I've come to understand as a key part of authenticity and deprogramming everything in the way of being truly ourselves is this: we have cultivated different personalities as survival or coping mechanisms to deal with whatever trauma was present, usually when we were little. But our authenticity—our true self is divinity—our unobstructed essence. Our personality can take many shapes and tends to be informed by reactivity to certain patterns that, again, happened when we were little but it's just a surface-level presentation of who we are. And usually we have far more masks on covering up our true essence than we are even aware of—and maybe the more we become aware, the more masks we notice remain to be taken off.

One of my favorite reflections on personality comes from Gabor Maté, a leading visionary on addiction, authenticity, and embodiment, in his book *In the Realm of Hungry Ghosts: Close Encounters with Addiction*. He says: "What we call the personality is often a jumble of genuine traits and adopted coping styles that do not reflect our true self at all but the loss of it." And similarly, John Bradshaw, in one of the foremost essential books on inner child healing, *Homecoming: Reclaiming and Championing Your Inner Child*, remarks: "The greatest wound a child can receive is the rejection of his authentic self." We are all simply here, attempting to remember who we were before we were made to forget by nature of the trauma we experienced in our families growing up. Our divinity, our essence, our authentic truth are already here, and now. There's nothing more to acquire; in fact, maybe in our present-moment, personal development world there's too much of selling us stories on what solutions and quick fixes we need to instantly gratify this desire to be ourselves. Take this course, take this program, read this book, do this training, learn this specific thing—stack on more knowledge and concepts to fill your consciousness with distractions away from simply being, feeling, and sitting with yourself. That's one way to look at it at least.

Funny for me to say that, as I've put a lot of my life force into creating this book—yet my intention isn't to fill your head with more concepts and ideas or distractions that pull you away from you. I hope by now you've gotten on board with the invitation here to do your own practices that help you connect in and through all the noise, that help you cultivate more presence, that help you see who you really are, beneath everything else.

I've worked with so many mentors, done so many trainings and courses, and admittedly probably invested multiple six figures' worth of my life savings into personal development, only to find the best teachers will guide you back to yourself (someone whose name I forget originally said this, in this way—but I love it so much, it's perfect). We are the medicine. We have the answers. We are the ones we are seeking. It's all already here. And it's free to do the work. No wonder the personal development industry isn't selling this message—otherwise we'd see a dismantling of so many people's entire careers.

Here's a big highlight for you. Authenticity now more than ever is equated with sexuality, our creative life force, and our aliveness. Consider this: to what extent do you feel safe to be completely as you are, to express your truth, your desires, your body's natural communication of pleasure and wants, to create what brings you the most joy and even ecstasy? All roads come back to sex, let's be honest. We were born from sex, and yet we spend a lot of our lives recovering, frankly, from all the backward repression inundated through society that skews our notion of sexuality, expression, and creativity—usually from a very young age. Catch my drift? We just opened a big old can of worms—or a door into an infinite rabbit hole, whichever you prefer—and we're going in.

> **"I am not what happened to me, I am**
> **what I choose to become."**
> **—Carl Jung**

Depending on how sexually repressed our parents are in their expression, we might have received projections from them very early on, maybe even before we could speak or make sense of concepts rationally (prelingual memory can inform a lot of our subconscious behavior until it's made conscious and integrated). Maybe we started touching ourselves and exploring our bodies really young, as innocent children do—without having had any sexual acculturation or context for what any of that means—but seeing that happen made our parents uncomfortable because it triggered their own repression. This certainly happened for me and most people I come into contact with who later on in life want to heal their repression and step into great authenticity and personal power.

Think of all the backward ways society programs us to think sex is bad, our desires are bad, and so much more in between just those two ideas. Our entire capitalistic system might even be based in large part around controlling our bodies—which is the gateway to controlling our minds. Or is it vice versa? What do you think? Considering everything we've learned so far in our journey together, can we see how the society we were born into—in the West for sure—is essentially engineered around our repressed traumas—playing into our inner critics and stories of insecurity, getting us to buy the things we think we need to feel better, complete, loved, like we belong, like we exist, like we are safe?

When it comes to sex, we've received so many mixed messages, though, it's wild. I know I was so confused about this for so long, not to mention already on top of the confusion I felt at just being in a body in general. I didn't come into my body for a long time because it didn't feel safe to feel the extent of what I could feel—I had no tools or awareness to regulate the amount of energy and data I could process, so I disassociated and became very good at playing the part others seemingly wanted me to play so they could feel comfortable and then maybe, just maybe, if they felt okay I could also feel okay. But I still wouldn't be totally there—my consciousness was more comfortable dissociating into the higher realms, other dimensions, or imagining potentials of the past or future—anywhere but here, anyplace but now.

Most people with trauma have this pattern in common. And it's wild to not know what you don't know, till you know. I had been teaching about authenticity and embodiment for years when I finally was guided to explore somatic therapy. In my initial sessions I realized I had been dissociating out of my body to avoid feeling all that was here, wanting to be felt and released. Nowadays we are all becoming more sensitized to energy, and we can usually tell from miles away if someone is really *here* or not. We can tell if they are speaking from truth or from their mind. The resonance of their words just feels different, and we don't have to explain it—we just know by the way it feels. And this is enough. We are resonance radars, designed to be divine antennas for pure truth.

When it came to losing my virginity at around eighteen years old, I was super dissociated, not to mention I had been drinking and doing drugs for almost four years at that point—my body underwent some serious trauma through that experience that has taken many years to unwind. I am grateful for the lessons, especially the awareness to always tune into the body for its authentic consent. Does the body really want this experience? Is this good for me? When we start asking and listening, we'll always be surprised at how clear our feedback becomes.

After many years of violation and nonconsensual sexual exchanges in many forms, all underscored by deep shame around my sexuality stemming from being very young when I started exploring masturbation (which is totally normal and maybe should even be celebrated and normalized more often!), my body began speaking to me, pretty loudly, through a recurring cyst (called a Bartholin cyst) on the right and then eventually on the left of my groin area. This was the only recurring medical problem I've ever had—and it was happening repeatedly while I was drinking and partying heavily amidst a series of pretty codependent relationships where I used sex as a way to validate my worth and value. I was so good at performing in the ways I thought my partners wanted to see me—anything I could do to get their positive attention, I'd do, usually completely discounting my own experience or feelings, which I wasn't connected to anyway.

I faked hundreds, maybe thousands of orgasms—and boy did I put on a great show. One of my first boyfriends asked me when we were teenagers—as he showed me the first porn I'd ever seen: *Can you be like this?* This left such a stark imprint on my consciousness about how I thought I had to be to be loved, enough, accepted. I didn't know what I was in for—and let's not leave the poor men out of the equation, who are also subjected to the porn industry at such a young age, and learn so many distortions about sexuality and performance too. About this an entire series of books could be written. Note: I did a great podcast on this topic with my friend Michael McPherson, *Everything You Never Learned about Sex,* if you'd like to explore more with us.

What I am getting at: all those years of faking orgasms, disassociated from my body, my pleasure, my authenticity—my expression of truth— compounded in such immense trapped energy that my body developed painful cysts to try to get my attention. But I wasn't willing to see the deeper meaning for many years to come. For the first few years it happened, I just wanted the cysts to go away so I could go back to what I was doing because the love addiction was so strong—I needed the attention and validation and the space to perform so I could get what I truly wanted—what I perceived to be love, at the time. Then, after getting sober, doing lots of spiritual work, and starting my own coaching-healing practice, I started to realize: faking orgasms all those years was strangely somehow connected to my inability to fully show up as my true self in all the ways I wanted to in my life—in relationships, in my business, with money, with my ability to receive, with my clients, with everything. Then it landed: the way you show up in sex is the way you show up for life. Boom. From here, everything had to change.

And years after this insight, I realized even more fully: what I was really harping on back then but still couldn't see because of how deeply enmeshed I was in the illusion of hierarchy, trauma bonding, validation seeking, and spiritual ego was how everything I wanted was on the other side of the par-alyzing fear I felt around actually being myself. The way I showed up in the bedroom was a good indicator of how in touch I was with my authenticity and ability to say what I wanted, express my truth in the moment, and, most of all, allow my body to express itself as it was naturally designed to, without any interference of my mind. Sexuality was much bigger than what I thought—it wasn't just the act of having sex with a partner or with yourself. Sexuality is the expression of our authentic being moving through the world and creating what it most desires. Sexuality is our life force energy embodying into form.

Maybe sexuality is actually all of life—making love to itself through all the various energy exchanges we're constantly playing into together. Maybe life is just one giant, erotic, holographic trip after all. And yet I love this understanding I am now committed to deepening in—will you join me? Our authenticity is our primal essence, our divine life force en-ergy and its capacity to move freely through our bodies and energy fields as unadulterated expressions of truth, love, and beauty.

**"True happiness . . . is not attained through self-gratification,
but through fidelity to a worthy purpose."**
—Helen Keller

AUTHENTICITY IS ALIGNMENT WITH DESTINY

My parents organized a sixth birthday party for me when we still lived in a small town in New Hampshire. Some of the neighbors thought I was strange and didn't want to walk to the bus stop for school with me because they didn't like that my mom had painted our front door purple—this was too much for our conservative New England neighborhood. That's what I was up against—oh, and I was loving wearing thrift store finds and cool fringe shirts and bell bottoms all up in first grade. This was my authentic being loving expressing herself. But once outside influences came into being, I started developing insecurity and questioning if my desires were okay. If other people didn't understand or, even worse, didn't like me because of what I wanted, then maybe what I wanted was bad. This lesson got anchored in very deeply by the end of my birthday party that year.

I did manage to have some friends, and I can remember having a lot of fun for a while—showing off my new nineties jean outfit with splattered paint designs on it. Then at one point, if you can remember from my story earlier on, in a moment of happiness and joy, I jumped onto my dad's knee and possibly started rubbing myself on him in a way that he perceived to be inappropriate. I didn't think this at all—of course, I was just allowing my body to express what felt good and natural, without any projection of sexualization on it at all. Pure innocence.

My dad's energy shifted immediately, however, and before he even could say, *don't do that* or *stop*, I could feel his energy contract and pull away from me like I had done something gravely wrong. I learned in that moment on the deepest level possible that when I allow my body to express its desires authentically—by listening to what feels good in the moment and allowing it to be as it is—that makes the people I love detach from me and even get mad at me, so I should never do this again. This is how much our early trauma programming gets set into stone at such a profound level—and it can be so hard to unravel because the memories get multilayered and stored deep within our unconscious, always wanting to protect us from facing the pain of being abandoned again.

I didn't remember that moment till years later in my healing path when I was receiving a hypnotherapy or intuitive session of some kind, trying to figure out this money block I had around receiving at higher levels while also feeling challenged at fully stepping out of the closet as an intuitive healer. Suddenly upon receiving this awareness, everything made so much sense—my entire life up until that point, actually. What if the entire path I had ended up following was actually a response to that initial trauma? All the choices I had made were for someone else—to make them comfortable, to seek their approval, to not bother them or make them mad. I had learned to repress my natural expression and full capacity of energy because my parents couldn't deal with it—so of course the rest of the world couldn't either. Better to not take the risk.

Until the pressure to try to contain my authentic energy became far too great to stand and I had to start shifting, I had to become curious about other possibilities. Part of the path involved a lot of depression and anxiety to be quite honest. I mean—existential crises, hello. Had my entire life been designed to appease others? It seemed like it. I was so cut off from my authentic needs and truth. Who even was I? What was it I actually wanted? What did I need? How could I even listen? Had I been playing the part of someone else for this long? How could I start over?

"If you can see your path laid out in front of you, step by step, you know it's not your path. Your own path you make with every step you take. That's why it's your path."
—Joseph Campbell

It really felt like that, and honestly, as I continue on this path, sometimes these cycles and similar questions can even still come up now. And I've learned to expect it. When we are growing and shedding so many layers so quickly, it's healthy to question everything—to be curious about our choices and motivations, to be okay with questioning it all. Can we be flexible and understanding with ourselves instead of rigid and controlling as if there is a perfect way? Whenever we are seeking the perfect way we are trying to live according to someone else's path or plan instead of our own, which actually always turns out to be perfect in the end, even if it seems messy while we're on it. Can you look back over your life and see any evidence of this being true?

That moment at my birthday party set into motion my destiny. I wouldn't be sharing these words with you now if that hadn't happened. So we remember: our greatest gifts, the gifts that we're designed to give, our sole purpose even, our divine assignment, is actually almost always connected to the greatest trauma, struggle, pain, and suffering that we've endured through this life. Here we have learned resilience, the meaning of truth, and what we are truly made of—all of which has brought us closer to the truth of who we really are.

> **"Don't look at your feet to see if you are doing it right. Just dance."**
> **—Anne Lamott**

FEARLESSLY OWN YOUR DESIRES

We are tuning forks or rather antennae for divine desire and creative expression to resolve itself through our human form in the physical plane. Our authenticity is the outgrowth of our desires—when we listen to what we truly want and follow what we are truly attracted to, that is our authenticity expressing itself. What gets in the way of us living our full potential and actualizing our deepest desires? Shame, guilt, fear, and other negative emotional experiences that carry past trauma imprints that prevent us from believing that we can go after what we truly want and desire it, receive it, and enjoy it. Now it's time to go deeper into fearlessly claiming our desires—to go after what we want and stop settling or playing small.

Could you believe that your desires are holy instincts pointing you to live your greatest alignment, destiny, and fully realized genius? Your desires are messages that come through your physical, emotional, and spiritual bodies, which are usually directing you to contribute your gifts in the ways that feel most fulfilling and nourishing for you in any given moment. Following your desires means honoring your truth, loving yourself so unconditionally that you put yourself first no matter what and honoring your needs above all else so that you give from overflow instead of depletion.

Attuning to your desires is a continual practice of attuning to your energy and emotions so that you can hear and honor your inner truth and intuition no matter what else is pulling for your attention in life. Here you are invited to choose light, expansion, and what's true for you even in the face of pressure or other people's desires or expectations guiding you elsewhere. Attuning to your true desires is a requirement for living a conscious life because your desires are the signature of what you are here to manifest in your own dream-life reality that you are here to actualize. You're always manifesting no matter what, and all of life is reflecting to you what you're outputting in your thoughts, emotions, and energy.

"The universe buries strange jewels deep within us all, and then stands back to see if we can find them."
—Elizabeth Gilbert

What you're seeing around you is a direct consequence of what you're putting out or programming in your reality, whether you're aware of it or not. Becoming consciously attuned to creating the reality you desire to experience in all moments starts with committed presence, listening to your heart and trusting your intuition above all else, especially when reason and the over-empowered mind or intellect wants to guide you elsewhere for the sake of supposed safety and security or something else based in linear time or space constraints. We are all being asked to attune to a new depth of truth. You know the truth by the way it feels: the truth feels good, the truth feels like being fully alive, the truth feels like being turned on, the truth feels beautiful, loving, welcoming, warm; even if it feels challenging at first, it's welcoming you to grow, evolve, expand, and feel.

You know the truth by how good it feels. And the way the truth feels good for you may be different than how it feels to anybody else and maybe everybody else. We are here in this life to become masters in discernment, which is how we embody and express our authenticity through our aligned choices and actions. So, in this moment especially, discernment is challenging you to trust in your truth, your knowing that you are receiving divine messages in divine timing, always signaling you to feel with your own heart, with your true self and to ask, is this choice point expansive? Is this choice point or potential inviting me into more love? Is this inviting me into joy? Is this inviting me into feeling the ways I want to feel in my life?

Even if it's hard to say or really capture in the moment—and resistance arises because a powerful insight is ready to be shared that will surely trigger or upset the accepted norms or status quo—the truth feels good to share and receive. Our bodies can feel the truth millions of miles away—and we can also feel dishonesty now more clearly than ever. As our bodies become more sensitized as the tuning forks they are, the frequency readers we are—we can sense dishonesty and inauthenticity so clearly now.

As you trust and allow more energy that feels good to emerge into your experience by following your truth and other resonances that feel true—you build momentum for more positive growth and expansion in all areas of life. You develop a greater capacity for your own authenticity and its unique expression. You build a stronger container within your body for the kinds of energy you are mean to transmit—you can radiate your light at higher and more potently felt levels of intensity and impact. Then life becomes a series of simpler steps of listening to how you are being guided and inspired—to show up, to do when you're called to do, to speak and to be, to share your message, to share your heart, to share your feelings, to share your medicine. We are remembering our inherent simplicity.

Make it a practice to strengthen your discernment and trust in your own intuition, which is always guiding you toward more truth and what is meant for you. Tune in with your own heart throughout the day, throughout your life, filling up, breathing in, enjoying yourself, connecting to the body, asking, what's so important for me to know in this moment? Is there any message that I'm called to receive? Is there any guidance that I can receive? What is the truth that I am meant to embody and integrate right now? How can I feel my very best? Is there any way that I can support myself and receive whatever I need to have right now to feel safe, supported and loved?

Whatever you hear in the moment, you must immediately follow up with an action; do not delay, do not wait, give yourself exactly what you need because you know how to give it to yourself better than anybody else can. The more you do this, the more your life becomes a series of miracles. More alignment naturally falls into place and suddenly there is more flow you start to enjoy. More ease and grace become your natural fate. This is where the game gets really fun—the game of fully living, in which there is no limit to how much more flow, ease, alignment, and grace we can experience and become conscious of. And we already won the game simply by being alive. Our incentive to keep playing is to embody more of ourselves, more of our aliveness, more of our authenticity—our miraculous capacity to create and radiate. The game is rigged in our favor, as always.

The current question that I'm in in this moment at my evolution: what is it actually like to be fully alive? We established this is a choice we make every day—and what's it like to actually move in each moment with this awareness, fully anchored in? It colors a completely different experience of reality, that's for sure. Suddenly life feels less noisy and little dramas seem far less significant. When we choose to be fully here and present for aliveness unfolding—our priorities become crystal clear. In this experience of curiosity—continually asking the question again and again (what is it like to be fully alive?), almost as a living meditation—I noticed that I am more open to receiving what feels like healing from my own body, from my own field, from the Earth—or maybe it's just a deeper attunement to my body's own natural state of ecstasy, finally allowed full permission to simply be, and flow.

SELF-LOVE IS BEING WHO YOU TRULY ARE

A few years ago I was in my first Akashic Records practitioner training as a student learning how to channel and share my gifts as an intuitive healer and guide. One of the exercises I was practicing invited the opportunity to work with a growing edge or pain point present at that time, which for me then was all about scarcity consciousness—particularly the fear that I'd run out of money, that I'd never make enough money and that I was always going to worry about money.

Anyone can do this exercise by the way, it's like a meditation practice. You can simply go into a meditative state and ask to be shown a version of you or a past-life version of you that was an expert in the thing that you're wanting to come into greater mastery in. I asked to be shown an aspect of myself that was an expert in abundance.

Immediately I saw, as though I was looking in the mirror, a version of me as a male figure who I felt to be a chief of a tribe. The scene I saw was beautiful, with mountains in the background, and the man's face was so captivating and familiar, it almost surprised me how close I felt to him. Then I essentially asked, looking deep into his eyes: *Hey, what's the deal? How do I receive more abundance? I'm suffering, I'm not happy. How can I be free? What's in my way? How do I transcend this mental slavery?*

"I've learned that people will forget what you said, people will forget what you did, but people will never forget how you made them feel."
—Maya Angelou

My experience was so profound because no words were really spoken, but there was more a feeling like I was looking into this person's eyes, really into myself, and the response I received was with a gesture that reminded me to look around at the world full of abundance, everywhere. It was a felt sensation and a sort of telepathic communication. No words. In fact my mirror's response actually conveyed a sense of confusion, as though he was responding with: *What are you talking about, how could you possibly think that, look around you, look at everything that's here, look at this world full of everything you could possibly ever need.*

And that hit me so deeply. My illusion of even buying into those kinds of stories and beliefs or false thoughts that scarcity even exists and the emotions associated therein suddenly fell apart. Our world is the embodiment of abundance. Look at this infinite expanse of the Earth and the land, the multidimensional access to different aspects of yourself. We already have it all.

There is so much wisdom available to us in any moment we choose to access it, especially within the higher consciousness and intuitive capacity we innately possess to interpret reality. Especially when we are living with the land or living in nature; it's so healing, just go listen. Honestly, we could solve so many issues, problems, struggles, and existential crises if we actually went into nature for a day and got off the screen, got off the phone, and allowed the body to do its natural process of healing, allowed the nervous system to just rest, which happens if you step outside. We could even envision this New Earth, how we're going to build it, and the timeline in which it will all unfold.

As soon as we step back into nature—we can't help but feel connected. We can't help but feel activated in our senses and intuition. We can't help but hear our inner voice become amplified, and I think that goes for all humans, all of us; there's such powerful healing in returning to the land. Bare feet on the ground, deep breaths into our cells—skin in the sunlight, wind blowing over and through. It's always an immediate cleansing. Imagine we're living like this with no obstruction, just with the land; we couldn't help but be in harmony. This is what we are remembering. This is our true nature—to be extensions of nature and its infinite intelligence.

Just like the forest, the trees, the soil, the mountains, and ocean— all the natural elements we are inherently connected to simply by being alive—we also have infinite access to the multidimensional world, the real intra-net. Here we have access to all that ever was, all that ever is, all that ever will be—transcendent of time and space and any limitations therein. My favorite modality for exploring the multiverse is the Akashic Records—or what I've come to know more personally as the quantum akashic field, or more simply: the known field. Here we see that we're simply energy beings. We're actually not a personality, not an ego, not even this body. We are energy, and we each have a unique energetic signature, like a snowflake's unique divine design. We are immortal, not matter. We are transcendant—we are infinite. And our lives are so malleable, our realities are there for the instantaneous creation. This is what we are here to remember and experiment upon. And we have everything we need to thrive and win at the game—in fact it's all already won because we are alive. Now, how do we want to play? I get so excited about what continues to be revealed in my explorations which are really more like initiations into deeper receiving—more of life, more of myself, more of the true nature of reality.

Abundance is a state of being. Our sense of abundance and capacity for it is directly related to our capacity for embodying our authenticity. The authentic frequency we emit is our ultimate abundance—our true expression, the space from which all of the gifts and contributions we're meant to share in this life are born. This is a frequency we attune to and re-attune to constantly, perhaps until we naturally embody our authentic state, our birthright, who we were when we first arrived to Earth in this lifetime. Maybe then we'll ascend in the old way we used to understand ascension—beaming up back into the celestial realms, having completed our human assignment.

Remember being a baby? When we are born we are pure joy, love, divinity embodied. Fear is a learned behavior that can actually be un-learned and deprogrammed if we'd only remember that we can choose to be free. Maybe it's that simple. But it's definitely not always easy to remember, let alone practice or embody this potential. So where can we make a beginning?

You can change any ways of being that don't feel good for you instantly if you'd like. It doesn't have to take years or process after process and digging to figure it all out. Your happiness and present moment–aligned life and full aliveness aren't conditional upon some future moment where finally all is well and fixed and you're healed at last. We are never healed and fixed because our natural state is perfection; there's nothing wrong and nowhere to get to except possibly deeper into now and deeper into your being and deeper into right here where we can finally meet, as our-selves. Then breathe, all the way in.

Do you feel yourself? Do you know what your true essence feels like and how to discern its guiding light from fear, other people's desires, scarcity, jealousy, or any other illusory frequencies that the ego and most societal frameworks that would love to run the show? Mastery is patience, observance, and discernment, and quite possibly boils down to presence in its simplest form. Are you present to allow old emotions to rise and clear out as they naturally will when given the space?

Are you present to allow and acknowledge density to process out of your system with grace and ease to allow space for abundance, love, power, and magnetism—your natural state of being to actualize? Most people are caught in an endless cycle of bait and switch—when I get *X* then I can feel *Y*—never getting there, and even if they do get there, wherever that is, usually they want something else or what they wanted before is never enough. **You can end the cycle of illusion whenever you choose.** Reclaim and restore your divinity, your royalty, your reverence and honor. Remember your sacredness and behold yourself in awe.

"Imagination is the primary gift of human consciousness."
—Ken Robinson

Feel Good Now

In June 2019 I hosted a retreat for an intimate group in Sedona, Arizona, focused on this invitation to *quantum leap our lives*, which now feels like a bit of a catchphrase, to be completely honest. But that was then, and this is now—and I am grateful for the experience, which at the end of the day was a lot of fun and created a lot of space for healing, connection, and presence to become more fully embodied. I certainly learned a lot as a facilitator, and as time goes on I am more and more grateful for all the beings that have shown up over the years for similar experiences, especially in immersions, where we can learn so much from one another and go so deep.

Sometimes I can feel embarrassed for how I was even a few years ago, because let's face it—we change so fast nowadays on our ascension path, especially if we're really doing the work, which today is pretty much a requirement. Doing the work might look like sleeping more to process all the energy we are receiving on a daily basis. It might look like a lot of things, but just remember: if you're here and alive and even thriving, you're doing the work, which means you're growing and evolving at the speed of light.

"Vulnerability is the birthplace of love, belonging, joy, courage, empathy, and creativity. It is the source of hope, empathy, accountability, and authenticity. If we want greater clarity in our purpose or deeper and more meaningful spiritual lives, vulnerability is the path."
—Brené Brown

So back to our Sedona retreat—at one point we were all enjoying some time in the sun at our beautiful saltwater pool and hot tub at one of the most gorgeous retreat spaces I'd ever hosted at, appropriately called the Light House. Then, someone in our retreat group asked if he could lead a small meditation activity. Everyone felt eager to participate and started closing their eyes, awaiting his guidance to take shape and formulate our intention. He then surprised everyone by saying almost immediately: "Feel good now." Queue brains breaking in unison—what did he just say? Can he say that? As if it's that easy—is that even allowed?

We all laughed and felt a bit duped, to say the least. The mind never thinks—the key word here being *thinks*—feeling good can be that easy. But the body, upon hearing this simple command, by then has already proven it knows how to listen when given a direction it can follow. This was such a pivotal moment of realization for us all—and for this lovely gentleman, because he was simply being his authentic self and in doing so, he activated an entirely new potential for the group. When we are completely ourselves, we can't help but make an impact, usually for the positive good of all in whatever field we find ourselves in. It's who we are and it's how we are wired to be.

The alternative title for this book was *Get Out of the Way of Being Yourself* because, really, isn't that the entire point? Maybe it'll be the next one. I can cry thinking about it now, how the title just dropped into my consciousness as if it had always been there waiting to be acknowledged. As if everything I had done in my life till then was a symptom of survival programming wrapped up in trying to prove my worth and value, get love, mean something, prove my existence, feel like I am enough—fill an unfillable void. And what if it was that simple all along: get out of the way of being who you already are?

Clean out all the noise and distraction, the efforting and trying—strip away all the agendas and personality dynamics that were formed to wrest a certain result out of relationships, that keep trauma loops continuing on and on—and simply be. Then listen and receive. And trust the next right steps always emerge. And if they don't, which is rare and temporary, you're just meant to be internal or at rest. Slow down and simply be. Why has it felt so impossible to follow this protocol? You know, the one we were wired from birth to follow? Why has it felt that up until now we've been replaying the first few years and trauma there in our early childhoods? Here's our wake-up call—no more groundhog day, no more personality agendas, no more getting stuck in the past or future, no more addictive cycles of giving our power away to anything outside of ourselves to give us something we already have within. Can we do it? Yes, of course. We wouldn't be given the invitation now if we weren't up for the challenge.

By now we're integrating so many crucial lessons in remembering our creator capacity, attuning our nervous systems, befriending our bodies, and allowing ourselves permission to simply be, as we are—as our true selves. We are tuning in and turning on, all the way up and IN. We are learning to feel good now, without condition or reason—other than the knowing that we are good, we are love and we deserve to radiate this truth. Cellularly, viscerally, without proving anything at all because our existence speaks for itself. Our presence and authenticity are our ultimate currency that speaks volumes about our potency and potential—more than our words can even convey, especially these days, amidst the most potent energies we've ever experienced before in a human body.

I honor you and acknowledge how far you've come on your path of fully awakening to your highest alignment, your authentic truth, your magnetism, your desires. We are wired for pure miracles, let us remember. Miracles are something we've been systematically conditioned to believe

are special or rare, when in fact they are completely natural and normal oc-
currences that happen as frequently as each conscious breath. Infinite bliss
is your natural state. We are love. And we're learning to allow ourselves to
simply be just that. It's not just a bumper sticker or spiritual meme—it's a
way of life we are welcoming ourselves home into embodying.

**Trust. Surrender. Relax. Repeat. We have all the answers we've been
seeking, here and now—inside. We have everything we need.** Maybe we
actually don't need any more tools. Maybe we have too many and they've
become a distraction from the point. Maybe the ultimate tool is whatever
practice that helps you tune in more deeply to being. Find what helps
you to simply be, at ease, as you, and practice that with great fervor—be
a disciple (in discipline) of what you hold to be more true and (w)holy.
We have so many infinite resources already. Let's use them.

Shift into higher frequencies, accentuate higher self-embodiment and
soul-aligned timelines. Imagine how we are constantly surrounded by
etheric stadiums filled with our spiritual support squad. They're always
waiting for us to ask for assistance for they can't intervene without our
conscious request. They love us so much that they'd love to let us grow
and make our own choices so we truly learn the lessons we sought to come
into embodiment to experience. It's time to actualize our dream timelines
and anchor our greatest visions. We have so much support to make it all
real. To bring Heaven into Earth. To be the beacons of divine essence we
are designed to be.

**We've never been more supported in actualizing our hearts' desires;
it feels so palpable, the amplifying energy we are receiving to play with
and transmit.** Working with these frequencies consciously invites us into
a new paradigm of nervous system stability and coherence. Presence is
the greatest currency at this time—the ability to sit in relaxed observance
of what is without attachment or judgment or any inner dialogue. Here
is where freedom lives: in creating the worlds we wish existed. Becoming
the beings we are destined to be.

Get out of the way of being ourselves. Eventually we find that the most
beautiful experience of being alive is to continue to not recognize ourselves from who we were yesterday, never mind last week or last year. And
yet simultaneously we feel even more deeply familiar and remembered—
the aspects that matter most shine through more clearly as we anchor into

our true selves and therefore into this present moment, fully home here on Earth in this being.

I wish all on the journey of authenticity and greater attunement to truth the utmost blessings on our unfolding paths. Here is where we are inevitably heading, I believe—clear fields meeting in complete coherence without attachment to external entities or dependencies on anything out-side to cultivate peace, presence, acceptance, and love. We are infinite beings capable of absolute magic when we start to use and trust the tech-nology embedded within our bodies without interference or obstruction. Grateful to be alive and thriving. Let's play.

AUTHENTICITY ATTUNEMENTS

One of my favorite quotes, which hit home so deeply it shook me to my core when I first heard it, is by none other than visionary actor Jim Car-rey, who reminds us that: "Depression is your avatar telling you it's tired of being the character you're trying to play." I love this reminder for so many reasons, one of them being his nonchalant way of demystifying and destigmatizing depression as something that we can shift depending on how willing we are to be in our authentic creative expression. How many of us have spent so much of our lives pretending to be someone else and not even knowing it?

That was the game I was playing for the first quarter of my life and even years into awakening. The layers of unconscious superficiality and survival mechanisms of fitting in and molding oneself to be understood and ac-cepted run so deep. Perhaps we could simplify the entire path of embodied ascension as one that guides us into our authenticity—how does our true life force and essence want to live, breathe, and create in this one beautiful life we're gifted to experience? How present do we want to be for all of it? As we've covered already, meeting ourselves, our real selves, is perhaps the most vulnerable aspect of our conscious life. Do we love ourselves unconditionally? Can we even?

Such a tall order indeed, yet there feels to be a sense of unity in this inquiry—perhaps this very question, and precisely whatever seems to stand in opposition to its resolution, is what unites us with our fellow human beings. Just like trauma and the universal wounds that bind us—we are so much more alike than we are different when we go a few layers deeper, beyond what we first see or judge. We can't help but fall in love with one another and more deeply with ourselves. What a cosmic comedy and divine game this life turns out to be again and again. Here are some of my favorite practices for attuning to our authenticity and welcoming our true selves to come out and play, more and more until it's the norm. Imagine the world we co-create when it is.

"We delight in the beauty of the butterfly, but rarely admit the changes it has gone through to achieve that beauty."
—Maya Angelou

Meeting Your True Self

Consider the following series of self-inquiries. You can journal your answers to these or meditate on them, whatever feels best for you: 1) What are you doing and how are you being when you feel most fulfilled? 2) Complete this sentence—whatever comes naturally is perfect: "I'll be aligned in my purpose when . . ." and/or "I'll know I'm living my purpose when . . ." Here's the trick—we just unearthed something deep in the unconscious here—the key: whatever comes up for you after is exactly what you are called to put your energy into now. Here we unravel the mystery of conditionality that keeps us trapped in the past and future instead of in the present, where we truly want to be (which is really the only place we truly are, as ourselves, now).

As we've explored already, a lot of our mental programming wants to orient us according to protection from past pain and prevention of projected future pain . . . which is estimated to potentially occur due to past evidence, keeping us outside of the present moment, where all our new potentials reside. If we see a way in which we have a conditioned attachment—for example, "I'll be happy or fulfilled when . . ."— we get to unravel this programming by reminding ourselves that our happiness and fulfillment are not dependent on a future result but instead are things we can source from within in this moment. If we have a material attachment—that is, we want something material to create a feeling state—we can fast-track to the end result by starting to practice attuning to that feeling right now.

Back to the first inquiry too—I didn't forget. When you name what you feel most fulfilled by, this is great information to guide what you are called to put more of your conscious energetic focus into. Can you dedicate more space in your life to practicing the activities that cultivate deep fulfillment within? Can you allow more space in your life to visit the environments where you feel most at home and relaxed as yourself too? When do you feel most alive? Let more of your life become designed around answering this exploration in real time— through the way you practice intentionally living.

Owning Responsibility

Another powerful self-reflection exercise invites us into a meditative space where we consider the following; either visualize your answer and state it to yourself or practice intuitively journaling it out so you can see it more directly: "I am not living my purpose right now because . . ." Complete the sentence with everything that comes up, naturally without a filter—be honest. Be present for what truth emerges—then challenge yourself to witness what resolution or counterbalance seems most authentic. I love this question because no matter how aligned we are with our fulfilled sense of purpose, we always have room to grow and evolve—and this inquiry helps us see where we can expand into even more depth and authenticity along the way. It might feel intense at first, but don't worry, we're not going after self-criticism or judgment here, just an honest, direct reality check of where we're presently residing and in which specific ways we might want to grow.

Time to Get Really Real

Similar to the above, here's another epic prompt I love—this one is really activating around our authenticity and seeing the ways in which we are potentially holding ourselves back from being in our full presence and power. Answer intuitively either in a meditative space or by free-flow journaling: "If I was allowing myself to be fully and completely myself, then what would be different about: (1) what I'm doing, (2) what I'm thinking, (3) what I'm feeling, (4) who I'm associating with, (5) what I'm dedicating my creative energy to, and (6) how I'm taking care of myself?" Talk about a life overhaul—this process can bring up a lot and it's a really good one to do when you feel inspired to do a deep dive inventory on ways you can cultivate more authenticity, alignment, and integrity in all dimensions of your life experience. As always, tune in with actions that help to cultivate the desired ways of being and feeling that emerge in each visualization.

Now, for each response on your list, make at least one commitment that creates space for improvement. You can do this by asking yourself honestly: What is my true self or higher consciousness guiding me to do here? How would my higher self approach this situation? What do I know in my heart is the right thing for me to commit to? And do it.

How do you most want to feel? What ways of being are you ready to embody? How does your physical reality shift accordingly when you are embodying these states more consistently? What actions arise as the next right step—no matter how big or small—to support you in actualizing these ways of being into form? To give you an idea, I'll answer the above questions, and I'll give you a true, in-the-moment reflection to show where I am honestly at in my path (how's that for authenticity!): If I was allowing myself to be fully and completely myself, (1) I would be playing in nature more and I'd be learning to DJ so I can have shows and create awesome dance parties, (2) I would be thinking more self-loving, creative, inspired thoughts about the set lists I want to create and how much fun I would have weaving together communities of coherence based in sound, movement, and breath, (3) I would feel deeply inspired, connected, supported, alive, sexy, and radiant, (4) I'd be hanging out with my soul family a lot more in person, and I would have a pet cat (!), (5) I would be dedicating my creativity to more fun, arts and crafts, painting, music production and composition, and dance, and (6) I would be doing more yoga and longer meditation sits and lots more time in silence, plus frequent sauna, ice bath, and hot tub soak sessions.

My commitments to myself that arise from these insights are: (1) this week I will play in nature off grid, off technology for a few hours at least one time, (2) I will research the equipment I want to get for my DJ setup, (3) I will write a gratitude list about what I am celebrating about myself this week at least once, (4) I will dress up one night in an outfit that makes me feel sexy and radiant and take myself on a date (or be taken out on one!), (5) I will set up at least one friend date this week to intimately, authentically connect with a soul friend I love, (6) I will paint for some uninterrupted time this week, and (7) I will explore potentials for visiting a nearby spa with at least a sauna and ice bath.

Commit to Yourself

One thing to keep in mind for the commitment piece—and this really helped me, as I was such an overachiever I'd frequently make way too many commitments and then stress myself out about not having enough time or bandwidth to do it all, catalyzing a self-criticism spiral and ultimately distracting from the point of self-care in the first place, do you relate?!—starting small and simple is a way of loving ourselves. Small actions build momentum and help us construct a strong foundation upon which to grow and build capacity for more. Give yourself lots of space. See how I said I'd do one thing over the week? That's more than enough. Maybe it feels good to even space your commitments out over the month. Whatever works for you—and feels good—is perfect. Most of all, have fun and enjoy the process. This is how we love ourselves into more wholeness and affirm ourselves in being more of who we already are.

**"Dreams are illustrations from the book
your soul is writing about you."
—Marsha Norman**

Wherever You Go, There You Are

When you're in a funk, there's something so healing and cleansing about laying everything out on the table, being seen, heard, and witnessed, especially by those you love and trust and want to grow with.

Whenever I have a spiritual tantrum or a few too many moments of mental chatter or inner criticism—all of which can be simplified as contractions—I wish I could remember to grab my closest friend or even call someone up to play a game that immediately snaps me into my heart, into what matters and into what's alive and now, aka where/how we are designed to truly reside and thrive.

Can you imagine if we all invited one another to play like this—maybe eventually co-creating a new way of being together, practicing presence as a collective?

Here's one way to play. This game is best played with a partner, but you can also play with yourself by looking at your own eyes in a mirror. It also works if you're on your phone—using the camera, you can make eye contact on screen. But you might find the mirror creates a more intimate presence with yourself.

1. Take a deep breath in to connect to self, your center, breathing all the way into your entire body. Clear your energy field on every exhale, feeling what's no longer yours melt into the Earth.
2. In silence slowly make eye contact with your partner.
3. Take a few breaths together at the same time. You can place hands on each other's hearts or on your own heart.
4. First person to share begins by saying one of the below prompts and completing the sentence with whatever is true for them. The other person simply receives and listens, holding eye contact.
5. You can use a timer for one-minute shares each as you volley the prompts below, maybe going in order.

Some of my favorite prompts for activating deepened intimacy, authenticity and presence are:

Being with you I feel . . .
Being with you I notice . . .
What I think others think about me is . . .
What I think you think about me is . . .
My biggest fear is . . .
My greatest strength is . . .
My vision for my life is . . .
The biggest thing in the way of being where I want to be right now is . . .
What I really get about you is . . .

Will you play? These are all also great writing prompts and potent for self mirror work.

11

TRUST YOUR KNOWING

"My religion is to trust myself."
—Yoko Ono

The foundation of every relationship is trust, but how can we trust anyone else if we don't trust ourselves? How can we develop trust? Trust is a felt sensation. It is a knowing. How do we build a body with the capacity for safety and trust? We've covered a lot of the practice and context for precisely this and still—of course, by now we're used to it—there's even deeper to go. Cultivating trust is another infinite part of our embodiment experience—with no end, only greater depths to explore and actualize. Let's explore how we can be in awe of our capacity to trust—in ourselves, in life, in each other, one relationship at a time, moment by moment. We'll start by considering how trust, especially when it comes to trusting our own guidance and intuiton, has everything to do with our self-worth, self-esteem, and our capability to truly love and accept ourselves in the present moment.

Everyone has the capacity to be psychic and gifted spiritually. Being spiritual and intuitive aren't special capacities reserved for only a select few. With the way energy is moving through our planet and through our beings now, we are all given immense access to dormant senses and multidimensional perceptual abilities that we can learn to harness for incredible healing, guidance, and support. Now that you have turned on and refined more of your innate sense capacities and perceptions through the practices and recalibration we've experienced thus far, we are ready to further explore the multidimensional self and the full spectrum of experience and insights that are now more accessible than ever. We are ready to deepen in trust of our true selves—and our unique abilities we came to enjoy and share.

> **"Ego says, 'Once everything falls into place, I'll feel peace.' Spirit says, 'Find your peace, and then everything will fall into place.'"**
> **—Marianne Williamson**

We don't have to go through years and years of healing in order for you to attune with the softer, loving, really wise intuitive voice within; this attunement and trust in your knowing can actually happen quickly. Maybe even instantly. It can happen right now. Years ago I had a friend in Los Angeles who was a psychic and occasionally taught classes on intuitive empowerment. I loved his class name so much: It's Okay to Be Right! Because honestly, that says it all. At around the same time I was connecting with people around the permission to be an energetic elitist—it's okay to be right when you know what works for you, when you know what information you're receiving and when you know what feels good. Who else are we living for, anyway? This class name has now more than ever become a mantra to remember whenever I might sink into self-doubt, especially in relaying any intuitive insight that may trigger others to rethink their realities (which is usually the point!).

What gets in the way of us trusting the naturally designed capacity we have within to listen to higher guidance and awesome multidimensional, extrasensory information, healing, and support? In addition to the trauma layers we've navigated up until now, there's another block, something you might have heard of often referred to as the *witch wound*. The witch wound refers to collectively felt trauma that we have usually tuned into unconsciously both collectively and individually following numerous experiences and expressions of persecution. Consider how in many contexts, perhaps in other lifetimes, you were simply a medicine man or woman, a healer, a mystic, but being who you were was simply not allowed and you were persecuted and even met in most cases with violence and death.

Let's zoom out for just a moment from our experience and identities therein on Earth. It's important for us all to know and receive ourselves at the soul level because our soul is a very vibrant being. It's a very powerful, potent, colorful frequency. As a sheer energetic being—an infinite immortal soul, you have spent so much more of your conscious experience in pure energetic form. For many at this time it can even feel very rare to have had the experience of being in a physical human body on Earth in this level of density.

Consider that there are timelines in your history on Earth that are ready to be brought into completion, and some of these are the timelines mirroring collective healing regarding persecution and disempowerment. There's an experience of slavery embedded in here as well that can be literal, but in this case it means more of a mental, spiritual slavery. Whenever we have been enslaved to follow doctrines that we do not believe in or authentically subscribe to, that we were persecuted by, there is repair to tend to. The oppression and persecution of being killed, enslaved, abused, or otherwise violated for being different or for questioning the status quo is a common trauma we are currently resolving in our collective and individual systems.

Part of our healing this wound of being in our power, of being magical, of trusting our unique truth to guide us involves first admitting that at some point in the path we didn't have a choice other than to be disempowered for a time. We definitely had other choice points available—but we couldn't yet see them consciously or else perhaps we would have chosen differently. In coming to terms with this trauma, we might reflect on how we were colonized to believe in and empower ideas and people that we really never trusted or wanted to engage with. It can even be helpful for the healing process to observe that over many lifetimes there were choices that were made, even before you came into Earth, that your soul chose to experience and explore, that were the opposite of what you really know to be true, the opposite of what you value most above all. Sometimes we choose to have these lifetimes in which we get to experience the complete opposite of what we actually want, of what we actually know as truth, so that we can come into greater appreciation, love, and gratitude for who we are and why we are here. Especially here in Earth School, we come to learn the core of our highest value and truth through the sometimes immense contrast of experiencing the opposite.

Another challenge to attuning to our natural state of intuitive knowing can be an often repressed fear of embracing multidimensionality—and the fear of becoming dislodged from the body and detached completely from our earthly experience. This tends to be a common fear of those with parents or ancestors who had what are referred to as psychiatric disorders or even depression. In my own personal experience I never had an officially diagnosed mental illness but instead an energetic challenge of managing an immense amount of intuitive data and insight that I had no tools, language, or awareness with which to support myself. If I had listened to Western medicine's diagnosis of what was "wrong" with me (which probably started way back when I was fourteen and got put on birth control), I would have been medicated and even more disconnected from my body and its intuitive wisdom and abilities—further disconnecting me from healing into wholeness.

> **"What do you love doing so much that the words failure
> and success essentially become irrelevant?"**
> **—Elizabeth Gilbert**

Nonetheless, this can be a very real fear if you grew up with a parent or with someone even far back in your family who was cast out as crazy, hysteric or labeled with some other kind of disorder probably for simply not knowing how to care for their psychic/intuitive/empathic selves and subsequently suffering in a society that wants them to be anything but who they are. Our society, our educational system, and our medical institution has systematically oppressed and disempowered intuitive, visionary people for centuries. Think back to the Crusades and all the religious indoctrination putting down mystics as heretics. **Remember the witch wound? Yes, we all have residue of this energy we are alchemizing in this lifetime—whether we've been the victim in the situation or the oppressor or both.**

If we have this fear, no matter how ancient, or embedded in our family lineage—that being intuitive means you'll die for being a witch, or you'll be cast out of Earth for being tuned into other dimensions and you'll be alone, abandoned, and unable to connect with other humans—this fear can prevent us from allowing our energy to evolve and expand in the ways we truly want it to. Especially if our soul path is designed for us to be healers with intuitive gifts to share. More and more I think this is actually everyone's path, as all humans are healers. First and foremost we are here to heal ourselves. And then some of us may be called to share these gifts with others in specific ways—but really, at the end of our day, when we heal ourselves, our presence communicates healing naturally without us having to do anything at all.

When we allow ourselves to explore multidimensionality—usually upon cultivating more inner stability and safety within—we recall that we have the capacity to be very conscious and aware of existing in simultaneous realities and that this awareness is one of our greatest gifts. **One of your greatest gifts as a channel and conduit of high-frequency energy is to see parallel timelines and realities from a very centered, grounded point.** And you have an innate ability to communicate what it is that you are receiving and seeing in these simultaneous realities. So, really, you are a bridge, you are a conduit, you're very well positioned to be a guide even beyond simply healing, because your presence in and of itself is healing. Your presence is healing whether you intend it to be or not. It's who you are.

Now more than ever, we have access to a switchboard of sorts—channels of different energies and communications that are available on Earth at this time. We really do have the capacity to transmit and interpret incredible healing, guiding energies that are meant to deeply support us through our ascension. Working consciously with these energies can sometimes require a level of energetic stability and training of sorts that you have received over many lifetimes in order to effectively know how to receive and attune to these transmissions. You might also simply recall how to receive high frequencies and intuitive guidance just from meditating or moving in a way that feels good. Everyone has a different intuitive expression and unique ways they are designed to transmit and play in the energetic realms. So many are remembering their gifts and callings every day now—it's such an exciting, expansive time to be fully alive to explore our embodied consciousness. I'm really glad I stuck around for this part of the show! Welcome to the multiverse—infinity is awaiting our eager exploration.

"Our bodies are one more way in which the Universe organizes itself. They are windows for consciousness to see through."
—Thomas Lloyd Qualls

Is not the greatest gift we can give ourselves the experience of being completely used? So many are asleep, half giving their gifts, which is depressing and so depleting. It's like pretending you're a lightbulb that needs something to power it instead of knowing and acting like you're the infinite sun that's always radiating like it's your job (because it is). You keep pretending you need all these external factors and future conditions to turn on. As if it's not up to you. But as we've established by now—we've had the power all along and we have everything we need to turn on all the way. What choice shall we make—are we all in, or not?

IT'S TIME TO TUNE IN

"The Game of Life and how to play it: Intuition is a spiritual faculty and does not explain, but simply points the way. As man becomes spiritually awakened he recognizes that any external inharmony is the correspondence of mental inharmony. If he stumbles or falls, he may know he is stumbling or falling in consciousness. All power is given man (through right thinking) to bring his Heaven upon his Earth, and this is the goal of the Game of Life."
—Florence Scovel Shinn

At a certain point, when your self-worth, self-esteem, and grounded presence have been built up a bit more—and you feel more stable in your authentic self, discernment happens pretty naturally. For a lot of my life that wasn't always the case at all. For most of my life, I was living in a lot of reactivity. I think most people are. It's reactivity just like *feedback and react, feedback and react.* Not a lot of thought. Not a lot of observation. Not a lot of mindfulness. Not a lot of presence. Instead my inner world was filled with a lot of: *here's what I think I should be doing, so I'll do that* and operating in this conveyor belt factory—autopilot, robotic mentality. **Like many, I learned discernment through pain.**

Frankly, that's been a long haul alright—seeing how discernment has been cultivated through discomfort and pain. Especially at the start of our awakening, this is how we grow and transform but from now on, I hope that growth isn't so often catalyzed by pain. With more examples of people sharing their healing journeys and transformation, maybe others won't have to go through the similar depths of pain and suffering to learn the same lessons, faster and sooner. All roads inevitably lead us back to ourselves regardless, no matter where we are on the path. How are we taking care of ourselves? How are we allowing and supporting our bodies to become finely attuned barometers for truth? How do we empower our systems to be the naturally discerning beacons of what's right and what's meant for us? When we take care of ourselves, mind-body-spirit-soul, when we are connected to our needs and do our best to meet them or ask for support to do so in the moment they arise, when we feel supported, safe, and secure to be ourselves—our discernment reflexes naturally strengthen.

How do you want to feel? Choose how you want to feel right now. Choose it, embody it, and don't engage in the mind for now, which might simply want to keep you in survival, fear, fight, or flight mode. Don't give in on autopilot. Instead go into an energetic movement, or breathe more deeply, tone or sing—feel your essence, your vibration, practice self-care, do something that gets you into a good feeling state and give yourself what you need right now to feel supported. Then, from a resourced space of self-connection and presence with your truth—and clarity to really listen and see it all as it is—consider engaging with whatever thought or mental images are wanting to be acknowledged. From here we can discern clearly our next right steps. New choice points will be visible that we couldn't see before until we become present. We aren't here to bypass anything—or escape from what's coming up to meet, no matter how painful or uncomfortable it might be; but we are here to fully resource ourselves first and foremost before doing anything else.

Let's remember that each and every one of us came into this life with a choice of what kinds of games we wanted to play—simply to learn and grow through, maybe even to master. My life lesson is unconditional love, I would say. So, I've selected a lot of lessons, triggers, painful situations and growing edges—to say the least—all oriented to show me the absolute contrast of true unconditional love which has manifested as wounds within abandonment, rejection, betrayal, shame, and scarcity. I choose these painful experiences again and again, these situations that reflect to me the opposite of unconditional love, so that I can find my discernment, awareness, understanding of what unconditional love actually is. I may never become an expert in this understanding and maybe that is beside the point anyway—maybe there is nothing to master when you accept that you are forever a student with new infinite depths to explore. The deeper you go, the more layers to peel through and alchemize reveal. There are infinite depths to dive through. For now, I am committed to peeling away more layers of distortions—of all that is no longer true—and simply allowing a greater understanding, a deeper truth, to emerge. And this is enough.

> **"It's impossible to live without failing at something—unless you live so cautiously that you might as well not have lived at all, in which case you have failed by default."**
> **—J. K. Rowling**

I'll always remember one of my biggest lessons in trusting my intuition. It was a series of commitments, really, that led me to this jump-off point and challenged me to transcend so much fear, doubt, worry, and immense conditioned belief around safety and security and doing the right thing. At that time, I was working for a public relations agency in New York—a job that absolutely checked all of the boxes in terms of everything I could have ever wanted. I worked with the best people. I had a beautiful office. I loved my role; it was so fun and allowed me to be creative while also being in a position of leadership. Things really couldn't have been better, and if you had asked me years ago what my dream job would be, this would certainly be it.

But a series of events lead me into realizing that I could no longer avoid the small, whispering voice that I had inside me all along, which was always saying things like, *you want to go out on your own, you want to work for yourself, it's time to take the leap, you're meant to do something else, you're meant to be of service in a different way, you're meant to feel more fulfilled.*

In hindsight, there was a recipe of sorts that ultimately led me to leaving my job and starting my company, setting me off on the wildest personal spiritual development journey I could have ever imagined. It started when I invested in my well-being for the first time in a tangible way beyond all the work I had done in AA. I started taking responsibility for feeling better emotionally and energetically and I made a huge commitment to taking care of my physical health. With my life coach I was receiving reiki treatments, I was attuning my energy, and I was being accountable to taking care of myself in ways that I had always wanted. I hired a holistic chiropractor to oversee a comprehensive cleanse and over those four months this in-depth protocol helped clear my system of heavy metals, remnants of birth control and synthetic substances, candida, and other foreign energies. I started to feel so clear—clearer than I ever had before. My skin was glowing, my hair and nails had never felt so strong, and my body felt so radiant and alive. Plus, my intuition was more striking than ever.

It was around the same time that I began speaking to a woman who was also a life coach who got my attention based on what she was sharing on social media. She was a friend of a friend that had participated in a similar personal development program I had done a few years prior that made a big impact on my life—definitely an important step on the awakening journey. She shared about traveling the world while launching her business and feeling so free and so full of life. Her energy spoke so much more than the actual words that she used. And I was magnetized to her—especially the example she was promoting of traveling while being of service, enjoying what felt like an abundant, purpose-filled, fun life. I wanted it all.

So, I messaged her and said, "Hey, I'd like to talk to you about how you got to be doing what you are doing," and sure enough, she suggested that in order for me to understand better how she's doing what she's doing, we might want to work together in a coaching container. In that conversation I remember feeling so triggered by the amount of money that was suggested I invest in this coaching, as I have never invested that much in myself before. It felt like a big stretch, but I knew that I wanted it and that something in me knew—I had to make this commitment in order to experience the next stage my life was welcoming me into. I wanted to travel, to be my own boss, to do purpose-filled healing work, to make an impact—to be free in more ways than one. So, I called in a teacher to help guide me along the steps to get there.

At my job, I had been trying to schedule more vacation time. I felt trapped because I had to keep track of the days that I took off and I wasn't really free to do what I wanted, even though my job offered me so much flexibility and a lot of incredible benefits. But the benefits that I valued most, such as traveling, exploring different cultures, and being free to create my own schedule, weren't fully accessible as long as I was working in someone else's company. Plus, because I was in a leadership role in the company, I needed to be very mindful of how I used my time and of the example I set for staff when it came to vacation.

So, I decided to start working with this mentor. I wanted to have support and I was ready to see how I could create more of the experiences I was calling into my life—I was ready for a big change and it felt good to have support along the leap into the unknown. In one of our first sessions, we mapped out my vision for my life, and I said, "You know, I'm going to give myself a year to leave my company and start my own business." I had already been a freelance marketing strategy consultant for a few months in between jobs about two years prior at that point. Plus I knew that I wanted to do more healing work, and I had already been offering reiki sessions and intuitive guidance sessions on the weekends (during this time, though, my weekend healing offerings always felt a bit undercover, like I was side-hustling with something that I actually wanted to be my full-time focus). I wanted to be doing what felt like my soul purpose work more openly and more regularly.

With all of my experience queued up, I was ready to press play. All my life experience, especially sponsoring so many people in AA and taking them through the steps, had brought me to this moment where all of life was showing me how my gifts were meant to be shared and how I could start living more into my true purpose and passions. I still thought that I would need a year to launch it. But what happened was my mentor asked, "Well, how soon do you want to be done? How soon do you want to start living the kind of life that you truly want to live?" "Well," I responded, "as soon as possible." And so suddenly my timeline, which had been a year, collapsed into two months. I had so much fear about leaving my job as I was so comfortable making the salary that I was making, having benefits and the stability and everything that I had been conditioned to really feel safe with. It was challenging to consider letting that all go for what felt like a complete unknown.

I wasn't sure how it was all going to work. But this is the amazing thing about listening to your intuition, listening to divine timing, listening to that nudge. I really felt the call to put my notice in sooner than I could have ever consciously planned, and I didn't have a very clear backup plan as to what was going to happen immediately following my last day of work. I just knew that as soon as I got more comfortable with this idea of leaving that I actually couldn't stay any longer. The voice moving me into action got louder—and more of my reality was giving me clear feed-back that I was ready to go—in sometimes almost funny moments that I couldn't ignore. My AA sponsorshop sessions started to feel more like life-coaching beyond the primary purpose of the program which was to focus on sobriety from alcohol. I started booking more energy healing and intuitive guidance sessions with clients on the weekends. I was invited serendipitously to events and workshops where I could host my offerings more publicly, without even trying to market or be seen more in that way.

Meanwhile at my job, I started to really feel more suffocated in terms of my gifts not being shared appropriately, and my energy, my creative life force potential, not being channeled effectively or in the ways that felt most aligned. I felt stifled by the box I was supposed to find myself so comfortable and safe residing in—with a fancy title, salary, and so much supposed stability. Underneath an entirely different being was trying to be birthed and set free. She needed space to expand and touch ground—to make the impact she was ready to make, to fully breathe and allow herself to simply be. Once I saw through what it was that I was subjecting myself to, I actually couldn't afford to be at my job for much longer. Every day felt so stretched out and time just moved slowly as I was waiting to leave.

**"If you want the best the world has to offer,
offer the world your best."
—Neale Donald Walsch**

So, eventually I put my notice in, and it was one of the most terrifying conversations I've ever had. I think I cried. I think I was shaking. I was so nervous to put my notice in at this company that I had loved so much, that I felt so much ownership in since I felt like I had helped build it from the beginning and watched it grow into such a beautiful vision. My boss at that time shocked me when he said, "Oh, we knew you were going to leave. This isn't a surprise at all. In fact, I had a bet going with the other managing partners that you would be leaving a couple of months from now. So, you just beat us to the chase," which made me laugh because isn't that true? The people that are around you in key transitional moments like this already know—they see and feel when you're ready to evolve beyond the boxes and confines you initially met in, usually before we can see it ourselves.

So, even though that conversation came as a huge shock to me, I put my notice in, and in doing so I let go of so much energy, control, and fear in that moment, to simply surrender to this higher plan that I knew involved me leaving. That I knew involved me being of service in a different way. That I knew involved me feeling free. But beyond that I really didn't know much of the specifics. I didn't have another job or even other opportunities lined up immediately. The next right step I was shown was simply to put my notice in and trust that the rest would reveal itself in due time, as I was ready to receive the next choice point. It felt a bit wreckless at the time, I'll admit it—but for whatever reason that's what I had to move through in order to learn and grow in the ways I was craving to experience.

I don't recommend this approach to others of course. In hindsight, knowing what I know now from this vantage point—I can see how I was orienting from a bit of impulsivity and potentially unnecessary stress where instead I could have created more structures for resource, support, stability, and overall calmness amidst such a big transition. I could have been more patient and planned a longer transition plan that gave more runway for next steps to emerge clearly and easily. I learned only later that the universe or our divine plan never wants us to feel stressed or rushed—we are meant to follow our aligned course with ease, presence, and peace. But at the time, I had to go through the intensity of living out the expedited timeline I set up and even still, I got to see the miracles of how supported I was as I listened and aligned my actions accordingly.

First things first, I had to put the notice in and create the space in which the universe could align so many moving parts to support me. Then, literally within a week of putting my notice in, an old consulting client of mine called me up and said, "Hey, I have a project for you. Come and meet me and let's talk about it." Interesting timing as he hadn't heard that I had put my notice in at my agency and that I was about to become a free agent once more. Funny enough I wasn't resonant with the project he had me in mind for, but I still had a sense there was something else he was brewing up and I asked him about it. Follow the intuitive nudge.

That *something else* turned into my first start-up marketing advisor role as a half-time consultant, creating this incredible company that felt so aligned with everything that I valued and felt like so much fun to be a part of. It was a platform for local tour guides to connect with visitors all across the world. And now, already years later, we see this business model has blown up in so many other reiterations. At that time, it was just such a gift to be a part of starting something that felt so new and energizing.

Then, another week later, I had two other job offers—really, I can't even believe the hilarious alignment of how this all unfolded at the time, so perfectly. One from a former client for another consulting role and another for a friend's start-up—both called me up seemingly out of the blue. So, suddenly within two weeks of putting in my notice, I had not just one but three new roles that were all in alignment with the kind of work I really wanted to be doing. I was utilizing my gifts, working half the time and getting paid the same amount, and working, in some cases, with some of my favorite people, with dear friends. And the rest is history.

It is fun to share that story now so many years later, after so many trials and tribulations of running my own business and experiencing some of the hardest initiations imaginable that come with the path of entrepreneurship. It really is not for the faint of heart—and let me be the first to tell you: entrepreneurship is the ultimate path of transformation and embodiment. When you sign up to bring your soul vision to the world you are signing up for intense alchemy on all levels so you can truly be prepared to be the vessel of your vision—who are you required to be to bring the thing you are meant to birth into this world through? In spite of—or perhaps it's better to say because of—all the lessons, the dark nights of the soul, the ego deaths, the hilarious experiences of giving my power away to those I thought could do it better than me, the incredible client collaborations and life-changing experiences, all of it—I wouldn't change a thing.

Then a fun reverberation started happening. The more I shared openly about my journey, celebrating how good it felt to have taken this leap into starting my own coaching and consulting practice, the more I magnetically attracted people who wanted to work with me, much like the same way in which I had felt attracted to my mentor way back when. And years later, hundreds of clients later, having created courses, hosted retreats, written books, created a podcast, built a few awesome brands, traveled all over the world, I just can't imagine how my life could have even unfolded any differently. It's almost like I never even had a choice, that leaving my job at that time—at that specific time—was part of my divine destiny.

"And, when you want something, all the universe
conspires in helping you to achieve it."
—Paulo Coelho

I only had to listen; all of life was just waiting to show up and support me. I would not have known that those other jobs existed had I not first created the opening and the space in which I was available to receive them. So often, when we're called to take a leap into the unknown, especially for growing into a new edge of our service, our power, and leadership, we don't know what's going to happen. We aren't supposed to really know—we are meant to trust and feel our capacity to allow life to show up for us in miraculous ways. We usually won't know what other opportunities will come and fill the space that we're creating—which are almost always better than we can even imagine.

Remember how our mind can only create and project based on past experiences—usually designed to create more of the same, familiar circumstances that will feel secure for us to navigate because we've done it all before? Well, when it comes to innovating new paths and pioneering new potentials, we must lean into our intuitive superpowers, our deeply felt sense of where we are meant to go and when—that usually emerges not through our intellectual mind but through our feelings, our gut sense, or other messages coming through our body's signaling. Here's another paradox of our human evolutionary process—we are meant to go through fearful circumstances in which we see we have no control and must let go and trust so we see how supported we are.

We never have control in the first place—at least not over the external circumstances we may find ourselves in. This is what life continually wants us to awaken more deeply into. The only thing we can control is our response to our reality, and even that isn't promised until we commit to repatterning and repairing the autopilot survival and protection strategies that prevent us from inevitably carving new paths into the unknown. This is why we are here—to create the future we wish existed. It starts from within, from listening and then resourcing ourselves fully so we can take stable, grounded action from a place of knowing precisely what is ours to do, at the right time, in the right way, with all the support required.

OUR PORTAL TO LIMITLESS LIVING

Do you know the voice or the feeling or the sense that you innately have that's always guiding you toward what's right for you? It may be that you haven't been aware of this innate sense until now or that you've known about it for quite some time but haven't felt like admitting to yourself that it's something to take seriously. Or perhaps you're like me and you've actually spent years trying to numb the voices and guiding sensations because you were afraid of what might happen if you actually listened and, beyond even that, actually followed suit in your commitments and actions.

If you're like me and you've been used to living from the outside in, if you haven't already gotten the point from reading this book thus far, it's time to reverse engineer your reality to operate more from the inside out. Your insides always reflect your outsides—it's a fundamental truth we must start to take more seriously as a culture. How we feel internally is a key element to how our physical reality is orienting around us. We see it when we believe it—not the other way around which says: I'll believe it when I see it. We're not just exploring spiritual philosophy here either; this way of living in total responsibility for our realities and experiences therein is quite pragmatic. In fact, cultivating our intuition plus ultimate discernment is a very practical path for allowing life to unfold as a series of aligned, even designed, next right step after next right step. It feels like ease, grace, and flow.

At this moment in our collective awakening each day, more and more people are waking up to their energetic sensitive and intuitive inklings, asking questions like: What is my purpose? How can I live a more meaningful life? What are my gifts and how can I share them? How can I be happy and fulfilled? and How can I trust my intuition and follow my heart? I get these questions all the time, and the rate at which they're being asked is increasing in frequency. I am often quite humbled to consider how I could even start to support someone in the very beginning of this journey that will bear so much wisdom and insight in the long run—words stop making sense when I try to articulate the meaning of my intention here. When I sink into more presence and silence—what I hear instead is: I wish for all of humanity to awaken to their innate wisdom and superpowers so that they can become their own best guides and extraordinary creators of their most desirable realities. This is the world we came here for.

This book is but a beginning in such an attempt—to define the indefinable perhaps. It's definitely a fun exploration trying—isn't it? Well, if there's one thing I hope to have conveyed clearly thus far, it's that awakening to higher consciousness is a deeply personal quest that's best followed through one's own guidance, through your discernment moment by moment of what feels best for you, and by taking everything in and leaving behind whatever doesn't completely feel resonant for you no matter what. You always have the best medicine, guidance, and discernment of what's true for you—no one else can ever take that away from you (unless you allow them to). Here's what matters most: you determine your values, you decide what you believe in, you're making this whole thing up anyways, aren't you? So why not choose moment by moment what feels best for you—why else are you here anyway?

Trusting your intuitive knowing is essential on your ascension journey into embodying your best self, living in alignment with your purpose, feeling fulfilled in giving your gifts, and enjoying abundant love, presence, and connection in all relationships. These are the fundamental aspects of why we are here on Earth, are they not? Or maybe that's the case for me: What do you believe is true for you? What do you value most? Why do you believe you are here? What is the story you are creating and therefore living into? What is your personal odyssey, your hero's journey, your unique why? These are the questions to be in constant inquiry of as you devote yourself to living a conscious life, actualized in your authentic self, sharing your greatest gifts, and having the most fun imaginable—enjoying every aspect of life as you've created it in perfect alignment with your deepest desires.

Trusting your knowing can happen through a gut feeling; an extrasensory perception you hear or simply feel, as though you're recalling a dream or a memory; a voice you hear, as though you're tuning into another channel, like on a radio; or a certain sensation like heat or coolness on your skin in response to a particular option being offered to you. The more you trust what feels true for you—which usually comes through based on what feels best for you, what feels expansive, what feels light, what feels nourishing—the more you notice synchronicity and even miracles as a very normal and perhaps even happenstance occurrence in life.

**"Let yourself be drawn by the stronger pull
of that which you truly love."
—Rumi**

In our Western culture we are predominantly conditioned to see miracles as rare; when they are noticed they're meant to be celebrated as extraordinary feats. The truth is, and for me I know this deep in my soul, miracles are a normal occurrence when you are living in alignment with the truth of who you are, trusting your intuition to guide you into alignment with your destiny and always in a more imaginative, easeful, fun way than you could have ever planned with your limited intellectual capacity.

Don't get me wrong, we love our minds, our intellect, our strategizing, and our superpowered gifts of organizing, planning, and projecting—all the great aspects of co-creating in the third dimension through our businesses, services, collaborative relationships, etc. How else would we build anything, especially the structure and systems that are required at this time of great change to support us in enjoying the more abundant, sustainable, beautiful, harmonious world that works for all beings? When you start to see yourself as intrinsically linked to all of life and you embody the creator that you are, it's quite natural to care for the Earth and all other living beings as though they are extensions of yourself, because seeing the world in any other way, certainly through the illusory story of separation, simply won't cut it.

We've done a fairly deep dive into understanding our core wounds and traumas by now—and in the context of turning on our intuition, we want to consider this brilliant statement: Learn to differentiate between the sound of your intuition guiding you and your traumas misleading you (not sure who it's by but it has always stuck with me). At a certain point on our path we start to turn up the volume on our intuitive voice or inner guidance—however that speaks to us, which might be as simple as a sensation through the body rather than a voice or what seems to be a thought or vision. We all have unique ways of perceiving and receiving intuitive insight.

We love our minds and we are grateful for how we've been taught and instructed over generations to think with our best foot forward, to learn from all the lessons of generations past, and to cultivate a great rationale with which to create incredible fears. Yet in the age of awakening that we are ushering in as our consciousness expands beyond the simple material realm into new dimensions of possibility and relationship, we are invited to trust our ability to create in the infinite quantum field far more easily and powerfully than the limits of our mental perception would allow.

Science is now catching up with what mystics for centuries, maybe even millennia, have known to be true—humans have energy fields that are essentially magnetic, and from their heart center, especially amplified by coherence, which signifies being at deep rest in the body and breath, they can manifest and attract desirable outcomes on the material plane quite instantaneously. It's not a surprise that one of the hottest trends in spirituality and even personal development now is manifestation and even the law of attraction.

Your intuition is speaking to you through your good feelings, through your desires, and through your heart's calling. The intuition, or perhaps an energy you may define as the voice of the divine, the soul, or even the higher self, communicates in timelessness. It knows time is an illusion, or simply an agreement we've collectively made up to measure our distance and to set arrangements into motion for—guess what—strategies, structure, and controllable outcomes to occur on a particularly benchmarked scale.

Trusting yourself and cultivating a habit of listening to your intuition is one of your greatest superpowers. Especially when it comes to manifesting your most desirable reality. Letting your intuition guide your path can result in faster, more efficient manifestation than you would ever imagine possible within the limited scope of your mind, which is programmed to operate within linear parameters that are naturally defined by scarcity and limitation.

"All suffering comes from the violation of intuition."
—Florence Scovel Shinn

Intuition on the other hand seems to speak most often in terms of beauty, play, joy, love, and celebration—at least this has been the case for me. Intuition for me often has the voice of the inner child—the voice of the divine that knows no limitation on what's possible, that speaks from pure genius imagination, that is motivated by the simple call to have more fun, to share more love, to experience more beauty, and to become more self-realized simply through learning and growing, sometimes without any seeming agenda at all, simply for the joy of it all.

I knew for a very long time, ever since I was little, actually, that I wanted to be involved in social justice and supporting humanity's collective consciousness awakening predominantly through education, diversity initiatives, and inclusion. When I was little I used to want to be president of the United States, and then even in middle school I pictured myself as a lawyer and social justice activist, thinking that if I could help change the laws that impacted separation and oppression I could help people feel more inclusive and empowered to live in more harmony and ease.

I was always drawn to study revolution and activism and always felt a huge pressure to really contribute in a massive way to social justice. But with all of my sensitivity and overwhelming experience as an empath—plus not knowing what that meant, not even being aware of *empath* being an indicator of what I was experiencing, and having no resources with which to support my evolution and integration of what I later came to understand as great gifts instead of painful burdens—I wasn't able to show up for any epic vision of service or contribution. For so long I was so caught up in numbing myself so I could survive and fit in and try my best to be a normal human. Leading the cause in social justice would have to wait till I could first learn to take care of myself. And once I did start awakening more as myself, I came into a completely different orientation to what social justice actually means and how I wanted to be a part of exemplifying positive change in the world. I came to see how the kind of change I was after was far more internally oriented than external. I started to understand how the massive shifts I saw we needed on the global scale couldn't be sustained until more people developed the consciousness and maturity to actualize the new behaviors and attitudes these new systems and structures required to effectively operate.

Our intuition is always guiding us to our soul purpose and our destiny. Just like how I knew from a young age that I was naturally drawn to social justice with a particular aim within inclusion and education and empowerment. You too have always had a calling and a destiny that's been communicated to you almost too easily through the activities and opportunities you feel most naturally drawn to. The issue most people have—and I know this was the case for me for quite a long time—is that our culture conditions us to think externally instead of internally. We are taught so young to look outside—what do you want to be? Who do you want to look like? What sounds like the coolest thing of all? I used to want to be president because I liked being in charge and I thought I could help a lot of people that way—actually the essence of this desire isn't totally far off even still. But what if we had been challenged early on instead to explore what gifts and natural curiosities were arising for us through how we most loved to play and create? Instead of immediately boxing ourselves into *astronaut* or *doctor* or some other socially acceptable profession—especially if our parents already had an idea about what they wanted us to grow up into—I wonder what we might have chosen or created anew instead.

If we were to prioritize our internal world, our desires, and our inner calling, and to listen to what's already being broadcast loud and clear, we'd find maybe obvious accessible direction showing us the next step. Now maybe we wouldn't be shown the whole ten-year plan, although that's certainly accessible to some degree when your intuition is more empowered and you can really hear yourself—but we'll be given what we are ready for, that's a promise. And isn't that all we really need anyway, the next right step? Having the whole ten-year plan can actually get in the way of us enjoying the present moment fully.

INTUITIVE AWAKENING ATTUNEMENTS

"Every time you allow life to leave you bored or indifferent or you feel this lack of energy and inertia, it is up to you and you alone to reconnect with your dream. Without a sense of higher purpose, human beings move in circles creating energy fields that prevent abundance. If your heart is not behind your every act, not only do you choose an inappropriate course in life, but you also continually wear down your health."
—Richard Rudd

Surrender your mind into completely opening, trusting, and following your heart. We've got this—we were made for this moment. Let's explore how we can tune into our inner truth and guidance system more clearly than ever and empower ourselves to start following more of our highest aligned paths in our dream realities. Are we in the dream awakening or are we ourselves the ones awakening the dream? Does it even matter anyway—if we are here to have fun, enjoy, create beauty, and architect brilliant visions into form? When we are so lost in the moment of this present now, time ceases to exist, thought forms are at a loss, and we deepen into new feelings and sensations that turn us even more on to new dimensions of this life. The deeper we go the more we realize there is to see, feel, and know. Let's see what our intuitive wisdom has to say.

Activate Your Intuition

Let's play a game to activate your intuitive awareness. This game is fun to play with a friend or if going solo you can try playing with yourself as your partner in the mirror or simply seated in a comfy meditative spot. If you're sharing with a friend, set the context for the game by saying something like, "This is a meditation, communication exercise and exchange in exercising our intuitive channeling capabilities! We'll each go for ten minutes using a timer, following the flow accordingly as I am about to lay out." Set the timer for ten minutes.

For two minutes, sitting across from one another, start syncing your breath with eyes closed, really becoming conscious of your own energy but also aware of the heart connection being formed. After two minutes, for the next one minute gaze in silence into each other's left eye. Breathing can be synced here also. Go into discomfort if it arises. There is so much to be learned here. Next five minutes: one person takes a turn channeling any wisdom that comes through to share for the other person's benefit, reflections in response to the prompts: What I really get about you is . . . , What I see in you is . . . , What I feel for you is . . . Trust that your truth will be delivered in the most perfect way in unconditional love.

After five minutes, the other person has three minutes to reflect and share what they received from the experience without interruption. Repeat the ten-minute cycle with the other person channeling. If you are doing this practice solo, it works basically the same—and can be a fun way to practice strengthening your connection to your own guidance and direction within.

Everyone Is a Channel—When We Allow It

Regardless of where you believe you fall on the intuitive scale and regardless of where you may be on your awakening path, in my experience we are all wired to be channels of the divine intuition we've been gifted. Have you ever heard of or perhaps even experienced being in a flow state?

That's another way to describe channeling. When you're operating as a channel for higher guidance and wisdom to come through you, you transcend time and space (which only exist in logical, linear understanding) and feel what it is like to be fully utilized in the fullest expression of your unique soul gifts. Practice. Time to put your gifts in full-throttle motion. You can do this solo or even invite a friend or loved one to play this intuitive mastery game with you.

A simple way to play is to set a timer for a few minutes—three can be good to start—and allow yourself to free-flow express whatever is arising, whatever is alive for you in this moment. It's kind of like a vocal meditation when you label what's coming up in the moment instead of labeling a thought internally or in a silent meditation practice. This is such a powerful way to cleanse the body and field of what I call *backlog* in consciousness—any stuck stuff we're allowing unconsciously to linger in our space that's preventing us from being fully present.

It's nice to put your thumb in your belly button with your palm facing downward against your body—take a deep breath into this space before beginning and feel yourself ground completely into your body and into the earth. Once you feel grounded, start the timer and then begin by saying, "I am allowing . . ."—insert after that phrase anything, absolutely anything, you are aware of floating in your consciousness—and just name it. Bring it into awareness so you can let it go. There is something so powerful about being witnessed in this process. Even after just a few minutes doing this I've experienced incredible emotional release and I've seen the same in others. We see a few layers in—after we allow some of the presenting superficial material we may be holding to finally surface and be let go of just by naming it and making it more conscious—how so many big feelings and energies are just waiting right there to be touched.

An example of this game might go like this, but trust it will be completely unique and different every time:

I am allowing ease.
I am allowing coffee.
I am allowing butter.
I am allowing writing.
I am allowing Mom.
I am allowing sadness.
I am allowing grief.
I am allowing not fair.
I am allowing lonely.
I am allowing red pants.
I am allowing green grass.
I am allowing blue laptop.
I am allowing alignment.

Continue on for the full duration of your timer and see what emerges—let it be a practice that is refined. The more you do it, the easier it will become and the greater releases might transpire too. I recommend this exercise as a prerequisite for channeling or doing any kind of public speaking or even energy healing work. It's a great way to cleanse the field and clean out one's consciousness to see more clearly what is here and now. Plus we get to be entertained by how much our mind is processing constantly—such a jumble of thoughts, ideas, and pictures. But there is a clearer voice underneath all that, waiting to be more empowered, wanting our attention. Here is how we can tap into our deeper, clearer, more direct truth.

Awaken Your Inner Oracle

Your intuition and any guides you may energetically receive support from will always speak to you in a way you can feel, promise. Your unique channel for guidance is designed to transmit messages to you sometimes in ways that are meant for only you and no one else—which is why discovering and exploring your intuition is a deeply personal practice. To get started, in your meditation or perhaps in your automatic writing (the practice of free-flow journaling without **trying** to make sense or create coherent full thoughts or sentences; for some this can be a potent tool for allowing intuition to translate sometimes very specific guidance), ask yourself: How can I strengthen my intuitive abilities? See what answers you receive. Some intuitive abilities are:

- Clairempathy (clear emotion): the ability to tune into the energy and emotions of other living beings, the collective consciousness, and other vibrational content.
- Clairsentience (clear sensation or feeling): an ability to receive intuitive, psychic insight through feeling and sensation communicated by the entire body.
- Claircognizance (clear knowing): If you've ever had a gut feeling or a simple knowing about something that was going to happen without any evidence to the fact, you're tuning into claircognizance.
- Clairtangency (clear touching): This expression is also commonly referred to as psychometry. If you've ever held an object or touched an area with your palms and received information about the owner of the object or its history that was previously unknown, you're tuning into clairtangency.
- Clairgustance (clear tasting): If you've ever been able to taste something without actually having it in your mouth to literally taste, you are accessing your clairgustance abilities.
- Clairaudience (clear hearing): the ability to perceive sounds or words from outside sources in the spirit world.
- Clairvoyance (clear vision): If you've ever had a vision of a past, present, or future occurrence or received information internally as though viewing a picture or movie within your consciousness, you are tuning into clairvoyance.

Our intuition speaks through us in infinite ways—which do you most identify with? The list above is by no means exhaustive—we have so many more ways our intuitive abilities can take form that I believe we simply don't have words for at this point in our collective lexicon. Perhaps we can ask our intuitive guidance for the new languages we require to describe the experiences we are meant to be having now! In the meantime, keep exploring: how can you strengthen your abilities now that you're more aware of how you receive intuitive guidance?

Your Supernatural Advisors

Just for fun, imagine how practical it is to play in a new reality in which you have a whole stadium full of your top advisors ready at your beck and call to help you in any and every possible way. Imagine each and every one of us has a whole board of advisors existing in all sorts of different planes and dimensions who have lived all these great life experiences full of incredible wisdom to share, and they want nothing more than to help us! You have a whole team of mentors for all of the very precise areas of mastery and expertise that you desire on your path. How can we start leveraging this great resource and making it work for us?

You can start by journaling out a question you'd love guidance on—or meditating on the question to see what is already emerging in terms of potential direction and support. Then go a bit deeper and picture yourself at a board meeting of your supernatural advisors, or in the middle of the stadium on center stage. Take the microphone, take the lead, and ask your question, no matter how big or small, if it matters to you, it matters to explore. Then picture your board of advisors—maybe you notice them as familiar figures from history, or from other lifetimes—and one by one go to them for their response and advice. You might picture them or actually hear them answering you with their unique tone and style—they're giving you precisely what's needed for the most ease and grace on your path, trust it. You might even feel the inspiration with some of them to press further and ask other related or unrelated questions in greater detail. Have fun with it—everyone is here to help you, just because—you deserve to be supported, and your path matters so much to the entire plan unfolding. You are that powerful.

This is another way of starting to look at past lives and all the experiences you have had that qualify you to be your own guide too. Somewhere out there perhaps you are even sitting on the board of someone else's advisory council—in another dimension, or elsewhere on Earth. You never know (but it's fun to imagine). I love exploring these topics especially as we see the guru dynamic totally falling apart in our society. How do you get to be your own guide? How do you start to trust yourself? How do you start to go to yourself for your own wisdom, for your own knowing, trusting again that you have so much power, you have so much wisdom. Whether or not you believe that you've lived in other lifetimes or even incarnated other experiences, just try it on and see how it feels.

But Wait, There's More!

I could go on and on—maybe there is a whole other book wanting to come forth in which we focus solely on intuition and awakening this fundamental superpower we all have within. For now, here are overflow attunements to explore and play with—to turn your knowing all the way on, all the way up, here and now. What beautiful world is possible when we start truly listening to the guidance moving through us? What kind of reality shall we choose to co-create?

- **Clear your space:** Strengthen your intuition by clearing your space, which entails not only your psychic space but also your physical space. Clean out all the old stuff that you don't use or need. Do you really need those punch cards for the coffee place you haven't been to in years? Stuff like that—let it go. Create space for what you really desire and space to receive what's meant for you.
- **Clear your being.** Remember what I shared about all that transpired when I did a holistic cleanse protocol, how my intuition came on so much stronger and I was able to hear so much more clearly? Consider doing a light cleanse, or even investing in support from a naturopath or holistic chiropractic like I did to get on a regimen to help cleanse your system more thoroughly. I like to do parasite cleanses a few times a year even still to keep everything running smoothly. Plus—colonics and coffee enemas are such wonderful self-healing practices that help us to feel more clearly by literally being able to access our gut instinct more directly. At the very least, make sure the water you are drinking is clean and free of chemicals. Hydrating with clean (structured is even better!) water that actually nourishes our cells is life changing.
- **Get grounded.** Your intuition, soul, higher self, inner child speaks

to you through your body. Your body can receive best when relaxed and grounded in this present moment. Ground yourself into your body so you can really listen.

- **Make affirmations:** I am free of all foreign energies. I am completely open to receiving divine guidance and inspiration. I listen to my powerful intuition that guides my every move. I am safe. I am protected. I am well. I am peaceful. I am powerful. I am free.

- **Explore.** Get curious. Get into creative imagination. How can you avail yourself to more flow and freedom and play? What if you committed two hours each day to free-flow creative fun and expression of your uniqueness? Paint, draw, sculpt, dance, cook, craft, vision board, knit, play music, sing, move, write—what intuitive expression feels best for you and can you honor that in this moment? This is when your soul is most apt to speak to you. Get outside. Play games.

- **Question everything.** Ask a question and allow yourself to respond creativity, intuitively. Allow a stream-of-consciousness automatic writing to take place—time yourself for ten minutes as you free flow your written response to any question that feels particularly pressing. Allow yourself to be surprised. What are you committing to this week to really go deep into your creative expression, through which your soul will most certainly speak? Declare it!

- **Is this true for me?** Next time you are taking in content or teachings from someone else—even as you're reading these words, practice the interruption of tuning into your intuition by asking yourself: Is this true for me? Then notice what comes up and see if any realignment or commitment emerges to respond with. You may be surprised by how many opportunities emerge here to take your power back.

12

EMBODIED ASCENSION

I forget who said this, but it still makes me smile: "We need a civil rights movement for the soul." It might feel really hard to be a human who feels this much right now. Just the other day I was even crying in the bath and curled in a ball a few times, feeling the immensity of trauma memories and densities being cleansed from my cells and DNA. So much for this body. All the layers so illuminated. Celebrating, not running away, not checking out—as if that's even an option anymore, it's not. Practicing loving ourselves unconditionally, interrupting the inner beat-up and voices of not-enough-ness when they arise, saying: I understand why you are here, you helped me survive in a family that was so hard to grow up in, but I am evolving out of survival and I am ready to feel supported, to receive, to trust, to love.

The complexity we all hold is sometimes overwhelming to fully consider—the layers of our programming, distortions, identity/personality structures, all the ways we had to perform to get what we needed. Welcoming all these parts. Honoring them. Not making them wrong. Saying: It's okay. I understand. I love you anyway. Thank you for all you did to arrive here in this moment as you. Going into the fire, holding hands with my soul family, who remember our mission at hand.

We are pioneering embodied ascension for the first time ever as awakening human beings—what is it like to embody multidimensionality in physical-emotional form? We are practicing being the examples for thousands of generations to come, paving the way as best we can. And it is enough. It's more than enough.

In this moment, our greatest requirement in our evolution is personal mastery and embodiment. This is the essence of ascension—allowing our true selves to become embodied in every cell, allowing our true presence to be felt beyond any words we say or personalities we don. We all have different journeys along that trajectory, but perhaps it's all as simple as:

be who you really are, do what you came here to do and have fun along the way.

Maybe, just maybe, from here together we start to create a world that happens to be pretty harmonious, unified, and innovative—in which more beings are awakened in their complete mastery, living their purpose, and bringing forth the gifts only they can bring in so many delightful ways that are all simply meant to be. It's such a wondrous puzzle we weave together. When everyone feels permission to be as they are and feels safety and trust in being truly present, there's no limit to what new potentials and realities we will be inspired to co-create and enjoy together.

HOLOGRAPHIC HAPPINESS

Your outer world always reflects your inner being. Unity consciousness is the state of oneness, the state of being at one with all that is, being at one with all of life. It means being completely present within and without—we are in the moment and we are the moment unfolding, all at once. Beyond time and space. We are. When we start to realize ourselves as creators of our reality—we see that life is happening as us, not only for us and through us, but really as ourselves, as us. At some level we start to see every single aspect of life as a reflection of our own consciousness. As something that we not only created but something that is, in fact, an extension of our being, especially when it comes to people we are in relationship with. As we awaken the higher consciousness, we really start to see every single other person in our life as a reflection of us, as an element of our consciousness, as an element of our personality. We might even notice that people in our lives start to even more closely resemble physical aspects of ourselves because we are, in fact, seeing more of our own physical energetic reflection in others.

As we awaken and continue on our paths of personal evolution, we must ask ourselves continually, especially if we are ever upset with what we see transpiring in the world around us: How am I abusing the planet? Where am I causing harm and how? I've come to find that when I notice something in the world I am not happy with—something that feels so out of alignment with what I value and believe, that's a sign to look within and see where I can create more space and coherence and congruence within my own being to more accurately reflect and project the kind of reality I want to be seeing and sensing more of. If we hear about environmental impact or devastation, could this also mean that we are not taking care of our body? We are a microcosm of the macrocosm—we are the planet, the ecosystem, a reflection of the whole. When we take better care of ourselves as though we are the world we want to experience—I have a strong sense that our outer reality will align accordingly and reflect more the values we hold most dear.

"Man cannot be anything other than what he is. Whatever he is, he will create a society that mirrors him."
—U. G. Krishnamurti

As I know is the case for a lot of activists, we're on the front lines doing the work of personal and collective healing and transformation, but to what extent is that outward drive to save the world actually a deep calling from within for us to pay attention to ourselves? Just take a moment and reflect. It's interesting that I'm upset about deforestation—the negligence, disrespect of natural resources, and disrespect of beauty—but where might that energy, that negligence, be present within me? Where am I not showing up for myself? Where am I not managing my resources effectively? Where am I not managing my energy appropriately? Where am I letting natural reserves go to waste or simply taking them for granted?

The experience of unity consciousness we are presently evolving into is requiring all of us to show up together and become masterful in our relationships so that we can truly thrive and live in a community together. Not just amongst ourselves and other humans, but with all living beings and with the planet itself. Maybe that doesn't mean that we're all living on communes—but maybe it does. Perhaps most of our issues when it comes to trauma and suffering have indeed seemed to germinate in the illusions of separation, from ourselves, from each other, and from the natural world and all its elemental healing beauty. We've learned to be so hyper-individualized especially over the last century—living in big houses, in busy cities, behind smartphones and computers. We've faced incredible loneliness throughout it all too—even while maintaining the appearance of having it all together on social media or in certain environments where we'd rather keep up an act rather than admit defeat, let the masks down, and actually, truly connect.

I know it's hard—trust me, I've lived it. And people—we can't live with them, but we definitely can't live without them. That was a funny reminder I had upon re-entering a communal living experience after living on my own for so long. It's so challenging to navigate group fields and such different energies, but alas: it's why we are here. Plus, growing up in most family dynamics can be wildly challenging too. Do we ever get a break? I can't help but think that the family as we understand it, especially in the West (as this is my experience and context), is actually a recent, modern development. In a typical American family dynamic—if there is such a thing, but I suppose I mean the one we are conditioned with in our media and culture—there is so much pressure assigned within various roles of the family unit. Dad is the breadwinner, Mom is at home with the kids, and everyone has their own room where they are expected to mostly keep to themselves and "be good." Sometimes you'll meet for dinner or for shared activities, but really the truth is we've never been more isolated from each other—especially with the mass adoption of social media and smartphones.

I wonder if kids these days are receiving the proper experiences and adequate attunement to learn effective social skills and emotional regulation. A remedy here of course is more conscious, embodied, awake parents who can interrupt social conditioning and create more space for intimacy and true presence in their families (and in all of life). Let this be a prayer for all the work we've shared thus far—that it makes its way through the family lines and impacts more young ones to also tap into their authenticity, intuitive knowing, and pioneering creativity so they can lead us one day soon!

Meanwhile, the majority of the world, the majority of our collective experience and history in family dyanmics, has actually been more tribal, has entailed living in communal groups and even sharing more intimate spaces together so people were actually kind of forced to rub up against each other, heal, and be present with one another. There wasn't so much isolation, avoidance, or repression possible when we were forced to live in closer quarters and actually had less distraction away from feeling and being with whatever was coming up. Plus it was more common for us to be immersed in nature—amidst the natural elements, which were healing in and of themselves to bask in and always supported us to be in better connection with our body's rhythms (and planetary rhythms too) and our intuitive guidance. We were more naturally out of time and in the flow of pure presence. For longer than not—this attunement, this way of being is in our cellular memory, in our DNA, even now. And we are simply remembering.

> **"Old paradigm: I'll teach you what you're here to learn.**
> **New paradigm: I'll be a mirror for you to remember**
> **what you already know."**
> **—Sydney Campos**

I spent a lot of my life feeling great suffering of the collective as a whole—things like racism, slavery, the prison industrial complex, and educational inequality always hurt the most to consider. How could we live in a world where this much pain was possible, seemingly for reasons that to me always felt so illusionary? I never understood the concept of skin color, for example—to me I always saw people as people, and just like people have different color eyes or hair or are different heights, shapes, and sizes—we have slightly varying skin tones. I never understood the concept of racism and systematically oppressing and institutionally separating people based on something as seemingly random as skin tone. This awareness at such a young age drove me nuts—it boggled my mind. How could people do this to each other? How did I end up on a planet where this kind of treatment was even possible? The weight of these questions was unbearable and would sometimes come out in endless crying bouts especially under the influence of a lot of alcohol or drugs, even as young as when I was in high school.

From as young as fourth grade or so, right after I moved to San Francisco especially and noticed more homeless and hungry people than I had ever come into contact with before, sometimes I would lose sleep at night worrying about why these people weren't being helped. I was wondering what I was going to do about it, how I could fix it, why did everyone just let it happen—and this drive to fix it (the world, society, people, and the ways they are) led me to study social justice, social movements, sociology, political theory, cultural theory, and everything in between—for what felt like so long, to no end. The more truth I'd uncover, the deeper I'd realize the whole game goes—that the system of inequality and oppression was definitely rigged and controlled by such a select, untouchable few. How could we ever fix such a mess? I still thought for a time being in politics or becoming a lawyer who could infiltrate the justice system might be the way. All the meanwhile I was still drinking and drugging, trying to turn off the immense sensitivity and overwhelm I felt about all of it, about all of life.

Upon awakening I started to see that the pain showcased throughout the outside world—in forms of oppression, systemic inequality, poverty, injustice, and all the other innumerable wounds we harbor collectively—was indeed a reflection of our inside world and the compounded unresolved traumas and wounds we individually still remained to resolve. For a few years I explored the path of advertising and media as a way to more directly infiltrate consciousness and perhaps incite cultural awakening and change—although I might not have called it that at the time. Advertising is like working in politics anyway but going direct—and it's a bit more efficient and expedient too when you look at the impact that's possible, especially in a capitalist society driven by marketing. Even further along in my awakening, closer to where I am residing now, I can see, for me, that the answer to world peace, justice, equality—whatever we wish to be actualized collectively—is within ourselves. I am here to clear the distortions in me that I no longer want to see perpetrated in the world—this is how I contribute most effectively to planetary healing.

What I see emerging now more than ever, so beautifully, is people who are devoted to embodying more coherence and more mastery while living their purpose and being turned on by life. More and more are opening up to their authenticity, exploring their intuition, and allowing themselves to be turned on all the way, fully awake and alive. And what I'm particularly excited about arising in our collective ascension process is this almost uncanny remembrance, uncanny knowing, that you're my family. We're in this together and none of us ever has to go it alone, ever again. In fact, we really can't even if we tried—we are all so innately connected and meant to be collaborating in this collective evolutionary experiment. There is no me without you.

We are at a tipping point in our collective consciousness evolution wherein more and more of us are seeing ourselves and each other as part of a unified whole. We are coming into deeper understanding of ourselves as souls that have lifetimes of experience and wisdom to source and share—that we are far more than the personality and masks we have learned to don in self protection and preservation. We are seeing how we are here to learn and grow, and there are no mistakes along the way—only lessons that help us transform and transcend in the ways we deeply desire actualizing, simply for the experience in and of itself. We are remembering we are here to deeply feel and attune to new sensations and perceptions within our reality—seeing our inherent multidimensionality and capacity to integrate far more insight into our experience than ever before. We are learning to forgive ourselves and each other more quickly—remembering we are like children learning to walk, in these highly evolved bodies that are recalling their ability to transmit exponential levels of energetic data, ushering us into pioneering new possibilities.

"We may not have it all together but together we have it all."
—sign on a cafe wall in Ubud, Bali

Let's be together. Let's see each other. Let's take care of each other. And let's see how doing so—starts with each of us making a commitment to do so, first within ourselves (every time I write that word I want to say *our cells*, perhaps holding the same or maybe even more true meaning). Being together—being in unity—with my collective human family, starts with me, walking the walk, talking the talk—supporting myself fully, feeling good, taking care of myself, being in full responsibility, being in truth, being authentic. We each must take care of all that good stuff before we can even think about coming together and playing let alone creating the new world we wish existed. We're not totally there yet. Even those of us who might claim to be in great mastery as teachers, facilitators, and stewards of great wealth and influence—or maybe all of us humans actually, we get to be really honest about whether or not we're actually who we say we are. Are we truly ready to play and collaborate together in this New Earth? I know for me, I personally still have my work cut out for me. I'll still keep practicing and collaborating in the ways that feel good and expansive—but I will always do my best to stay humble and willing to learn, grow, and improve. This is the best we can do.

What we all really want deep down is connection. We all really want unity, but we have to experience that within ourselves first. We have to experience being with ourselves, fully accepting ourselves, and maybe even fully loving ourselves first. Such a seemingly simple, yet also impossible task—this invitation to unconditionally love ourselves and truly come home within. Can we be an unshakable foundation of self-love and affirmation, of power and confidence, of knowing our truth and our purpose, no matter what might come up in our path? Can we be the eye of the storm? Can we be stable and secure despite what waves might come? Especially when we are in intimate and creative partnership with other complex human beings—mirroring back to us our unconsciousness and opportunities to repattern and further embody our truth—how do we meet the moments of opportunity to face what's uncomfortable and see it through to completion?

Embodied ascension means going willingly into the fires of purification again and again to burn away all that can no longer burden our paths into deeper presence. Here we are—and we can't escape the inevitable if we tried. Checking out is no longer an option, as if it really ever was. We can't pretend to be heavy when we are made to feel the fullness of light that we are. It hurts burning like this; the layers to clear go deeper than we imagined. But what if we are meant to feel completely clear?

What is it like to be in a body free of trauma, density, distortion, survival, protection, and all the strategies therein that carry such a heavy weight? Who are we when we drop the baggage, for good? When we are ourselves, present, available, open, receptive, fearless, infinite? Here we are in a grand experiment that's never been attempted before like this: as us, in this moment. The conditions for our practice have never entailed such immense challenges for our physicality, with energy moving this fast, this bright, this strong.

We are like babies, learning to walk in new bodies in a new world, speaking new languages, using new senses, breathing new breaths, seeing through new eyes, hearing and knowing through new channels all at once and then some. No wonder it feels overwhelming. We are learning to love ourselves no matter what and accept who we are as we are now, as absolutely perfect. We are learning true unconditional love. We are learning to meet our own needs completely. We are learning our true worth and value. We are feeling more of our power flowing through our sovereign body-soul systems. We are learning to deeply, presently listen and trust. We are learning what it means to be fully alive. We are learning how to be ourselves, in connection and collaboration with each other, in a reality purely existent in truth and nothing but the truth. Everything in the way will come up to burn. Into the fire we go, as long as it takes, no matter what.

> **"You can't use up creativity. The more you**
> **use, the more you have."**
> **—Maya Angelou**

When we try to make it happen, we get in the way of what's meant to happen. Here we are—within another initiation unfolding into greater presence, self-acceptance, honoring one's value from deep within—getting into the root of what is raw and real. The truth, and nothing less. Energy here feels simultaneously like being entrenched in the Earth's deepest layers—in the core of her fiery flows from which all creation stems—while also expanding into layers of consciousness that feel quite far out literally and figuratively. The cycles of death and rebirth are in your face everywhere you go—reminders of our smallness in the great scheme of nature's divine plans. In an instant everything you know as familiar and safe—externals—could be destroyed and birthed again anew. So how is your internal stability, safety, and core sense of self? How deep do your roots really go? Are you unshakably stable, strong, and resilient despite what's happening outside?

Here I am reminded to feel simple yet profound gratitude for being alive—having fresh, clean air to breathe, a home and all my needs met—not to mention a purpose, a mission, awareness, empowerment to make choices, and take action in alignment with desires. Funny how wrapped up we can get in purpose when maybe our simple purpose might just be to live and enjoy our lives completely. When anxiety and self-criticism and insurmountable grief arise to speak their piece, as they have been rather loudly doing lately, do we give them air time? Or, do we speak as the strong protector we are who is choosing consciously what energy to empower and embody?

> **"The purpose of life is to watch and experience living. To enjoy living every moment of it. The ideal purpose of your life is that you are grateful—great and full—that you are alive, and you enjoy it."**
> **—Yogi Bhajan**

We may have been building new nervous systems capable of sustaining the energy we are meant to channel, and yet here we venture into the depths of real emotional stability, maturity, and actual energetic mastery. We are burning away all that is not true from the deepest layers of our beings all the way to the core essence we are. Overexposure used to catalyze shame and all its inherent survival strategies and personas. Now perhaps we are invited to willingly practice being exposed and revealed as a means of self-liberation—building capacity to sustain our own raw power, presence, and authentic expression. No longer holding back.

No longer strategizing ways to titrate the depths we feel safe emanating. It feels like un-damning/un-damming the energy we've held back for lifetimes, venting out breath by breath all that's been held back and in for too long. All of reality is catalyzing the perfect opportunities for us to receive, affirm, and express our unique truths (especially in high contrast to the material worlds unfolding) more deeply. Are we willing to allow what's wanting to live through us to express as us? Keep practicing.

There's no me without you. I see myself in your reflection and you see yourself in mine. We are here on Earth to master being in a relationship so that we can better see and understand ourselves and arrive into more of our true essence which knows its inherent perfection, majesty, and wholeness. We are practicing embodying and remembering more of our power, remembering more of our innate infinite wisdom, remembering divinity, remembering that we are aspects of god. And only from here—how do we want to play?

HEAVEN ON EARTH IS HERE

Heaven on Earth is here when we choose it. In an Akashic Records journey we shared recently, a student in the facilitator training program I host a few times a year brought through an insight so poignant, so beautiful you almost could have missed it: "The mind understanding is the least important thing." We are evolving into a 5D consciousness that invites ultimate presence in all moments, transcending time, welcoming an entirely new creation process rooted more in pure being rather than in thinking or action. We are reconditioning ourselves to embody highly attuned states of faith, trust in uncertainty and even joyfulness in admitting we have no idea what's happening and we never have and never will and it's not our job to pretend we do anymore. What a sweet relief.

When we let go of the pressure to know and manage and track and strategize and control, how much more creative energy do we channel into genius innovation; playful, magical, beautiful contribution; healing ourselves and the collective, and connecting more deeply within and without? What kind of world do we experience in truly infinite possibility wherein all roads lead to collective thrive-al (instead of survival), harmony, expansion and quantum leaps, miracles, abundance beyond our wildest dreams? All the new norms, yes, absolutely. We are attuning to deeply receiving ourselves and each other.

"Your soul doesn't care what you do for a living—and when your life is over, neither will you. Your soul cares only about what you are being while you are doing whatever you are doing."
—Neale Donald Walsch

There is a profound intimacy in presence with yourself and all of life. Some would call it tantra or unity consciousness, but I like saying it's all about purely being. Here and now. Honesty. Authenticity. Transparent like water. Detached, powerfully flowing like a massive river with no end and no beginning. Remembering our infinite nature and remembering to enjoy the cosmic ride of this embodiment. It's never been a more ripe moment to launch into our dreams. Our New Earth is craving our genius contributions. Your multidimensional support team is here rooting for you, ready to assist, awaiting your order. Place your order, humanity, you can have anything you desire. What are you waiting for? Give yourself permission to really live and expand from here. There is so much beauty, abundance, love, and fulfillment to enjoy and share. Life is a ceremony of celebration and divine play. Can we let this be our practice and let it be filled with ease and grace?

Heaven on Earth anchors through your pure loving presence. Your being is all that is required. Rest into stillness and receptivity. Our new paradigm of teaching is being who you truly are and embodying wisdom through your presence. Your being is the direct transmission of your mission. Your life and how deeply you love is your message.

> **"So I ask again, what is the Great Work before us? Be fierce in rejecting any answer that your soul knows is untrue, however flattering it may be to your righteousness. Be gentle in your judgments, so that clarity of purpose has room to grow. Be grateful as you discover the joy, ease, and humor that the Great Work makes available. Be confident in the true knowledge that we are ready to accomplish it. Rejoice in the renewal of our love affair with the world of matter and flesh."**
> **—Charles Eisenstein**

Heaven on Earth Means Going Through Hell

By now we've hopefully established that to arrive in Heaven on Earth, we've got to go through hell. I am so grateful to journey with those who are up for the challenge of meeting our true selves, being with what is, accepting the moment as perfection, forgiving the parts of ourselves that act out in protection and survival, holding the complexity of our multi-dimensional selves. It's a miracle to practice presence in this way and shed so many layers in a few days that feel like infinite lifetimes.

Words don't ever do justice to the healing and awakening we share in this path into embodied ascension. It is a way of being, a feeling, a knowing, a remembering more so than an intellectual concept or idea that fits neatly into a box. Who are we outside of the boxes we've learned to put ourselves and each other in? Who are we beyond the voices we've learned to listen to above the voices of our hearts and souls? Who are we when we see the other as a mirror of our innermost being who has been long forgotten, repressed, abandoned? Who are we when we start to let our true presence—our light—completely radiate without diminishing the aliveness we incarnated to embody? Who are we when we meet our deepest fears and core wounds, the ones that make us feel like we are dying in the process of allowing the energy to actually metabolize through our systems, letting us welcome space for something new to happen? When we own our experiences and drop all projections, judgments, control mechanisms, and expectations?

It can be the most arduous process. Some think they are ready and even seek it out, but when shit gets real and the shadow parts you haven't felt since you were a child or even in this lifetime emerge and you feel exposed—do you run away and escape the opportunity to truly heal? We all want to be seen and feel true love and connection, but few in my experience are actually willing to do the work that requires holding space for oneself to die a few times and fall apart so that the true parts of your divinity can integrate and emerge as whole.

I'm sorry for any ways I've ever incongruently sold spirituality and ascension as some levity-filled journey into 5D and the vortex of liberation and lightness. I was afraid that no one would come to do the work unless it was sold under the moniker of fun and magic and Heaven on Earth. Are we really—collectively—ready to do the work at the level of depth that is required to truly be free? Free of personality, superficial games, wounding that binds us in projection and separation? Would anyone care to try if the invitation led with the real promise that doing the work actually means staying present with the most uncomfortable feelings and memories and traumas, the ones you never wanted to feel, that sometimes feel like they'll kill you (your ego) when you actually allow the energy to digest?

It's not all love and light on this path—it's the most painful, un-damning, and exhausting work there is that we have on this human journey, and it's truly a testament to what one is made of . . . we meet our true capacity and see what we are really here for. Yes, it's true our greatest gifts arise out of our deepest wounds, usually not in the ways we imagine. Ascension doesn't fit into a neat little body with easily categorizable chapters and easy-to-follow steps. It is a personal journey deep into one's own depths to meet one's divinity beyond all falsity and limitation. It looks like dying over and over again to awaken more of one's true, humble presence.

There is a quiet and peace here that triggers many—illuminating the ways in which their own inner agitation is actually screaming at them, criticizing, judging, controlling, dying. I love to explore these subtle realms of our consciousness and embodiment that guide us—when we allow and listen and receive—into more of our truth. We can never do wrong as long as we are listening and sharing from our heart what our authentic experience is in this present moment, in this body.

I overflow with gratitude for the souls that are here for the journey, here for the invitation into the depths, honoring the perfection of it all. I am here to live life as a transformational immersion, as a healing retreat, not to compartmentalize it as some other game that I need to get away from to go practice and heal. Life is the ultimate practice—are we receiving the invitations along the way to do the work, to meet ourselves, to drop the masks? From now on I am only available for relationships with others who are willing to be in this unmasking, un-damning practice no matter what—authenticity at all costs. This is how we build safety and trust and reverberate through the world a transcendent example of actual unity, connection, and collaboration.

When I say "let's play," what I really mean is—let's go into the depths of who we are beyond all stories and ideas and feel what's actually underlying, allowing our true essence to actually embody. Let's become comfortable and maybe even at ease in the silence and stillness amidst the most powerful transmission of loving presence—god—we've ever felt. I am here for more of this, and nothing less. And I am honored to co-create with others who are ready to play in the depths of our darkness, our authenticity, our core wounds, our fragmented selves, our divinity, and everything in between—all of it—allowing complete permission to be as we are. Here is where true healing and remembering happen.

WHAT SHALL WE CHOOSE?

It is a miracle that you and I are able to communicate and actually make sense let alone make anything together. With how different and unique we each are and with how differently we see the world—isn't it wild to imagine we are able to co-exist from within such unique universes, each with their own ways of seeing, being, and feeling? This is part of the learning, the remembering and the deconditioning that we get to go into together as New Earth architects. We get to be on a healing process together, we get to be in transformation together, we get to be the bridges between science and business and spirituality and mysticism and bring it all together. So that we can really share a common language, a common understanding without assumptions or projections.

We are stepping into more maturity and mastery which means we can welcome each other's uniqueness and differences in opinions and viewpoints—understanding that we don't have to agree or see things the same way to get along. In fact, maybe we're meant to see things completely differently and learn from the contrast—through empathy and compassion. From here perhaps we can see so many new potentials we wouldn't have otherwise considered, that broaden our realities in beautiful ways with so many new choices for creative expression.

We've never had more at our disposal in terms of innovation, technology, resources. I mean human capital, genius. We have everything we need to thrive. Most of all, we have our hearts, our truth, our intuitive genius, and out of this world creativity and vision. Plus, can we remember this reflection from someone I can't recall—but who impacted me deeply: "Innocence is the one that forgets to wear any masks." When we are being our true selves, there is no mask to don, no density to carry, nothing to worry about and very little to even think about or strategize. We can simply be.

We've done the work to arrive at this moment, initiated to receive all that's destined to unfold. Yet always there remains your invitation to make a conscious choice to step forward. Awakening is happening whether you're ready or not. You decide to be ready as soon as you let go of all that's weighing you down. You decide to be ready as soon as you consciously choose to step through the door into your new desired dimension, your new embodiment. What do you stand for? In your dream life, the vision you've held in your heart for perhaps too long, who do you get to be?

What does your presence communicate more accurately than any of your words possibly could? What do you believe in? What do you value? Are you acting out of integrity in even small ways? Are you hiding anything out of shame or fear? Are you still using other people's words instead of your own, worrying deep down that you have nothing to say or that you can't trust your own heart to fully guide you? Letting these old ways of being go can happen instantly, love—it doesn't have to be a long arduous process unless you want it to be. Careful of overly identifying with processing and being in process forever.

This can be a cop-out from being fully present and responsible for creating the life you want. Addiction to overprocessing is actually self-sabotage and the ultimate game of victim consciousness, which is actually spiritual bypassing in most cases masquerading as *doing the work*. You know when you're playing the avoidance game or if you're actually facing yourself and genuinely welcoming liberation. So as we walk through the doorway to Heaven on Earth, to presence in this moment, to liberation and expansion beyond our wildest dreams—a feeling so familiar to our deepest soul's memory—what are you leaving behind forever? What's heavy? What's been too effortful? What's confusing? What relationships must end? And most important, where and who can you forgive? **We have the keys . . . we are the keys.**

You experience heightened anxiety and depression so you can relate to what the average person is going through and see how they can come out of it because you are resourced to do so. Do not forget yourself along the way. We choose to play into the collective theater, to empathize with the mass experience unfolding, so we can more effectively navigate into the realms of choice, freedom, and clarity we are much more accustomed to operating in as sovereign souls. You are choosing to continue experiencing this intensity because it feels familiar and it is is communicated most loudly in the collective current, yet you can tune out of it whenever you'd like, for this current is not natural to you at the soul level.

"Make yourself so happy so that when others look at you they become happy too."
—Yogi Bhajan

We had to learn these states to mold ourselves along the human experience, but these states are not present where we come from. In fact they have always felt foreign and inherently broken, dubious, and dense. This conditioned experience runs very deep and has taken a strong hold on our bodies, fields, and neurobiologies—even still, do not forget that we are in control of what we are choosing to emanate and amplify. You are the director and conscious conductor of the frequency signaling in, out and through. You were lied to in this lifetime and many others and told you were a victim to your emotions and to the outside world. You were lied to about needing to fit in and be like everyone else to make sense and be safe. You were taught distorted strategies of control and manipulation, mimicking the powers that be who have always merely played out the same patterns on the global scale.

Can we see how the microcosms we propagate through our own distortions only empower the macrocosmic systems of control and oppression we claim we're ready to dismantle? Time to forgive ourselves for playing their game all along instead of our own, perpetuating more of the same dissonances we've always doubted and seen through. No more. Separation tactics will not stand as building blocks of an Earth game that feels truly new. Disconnect from the falsity and choose your core truth, which knows inner stability, truth, and wholeness are yours and you. You are free. You are sovereign. You are liberation in form. Feel yourself and remember. Open to receive more now. It's time to meet our own immensity.

HEAVEN ON EARTH ATTUNEMENTS

For our culminating energetic practice, let's explore the Akashic Records and the beloved realm of quantum healing. Get into a meditative space and allow the energy of these words to permeate your being in whatever way feels best for you to receive.

Let's connect in the heart space again and relax. Connect with the Earth, connect with your roots. We will also be working on the sacral energy; this is the space right below the belly button, and the color is orange. The fiery space in the belly. Disperse your energy through your whole body, through your whole field, and allow your breath to expand and slow down. Open up the heart, expand the field around the heart out into your energy fields, maybe feel the color green starting to radiate. Let's see what's here. Deepen the breath, bringing the energy down from the head space, down through the heart, down through the sacral, down to the root, down to the Earth. Relaxing. Letting go, letting go of what's tightened up. Just letting go, just letting go of that grip. Imagining that sensation of letting go of the tight grip happening through your whole body.

Imagine a current falling through your crown at the top of your head to your whole body, to your own source connection. You can receive it whenever you like, just say, *I am ready. I am now receiving.* This is a current of divine abundance, divine value, embodied value, true value, authentic value. Just open your heart to receive.

Think of any time that it felt unsafe for you to feel what you truly felt. Any time in your life or in any other lifetime that you felt like it was not fully welcome for you to feel how you wanted to feel. Now feel what you're feeling to allow the energy to arise and to land, to be expressed, to be transmitted. Allow these memories to surface right now. Allow these memories to clear out of your cellular memory and out of your energy field. You can imagine this energy, these memories, going into another box.

Imagine a rose gold box that's quite big and it's collecting all these memories, collecting all of the cellular residue of all the times that you felt unsafe, unsupported, and scared of expressing exactly what you were feeling in the moment you were feeling it. We ask for these memories to be resurfaced right now, to be highlighted. Without attaching to any stories or specifics, simply imagine all of these memories clearing out of the field like they are just being magnetized out of the cells. You might even hear a *pop, pop, pop* as each memory flows into little bubbles of golden light.

All the bubbles of golden light are being effortlessly magnetized into this rose gold box that can hold them all, all of these little memories that are ready to be cleared from our cellular programming, from our neural circuitry from all the weak systems. Many memories in which you felt like your value was not appreciated or acknowledged by yourself or by anyone else. Any memories in which you feel like you've given power away or prostituted your value, or given your power away to someone in a way that felt like an unequal exchange of energy that felt exhausting, draining.

Any energetics around slavery or feeling like you were a slave to someone else's desires instead of your own. Any energetic relational patterns of this and any other lifetime that show how much you felt like you had to sacrifice yourself for the benefit of others, in which you felt like that was your role, your purpose, and you lost sight of your true purpose. You lost sight of yourself, you completely lost yourself in the presence of others. Any lifetimes and this lifetime in particular in which you felt enmeshed with the energetics of someone else, particularly a parental figure or in an intimate relationship in which you lost sense of your own center and became colluded with the energy of another. All these memories are now surfacing and bubbling up until little golden bubbles of light will magnetize them into this rose gold box.

Any feelings of needing to continue to suffer because those who came before you suffered and self-sacrificed and gave so much so that you could be who you are and how you are and where you are. Any feelings like you need to repay a debt. A debt that has been owed to others that have somehow allowed for you to exist. Any feelings of inheriting a debt that is not actually yours to carry but is just simply an inheritance of the feeling of indebtedness and of giving your own power away, of giving your creator consciousness away to someone else. Believing that your existence is the result of someone else, that someone allowed you to exist. Any of this energy is now being activated and magnetized into these little golden balls of light, magnetized into this rose gold box.

Any connections with your ancestors or lineage in this dimension or any other lifetimes, any other timelines, around the energetics related to servitude, around being an indentured servant, being told in that context that it was of higher service to all for you to play the role of the slave or servant and completely lose touch of your personal desire, learn in fact masterfully how to repress and forget your desires. Even in the misguided context of being a servant of the divine, or servant of higher consciousness or awakening, any of the distortions around repressing one's own power or creative expression or sexual desires in service of the light or in service of this false light.

This idea that light means one thing and only welcomes certain expressions of desire, therefore leading you to filter your true desires or experience feelings of guilt or repression or shame around your desires. Any memories in which you felt ashamed of what you truly desired and felt ashamed of what the expression of your desire may bring. Any moments in which other people felt uncomfortable when you expressed your desire or truth and you felt ashamed because their response was not what you wanted at that time.

Let all that energy arise, especially clearing out through the sacral center, the womb, the belly, through the throat, all along this entire energetic channel. Clear out all of these memories of shame and guilt around desire and particularly regarding the body. Any shame that you felt in any timeline, any other dimension onto the lineage of repression or shame around sensuality and enjoyment and pleasure through the body. Repression of sexual energy, creative energy, any feelings or conditioned ways of being in which you learned that it was wrong or bad to express the way that your body feels good, the way your body experiences pleasure. Let all those memories bubble up to the surface and go into these little golden balls of light, magnetized into this rose gold box.

"Feel good, be good, and do good."
—Yogi Bhajan

Feel any energetic cysts now pressing in the energy fields or in the body or in any of the internal organs, particularly in the sexual repro-ductive system. Allow these energetic cysts or blockages or resistances to surface into the light and dissolve out of the field of the body, above the layers of our beings. Clear the cellular memory now and forever through this and any other timeline. See these cysts be wrapped into bubbles of golden light, moving into the rose gold box.

Tune in now through this and any other timeline the experience of not feeling like you were allowed to love who you loved or to love how you wanted to love. This may include having been attracted to different gen-ders or different energetics and feeling judgment, shame, or guilt around how attraction was arising and feeling the repression of your creative ex-pression, feeling wrong or bad or dirty or ashamed. Let these memories arise especially from early on in life and as a child and even later on. Allow these memories to arise and be encapsulated by these golden balls of light anchoring into this rose gold box.

Any time in which you said to yourself in this and any other lifetime that what you want is not possible, what you want is not available, what you want does not exist, what you truly desire to see or envision yourself creating cannot come to pass or you do not have what it takes. That you must be imagining things, in times in which you have judged, criticized, or repressed your own inner guidance that has guided you to receive a partic-ular vision, in times that you have withheld yourself from receiving it fully or supporting yourself in knowing that of course this vision is here for you to bring through, surfacing any memories in this or any other timeline, in any other dimension. The experience of self-judgment and criticism that has shown in the path of you orchestrating precisely the creative vision that wants to be born through you, knowing that you have exactly what it takes and that you can expand to hold whatever it is infinitely.

Let's clear for the collective, for ourselves through any timelines, di-mensions, space and reality, the belief system, the platforms associated with limitations of time and space when it comes to creating the infinite po-tential that is expressed through us, all of the thought forms, all of the belief systems that will arise as limitations wanting to operate in our time and finite space or in the finite measurement of resources that can arise as obstacles or impossibilities in the way of allowing what comes through our hearts to simply be. Any ideas that we have to work hard, struggle, extend effort, prove ourselves, prove our worth, validate why we are capable. Any of these energetics that are associated with the current political system, economic system, social system, or capitalism. Ask for these power distortions to be completely cleared from the collective consciousness of this time; cleared from the collective consciousness of all beings connected to us, connected to Earth at this time. Ask to see reality clearly, ask to see our infinite potential clearly, ask to know ourselves more clearly.

All of these energies are still being magnetized into these little balls of light. All of them are collected effortlessly into this rose gold box. These processes are approaching completion. This is complete. Now, close the box. Lock it away. Close it up securely. Imagine yourself now burying the box in a sacred place in the Earth. This box has a highly energetic nature and will be instantaneously absorbed into the Earth, into the inner Earth grid, and most likely it is meant to be received by this particular space where you are called to plant it.

And it just effortlessly gets placed back into this perfect circuit that pulls apart every single unique aspect of what you just put forth and transmutes this energy in the most perfect way, transmutes these lessons for the collective consciousness of the awakened beings that are ready to receive it. It's now available for them to receive these lessons, these potentials, these templates. This is all happening so effortlessly and you are just watching this energy flow like water through the Earth. Planting seeds of new attention, of new potentials for all those who are ready to simply receive without even knowing about it. And all this energy has completely left your body, has left your memory, allowing a spaciousness that wasn't there before. Feel your expansiveness, feel your lightness.

Now receive a current of white light through your heart center. White, purifying, hot, bright light emanates through the heart and out through the whole energy field until it clears out any lingering residue from around the DNA, cellular structure, cellular membranes, and subatomic structure of the body. It clears lineage, residue of lineage, inheritance regarding abundance of divine value and authentic value. Know this new attunement of the true nature of abundance for you to incur your being at the deepest possible level.

We will complete this process with some toning. Take some deep, activating, energizing breaths and tone as long as your body can. We'll practice by first toning the heart space and then bringing the sound to lower down into the body, ideally through the solar plexus to the sacral and through the root. See how low you can bring your sound with the breath, just for a few moments together, and this will be for you to really enjoy and integrate all that has been received. You may place a hand on your heart and on your belly, if you like, to really feel the vibration moving down the body.

Just feel what is present here and now. How your energy feels, how your body feels. Now, when you're ready, take a little more of an energizing breath. You'll come out of this very slowly. Let the next breath be deeper than the next. Full body breath.

On your next inhale, raise your hands up to the sky and just stretch up the side body. Maybe moving from side to side a little bit, start to shake the palms. Shake the body gently. Roll up the neck, especially, tilting the head back and opening up the front of the throat as you roll around. And the other direction eventually.

Now, let's explore tapping. Tap wherever you intuitively feel guided to tap, wherever your energy is moving. Make sure you keep breathing deeply and just tapping on whatever space feels like it's calling for your attention, especially around the base of the spine and the front and the back. And the womb space, the sacral chakra below the belly button, the circumference of the body.

Making long, loud sighs is really helpful. And when you feel complete with the tapping, we're going to do something specific: make a light fist and just start tapping in the inner meridian line of the arm and the outside of the arm. It's a light fist, so it's not too intense, just kind of knuckling along the inside and the outside of the arm. You might want to do this along the outside of the legs, all the way down into the inside of the legs, stimulating your immune system meridian channels. Then along the base of the feet, just tap on the soles of the feet with the fist, especially toward the arches.

When you feel complete with that, make three loud powerful claps of the palms together. Generate a lot of heat, generate a lot of light. Rub your palms together for a while—then once you feel them heat up, bring your palms over your eyes. Feel that energy exchange, then move your palms over your whole body as though you're giving yourself an energetic bath in luminous healing energy.

Notice how you may feel different and consider moving more slowly in the moments to follow. Drink lots of water, perhaps reside in a more meditative space to integrate and further reflect. Most of all, celebrate yourself for being willing to have a new experience and simply receive. Celebrate the being that you are—who is a powerful healer, capable of alchemizing lifetimes of density into more purpose, light-filled presence, and spaciousness in which something new—and more true—can arise. Thank you for playing.

CONCLUSION

*"At the center of your being you have the answer. You know who
you are and you know what you want. There is no need
to run outside for better seeing, nor to peer from a window.
Rather abide at the center of your being, for the more
you leave it, the less you learn."*
—Lau Tzu

We have our work cut out for ourselves, yes, we sure do. Welcome to Earth School. By now hopefully we better understand our assignment and how to move through our paths with a little more grace and maybe even just a little more lightness. My prayer for this book and for every soul that gets to share in this journey with me is that we take what we've learned and put it into practice—for real. This is just the conceptual, integrative learning process—life is going to now give us even more opportunities to train and practice in real time to see what we're really made of. Ready?

Amma, who is known as the hugging saint, says: "Our efforts to remove hatred and indifference from the world begin by trying to remove them from our own mind." She really does give powerful hugs—I can attest to this after having received two myself over the years. The first one brought me to immense tears at feeling such a profound wave of unconditional love wash through me. My heart was broken open. Her reminder is everything—can we consider: to what extent is the turmoil we perceive to be inundating the world actually a result of our own internal turmoils attempting to be made conscious in our awareness through these external showings of drama in the world theater?

As they say: whatever is in the way, is the way. If we see something happening in the world that feels off, can we look to where that same energetic is maybe feeling off within ourselves? The entire world is rigged to distract us away from our center, remember: so can we make our training intentionally focused on staying in ourselves no matter what? Maybe we can call Earth School Ninja-Wizard-Jedi training instead, as it feels more appropriate for the level of initiations we're destined to experience here in these bodies, especially now.

Embodied ascension is an inner journey deep into your darkest shadows to illuminate your brightest light, to remember the wholeness that you are. It's time. Align your mind to serve your soul. All is given to those who give all. Giving your divine gifts effortlessly instantaneously becomes indistinguishable from the receiving of all that is meant for you. We soon see giving and receiving are the same circuit of energy flowing—when we are in alignment, giving our gifts is the ultimate way we are receiving: abundance, our own light, our own aliveness, our own love.

Can it be easy? To desire. Receive. Intend. Imagine. Play. Co-create. Allow. Surrender. Trust. Know it is done. Love. Pause. Enjoy. Repeat.

How much love are you open to experiencing and sharing now? In every moment?

How deeply do you allow all of what life is always flowing to you to simply arise and arrive into your awareness, easier than you could have ever possibly planned or strategized?

What's your dream beyond a dream?
Your deepest desires?
What sets your soul on fire?
What makes you feel most alive?
What experiences remind you of your essence?

What is your greatest gift?
What would feel most beautiful to experience in this perfect present moment?
How's your heart?
What is your beautiful body communicating to you now, in essence guiding you into alignment with your divine path?

How's your listening and trusting all that arises as your divine
    guidance?

How easy can it all be?

How much space can you hold for miracles to continue expanding
    into your field?

How much capacity do you have to surrender into deeper levels of
    pleasure, bliss, ecstasy and orgasmic power?

How radiant would you like to BE, turned on completely, as alive as
can be, completely utilized, fulfilled beyond measure, in service to the
divine plan unfolding, infinite intelligence and power flowing through
your every cell?

You've been prepared and initiated for lifetimes over and over for this
moment.

You wouldn't be here in this divine time otherwise.

You are awake, you are awakening even deeper into the dream beyond
the dream—remembering it's time to fly again, just like we were made to
dance with the divine.

Do you feel your truth in your heart?

Can you trust its timeless, transcendent wisdom?

Heaven on Earth is here when we choose to Be (present, as ourselves).

We are not seekers: stop seeking what you've already had all along.
You're a finder, you've found it already—everything you've been taught
to seek outside yourself. Now trust that you always have the answer and
continue to ask yourself for more guidance so it can fully land and embody in this beautiful reality.

Reorientation to trusting oneself and deeply listening to the body's
wisdom is the powerful invitation on offer. Listening without judgment
and holding space for yourself requires spiritual and emotional maturity,
which so many haven't been held to rising into for lifetimes. That struggle
stops now. Let it be that easy.

What do you need right now to feel your best?

What do you celebrate about you right now simply for being alive in
your essence?

What's the most nourishing, loving way you can be for you right now
at this moment?

Everything you want starts with you loving yourself, forgiving yourself, and accepting that everything in this perfect existence has always been here all along to help you thrive, grow, and evolve into even greater truth.

Assemble your support, reevaluate priorities, take your power back from anything or anyone you've outsourced to unconsciously. Tune in with your deepest desires—what wants to be birthed through you, now? Reclaim your grounding here on Earth in this body. Detox.

Where have you fallen out of integrity even a tiny, little bit? How you show up for anything is how you show up for everything, beloved, and the stakes are too high for you to cut corners in the ways you used to get away with.

Do what you say and be who you talk about all day in alignment, integrity, courage—telling the truth is so vulnerable and so powerful because in doing so you can finally disarm the charge and regain the energy you've been rerouting away from your soul, vision, purpose, power and fulfillment, now. Be honest: What needs to get back in integrity? Where have you been dishonest? What doesn't feel like it's sitting right? Make amends, forgive yourself, practice compassion—can you love yourself anyway? Even more? Can you love your human self learning and growing and doing its best? What are you learning? How are you evolving? How is this a gift?

Where can you practice acceptance even if it's all so awkward and weird and unknown?

I love this reminder most of all (source unknown—maybe direct from source?!): **We are the ancestors who rewrite our families' cellular blueprint.** Our trajectory in this whole journey of our destiny on Earth at this time and all time, all timelines, is a spiral. It's an upward spiral. We are always evolving. We are always expanding. We are always moving. We are never going back. We can never go back. It's not how it works. This is a paradox. It may feel that you are moving backward because you may still be orienting very much in the mental frame, the mental capacity, the mental view, which again is only able to orient itself in terms of the future, the past, predominantly the past.

Whenever you feel that you are moving backward, that is a sign that you are living in the very limited mental frame and it is really a reminder

not to judge or criticize but to come into presence, to come into attunement to what is here now in this moment, to breathe all the way into your
body. Let go of any critical thought.

Remember: you are only ever going up the spiral. Imagine yourself
cycling through different circles, just like a spiral. Sometimes, you go
through a circle that has an echo of a spiral beneath it, something you've
experienced in the past. It's a déjà vu. It's a similar experience. It's a deeper
understanding of a lesson you've already transcended. But you are never
going back, you are just going deeper. You are going deeper into the experience and so bring yourself present. How do you do that for yourself?
How do you take care of yourself? How do you connect with your inner
being? What is this process that we just shared like for you?

So much is here, happening in your inner being in this present moment. **And your purpose is here. Your purpose is who you are.** Maybe your
purpose is to be your true self. Too often we are conditioned to believe
that our purpose must be this external expression of productivity and
some kind of material contribution to society. This is a distortion of the
old world that we are evolving out of at the speed of light.

Your purpose perhaps is to be you and to be. To be the unique frequency that you are. That only you can contribute in this collective unfoldment of unity, in this collective unfoldment of harmony. And again
this statement is probably not satisfactory to the mind, which wants to
know its place and have a system, a structure, vanity, and construct. It's a
lot to let go of all of that. To be formless. To feel nothing. To feel empty.
But think about emptiness as all that is possible. In the space that you are,
all is possible, all is accessible, all is here. And we practice quite simply by
breathing. Breathe all the way into your body.

Usually, through very short breathing we activate a nervous system
that's operating in fear, in flight or fight and survival. We reprogram this
old operating system and restore our divine operating system, which is
rested and restored and receptive and intuitive, by calming the nervous
system through the breath. Can you imagine that it's that simple? And
it's free.

If anything, we can always feel resolute in this reminder channeled by
one of my best friend's daughters who I've known since she was a little

baby. These words came via text one day—in the perfect moment when I really needed some cheering up: "In case you need some self-love/inner child inspiration, Olympia just said, 'I'm funny, and I got a naked butt, and I got a belly button. I got what I need,' in a sing-song voice." Maybe this is the grandest teaching we could ever hope to truly master.

RESOURCES

I am beyond grateful to have received such immense support on my path in becoming who I am today. From teachers, to books, to modalities to power portals on Earth and everything in between, here are some of my favorite resources to assist and inspire you along your journey.

Books

Jonathan Livingston Seagull by Richard Bach
Healing the Shame That Binds You by John Bradshaw
Homecoming: Reclaiming and Healing Your Inner Child by John Bradshaw
The Three Waves of Volunteers and the New Earth: Three Generations of New Souls by Dolores Cannon
Intuitive Dance by Atherton Drenth
Conflict = Energy: The Transformative Practice of Authentic Relating by Jason Digges
Sacred Economics and *The More Beautiful World Our Hearts Know Is Possible* by Charles Eisenstein
Letting Go: The Pathway of Surrender by David Hawkins
Conscious Loving: The Journey to Co-Commitment by Gay and Kathlyn Hendricks
How to Read the Akashic Records by Linda Howe
Adult Children of Emotionally Immature Parents: How to Heal from Distant, Rejecting, or Self-Involved Parents by Lindsay C. Gibson
The Magdalen Manuscript: The Alchemies of Horus and the Sex Magic of Isis by Tom Kenyon and Judi Sion
Bringers of the Dawn by Barbara Marciniak
When the Body Says No: Understanding the Stress-Disease Connection by Gabor Maté

The Life You Were Born to Live and *Way of the Peaceful Warrior* by Dan Millman

Anatomy of the Spirit by Caroline Myss

The Pocket Guide to the Polyvagal Theory: The Transformative Power of Feeling Safe by Stephen Porges

Creating Money: Keys to Abundance by Sanaya Roman and Duane Packer

The Untethered Soul and *The Surrender Experiment* by Michael Alan Singer

The Body Keeps the Score: Brain, Mind, and Body in the Healing of Trauma by Bessel van der Kolk

Messages from the Masters by Brian Weiss

It Didn't Start with You: How Inherited Family Trauma Shapes Who We Are and How to End the Cycle by Mark Wolynn

The Pleiadian Tantric Workbook: Awakening Your Divine Ba by Amorah Quan Yin

Movies & TV Shows

Beautiful Boy (2018)

Being Erica (2009)

The Celestine Prophecy (2006)

Everything Everywhere All at Once (2022)

The Good Place (2016)

Harold and Maude (1971)

His Dark Materials (2019)

Inside Out (2015)

The Matrix (1999)

Merlin (2008)

The OA (2016)

Peaceful Warrior (2006)

Sense8 (2015)

Soul (2020)

Up (2009)

Power Portals

Thank you to Sedona, Mount Shasta, Bali, Hawaii Island, Maui, Kauai, Koh Phangan, Barcelona, Tulum, Costa Rica, Venice Beach, Italy, New York City, and Santa Cruz. To the lands of my birth and my childhood: Concord, Tilton, and Dover, New Hampshire; Newburyport, Massachusetts, and San Francisco, California. To all dimensions beyond time and space—and all my infinite allies, teachers, and family therein—where we explore, expand, and remember.

Key Inspiration

Dolores Cannon, quantum healing hypnosis therapy (QHHT)
David Elliott, breathwork training and his book, *The Recluctant Healer*
Christina Cross and Linda Howe, Akashic Records
Laughing Lotus Love School Yoga Teacher Training, New York City
Mark Wolynn, inherited family trauma therapy and family constellations
Richard Rudd, creator (and author) of *The Gene Keys*
Lor Fjerkenstad, somatic therapy

Healing and Facilitation Modalities

Akashic Records
Authentic relating
(Biodynamic) craniosacral therapy
Chinese medicine: acupressure, cupping, acupuncture
Emotional freedom technique (EFT/tapping)
Family constellations
Hypnotherapy
Holotropic breathwork
Inherited family trauma therapy
Internal family systems (IFS) therapy
Neuro-linguistic programming (NLP)

Network spinal analysis

Quantum healing hypnosis therapy (QHHT)

Quantum energy wellness bed (QEWB)

Quantum healing bed (Golden Light Alchemy)

Rapid transformational therapy (RTT)

Rife frequencies

Reiki energy healing

Structural integration bodywork

Shiatsu bodywork

Somatic experiencing (SE)

Sound healing

Yoga, particuarly the practices of Yoga Nidra, Yin Yoga, Kundalini
    Yoga, Bhakti Yoga

ACKNOWLEDGMENTS

Thank you to my guides and to my higher self that gave me such a clear vision for the 12-step program for ascension that turned out to be so much more. Thank you to my inner being who has shown up to live the life required to tell these stories and embody this shared wisdom. Thank you to all my angels who supported me in this Earth life and didn't make it easy for me to leave all the times I wanted to; I am truly glad I am here for this moment.

Thank you to my family: Roger, Sue-Ellen, and Silas. Thank you for being the perfect family for me to be born into and grow up with to learn precisely what I am here to learn, remember, and radiate. Thank you to my sisters who have supported me through this process of alchemy and expansion—burning away what is no longer true or real: Kyle, April, Zoe, Dayana, Joy, Becki. Thank you to my support team, all my bodyworker angels, human and etheric. Thank you to the lands of Venice Beach, Maui and Big Island and Tulum. Thank you for welcoming me home again and again.

Thank you to my clients, students, collaborators—to anyone and everyone I've had the absolute honor and privilege to connect with and support in session, training, mentorship, retreats, and events. Thank you for your willingness to connect, to see, to remember, to reveal, and to explore together in such depth, intimacy, and authenticity. I live for the moments with you when we touch into the deepest presence we've ever tasted, from which new worlds, bodies, and realities are birthed before our eyes.

Thank you to Lor, my cosmic Ma and mirror. In, Back, and Down, forever and ever over, practicing being in the in-between, deepening in presence and patience, seeing and feeling more clearly. Thank you for helping me remember how to trust and know. To David, my ASCEND cofounder and spiritual ally on this wild visionary ascension path—thank you for your patience, love, and support throughout this journey.

Thank you to Joel, Gwen, and the entire St. Martin's team who helped to bring this book into being. Thank you for seeing the future and believing in something new being possible—before anyone else could trust this new path unfolding.

Thank you, Bill, for your spirit, your generosity, and your kindness, and for saying to me in our first conversation: "I'm excited to see what books you'll write twenty years from now." I'm so grateful that god guided me to that back-channel website where I miraculously got directly connected with you—at the perfect moment, right on time.

Thank you to awakening humanity, to the Earth, to the plants, animals, and all living beings anchoring ascension into this now. We may not have it all together, but together we have it all! I love you, keep going.

We're just getting started. Let's play.

INDEX